THE WORLD

ONLY

SPINS FORWARD

THE ASCENT OF
ANGELS IN AMERICA

THE WORLD
ONLY
SPINS FORWARD

ISAAC BUTLER and DAN KOIS

BLOOMSBURY

NEW YORK · LONDON · OXFORD · NEW DELHI · SYDNEY

Bloomsbury USA
An imprint of Bloomsbury Publishing Plc
1385 Broadway, New York, NY 10018 USA
50 Bedford Square, London WC1B 3DP UK

www.bloomsbury.com

BLOOMSBURY and the Diana logo are trademarks of Bloomsbury Publishing Plc

First published 2018
© Isaac Butler and Dan Kois, 2018

ISBN: HB: 978-1-63557-176-9; ePub: 978-1-63557-177-6

Library of Congress Cataloging-in-Publication Data is available.

4 6 8 10 9 7 5

Designed by Elizabeth Van Itallie

Printed and bound in the U.S.A. by Berryville Graphics Inc., Berryville, Virginia

To Kathleen Chalfant and Ellen McLaughlin

If I've made a fool of myself, I have at least made
of myself the kind of fool I want to be:
That is the virtue and power of pretentiousness.

–Tony Kushner

CONTENTS

ACT 4: 1994–2003

ACT 5: 1998–2018

TONY KUSHNER: Around November of 1985, the first person that I knew personally died of AIDS. A dancer that I had a huge crush on, a very sweet man and very beautiful. I got an NEA directing fellowship at the repertory theater in St. Louis, and right before I left New York, I heard through the grapevine that he had gotten sick. And then, in November, he died.

And I had this dream: Bill dying—I don't know if he was actually dying, but he was in his pajamas and sick on his bed—and the ceiling collapsed and this angel comes into the room. And then I wrote a poem. I'm not a poet, but I wrote this *thing*. It was many pages long. After I finished it, I put it away. No one will ever see it.

Its title was "Angels in America."

ACT I

1978–1990

NOVEMBER
The Briggs Initiative, an anti-gay law in California, fails

——

Gay rights activist Harvey Milk assassinated in San Francisco

NOVEMBER
Ronald Reagan elected president

JULY
The *New York Times* publishes "Rare Cancer Seen in 41 Homosexuals"

JANUARY
Gay Men's Health Crisis founded

APRIL
Larry Kramer's *The Normal Heart* premieres at the Public Theater in New York

SEPTEMBER
AIDS is now the leading cause of death among men in New York in their twenties and thirties

JUNE
Supreme Court rules anti-sodomy laws constitutional in *Bowers v. Hardwick*

1978 — 1980 — 1981 — 1982 — 1984 — 1985 — 1986

OCTOBER
San Francisco's Eureka Theatre, in the basement of the Trinity Methodist Church, is destroyed in a fire

OCTOBER
Kimberly Flynn's taxicab crashes on the West Side Highway

APRIL
A Bright Room Called Day has first production in New York; Oskar Eustis attends

SEPTEMBER
Tony Kushner begins a directing fellowship at the Repertory Theatre of St. Louis

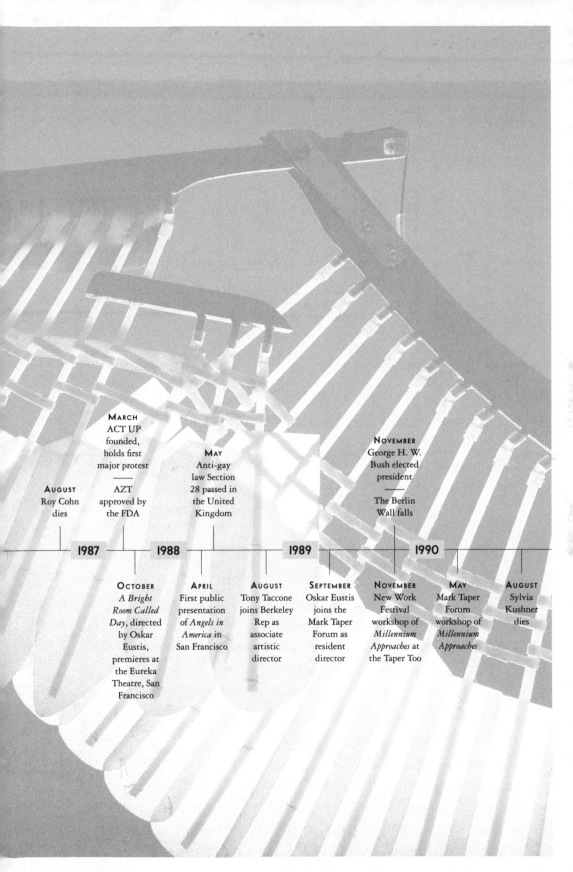

MARCH
ACT UP
founded,
holds first
major protest
—
AZT
approved by
the FDA

AUGUST
Roy Cohn
dies

MAY
Anti-gay
law Section
28 passed in
the United
Kingdom

NOVEMBER
George H. W.
Bush elected
president
—
The Berlin
Wall falls

1987   **1988**   **1989**   **1990**

OCTOBER
*A Bright
Room Called
Day*, directed
by Oskar
Eustis,
premieres at
the Eureka
Theatre, San
Francisco

APRIL
First public
presentation
of *Angels in
America* in
San Francisco

AUGUST
Tony Taccone
joins Berkeley
Rep as
associate
artistic
director

SEPTEMBER
Oskar Eustis
joins the
Mark Taper
Forum as
resident
director

NOVEMBER
New Work
Festival
workshop of
*Millennium
Approaches* at
the Taper Too

MAY
Mark Taper
Forum
workshop of
*Millennium
Approaches*

AUGUST
Sylvia
Kushner
dies

CHAPTER I

BAD NEWS

THE REAGAN REVOLUTION
AND THE END OF THE WORLD

—————————

BARNEY FRANK (congressman from Massachusetts, 1981–2013): It was a bad time.

DAVID FRANCE (director and writer, *How to Survive a Plague*): Ronald Reagan was brought to power by the religious right. And it was the first time the religious right got power. The Moral Majority kind of swept the slate into Washington.

FRANK: I remember having very mixed emotions the night I won in 1980—I was obviously very happy that I got elected to Congress, but it was a slaughter. Not only did Reagan win by a big margin, but they controlled the Senate.

RICK PERLSTEIN (historian; author of *The Invisible Bridge: The Fall of Nixon and the Rise of Reagan*): The religious right wasn't as mature as a political formation until the latter part of the 1970s, when so many of these social issues were thrust into the center of politics.

FRANK: Things began to change in the mid-'70s when the rest of the world began to regain its economic footing, when America's dominant role eroded, and that began the process of people who were not highly skilled and not highly educated losing out in relative terms economically.

PERLSTEIN: Through 1977 to 1978, there were the gay rights fights in Miami, the Briggs Initiative in California, the Equal Rights Amendment, and abortion—the movement is beginning to take shape, and it's taking shape in parallel to Reagan's very aggressive, full-time efforts to begin working for the Republican nomination.

There'd been the successful campaign to overturn the gay rights ordinance in Miami in 1977.

> Unfortunately, the battle that we won today is only that, a battle.
> The war goes on to save our children, because the seed of sexual
> sickness that germinated in Dade County has already been trans-
> planted by misguided liberals in the U.S. Congress.
>
> –Anita Bryant, President, Save Our Children, April 1977

PERLSTEIN: Right around the corner on the general election ballot in California, you have the Briggs Initiative, the first statewide attack on gay rights. Not only that, but in the biggest state. It was an incredibly, incredibly scary prospect. This was a law that would have made it illegal for gays to teach in

Religious protestors on the route of the Gay Pride parade in New York, June 1983. (*Barbara Alper/Getty Images*)

the schools and also illegal for supporters of gays to teach in schools. It was a very, very creepy law.

DAVID WEISSMAN (director, *We Were Here*): From the beginning the numbers looked very bad.

CLEVE JONES (founder, NAMES Project AIDS Memorial Quilt): Yeah, I don't think anybody thought we could win it when we started organizing, but we saw it as a great opportunity to organize. You know, this was before we had any really strong statewide or national organizations. That kind of infrastructure hadn't been built. So Harvey Milk and I and our counterparts in L.A. saw this as an opportunity to organize and not be passive.

PERLSTEIN: One of the organizers of the anti-Briggs campaign was David Mixner, who is this absolutely legendary organizer. He organized an anti-war demonstration in 1969 that got two million people. Federal agents set him up with a honey trap and showed him pictures of him with a man when he was still in the closet, and said, "Unless you basically give us intelligence on the anti-war movement, we're going to release these pictures." This was in 1969. He refused.

So he's back, he's out of the closet, he's leading this movement. They're thinking about this Hail Mary pass: What if we reach out to Ronald Reagan?

JONES: I was surprised when they said they were going to do it.

PERLSTEIN: It turned out that Mixner knew a leading Reagan advisor who was part of the gay underground. This guy, [Don] Livingston, was intrigued by the argument. An even more senior Reagan advisor, unnamed, who was married and gay, might be sympathetic, but couldn't even be seen with these people. So they met at a Denny's in East L.A., where nobody would spot them. What Mixner said was "We don't want you to lobby Reagan, we just want a meeting with him to make our case."

Mixner bought a new suit. They made the argument that the Briggs Initiative would allow students to blackmail teachers, that it would destroy school discipline, and that it would waste taxpayer money in pointless litigation—which would have been a striking argument for Reagan, because he was very much a budget hawk in his mind.

Whatever it is, homosexuality is not a contagious disease like the measles. Prevailing scientific opinion is that an individual's homosexuality is determined at a very early age and that a child's teachers do not really influence it.

–Ronald Reagan, *Los Angeles Herald Examiner*, November 1, 1978

JONES: The main lesson that I learned from that was the power of retail politics. The power of ordinary gay people knocking on doors, precinct after precinct after precinct, saying, "Hey. I'm Cleve, I live down the street, there's this scary bill that will hurt me and my family."

Harvey's constant exhortation to people to *come out*, I really think, became the main driving force behind everything we've achieved in the decades that followed. If you come out, if you live your life honestly at work, at church, everywhere, those people are less likely to fear and hate us and vote against us. One of the words we used a lot was *demystify*. You know, we needed to demystify homosexuality with the boring reality of our ordinariness.

BRIAN HERRERA (assistant professor of theater, Princeton University): In that moment, that period of Briggs until Reagan's second election, this period before AIDS goes wide, is the period where gay culture goes big. There was an incredible cultural dynamism where you could live a gay life in certain subcultures in some cities. Those subcultures, whether it be music, or erotica, or fashion, or literature, they could travel out into other enclaves in Dallas or Atlanta or Chicago.

STEPHEN SPINELLA (actor): Being gay, because it is something hideable, because it is something that can be masked and hidden, there are issues of a dual nature to your presence. You're living a double life. There is something fabulous about that. There is something outside the norm of living in that mysterious mind-set.

MADISON MOORE (author of *Fabulous: The Rise of the Beautiful Eccentric*): Fabulousness becomes, if I may, a giant *fuck you* to the norms. People emerge out of that. You emerge because you're tired of hiding. It's so much easier to be normal, to fit in, repress yourself, not, sort of, you know, be over-the-top. A lot of folks, people who may embrace fabulousness, are attacked on the street and feel the need to wear men's clothing, "safe" clothing, as a way to get from A to B, and then when they get there, they bust out.

HERRERA: You could see the cues, the winks, ways to tell that someone was gay, and you could read that as speaking to you as a gay male person without ever having to name it. In that register, the realm of the fabulous became one of the ways that you could signal that you were in on the joke, you got the joke, you were in some ways making the joke. People like Sylvester. The Village People. Camp was a building of a vocabulary of critical connoisseurship that was celebratory, that was *ours*. Isn't it fascinating that no one in America seems to realize how much *Dynasty* knows that it is speaking to us?

PERLSTEIN: You begin to see Christian conservatives bursting on the political scene starting in 1979. That's when you begin to see Ronald Reagan courting them quite explicitly.

FRANK: There's a great irony in that because Reagan was a man whose personal life showed no confluence with the religious right.

HENRY OLSEN (author of _The Working Class Republican: Ronald Reagan and the Return of Blue-Collar Conservatism_): Reagan saw their quest as being very similar to other people. They were trying to resist, in his view, the efforts by the elite to force them to live lives of the elite's choosing.

PERLSTEIN: It wasn't a difficult fit. He believed what they believed. He talks about the rising tide of secularism: That was straight-up religious right language, and it was one of the coalitions that he kind of maneuvered into place behind him.

OLSEN: He didn't necessarily ratify the Christocentric worldview that many seem to hold today. You'll almost never see Reagan talking about Christ or the importance of the Bible, the sort of things you'll see Republicans do when they want to court the religious right. It's very rare, if you go through his speeches, where he'll say something broadly denominational, let alone narrowly denominational.

FRANK: Yeah, he was very clever about it.

PERLSTEIN: Jerry Falwell by 1980 was a very close Reagan ally, and Falwell was absolutely savage as an opponent of gay rights. He gave a televised sermon in which he said, "Like a spiritual cancer, homosexuality spreads, and like the city of Sodom was destroyed, can we believe that God will spare the United States if homosexuality continues to spread?"

ALICE KRASINSKI (production manager): This is my iconic memory of that time period. I was living in a converted warehouse in the South Market area of San Francisco with a group of about a dozen of us. We got this raw space and divided it up into multiple live/work spaces. It was entirely illegal. The night that Reagan was elected for his first term, we were painting the walls of this studio and watching *Citizen Kane* play on one of the four channels that existed then. We were flipping between watching *Citizen Kane* and the election results. At the time, the fact that we were electing a B-movie actor to be president of our country was horrifying.

EMILY MANN (playwright): Reagan felt like the beginning of the end for the left. We watched people really financially start to fall off the cliff and to be marginalized again. It was a grim time.

FRANK: There was a real fear that Reagan was gonna dismantle much of what we had been able to put on the books to improve the quality of life, and in fact he did make some serious inroads.

JONATHAN LETHEM (novelist): Reagan was abhorrent and a joke to me. The world had gone beyond the pale, much the way we feel now about Trump. It was both ideological nightmare and cartoon, an American reactionary regressivist horror, like, "Oh wait, we're gonna go back to nonsense cowboy bullshit?"

TOM KAMM (set designer): There's so much about Reagan that was heinous. The busting of the air traffic control union. The buildup of arms, the arms race, the Star Wars initiative, the scariness of the nuclear threat. Reagan militarized our society. It was scary, it was not popular. Much of that is completely reinterpreted. History has been rewritten by the Republicans.

KIMBERLY FLYNN (activist and scholar): In the '80s, in cities like New York, the wreckage and the sense of mounting catastrophe was impossible to miss. As the Reagan years began, apocalypse was in the air. In New York City, the economic recession of the early '80s would combine with Reagan's draconian cuts to federal housing dollars to throw thousands of families onto the streets. Tax cuts, resurgence of military spending, cuts to social programs, deregulation. Also, people believed that Reagan would blow up the world. In 1981, the minute hand of the Bulletin of Atomic Scientists' Doomsday Clock was pushed forward to just four minutes short of midnight.

PERLSTEIN: Reagan's history-making contribution to this stew was an excess of optimism: that there's nothing America can't do. That's absolute catnip to the American population, especially by 1980, especially when America has been humiliated by Iran holding all these hostages at the American embassy.

> In this present crisis, government is not the solution to our problem; government *is* the problem.
>
> –Ronald Reagan, First Inaugural Address, January 20, 1981

OLSEN: The thing is, without Ronald Reagan the anti-government right has no standing in American political life. He's the only person who has made any sort of political impact by being rhetorically relevant to that cause. Without Reagan, they have no legitimacy in participating in political discourse. It's absolutely crucial for the anti-government right to glom onto him.

Reagan was always very careful about saying what he wanted to shrink. He wasn't Grover Norquist trying to drown government in the bathtub. Reagan wanted to set an amount of taxes, and he wanted to see spending pared down to that level. He didn't want to go to a world where people in genuine need would not see public support. Now, clearly, Barney Frank and Ronald Reagan might differ on what "need" meant.

FRANK: David Stockman, Reagan's budget director, wrote a book in which he said that he was surprised that a lot of the liberal programs turned out to be popular. He thought that all these things, housing programs, Medicare, that this was some liberal conspiracy, and he found out when politicians expanded these government programs that provided benefits to people, they were responding to public demand. They were popular.

So how do you cut off things that are popular? You cut taxes and increase military spending. Then there's that much less to pay for all these government programs, so you were able to defeat them not because they are, on the merits, wrong or unpopular, but because you then say "We can't have such a big deficit, we have to cut them." Reagan was very skillful at that.

They called it "starving the beast."

• • •

Doctors in New York and California have diagnosed among homosexual men 41 cases of a rare and often rapidly fatal form of cancer. Eight of the victims died less than 24 months after the diagnosis was made.

The cause of the outbreak is unknown, and there is as yet no evidence of contagion.

–Lawrence K. Altman, "Rare Cancer Seen in 41 Homosexuals," *New York Times*, July 3, 1981

WEISSMAN: AIDS hit eleven years after Stonewall. I mean, it's just mind-boggling to think that the vast bulk of gay history since Stonewall has been about AIDS. It happened so quickly after this first blossoming of liberation.

JONES: As we left our homes and came to San Francisco, or Manhattan, or West Hollywood, to be gay, we came with a real deep yearning to belong. We got to be sexual, we got to be ourselves. We got to fall in love and have these things we thought we'd never have because of these things that made us different.

ROBIN HAUETER (member and spokesman, ACT UP, 1989–92): I left Milwaukee, Wisconsin, in 1974 at the age of seventeen and moved to New York City. Yeah. *(Laughs.)* I was, you know, really young and breathed a great sigh of relief to come to New York. I was incredibly naïve, I hardly knew anything about the world, that's for sure. I came to New York in that frame of mind and lived my life as a young gay boy in the '70s, trying everything.

One of the hardest things for people who didn't live through that time to understand about gay culture was what it was like to be underground. In a big city like New York, you could hang around gay people and live in a pretty gay world and feel like you were "out," but the reality was you were in a bubble. The real world, no one was "out" in the larger world. Even someone like Charles Nelson Reilly, people who were so plainly gay, they were pretending not to be. Or rather, it's that everyone was pretending they were not gay. Society, culture, was pretending these people weren't gay, even when they displayed it fully.

So that's the world. And then, of course, anything goes. Having sex with anyone you wanted was considered normal. Having sex with several people on the same day was considered normal. It was just what we did. There was no manual, there wasn't much help you could get. During the '70s, we were all going to the clinic all the time to have STDs treated. Gonorrhea was everywhere. Syphilis. And then it started expanding. Everyone's getting amoebas. Everyone's getting—these STDs were everywhere, and it was a burden. Every thinking person—I mean, even myself as a naïve person—thought: This isn't really OK. It's not right. When Larry Kramer published *Faggots*, he got attacked *politically* at the time, but he wasn't exactly *wrong*. There were people who were questioning, who were concerned about disease.

> *Faggots* is basically about a person looking for love at that time in our history and not finding it. He comes to the conclusion at the end of a weekend of high living that having so much sex makes finding love impossible.
>
> I question that it's always called controversial; it really wasn't. It created a big stir and made a lot of people quite angry, but it also made a lot of people very happy . . . The controversy, such as it was, came from the entrenched people who believe that fucking is a civil right and that I was imposing on that.
>
> –Larry Kramer, interview with *Frontline*, May 2006

HAUETER: And then of course GRID comes along, the first name for AIDS. It's being whispered about. You hear about a friend, a friend of a friend, they have this weird new thing. But it's talked about in this context of STDs: "Oh, we've got another STD and it's *worse*." At the beginning, who knew that it would be so much worse, and fatal? None of the other STDs were fatal.

WEISSMAN: It took a while before people started to really grasp that this was a significant issue.

HARRY WATERS JR. (actor): I especially remember, in like '78, especially in the business—the number of black gay men that were literally disappearing. And nobody was talking about what it was.

JESSE GREEN (theater critic, New York Times): I came to New York in 1980, you know, the first *Times* story about AIDS was in '81. "Welcome to your young adulthood!" And I immediately knew people who were sick. I had always been prissy, prudish. It saved my life, I guess.

FRANCE: If you were in the crisis, meaning if you were in the community of the people impacted by it, it affected you every moment of every day. There was no way to get away from it. But oddly, if you were outside that community, it was as though it wasn't happening at all. I was navigating that double consciousness very directly, because I was trying to get those stories told and to convince editors that those stories were important. So I was engaged in the campaign to break through that barrier, but I meet people my age now who were living in the city at the same time who were shocked to know this was going on.

FRANK RICH (chief theater critic, New York Times, 1980-93): By the time [Larry Kramer's play] *The Normal Heart* arrived in 1985, public awareness of AIDS was enormous, as was the political battle that Kramer described going on around it. It was so contentious that, in a break with precedent, the *Times* sent a reporter to *The Normal Heart* to write a piece that was tacked on to the end of mine to say Kramer's accusations about the *Times* and the [Ed] Koch administration in the play were erroneous. Which, by the way, was wrong. Kramer was not erroneous.

"I haven't seen the play," Mayor Koch said through a spokesman, Leland Jones. "But I hope it's as good as 'As Is,' which is superb."

—from a note appended to Frank Rich's review of *The Normal Heart*, *New York Times*, April 22, 1985

ROBERT STANTON (actor): At this point, I'm having my first sexual relationship. All of this energy that I had pent up through my teenage years, through my college years, through my years at grad school, I released with this guy during a very brief affair. Basically, he's fucking me. We're having unprotected sex, and it was—I was really enjoying it.

There are those of us who are of a certain generation who owe our freedom to people who came to the city a couple of decades before us, or generations before us, who put their necks on the line. And there were freedoms that I enjoyed. But still I carry these scars from growing up in high school where I was constantly getting messages from people that I was worthless, and I was told every day repeatedly that I was a faggot, before I even knew what a faggot was, and I don't think they even knew what it was, but still it's the message that I'm not quite a human being. At the same time, I'm enjoying this very human pleasure with this guy.

I'm sitting in the audience watching *The Normal Heart*, and it's like AIDS 101, and it was effective. There's the scene between the doctor and Brad Davis, and she asks what his sexual behavior with his partner is, and she basically says, all caps, "WHAT ARE YOU DOING?" and my blood ran cold. I never called that guy back. I'm ashamed of it—I will say in my defense that I was twenty-two years old and my frontal lobes hadn't fully formed. After that I was celibate for about five years.

GREEN: There was a feeling of being picked on by the universe as a continuation of having been picked on in gym. It just seemed, like, great, now I've got away from that, so now we get the cosmic version of having a towel snapped at me.

HAUETER: The people who were activists, those were the people who did not disappear. Once that happened, you would know what was happening: People would be visited in the hospital, it allowed people who were sick to take control in a way that people who got sick before that activism could not do.

JONES: I knew a few people who tried to run away from it. They were the rare exception. One of the most amazing things about it was the way everyone pitched in. Some were political, some were organizers, some were with ACT UP, some were with the Shanti Project being buddies to people. You could make a fist and raise it in the air and march or you could open it and take the hand of someone who was dying. Everybody did something. And out of that came this great infrastructure that we never had before.

I didn't think that I was going to live, so what I did with those years really mattered, that was all I had. That's why the Quilt was important to people, because we thought we'd be wiped out and our names would not be known.

HERRERA: Camp as a tool of survival became increasingly necessary in the AIDS era. What's great about glitter is that it's light and dark. You see the flicker of the light and dark simultaneously. What camp really let me do was be present with what was scary but also be present with incisive delight.

SPINELLA: There was a quality of fabulousness that really was political. That could be marshaled to support you in your struggles.

Tony Kushner and Stephen Spinella at a New York City Pride March, mid-1980s. (*Mark Bronnenberg*)

I think there is a way in which people take hatred and transform it into some kind of a style that is profoundly moving to me because it shows people's enormous capacity, or the enormous power of the imagination to transform suffering into something powerful and great. For Jews, it's called menschlikeit and for African Americans it used to be called soul and now I think for younger African Americans it's called badness, and for gay people it's fabulousness.

–Tony Kushner, interview with Michael Cunningham, February 1994, quoted in Robert Vorlicky's *Tony Kushner in Conversation*

HERRERA: It was deployed as a tool of survival and resistance.

MOORE: Disenfranchised people don't take that disenfranchised script at face value.

HERRERA: When you'd go to a benefit or a concert, they were always filled with drag queens from the community, they would sing these ridiculous and silly songs about gay life. They would do the standard making-jokes-about-gay-life songs, but then they'd sing love songs, and then they'd sing songs describing the emotional devastation of grief. These were not contradictory. They were simultaneous.

MOORE: It's about rising up out of the ashes. No matter what systems oppress us, no matter what laws or lawmakers try to decimate us, we still will be amazing.

SPINELLA: Fabulousness, oh God, it's a kind of an engine, it gives you force, it gives you power, it comes to life when it is in opposition to something. It's a response to the mundane, a response to what is holding you back.

HERRERA: You know, when people say today "That queen *gives me life*"? When your soul is broken down, it can be replenished. This is part of why camp was so sustaining as a tactic.

WATERS: Once the gay community was able to bond together—not only in their ranks but in the finances—there was very little space for the black body in that discussion. All the PR about protesting, about raising money—it wasn't on the agenda. And in the black gay community, people didn't really want to acknowledge it because black gay people were a hidden culture. So it was a hidden gay disease affecting a hidden culture.

MANN: I watched so many people who I'd worked with—actors, designers—the theater was devastated by the AIDS epidemic. It was terrifying, you never knew who was going to get hit next.

> Leaders like Reagan and Bush are essentially as morally debased as the people who followed Hitler. Bush may not be as psychotic—I think Reagan probably is—but whether or not they sound as crazy or have the same mustache, these are people who fundamentally place all sorts of ideological agendas and personal success above human rights.
>
> –Tony Kushner, *Theater Week*, 1991

FRANK: Absent the religious right, the "starve the beast" thing wouldn't have been as popular. But, yeah, it clearly hurt with regards to AIDS. The response to AIDS was very much slower than it could have been for two reasons: One, they didn't want to spend any money, on either the research or the care. And two, they were claiming that people who were gay—obviously we represented a very large percentage of the people getting AIDS—that we were bad people doing immoral things. And with some vicious bigots like [North Carolina senator] Jesse Helms, it was: "They got what they deserved, don't help them."

FRANCE: "It was revolting behavior that led to the proliferation of AIDS." That was Jesse Helms's quote. And that was understood in the '80s.

STANTON: William F. Buckley said people with AIDS should be tattooed! Part of the reason the political environment was insane back then was because the social environment was insane back then.

FRANCE: The underlying problem as I came to see it was that the humanity of people with AIDS wasn't recognized. That was embodied by Jesse Helms's public statements. He blocked all money for the prevention of AIDS, blocked all money for research into the treatment of HIV, because we're not gonna spend our money in any way that would seem to promote this revolting behavior. And we were being buried by the hundreds. The *Times* wasn't covering it for the same reason, our surviving partners weren't being mentioned in obituaries for the same reason.

STANTON: In 1990 or 1991, I remember going to my medical practice. I remember saying, "I wanna get an HIV test," and he said, "Why? If you've got it, you're gonna die, so what's the point in knowing?" Literally, a doctor said that to me.

FRANCE: By 1990—so that's, like, nine years of the epidemic—modern science had managed to change life expectancy with the disease from eighteen months to twenty months. So nothing was happening. And the discovery of the virus was only cause for more alarm among us, because it gave them a way to find out who we were, and at the time they were discussing bills in twenty states to quarantine us.

WATERS: Everyone in New York was scared they were going to get sent to a camp. The AIDS crisis was the opening that brought everything terrible about our culture through. It felt like the end of the world.

CHAPTER 2

THE GREAT WORK BEGINS

NEW YORK AND SAN FRANCISCO, 1980–1987

KIMBERLY FLYNN (Tony Kushner's friend): I met Tony in 1975 in a life drawing class at Columbia. We first struck up a conversation when we realized we were both from southern Louisiana and soon discovered that we both had a strong interest in theater. We got to know each other better as we became involved in Columbia Players, which at that time was the main vehicle for students who wanted to make theater from the ground up. There was not much of a budget—but there was no censor and no one to tell you how preposterous your ideas were. You had the sense the university really didn't care what you put on as long as you didn't trash the place.

STEPHEN SPINELLA (actor, NYU classmate of Kushner): I guess we met the fall of 1981, I wanna say? We were both students at NYU's graduate program. We had an argument about the *New York Review of Books* versus the *Village Voice*. He was on the side of the *Village Voice*.

DAVID ESBJORNSON (director, NYU classmate of Kushner): Tony was in the directing program, but at the end of those three years he started writing, and he wrote and directed his final thesis.

MICHAEL MAYER (director, NYU classmate of Kushner): We were inseparable at NYU. Whatever his directing projects were, I would always just hang around and help.

MARK BRONNENBERG (Kushner's partner, 1982–86): He was directing a play I acted in called *The Age of Assassins*. It was a wonderful play about Emma Goldman and these five anarchist assassinations, William McKinley being the American one. The Italian premier. Archduke Ferdinand.

SPINELLA: I had to kill the empress of Austria.

BRONNENBERG: We moved in together in Brooklyn, like, six months later. We were on Clinton Street down near Luquer.

SPINELLA: He was really super-smart, and I became really good friends with him and Kimberly Flynn.

FLYNN: In the late '70s and early '80s, some of us were discovering experimental theater downtown, which was really in a renaissance. The Performing

Tony Kushner (far right) in rehearsal for 3P's *The Age of Assassins*, 1982. *(Photographer unknown, courtesy of Mark Bronnenberg)*

Garage, Mabou Mines, La MaMa, Richard Foreman, Anne Bogart. Before Tony and I ever heard the word "deconstruction" we watched deconstruction-in-action, not only of theatrical convention but also of social, cultural, and political convention.

TONY KUSHNER: Kimberly had a huge impact, she's just terrifyingly smart and she was devouring stuff that I can now read with difficulty but back then I found completely incomprehensible. Derrida and Kant and even Marx to a certain extent. Kimberly just had a miraculous degree of fluency in theoretics and an incredibly synthetic mind—someone who could really hold together strands from different places.

FLYNN: This extended dialogue involving the work of major left thinkers of the past half century helped form the intellectual ground floor for the plays Tony created in the 1980s and early '90s.

KUSHNER: I was introduced to Walter Benjamin by Kimberly, and he became—as he does for most people who have read him—central. The Angel of History. Staggering.

FLYNN: According to Benjamin, "One reason Fascism has a chance is that in the name of progress its opponents treat it as a historical norm," a developmental phase on the way to something better. Opposing this notion, Benjamin wrote, "The tradition of the oppressed teaches us that 'the state of emergency' in which we live is not the exception but the rule." This is the insight that should inform the conception of history. This, not incidentally, is the way in which ACT UP, operating in the tradition of the oppressed, understood the emergency of AIDS.

KUSHNER: There's no one on earth who's smarter than she is, this kind of frightening brain, and I didn't have that, and I was scrambling a lot to catch up, I realized in later years that I just hadn't had very good academic training in high school and she was a crash course in that. It was thrilling.

SPINELLA: We formed a theater company with a number of other people.

BRONNENBERG: It was called 3P Productions, which stood for "Politics, Poetry, and Popcorn," which he felt were the essentials for good theater.

ESBJORNSON: Tony was very political.

MAYER: Tony was obviously the leader. He was this unbelievable advocate for humanism in the face of some really terrible times that we were all suffering through. That horrible morning in America we were all trying to survive.

SPINELLA: It was just a ragtag group. Three of them were people he met at the UN Plaza Hotel, where he used to work in the switchboard office. All of us were pulled pretty much into his vortex.

ESBJORNSON: Stephen was kind of his muse, in an early sense.

KUSHNER: I loved writing for him.

BRONNENBERG: They did a show called *La Fin de la Baleine, The End of the Whale*.

SPINELLA: "An opera for the apocalypse." There was a whale ballet in which a choreographer danced *en pointe* with a sousaphone.

FLYNN: On a rainy Monday in October 1984, I grabbed a taxi to City College, where I was a new doctoral student in clinical psychology. Heading north on the West Side Highway the cab careened out of control, coming to a halt only when it slammed into a tree in Riverside Park. When I came to, there were tree branches inside the cab, glass fragments everywhere, including in my mouth, and my shoulder was broken.

I sustained a host of orthopedic injuries, some that required surgery. From the head trauma came cognitive deficits that at first I thought were temporary, but that for several years left me struggling to read, remember, and find words. This experience was entirely new—not only something that had never happened to me or anyone I knew, it was something I had no idea was possible.

It took Kushner some time to concede that Flynn's injuries were severe and, to some extent, permanent. As she wrestled to understand what was wrong with her and how to begin to remedy it, he became her sounding board, her medical guide, her companion in doctors' offices.

–Arthur Lubow, "Tony Kushner's Paradise Lost," *New Yorker*, November 30, 1992

FLYNN: Recognizing my deepening despair, Tony would tell me about dreams he had that featured portents of my recovery, like one where all of his house plants were suddenly growing in fast motion, sprouting new leaves that the pots could no longer contain. I was pretty sure he was making it up, but I loved him for it.

KUSHNER: I got an NEA directing fellowship in 1985, at the Repertory Theatre of St. Louis.

For an insecure aspiring director who was toiling at a hotel switchboard, the fellowship was a godsend. However, it required him to be separated from Flynn. As their interpersonal style dictates, they argued back and forth over whether he should go. In the end, he did.

–Arthur Lubow, "Tony Kushner's Paradise Lost," *New Yorker*, November 30, 1992

Tony Kushner and Kimberly Flynn, as seen in the WNET documentary "Great Performances in the Wings: *Angels in America* on Broadway," 1993. (*Michael Petshaft*)

JEFF KING (company member, Eureka Theatre, San Francisco, 1987–90): I met Tony Kushner at the Repertory Theatre of St. Louis, where he directed Clifford Odets's *Golden Boy*. That was the most intense production of *Golden Boy* ever staged. There was a character that wasn't in the play, a Russian woman running around with the casket of a baby. I don't know what this was meant to signify, but it was important to Tony. A giant stoplight came out, going red to green to yellow to signify where the characters were in their relationships. It was very Expressionistic.

JOYCE KETAY (Kushner's theatrical agent): Tony called me and had at that time—I remember this—he had a musical called *The Heavenly Theater* and he had a play called *A Bright Room Called Day*. I told him that I don't know how to read musicals, so the play was really what affected me. He told me years later that all the other agents told him, "Oh, I love the musical," and no one mentioned the play. So that's how I got him.

ELLEN McLAUGHLIN (actor and playwright): We met at New York Theatre Workshop in '85, I think. They were doing my play *A Narrow Bed*. Tony was the associate artistic director. He kept giving me dramaturgical ideas, notes about my play, which were quite good. He was couching them as coming from him as a director. But at one point I said, "Hang on, you're not a director, you're a playwright, aren't you?"

And he said, "Yeah, I am, I have a company of actors who do my work."

I thought, oh, how sweet. Then he showed me *A Bright Room Called Day* and I thought, *Oh fuck, he's a genius!*

KUSHNER: We rented a theater on Twenty-Second Street, one floor below a Korean S&M bordello, At the King's Pleasure.

SPINELLA: It sat twenty-eight people. And that thing was packed out every night. This beautiful redheaded dancer with a little moustache would come in and quote some Hitler. We would dance around in pig masks singing songs called "Eat the Rich."

BRONNENBERG: I can remember how disappointed Tony was. They couldn't even get the *Village Voice*'s critic to come see his work.

• • •

LORRI HOLT (company member, Eureka Theatre, San Francisco, 1980–90): Talking about all of this is painful. There was so much of an intense bond between those of us who worked at the Eureka. It was our *lives*. But it was fraught with difficulty because we were human beings trying to figure out how to be artists together and take care of each other.

ANDY HOLTZ (business manager, Eureka Theatre, 1987–89): The Eureka Theatre is named for the Eureka Valley section of San Francisco, which is now better known as the Castro. It started in a church basement in the early 1970s.

TONY TACCONE (artistic director, Eureka Theatre, 1981–88): I had met Oskar Eustis years before. He was a wunderkind in Europe. Oskar's a weird dude. A brilliant brilliant guy with big ideas and a big heart.

EMILY MANN (playwright, *Still Life* and *Execution of Justice*): Both Oskar and Tony were red diaper babies, and so they had an immediate connection.

TACCONE: Fast-forward a few years, I'm at the Eureka as a resident director. My friend and colleague Richard E. T. White was artistic director. It was semi-professional, very robust, largely volunteer. It was young people interested in doing modern, edgy, overtly political, post-'60s theater. We found each other.

ALICE KRASINSKI (production manager, Eureka Theatre, 1984–86): They were doing interesting, radical things. Everyone had a big personality.

JACK CARPENTER (lighting designer): This was a time when theater was hugely politicized, and galvanizing. The thing that is hard for people to understand now is how theater was a major part of people's lives, partly because there were fewer distractions. Theater was viable for so many people, across so many economic barriers. That's just not necessarily true anymore.

TACCONE: The board ousted Richard but had forgotten there was a process to hire a new AD, and the board was responsible for that! So Oskar basically persuaded me to go after the job. I got it, which was a real shock. About half the theater quit the day after I took the job.

RICHARD SEYD (company member, Eureka Theatre, 1980–88): Oskar came on shortly after that.

OSKAR EUSTIS (dramaturg, Eureka Theatre, 1981–88): I had, as a young man, become very deeply committed to the avant-garde. I fell in love with the experimental theater scene in SoHo. At sixteen, I moved to New York and lived at the Performance Garage and loved Mabou Mines and Richard Foreman. That led me to get hired to found an experimental second stage at the Schauspielhaus Zürich.

I found a contradiction. I became very excited by the socially engaged, experimental scene the German-speaking world had. But I realized I was growing more and more contemptuous of my own work, which I realized was designed to intimidate the audience into liking it.

Christmas of 1978 I was in East Berlin visiting my mother and I was listening to Patti Smith's "Babelogue," and there's the part where she says, "In heart, I am a Muslim, in heart, I am an American artist and I have no guilt . . ." and I realized that I had to go back to the United States and speak to my people. I had to work with playwrights, do something much more mainstream, because writers were the ones who could carry ideas of complexity and convey them to audiences.

My company, Red Wing, had had a very successful residency at the Eureka. They knew me, I knew them. I walked into the Eureka and said, "What I want to do is be your assistant." And I wound up at the Eureka for ten years.

SEYD: The company was Tony Taccone, Oskar Eustis, myself, Oskar's then partner Susan Marsden, my partner Sigrid Wurschmidt, Lorri Holt, Abigail Van Alyn, and a little later Jeff King.

KING: I came to the Bay Area in '86 to do a production of *The Normal Heart* at Berkeley Rep. If you're thinking about the Reagan years in San Francisco, doing *The Normal Heart* was a hugely exciting thing to do. I met Oskar, who came to see the show. He had this big silver feather earring hanging out of one ear, and he had a long shag and a leather jacket. We really hit it off. They were this interesting, smart, political group of people. I was the first male to be asked to be part of the acting company! That was a great honor to me.

ABIGAIL VAN ALYN (company member, Eureka Theatre, 1981–91): My vision of a theater, what we were working towards, was Joint Stock, the Berliner Ensemble, Shakespeare's theater. I had come to feel that what theater needed was for a writer and an actor to get together. Directors were a bother. And then I had four to deal with! *(Laughs.)*

HOLT: It was sort of a collective, but the directors had more power than the actors. But we fought against that; we wanted equal time to critique the directors. We eventually got that privilege.

MANN: Oskar and Tony were just filled with idealism and a passion for the work. They had the feeling that the theater could make a difference in people's lives. You could change people's mind in the theater, you could make a huge impact in social and political significance, through the stories that you told onstage. I think they truly believed it.

SEYD: I think that Reagan's election galvanized us. We saw ourselves as part of the opposition.

KRASINSKI: Mary Mason was our managing director. She was the pragmatist of the group. She had a very dry sense of humor. She was the counterbalance to Tony as artistic director. She had to be, because she was responsible for the bottom line.

HOLT: Mary Mason was in charge of all the finances, and she worked her butt off trying to keep us afloat.

TACCONE: A few months after I became artistic director, the Eureka burnt to the ground thanks to an arsonist. The theater burnt down after we did a play by David Edgar, a documentary play about the incarceration of Albie Sachs, who had been incarcerated for being a Jewish, Communist, anti-apartheid lawyer.

SEYD: I was playing Albie. Oskar was directing. The night before the theater burnt down, I got a call threatening my life. I assumed it was just a crank call.

HOLT: I had been at the theater, and so had Sigrid, and then we went out to the movies. Someone came pounding on our door and said, "Your theater is burning down."

CARPENTER: I was on a plane going to France with Bill Talen, who is now Reverend Billy of the Church of Stop Shopping. We landed and got a postcard—there's no cell phones in those days. We got a postcard that said the Eureka had burned down.

KRASINSKI: The idea that it was firebombed always seemed a little bit of a stretch to me. Although it was a wild, volatile time.

HOLT: We're wading through the smoke and the space trying to salvage anything we could. Then we had to resurrect ourselves.

TACCONE: We were itinerant. We spent a year at the Magic Theatre. Then we used a dance company space on Mission Street.

SEYD: The community rallied around the Eureka tremendously.

VAN ALYN: And then the next show was [Caryl Churchill's] *Cloud 9*. Richard directed that.

SEYD: We produced it in this fifty-seat space, and a couple of commercial producers wanted to do it, and we moved it to the Marines' Memorial Theatre. It ran there for about a year and a half.

TACCONE: We spent close to a year meeting regularly without the burden of having to produce anything, talking about theater, trying to marry our conceptual ambitions and our ideals with how the theater was actually run. For me it was a very formative time. You only get one shot to be formative. It was really cool.

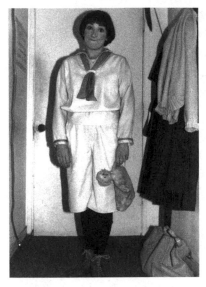

HOLT: It was pretty all-consuming. It was also mixed up with personal relationships. Oskar and I left our partners for each other—he was with Susan Marsden, who later got together with Jeff King and got married. Oskar and I were together, off and on, for four and a half years. There was an incestuous quality to it.

It became unfair, because the men were mostly the directors. So they would be deciding, and giving the actors critiques of what they felt they needed to work on for next season. Once we reached a point where we couldn't have a meeting because of all the resentments, we'd have a mediation and people from the Bay Area Radical Psychiatry Collective would come in.

KRASINSKI: I remember staff meetings where there were a dozen of us, including the core acting company, and we were all sitting in a conference room on the floor because there was no furniture, envisioning the future, discussing what was important.

KING: The decision-making processes that people went through could be grueling, they could be filled with people's baggage.

HOLT: There's this line in *Fanshen* where they say "and they talked for days." That's what it felt like. We deeply cared about each other and the art we were making. But we were just human beings, with ordinary foibles, and we had to find ways to grow together.

VAN ALYN: There were a lot of strains from the beginning of the theater, in terms of our not being able to establish a collective, because we couldn't be equally paid. Actors were sinking to the bottom of the pyramid.

Lorri Holt in costume backstage at *Cloud 9*, 1983. (*Richard Seyd*)

TACCONE: We felt like imitators. We were doing the best of the Brits, mixed in with Dario Fo, a Strauss piece; Oskar had a big affinity for German theater. And then there was this incredible, glaring lack of American plays. And so we did Emily Mann's *Still Life*, which was a turning point for me in terms of immersing you in American drama.

MANN: Oskar and Tony got on the phone to invite me out to see their production. It had taken a lot out of me writing and directing that play, so I wasn't sure that I wanted to see another production at that point. I got on the phone with them to talk with them, basically to say, "I just can't, I can't come to San Francisco," and then the two of them launched into this analysis of the play which was so brilliant! It was the most articulate and wise look at the play that I'd ever heard. I thought: *Oh my God, who are these guys? I have to go out just to meet THEM.* And I did.

TACCONE: Oskar and I talked to her about doing a play together.

MANN: They wanted more American political theater, as opposed to "the Davids"—Edgar and Hare. What they said to me is don't worry about the size of the cast, don't worry about it being one-sided. No holds barred.

TACCONE: Dan White had shot Harvey Milk, and we said wouldn't it be amazing if we did a play about this.

MANN: I came back to Tony and Oskar and said, "I have a feeling that the story is in the trial transcripts." Oskar somehow got a copy of those transcripts, I think he sweet-talked the clerk or something because it cost a fortune.

TACCONE: We interviewed everyone involved, and that became *Execution of Justice* [at Berkeley Rep, in co-production with the Eureka in 1985]. The immediacy of the event, the absolute, visceral, overwhelming emotion of the audience, many of whom were characters in the play—there was a kind of tsunami of feelings that was almost overwhelming. It validated our ideas, what we wanted to do and say about creating American work.

All of that is a prologue to saying we were then on the prowl—seriously, a search—for American writers with a political sensibility in concert with ours, a band of lefties ranging from anarcho-syndicalists to Marxist-Leninists. The whole spectrum. We were in a serious discourse about what the political aspirations of a theater might be.

Carl Weber was a professor at Stanford and a mentor of Oskar's. He said, "There's this kid in New York, this former student of mine. You have to check him out." We dispatched Oskar and said, "Go east and find this Tony Kushner!"

• • •

EUSTIS: It was the spring of 1985. We were supposed to see a show at the Public and we'd missed the curtain. There was no late seating. I was furious, I had no money at the time, and trips to New York were expensive. But we could make it up to this little room in Chelsea and see this first presentation of *A Bright Room Called Day* because that was an 8:30 curtain.

KUSHNER: And the set fell down, and somebody in the audience—

EUSTIS: At that point the first act ended with the singing of the Internationale—

KUSHNER: —somebody in the audience started singing along and knew all the words—

EUSTIS: I sang along with it! It was a eureka moment. I just knew I was in the presence of a major artist, and one that had the same concerns I have.

KUSHNER: Oskar called me the next day and said, "I want to have a reading of *A Bright Room Called Day* in San Francisco."

EUSTIS: In what should've been a clue as to the future of our relationship, it took five months for Tony to send me the script.

KUSHNER: Oskar was kind of already something of a legendary figure in theater. The Eureka had interested me, because it was kind of a progressive, serious left theater in San Francisco, where I had never been.

EUSTIS: I flew Tony out to meet the company and talk about *Bright Room*. I was innocent enough to think what a gay writer wanted to do as soon as I picked him up was go to Candlestick Park and watch a Giants game. He was very polite about it.

TACCONE: We produced *Bright Room Called Day*. It bore many of the hallmarks of Kushner's work, from the soaring language to the incisive intelligence, the comprehensive worldview, the interstitial connections between social systems and systems of thought that nobody else was doing. We were just—*Who is this kid?* Oskar directed the show. Spinella was in it. It was a seminal event for us. It featured our company, we were introducing a writer into the field. We were saying, "We believe in this guy."

KING: I had known Tony before I came to San Francisco. We were already friends. Way beyond my ability to understand as an intellect, but that's also appealing. It was a big shift in his career for a professional theater to be doing his play.

VAN ALYN: It was so wildly creative, doing *Bright Room*.

ANNE DARRAGH (actor): I was a production assistant on *Bright Room*. I loved it. Sigrid played Agnes and I would sit backstage and listen to her speak, and fall more and more in love with the play.

HOLT: It was as we were doing *Bright Room* that Sigrid first found out.

VAN ALYN: This is so vivid to me. She came to me and said, "Would you take a look at this lump?" And I went, "Oh my God. Oh my God."

HOLT: I can remember her coming into the dressing room and saying, "I have this lump—I have this lump in my breast." And Abigail and myself feeling the lump and going, "I don't—I think it's fine."
  I said, "Is it sore?"
  "Yes, it's sore."
  I said, "Well, that's probably a good sign, because usually they're not sore."

VAN ALYN: I said, "We are going tomorrow to the doctor. You are having this biopsied." Then the whole thing just cascaded from there.

HOLT: During the previous year Mary Mason, our general manager, got sick. Mary was the steady, always dependable one. She refused to panic when we had money troubles. She was the very picture of lucidity, clarity, calm in the storm.

Sigrid found out she had breast cancer right after Mary died. We closed the show early because of it.

> Sigrid's lump was malignant, and after two days of fear and misery we've closed the show and it's all happened so fast. . . . Sigrid will go for a second opinion this week but will probably have surgery again on Thursday and will find out then if the cancer—God I hate writing that word—has spread to the lymph nodes.
>
> –from Lorri Holt's journals, November 15–16, 1986

McLAUGHLIN: The whole community just reeled. She was such a vital, crucial member of the theater.

SEYD: Sigrid went into treatment after *Bright Room*.

KUSHNER: Oskar asked me if I would do a play on commission.

HOLTZ: Tony Taccone and Oskar were aware that Larry Kramer had written a very political play about the AIDS crisis called *The Normal Heart*. Here we are, the political theater founded in the epicenter of this epidemic, we have to do this play! And the rights went to Berkeley Rep. And Tony and Oskar were so angry, they said, "We're gonna write our own AIDS play!"

KUSHNER: I wanted to call it *Angels in America*.

EUSTIS: I thought that was great.

KUSHNER: My titles usually suck. I'm sure he was, like, thrilled.

VAN ALYN: "It attempts to place the AIDS epidemic in the context of Mormonism and the wild religious seeking of America and *bah* bah *bah* bah *bah* bah *bah* bah *bah*." We're all going, "Wow!" *(Laughs.)* "That's a lot."

KUSHNER: *A Bright Room Called Day* was three hours long, and Oskar felt very strongly that it would be better if it had been shorter. So he made me sign a contract. Not *made* me, but the contract stipulated that the new play could not be longer than two hours. And I wanted songs in it, so I made them include that it would have songs. So it was gonna be a two-hour play, with songs.

The NEA offered this $50,000 grant, and $40,000 would go to production, and $10,000 went to the playwright. That was more money than I'd ever made for anything.

GREG REINER (director, theater and musical theater, National Endowment for the Arts): I'm sure *Angels* was just one of many grants we gave that year. We give grants widely because you never know. It's like when I hear all these interviews with people at Google and they talk about all those projects they invested in that *don't* work to get to the thing that *does* work.

KUSHNER: We had to submit a description of the play, and I said, "It's gonna have five gay men and an angel," but the grant was specifically to write a play for the Eureka Theatre Company, which was three straight women and a straight man.

SEYD: The intention was to link it to the Caryl Churchill, David Edgar way of working, to write a play for the company of actors.

EUSTIS: We had four actors, three of them were women, so it had to have parts for three women. Tony complained for a long time, "What is this play about gay men doing with these women?"

KUSHNER: Anyway, then we got the grant, and I got a check for, I think, $3,000 or $5,000—this really impressive check, and it had the seal of the people of the United States on it, and it was a big moment for me. I was really moved by it.

REINER: To think that then the U.S. government was part of the support of that is exactly why I'm so proud to work at a place like the NEA. To do work that speaks to every person in this country.

KUSHNER: I was sort of being commissioned to write—the federal government's commissioning me to write—a play. So I should really . . . You've got people of the WPA, and James Agee, and all these people that had done things on federal paychecks. And I'm a patriot, and it just meant a lot to me. So I think that's sort of where it started.

CHAPTER 3

I LIKE YOUR COSMOLOGY, BABY

AIDS, ROY COHN, AND MORMONS

TONY KUSHNER: The title didn't seem grandiose or anything to me.

STEPHEN SPINELLA (Prior in workshops, San Francisco, Los Angeles, New York, 1988–94): Tony said, "I have this great idea for a play about Mormons, and it'll have Roy Cohn, and it'll be all gay men, and it'll be about AIDS." I remember him talking about Mormons, Roy Cohn, and AIDS.

OSKAR EUSTIS (dramaturg, Eureka Theatre, San Francisco, 1981–88; artistic director, 1988–89): This was 1986, in the heart of San Francisco. We knew it had to be responsive to the AIDS crisis.

CLEVE JONES (founder, NAMES Project AIDS Memorial Quilt): Between '85 and '95, when the first wave of protease inhibitors started hitting, I think we lost about two thousand a year in San Francisco. The greatest concentration was in the Castro. And it was so immediate, so in your face, so . . . and at the same time, kind of invisible.

DAVID WEISSMAN (director, *We Were Here*): As things got worse and worse, you could not be in the Castro without being confronted by AIDS all the time. You would see someone walking up the street in those sagging sweatpants, which was kind of the most common look, those skeletal bodies with sagging sweatpants covering just the most bony frame, carrying a cane. You'd think this person was, like, seventy-five years old and then you'd realize they were thirty and they were someone you had slept with.

ANNE DARRAGH (Harper in San Francisco, 1991): AIDS was so horrible, it was so horrible, it was a lethal diagnosis.

JEFFREY WRIGHT (Belize in New York, 1993–94; on HBO, 2003): That visit to Prior's hospital bed was something I had experience of, as everyone had.

JOE MANTELLO (Louis in Los Angeles and New York, 1992–94): It was really, it was really harrowing. It felt like people were just disappearing.

MARK BRONNENBERG (Kushner's partner, 1982–86): At the time, my best friend, a college roommate from Iowa, had AIDS. He was diagnosed in '82, before they even had discovered HIV. He died in 1984.

FRANK RICH (chief theater critic, *New York Times*, 1980–93): The *Times* had done such a poor job of covering AIDS, many people like myself were unaware of it. This was a period where, under the dictates of Abe Rosenthal, you were not allowed to use the word *gay* in the *Times*. Gradually what happened was, if you were on the theater beat, you had to notice that young men, featured actors, no one quite famous yet, or super-famous, were dying. Something was going on. Then it became quite clear that there was this lethal epidemic. The theater caught up with it relatively fast, at least by the standards of American pop culture. There were some early plays, probably by '84-ish you have William Hoffman's *As Is* and Larry Kramer's *The Normal Heart*.

MANTELLO: *The Normal Heart* was very, very instrumental in propelling me to become a volunteer at Gay Men's Health Crisis. I became a buddy to several people over a few years. You'd be assigned a case. Sometimes you'd shop for them. Sometimes you'd spend time with them. I remember going to sit with a man I was working with in the hospital, and I remember it was at the time when the food service people were not required to come into the room. They could leave the trays outside the door. They would wear masks, they were covered like astronauts.

BRONNENBERG: Back then it was still not clear how it was transmitted. It was horrible. You'd go into a hospital room and you'd wear a mask and rubber gloves.

MANTELLO: I was one of several people in his life, but he was very, very ill. After he died, I just couldn't do it anymore. It was too much. It was too much.

SPINELLA: In the summer of 1988, right after the Gay Pride March, my best friend Reno Dakota took me to these ACT UP meetings. So starting then I was a full-on member of ACT UP. I wasn't a core member, but I was on the issues committee and knew all those people. So I started to get a really more politicized view of AIDS issues. I was HIV-negative, and most of the people I

A 1989 ACT UP protest at Kings County Hospital, New York, including Tony Kushner (KILLED BY BIGOTRY) and Mark Bronnenberg (WOMEN DIE TWICE AS FAST). (*T. L. Litt*)

knew were HIV-negative. Then I found out one of my good friends, a teacher at NYU, Paul Walker, was sick.

WRIGHT: The first director who hired me in a legitimate role at Arena Stage in D.C., Hal Scott; the first director to hire me when I moved back to New York, Dennis Scott; my favorite teacher at NYU, Paul Walker—these people were so important to me in my early days, and they all died of AIDS.

MARCIA GAY HARDEN (Harper in New York, 1993–94): The first person I knew who died of AIDS died in 1986. He was my first boyfriend. His mother was Catholic. She was telling him to repent on his deathbed. And he was so sick. And so scared.

SEAN CHAPMAN (Prior in London, 1992): My godfather had worked for a major airline. He was gay, and he died a couple of years before the play. It was referred to as cancer. It wasn't considered acceptable for some of his family members to know.

NICK REDING (Joe in London, 1992): You had this sense of a, a plague going through our community. The arts community was *hammered* by AIDS.

F. MURRAY ABRAHAM (Roy in New York replacement cast, 1994): When I did *The Ritz*, that was a big cast. Eighty percent of that cast died of AIDS. It was awful. There was no support system. Because of the ignorance, when the parents of these dying kids were there, they must've thought it was some form of retribution, a scourge from God.

BRONNENBERG: During the writing, he would occasionally either read me something or have me read something. I remember one time in particular, I think it's the first scene in Act 2 where Prior really breaks down physically, where Louis comes to the conclusion that he can't deal with it, that he's going to abandon Prior. The power of that scene is that Prior shits his pants and has blood all over him. And Tony said, "I don't want this to just be *about* AIDS. I want people to see AIDS, to see the horror." He wanted a scene that was viscerally horrifying.

ELLEN McLAUGHLIN (the Angel in San Francisco, Los Angeles, and New York, 1990–94): If AIDS is a plague that is intentional on God's part, then it's horrifying. But in *Angels*, it's due to abandonment and incompetence by the stacked bureaucracy of angels. That's so terrifying. There's no negotiation with the divine. But Tony being Tony, there *is* ultimately negotiation with the divine, because ultimately Prior asks for more life and gets it. Tony can't imagine a God you can't argue with. That's part of what makes the play bearable.

EUSTIS: Tony knew he wanted to write about Roy Cohn.

> *Roy Cohn.* Born in 1927, Cohn became a lawyer and rose rapidly by ruthless use of influence and self-publicising. Violently right wing, he helped prosecute the Rosenbergs and became Senator McCarthy's number 2. . . . His secret homosexual life stopped him from running for the Senate, so he worked as a political fixer, helping to sabotage several Democratic Presidential campaigns.
>
> —"Real Life Characters in the Play," Royal National Theatre program, 1992

EUSTIS: He made specific reference to a piece that Robert Sherrill had written in the *Nation*. It's a particularly nasty piece of homophobic leftism.

> Cohn was rumored to have humped, or been humped by, [G. David] Schine, his colleague of the McCarthy days, but [biographer Nicholas] von Hoffman says there is no evidence of such a relationship. Ditto the rumors that he humped, or was humped by, his dirt-supplying pal J. Edgar Hoover. Ditto the rumors that he humped, or was humped by, Cardinal Spellman (who reputedly was hot for choir boys), all very, very close friends of Cohn, to be sure . . . To his death he denied that he was homosexual, but the Dorian Gray scene of his dying of AIDS said it all: "Roy . . . lay in bed, unheeding, his flesh cracking open, sores on his body, his faculties waning" and with a one-inch "slit-like wound above [his] anus."
>
> —Robert Sherrill, "King Cohn," the *Nation*, May 21, 1988

EUSTIS: While we were working on the play, the AIDS Quilt had its first public display at the Moscone Center. We came across a panel:

EUSTIS: Tony looked at it and said, "If I can write something half as dialectical as that, it'll be a great character."

JONES: I remember when that panel was made. One of the volunteers told me there's someone behaving oddly here, come check it out.

I went up to him and he was super-secretive and flipped the panel over and I said, "You know, if it's going to be in the quilt, I'm going to have to see it, so why don't you show it to me?" and he did. My hair just stood on end. It was the first of the . . . eventually there would be many very *harsh* panels, you know, but this was kind of in a league of its own. The first thing I asked him was "Did you actually know Roy Cohn?" and he said, "I knew him *very well*," and so I said, "Fine."

WESLEY MORRIS (critic-at-large, *New York Times*): It would've been so easy to make a play about Roy Cohn, maybe even him having AIDS. But for a gay Jewish man to completely re-appropriate Roy Cohn's story, to tell this larger story about the AIDS crisis in the 1980s, is really incredible. To have a gay man who is also a Jew wrestling with the legacies of shame and hypocrisy among his own people, on his own terms, is really powerful.

BRONNENBERG: I knew it was about Roy Cohn. I knew it was about AIDS. I knew it was about the Reagan era, but I couldn't quite grasp where the Mormons fit in. I'm not sure he did, either.

Roy Cohn's square on the AIDS Memorial Quilt. (*Tony Kushner*)

KUSHNER: I think if you have a title *Angels in America*, you're gonna start to think about American angels.

EUSTIS: The Book of Mormon was there from the beginning. He had read it, he had an intuitive sense that Mormonism was going to be important to the play, but we didn't know how.

KUSHNER: When I was a kid in Louisiana, I went to this summer program at McNeese State University, which was in my hometown, Lake Charles. Kids came from all over the state, and you lived there for six weeks. In the summer of my first year in college, I applied for a job as a dorm counselor at the program. My favorite student of all the kids, her name was Mary Fanning, her father ran the local Boy Scout troop, and they were a Mormon family. She is a really incredibly warm, lovely person. And I adored her. And she adored me.

At the end of her last year of the program, she gave me, as a parting gift, the Book of Mormon, with this very impassioned inscription: "If you think this is false, then this must mean that I and millions of other fools are stumbling around in the darkness." Or something devastating like that. It was so daunting, and it took me like a year and a half to get around to starting to read it. And then I read it, and it's—Mark Twain famously called it "chloroform in print." It's just terrible. It's a terrible book.

JOSEPH MYDELL (Belize in London, 1992–93): Mormons knocked on my door in Hackney before I did the play, wanting to talk to me about the church. These two very blond, well-dressed lads, they came in and at the time I smoked, and they said, "The holy spirit won't come if you have that cigarette, and we'll pray for you," so I said, "Oh yes, I'll put it out." They preached to me as if I was a child. And as they left I said, "Why are blacks told that they have to go to a separate heaven? And why are blacks not allowed to be elected to higher office in the church?" And they were *flabbergasted*. They said, "Oh, uh, well, just at this moment there's a new revelation and a lot of that is going to change."

KUSHNER: I took the F train into Manhattan daily to go to grad school. And the summer before I left to go to St. Louis, these incredibly adorable Mormon missionaries—these two guys—showed up at the entrance of the subway station, with their little white shirts and their little ties, and their "Elder this" and "Elder that." I, of course, always loved stopping and talking to them, 'cause I'd actually read this stuff. One of them, especially, was just—I couldn't wait to get to the subway station.

I'm sure that also had a role.

McLAUGHLIN: One show, there was a group of students from *Brigham Young*! Like *the* Mormon kids! And this beautiful, corn-fed girl said to Stephen Spinella, "Everyone in my life, my family, my church, my school, my entire society, has taught me to hate you, and I love you." And she burst into tears. And Stephen burst into tears and they hugged. And I thought, *If we've done nothing else, we changed that young woman's life.*

RICH: It's a history play, in the sense that it transcends what AIDS means in our culture now, or what it meant when the epidemic first hit, but it brings it back for audiences who are open to the experience and puts it in the context of America in general, not just the Cold War. Not just even in terms of Roy Cohn and certain kinds of overlaps with the McCarthy era. But also the Mormon Church, the most American creation among religions. And the sense of the sweep of the country over roughly a century, going back to immigration in the nineteenth century. It's all there.

CHAPTER 4

NOT-YET-CONSCIOUS, FORWARD DAWNING

DEVELOPING THE PLAY IN SAN FRANCISCO AND LOS ANGELES, 1987–1990

ANDY HOLTZ (business manager, Eureka Theatre, San Francisco, 1987–89): We got the grant and figured out, *Wow, I guess we better write the play, then.*

TONY KUSHNER: I'd left New York Theatre Workshop around '87 when Jim Nicola took over and went to work as director of literary services for Theatre Communications Group. But it became sort of clear to me that I needed to stop having a full-time job. So I borrowed $6,000 from Stephen Graham, who I knew from New York Theatre Workshop, so that I could just work on *Angels* exclusively. And then I ran through that money—and I needed more money, 'cause I had no job. And people were getting excited about the play, but that didn't pay anything.

Jim Nicola called me and said, "We have a director who wants to do this play by Pierre Corneille called *The Illusion*, and there's no good English translation of it. Would you be willing to do one?" And so I did *The Illusion*. And the Workshop did it, and I think they paid me enough for two months' rent. And then Mark Lamos at Hartford Stage asked if he could do it. And then Mel Gussow for the *Times* went and reviewed it in Hartford and loved it, and suddenly it got done all over the United States, and it paid for the rest of the writing.

JEFF KING (company member, Eureka Theatre; Joe in workshops): We all had to do a musical audition. I did so poorly that I credit myself with keeping it from being a musical.

KUSHNER: I wrote the part of Harper for Lorri Holt, Hannah for Abigail Van Alyn, Sigrid was the Angel. And Jeff King, I wrote the part of Joe for him. And that took care of the Eureka company. My first year at NYU, I became friends with Stephen Spinella. I thought then, as I think now, that he was one of the most remarkable actors I'd ever met, and I loved writing for him, and so I wrote Prior Walter for him.

KING: I think, honestly, all of us are so in those parts. No matter who does them, they're doing us in a way. Tony was writing them for us to do, so there's some DNA strain from those four people, five including Spinella, that lives through those parts.

ABIGAIL VAN ALYN (company member, Eureka Theatre; Hannah in workshops): Lorri is sharp as a razor. She is so smart.

KING: Lorri had a strong connection to her emotional life; she could bring a lot of emotion onstage. With Harper, you know, her fragility and need and imagination was really strong in her. I think that's why it was written for her.

RICHARD SEYD (company member and director, Eureka Theatre; Sigrid Wurschmidt's partner): Jeff was very quintessentially Middle America, I would say. That's very much how he read. He's a very subtle actor, I thought.

JOE MANTELLO (Louis in Los Angeles and New York, 1992–94): Jeff was like a redwood. He was *massive*. And sweet. And very straightforward, a kind, kind, kind man.

VAN ALYN: Oh, Jeff is a delight. He's an interesting combination of a vibrant, still presence and then suddenly being really smart in the way he understands a character.

SEYD: Abigail is a very grounded actor.

ALICE KRASINSKI (Eureka production manager, 1984–86): Abigail was a little bit older than everyone else, although I can't remember how much older. It seemed like the rest of us were such kids.

KING: Abigail was smart. She was very politically committed. There's a character that she played in *A Bright Room Called Day* named Gosling—she goes around putting posters on telephone poles—and the other characters say they're going to tear 'em down and she says, "I don't care what they do, I care what *I* do." She was like that.

KRASINSKI: Sigrid was such a—just a beautiful person. She was so talented. I remember when we were . . . *(Pause.)* This is when we were still moving into the theater. There was this dreadful pea-green color on the walls so we were painting the offices. Sigrid and I were there one night painting, and the main stairwell leading to the street, leading up to the office area, had pretty high and unreachable upper walls and ceiling. Sigrid was in her painting overalls, and she said "Here, Alice, I'll be Lucy and you be Ethel. Hold my belt while I lean out and paint."

KING: Sigrid was absolutely *fearless*. She was—along with all these other great qualities—she, onstage, was not afraid of *anything*, and would go where she had to go.

ELLEN McLAUGHLIN (actor; Sigrid Wurschmidt's friend): Sigrid was a great actor, someone equally fine in comic and tragic roles, a huge-hearted, smart, and passionate artist. She was immensely important to Tony's development of the idea of that character and what that play was. She was a light of a human being. She was one of those people who create communities wherever they are, because people just want to circle around where they are standing. She was beloved.

KUSHNER: The second act of *Perestroika* was dedicated to her. She was an amazing actress, and just completely luminous.

• • •

OSKAR EUSTIS (dramaturg, Eureka Theatre, 1981–88; artistic director, 1988–89): Tony has patience. And "patience" is, of course, a synonym for "blown deadlines."

MARK BRONNENBERG (Kushner's partner, 1982–86): I think he worries about finishing a paragraph. A page. An act of it. But the thing is that he doesn't give up.

STEPHEN SPINELLA (Prior in workshops): There was no play. We all gathered together in San Francisco and there was no script. It was the group that would become the cast at the Eureka. We hung out and we talked about stuff.

> We began meeting tonight about "Angels." Tony laid out the plot, and the basic scenes, it's very exciting, fascinating, and somewhat chaotic, at this point in time. But it did get me excited again about acting.
>
> –from Lorri Holt's journals, June 1988

HOLTZ: The clock ticked and we did our first and second productions and it was getting to be later winter, and no one had seen any pages of this play, and rehearsal was supposed to start April of '89. And we had sold subscriptions based on this world premiere.

KUSHNER: Oskar had decided he'd had enough of waiting for the play, so he summoned me over to read what I had, which turned out to be a very important moment. Sigrid Wurschmidt played the Angel. Ellen was her best friend, so Ellen read Prior.

HOLTZ: I poked my head out of the office and the first draft had come out of our laser printer and it looked like a phone book.

LORRI HOLT (company member, Eureka Theatre; Harper in workshops): I think the very first time we read a draft of *Millennium* at the theater, afterwards it was like, oh my God, this is going to be amazing.

VAN ALYN: I was extremely disappointed in the process. I didn't see us as developing it at all. I saw it as Oskar and Tony developing the play with us as a sounding board. Sort of.

KUSHNER: I really had gotten into trouble, I knew, because my outline said that the Angel was gonna come through the ceiling before intermission, and I had written 120 pages, which is the length of—that's two hours at a minute per page. And I wasn't—she hadn't come through the ceiling yet.

EUSTIS: He came to me and said, "Oskar, I can't get these people to change fast enough!"

KUSHNER: Sigrid told me to walk with her. She said, "Well, what happens next?" I told her what I knew of the plot, and she said, "Have you written any of it?" And I showed her, in my notebook, when we got to her house, this thing that I had written just sitting in the park that turned into Harper's monologue on the flight to San Francisco at the end.

HARPER

Souls were rising, from the earth far below, souls of the dead, of people who had perished, from famine, from war, from the plague, and they floated up, like skydivers in reverse, limbs all akimbo, wheeling and spinning. And the souls of these departed joined hands, clasped ankles, and formed a web, a great net of souls, and the souls were three-atom oxygen molecules, of the stuff of ozone, and the outer rim absorbed them, and was repaired.

–*Perestroika*, Act 5, Scene 8

KUSHNER: And she read it, and she cried a little, and she said, "This is wonderful," and she said, "This is gonna have to be in the play." And I said, "I know, but I don't know what to do—what am I gonna cut?" And she said, "Well, why do you have to cut anything? Why don't you make it two plays?"

EUSTIS: I had no idea it was Sigrid's idea to make it two plays! Either I've repressed that or Tony's blaming a dead girl. (*Laughs.*)

VAN ALYN: I said, "Why don't you make it two plays?" I remember Oskar and Tony looking at each other and going, "Huh, there's a thought."

> Kushner says it was Robert Egan, the [Mark Taper Forum's] associate artistic director, who first suggested to him that his play wasn't half done; rather, Egan told Kushner, there were two related plays and that Part 1 could stand alone.
>
> –Bruce Weber, "Angels' Angels," *New York Times Magazine*, April 25, 1993

EUSTIS: When he wanted to split the show in two, we had a fight, and it lasted a couple of weeks. None of us had heard of a two-evening play other than *Nicholas Nickleby*, and I said to Tony, "That was the Royal Shakespeare Company, and that was Dickens."

HOLTZ: We had to have a company meeting and decide what we were going to do. We all gathered, the management of the theater and the actors, and

Oskar said, "I think this is a really significant piece, but we don't have the resources to mount this in six weeks."

> "Angels in America" is in another state of flux. It looks now as though we'll just be doing a workshop production in March/April . . . The script . . . is outrageously long, and the first part alone is 200 pg.
>
> –from Lorri Holt's journals, December 1988

HOLTZ: We substituted the season-closing play with something else, and we did a staged reading in some other place, and it was the first time anyone had heard *Angels* out loud.

KING: It was a weeklong rehearsal process in some weird former military installation in the Marin Headlands. Then we put it on over the course of two days at this dance workshop. It was a reading, nothing was staged, but the reading took five hours. Then we had an audience talkback afterwards, and there was a guy who said, "It's not a play, it's a novel!"

HOLTZ: The fact that we couldn't do that play when we had promised it really affected subscription sales for the following season. Tony Taccone left; Oskar hung around for a season and then he left.

TONY TACCONE (artistic director, Eureka Theatre, 1981–88): The problem was everybody was getting older, moving from their twenties to their thirties. They needed money to live. I had two kids, I needed a health plan.

VAN ALYN: I know that Tony Taccone sees this as fundamentally a function of the economic forces pushing and pulling us. I'm sure that's partly true, but there was also the ambition—even as far left as we were—all of the men were wanting to fulfill what they felt they had in them in theater. And here we are in America. What are you going to do?

TACCONE: Our aesthetic—it was like we were a little out of step. George Bush was elected president; we were not going to reach that next level of the promised land. I left for Berkeley Rep, which at that point was like the bourgeois house on the hill. I know Oskar was disappointed. It was the

A

E U R E K A

THEATRE COMPANY

production

OUR SYSTEMS ARE BREAKING DOWN:

AIDS —
   the OZONE —
     the GOVERNMENT—

and GOD HAS DISAPPEARED!

A staged reading in two parts

ANGELS IN AMERICA

a new epic drama
by **Tony Kushner**
directed by **Oskar Eustis**

Performance A/ $12   Performance B/ $12

I. Friday	II. Saturday	I. Sunday	II. Sunday
April 14	April 15	April 16	April 16
7:30 p.m.	7:30 p.m.	2:30 p.m.	7:30 p.m.

Discussions following each Part II presentation.

at FOOTWORK STUDIO

3221 22nd Street at Mission Street

call Eureka Theatre Box Office

558-9898

for tickets and information.

hardest decision I've ever made, leaving the Eureka. Within a year, Oskar was at the Taper.

KUSHNER: Oskar was headhunted away by Gordon Davidson and brought down to L.A. to work at the Taper, which was a very big— the largest—regional theater in the United States at that point. Gordon Davidson was like Joe Papp.

BOB EGAN (producing artistic director, Mark Taper Forum, 1983–2003): I was looking to beef up our new play development staff, which was pretty healthy and robust, but Oskar has unique and enviable dramaturgical skills—he's, you know, pretty great. Gordon had this lovely tendency when he was out in the world, he'd come back and say, "You know, Bob, I just had this lovely conversation with Oskar Eustis, and I think we should think about bringing him on staff."

EUSTIS: When I went to Los Angeles, I left my theater in effect to protect *Angels*, because the Eureka didn't have the resources to develop it. I could either throw my hat into the ring with *Angels* or I could stay in San Francisco and keep the Eureka going, and I chose *Angels*.

A flier for the first Eureka Theatre reading of *Angels in America*, 1989. (*Jeff King*)

EGAN: If my memory serves me correctly, he wanted to bring a project with him. Only one.

EUSTIS: I sent Gordon *Angels* in a somewhat hyperbolic fashion. I said, "Gordon, my theater company is falling apart, the Berlin Wall has fallen, my father has died, my girlfriend"—Lorri Holt by the way—"has left me, and I don't know what I believe in, but I believe in this play. If you produce this play, I'll come to your theater."

EGAN: I read it right away, as did Gordon, and Gordon and I, I don't think we had a conversation, we just both independently called Oskar. I told Oskar, "This is one of the best plays I've ever read. We'd be foolish not to say yes."

KUSHNER: Suddenly, Gordon Davidson had read my play and was calling me up. I mean, things started happening.

> Debra Ballinger is the new executive director of the Eureka.
> Oskar is going to Los Angeles. I have not written about any of
> this—not any of it. . . . I am suffering from complete burnout
> with regard to the Eureka.
>
> –from Lorri Holt's journals, July 9, 1989

DEBRA BALLINGER BERNSTEIN (executive director, Eureka Theatre, 1989–92): I had been teaching at NYU. My mom had breast cancer, and I was on a leave to take care of her, because I'm from the Bay Area. I had decided I wasn't going back to New York, and then in May or June I was recruited. Probably not the best time to be recruited to be the executive director of a theater.

KATHLEEN CHALFANT (Hannah in workshops): We did all the developmental work at the Taper starting in 1989. We did a whole version of *Millennium* in their theater up in the Hollywood Hills. It was sort of like our day job.

CASEY COWAN (lighting designer at Taper Too *Millennium* workshop, 1989–90): First was a workshop at the Taper Too, with Oskar, Tony, and Bob Egan, as part of a New Work Festival that Bob Egan produced.

EGAN: Hold on, I'm looking at it because I have the posters in my bathroom . . . "*Angels in America* Part 1 by Tony Kushner, Taper Lab, '89: The Presiding Demon is Roy Cohn in this incandescent tapestry of Mormons, AIDS, Perestroika, and Redemption, as we hurtle towards the Millennium, yearning to find those Angels in America."

COWAN: We had one week to load it in, tech it, and open it. I am famous for writing light cues really fast. There's over three hundred light cues in that show because of all the scenes, and that was just *Millennium Approaches*! We really slammed that thing in.

EGAN: Shows in the festival, we tried to really accentuate to everybody, top to bottom, the board, the staff, the artists, the audiences, that this whole process was about plays in the process of becoming. So to encumber too much production would stop that spirit of exploration and experimentation.

SEYD: In 1989 the earthquake happened in San Francisco during the World Series. Everyone ran out of their apartments and houses. I got a call from Sigrid in L.A., five minutes after the earthquake ended. She had gone to the doctor to have an eye exam because she was having a problem with her eye. The doctor said, "Look, I hate to say this to you, but have you experienced cancer?" And she said yes, and he said, "I'm afraid that it's come back in your eyes."

VAN ALYN: I have very little memory of that whole rehearsal process. I have no idea how I was! Probably not very good (*laughs*). I would say I was pretty checked out, worried about Sigrid.

EUSTIS: Sigrid remained doing the part through the first workshop we did of *Millennium* at the Taper Too. It was one of the grimmest nights. The cancer had returned, it was affecting her eyesight.

KUSHNER: She had these huge, really thick spectacles. We had to blow up every page of her script to these giant pages, 'cause she couldn't really see anymore. That's why the Angel in the play calls herself the bald eagle—'cause I was hoping that Sigrid would make it, and I thought, *Look, she's bald.*

EUSTIS: There was one point where she missed an entrance. I was sitting in the far house right; I could see backstage. Sigrid was sitting with her head in her hands, she had completely missed her entrance, there was maybe twenty seconds of silence, and then she put her head up, realized what was going on, and ran on.

EGAN: I remember very clearly, when the Angel appears, she walked out onstage and stood on a box, and spread her—I think Oskar had done some minimal thing—she put her arms out and was the Angel. People talk about that moment to this day. It was unbelievably powerful.

EUSTIS: That was the last time she went onstage.

TACCONE: She was in so much pain, she barely made it through.

Sigrid Wurschmidt. (*Richard Seyd*)

VAN ALYN: At the end we came offstage, and she was lying on the floor. I stuck my head out and Tony Taccone was sitting in the front row and he said "What?" and I said "Sigrid"—

TACCONE: —and we carried her out and I drove her to the hospital. And then we went back to the apartment and stayed up talking all night. One of our closest friends was dying.

SEYD: After the workshop, we came back up to the Bay Area. She passed away in April of 1990. What was extraordinary was the outpouring of love and affection for her. I still have a box with all of the letters that people wrote her when it was publicly announced that she was really sick. She really got to *know* and *understand* how much she was loved by the community of audiences that saw her work over the years in San Francisco. It made a difference to her.

And then, of course, it's ironic that she was playing an angel. Her best friend at the time was Ellen McLaughlin. Ellen took over the role. Ellen said that every second of the time that she performed it, Sigrid was there with her.

McLAUGHLIN: It was a terrible thing to get a part that way.

> I remember a plane trip that we took together from New York to San Francisco. You were wearing newly purchased green boots, and we sat together, talking for a long time. It was an evening flight, and somewhere over the vast mid-reaches of the country, a miracle occurred. The northern lights were suddenly, vividly, brilliantly visible out our little round window. The cabin was dimmed and the passengers watched as these extravagant washes of green light vaulted across the sky for about a half an hour.
>
> We were transfixed, leaning together, cheeks touching, holding hands. I think of that often, perhaps because it was so like what happened when I was with you. The world became this wild and generous stranger that was constantly bestowing gifts. The world through your eyes was like that, and just sitting next to you was enough to endow what one saw with magnitude and grace.
>
> –from Ellen McLaughlin's eulogy for Sigrid Wurschmidt, San Francisco, April 16, 1990

KING: There were eleven thousand workshops. It was well developed.

EUSTIS: What we were trying to do was provide the ground for the piece to continue developing. Overwhelmingly what that meant was for Tony to keep writing. What I found was a very effective way to keep him writing was to keep having deadlines for readings and workshops and readings and workshops.

JON MATTHEWS (Louis in Taper Too *Millennium* workshop, 1990)**:** For a while I kept a file and there were seven wholly different scenes for the hot dog scene. That was exciting. That's the appeal of this part of the process.

CYNTHIA MACE (Harper in workshops)**:** There were so many of them. Sometimes it would be a two-week workshop, sometimes it would be a week when everyone would get together and try out new things. Many of them weren't for the public; they'd just be for Gordon Davidson and his staff, a few invited people. I loved Gordon. He said, "I don't know what this is, but this is something, and this is our mission," and he was right. But sometimes he'd sit there with this kind of "What *is* this?" look on his face.

KUSHNER: I had been associate artistic director at New York Theatre Workshop. I was working with a director, and the first person who walked in to audition was Kathy Chalfant, and nobody knew who she was, and she was astonishing. And so, secretly, I think I actually started working on Hannah more for her.

CHALFANT: In the spring of 1988 I ran into Tony on the street and he told me he was writing a play and he had a part for me in it.

KUSHNER: The very first reading of the completed script of *Millennium Approaches* was at New York Theatre Workshop. It was the first time Kathy, who had never seen the script before, she was doing some other play, and finished it two minutes before she did the reading. I kind of hand-delivered the script to the actors; Kathy was performing, so I couldn't get it to her.

CHALFANT: For some reason I was slightly late and I just got handed the script and they said, "You'll be playing the rabbi, the doctor, the Mormon mother, and Ethel Rosenberg," and I said, "OK." Out came the rabbi from my Christmas-and-Easter Episcopalian mouth!

KUSHNER: She came in, and sat down, and didn't miss a beat. She pulled Ethel out of her back pocket. It was dazzling. It was dazzling.

McLAUGHLIN: Kathy's part had been done by Abigail Van Alyn in the first few workshops. So I met Kathy for the first time when we did the full staging of *Millennium* at the Taper after Sig's death.

Louis (Jon Matthews) and Prior (Stephen Spinella) in the Taper Too workshop, 1990. (*Casey Cowan*)

MATTHEWS: I have a very strong memory of sitting at the first rehearsal, and it really blew my mind that somebody that brilliant was someone I had never seen in New York or L.A. theater. I couldn't believe that Kathy was so brilliant, and I had never seen her work.

EGAN: We had a pretty coherent path for big plays that were finding their sea legs. The next stage was then it was done fully at the Taper Too, this really small ninety-nine-seat theater. And then it went to the mainstage.

COWAN: We did it as part of the regular season of the Taper Too, same group, probably within a year. We had more time. We had more money.

EUSTIS: *Perestroika* wasn't written yet. We had basically thrown up our hands. *Perestroika* was not being finished, so let's put up *Millennium* and see what it does.

KING: Rick Frank played Roy, he was wonderful, he's since passed. I remember telling my wife after one of the first rehearsals, "I feel like Rick by himself is raising the game here." Roy and Joe have these exciting scenes together, I felt like I had to step up.

MATTHEWS: Rick Frank was amazing.

McLAUGHLIN: He was already sick [with AIDS] while we were doing the show. He was on a TV show [*Anything But Love*] at the time. People would recognize him on the street because he was a pretty big star. And I thought he really understood something about Roy Cohn. There was a kind of sensual sneer and whine to him that seemed right. He was important to the development of that character.

HARRY WATERS JR. (Belize in Taper Too *Millennium* workshop): Suddenly I'm in the room with all these people. I was a journeyman actor in L.A.

MATTHEWS: It was a fucking shitstorm of energy.

HOLT: I was in L.A., living in this house in Pasadena. Playing Harper, who is pretending to be pregnant, and here I was pregnant, living in this house full of mothballs to keep the skunks away, and they were spraying Malathion every night to kill the fruit flies, and I was getting soaked with it and I thought I was poisoning my son.

MATTHEWS: It was clear that Tony felt that Oskar needed a different eye on it.

DAVID ESBJORNSON (associate director at Taper Too *Millennium* workshop, 1990): When I arrived in Los Angeles I realized that Tony was out there to do this workshop. That's when he invited me to be part of the development process. And Oskar was very welcoming and gracious about that.

MATTHEWS: We had three and a half weeks to put up a full production, the biggest production the Taper Too'd ever had, and there were huge rewrites. It was an impossible situation. Tony had all this pressure on him, and so there was a lot of pressure on Oskar.

COWAN: The Taper Too is basically a basement below an amphitheater. There's hardly any fly space. There's barely any offstage space left or right. Figuring out how to fly in an angel or have a wall crack open—that was more than just an exercise in physics.

BRONNENBERG: Tony called me and said, "Something really strange is happening. At the end, people are just going crazy. They're cheering and applauding." He seemed surprised, kind of befuddled by it in a way.

MATTHEWS: The reviewers weren't over the moon. The audience got it, that's what was exciting.

> There's an overabundance of good stuff, but too much is too much.
> It undercuts focus. The real chaff here is a gratuitous and luridly
> graphic scene (verbally and visually) of street sodomy in Act II
> (there are *three* acts, folks, and *two* intermissions). It adds nothing

and is jarring in a play that has been outspoken and direct until then, but a great deal more subtle.

–Sylvie Drake, "Stage Review: A Novel 'Millennium,'" *Los Angeles Times*, May 21, 1990

DAVID MARSHALL GRANT (Joe in New York, 1993–94): I walked in having no idea of what I was going to see. It was astonishing. It just blew my mind. I just couldn't get over how funny it was. I couldn't get over how moving it was. I knew I had seen something that would live forever.

And apparently there was a second play that he was working on! I couldn't imagine what Part 2 was going to be.

In the summer of 1990, with no warning, Sylvia Kushner was found to have inoperable lung cancer. She died six weeks later. . . . "One thing I learned from my mother's death is that until you go through a major loss you don't realize what is taken from you," he says.

–Arthur Lubow, "Tony Kushner's Paradise Lost," *New Yorker*, November 30, 1992

SPINELLA: Sigrid was a big deal. Kimberly's accident was a big deal. And Tony losing his mother was a very big deal. All of that stuff went into that play.

KUSHNER: I came out to my mother in 1981. This was before NYU took over the giant building at 721 Broadway, and the directing program was in this little crummy two-story building on Seventh Street between Third Avenue and Second Avenue. There was a pay phone across the street from the building, and I was sort of trying to work my nerve up to do it, and between classes I decided it was time so I just went across and made a collect phone call. And I told her that I was gay and I was coming out of the closet. She was very upset. She started crying. She cried through the whole phone call. And pretty much for several weeks after every time I called her, she would start crying. So I told her to stop or I wasn't going to call her anymore because I was—it began to feel like she was in mourning for someone and I found it too disturbing.

I think when she saw the play, read the play—she only ever saw *Millen-nium*; she died before I wrote *Perestroika*. She came to see it at the Taper Too production and I think—my mother was always very eager to feel guilty about things, though in my opinion she really didn't have all that much to feel guilty about. She was a really wonderful mother. But she was very thin-skinned about some stuff, and I think that because I had used that—the phone call—in the play, she felt that I was saying something to her about her reaction to my being gay. In fact her reaction was nothing at all like Hannah's. She didn't deny . . . She didn't refuse to hear what I was saying. She heard it loud and clear.

ACT 2

1991–1992

JANUARY
The death toll
from AIDS
in the United
States reaches
100,000

AUGUST
ACT UP covers
Senator Jesse
Helms's house
in a giant
condom

NOVEMBER
Los Angeles
Lakers star
Earvin "Magic"
Johnson reveals
that he is HIV-
positive and
retires from the
NBA

1991

APRIL
Tony Kushner
completes the
first draft of
Perestroika

MAY
Eureka
premiere of
*Millennium
Approaches* and
staged reading
of *Perestroika*

OCTOBER
Joseph Papp,
founder of the
Public Theater
in New York,
dies

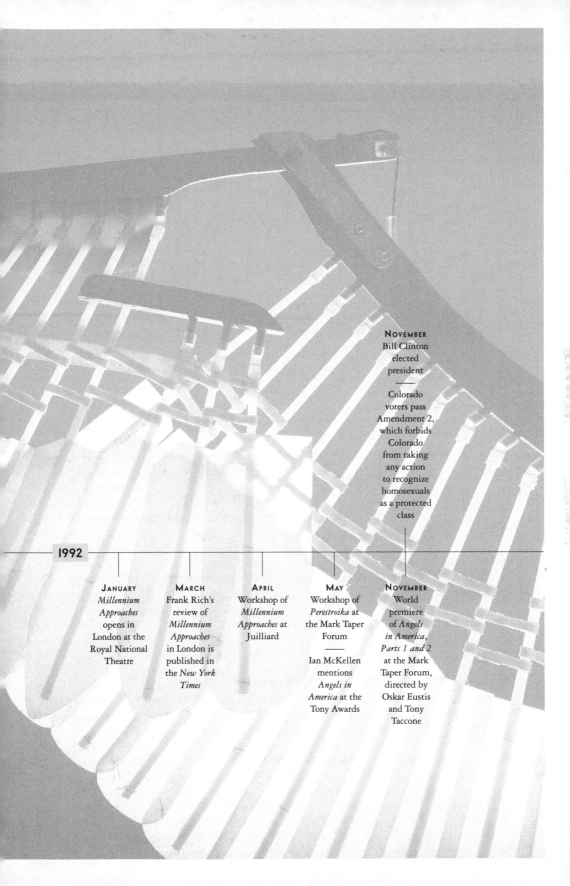

NOVEMBER
Bill Clinton
elected
president

—

Colorado
voters pass
Amendment 2,
which forbids
Colorado
from taking
any action
to recognize
homosexuals
as a protected
class

1992

JANUARY
*Millennium
Approaches*
opens in
London at the
Royal National
Theatre

MARCH
Frank Rich's
review of
*Millennium
Approaches*
in London is
published in
the *New York
Times*

APRIL
Workshop of
*Millennium
Approaches* at
Juilliard

MAY
Workshop of
Perestroika at
the Mark Taper
Forum

—

Ian McKellen
mentions
*Angels in
America* at the
Tony Awards

NOVEMBER
World
premiere
of *Angels
in America*,
Parts 1 and 2
at the Mark
Taper Forum,
directed by
Oskar Eustis
and Tony
Taccone

CHAPTER I

HEAVEN IS A CITY MUCH LIKE SAN FRANCISCO

EUREKA THEATRE COMPANY, 1991

DEBRA BALLINGER BERNSTEIN (executive director, Eureka Theatre, San Francisco, 1989-92): When I took the company over, everyone was leaving. I was walking into a period where there was lots of resentment. Resentment that everyone had left. Resentment that the Eureka had the rights to the play.

TONY TACCONE (former artistic director, Eureka Theatre): We tried to wrestle the rights from the Eureka. The Eureka, wisely, did not allow that to happen, and forced Tony's hand, and forced him to let the theater do the first incarnation of *Angels*.

ABIGAIL VAN ALYN (Eureka company member, 1981-91): Oskar was going with Tony and this play wherever it went. And the idea was that we were *all* supposed to go with it wherever it went as a Eureka production . . . I guess from their perspective, you know, what do we have to offer? They have actors. They have lots of money. Why would they do that? Why wouldn't they get the best of the best wherever they go?

JOYCE KETAY (Kushner's theatrical agent): The contract was with the Eureka Theatre, not with Oskar.

ANNE DARRAGH (Harper in San Francisco, 1991): The new administration didn't have the collectivist ideals, it wasn't their mission, they didn't commission that play.

KETAY: They didn't have an artistic director; they had a board, which was mostly lawyers.

DAVID ESBJORNSON (director in San Francisco, 1991): There wasn't a lot of goodwill.

TONY KUSHNER: It turned into this very ugly struggle. I hadn't written *Perestroika* yet, but to fulfill my contract the Eureka insisted that we do a production of *Angels*. The two lawyers for the board of the Eureka, who'd taken over the theater, insisted that they were gonna sue me if I didn't.

ELIZABETH ZITRIN (attorney; board member, Eureka Theatre, early 1990s): My fiduciary responsibility was to the Eureka Theatre Company. Oskar was my good friend, and I certainly cared about him. He said he thought it would be difficult for the Eureka to produce *Angels* and he could take it to the Taper. I opposed that. I was not the only one.

BERNSTEIN: I made the case to the board that we should downsize. We should become a smaller theater company, maybe even give up the space. But we had this thing: *Angels in America*. The board thought it would be a cash cow.

ZITRIN: There was no question but that it was the most important thing by far

---

Program cover and ticket stub, Eureka Theatre, 1991. (*Program: David Esbjornson. Ticket: Jack Carpenter.*)

that the Eureka had going on. I was convinced very early on that its potential was limitless. I don't think I'm particularly brilliant to have been right about that. It was just so good!

ESBJORNSON: I don't think Tony and the Taper thought that was going to materialize. And then it became clear it was going to. I was the associate director of the Taper workshop, or something like that. I didn't lobby for the Eureka job. But I was there and I was jonesing to direct it.

KUSHNER: So David, who I went to graduate school with, came to San Francisco.

• • •

DAVID WEISSMAN (director, *We Were Here*): What surprised me the most in revisiting that period, I think, was how much *fun* we were having in the midst of it all. At a certain point you just had to accept that this is the new normal, that this is the reality we're living in, and that's not going to change. You live your life accordingly, because you can't live in a state of constant heightened panic, because it's just not sustainable.

CLEVE JONES (founder, NAMES Project AIDS Memorial Quilt): By 1991 it was really hard to walk through the neighborhood and not be aware. You saw people with KS lesions. We were already skinny—by the late '70s, everyone was skinny—but you saw people wasting away. It wasn't a regular occurrence, but it wasn't unheard-of to see people die on the street.

WEISSMAN: As it got into the late '80s and early '90s, that scene started to have a lot more of a presence of ACT UP, in the nightlife and in the Cafe Flore particularly. There was a lot of overlap with artists and ACT UP types.

JONATHAN LETHEM (novelist): Going to a Halloween parade, which I did many successive years in the Castro, was the most extraordinary experience of feeling myself to be part of a living and growing countercultural consciousness.

DAVID FRANCE (director and author, *How to Survive a Plague*): When activism took the ground in 1987, one of its first goals was to establish the humanity of gay people. The first gay kiss on national television was an ACT UP protest event. They would do these kiss-ins where they would make their opponents see them kissing: Just look at us kissing, and the world is not gonna fall apart.

ESBJORNSON: I didn't have a script when I went into *Perestroika* rehearsal.

BERNSTEIN: Spring was rolling around, we were in rehearsals. Tony hadn't finished *Perestroika*. It was a nail-biter: Was it going to be done? Was it *not* going to be done?

KUSHNER: During that rehearsal period, someone on the board gave me their spider-infested cabin on the Russian River, and I went away for ten days—it was early April—and I sat down, and I started writing. And I wrote seven hundred pages of *Perestroika* in ten days—I just wrote the whole . . . three times as much as would ultimately be in it, all by hand. And it was literally like *The Red Shoes*—I could not stop writing. If I tried to go to sleep, I would wake up two minutes later and just *go*. And a lot of the best stuff that's in the play now was in that first draft. And when I'd finished, I realized I had finished on my mother and father's wedding anniversary. And I'm not making this up: I got in the car to drive back, even though I hadn't slept in eleven days and I was literally shaking from exhaustion. I didn't have a computer—it was just a big stack of legal paper. And I thought, *If I go off the cliff into the Pacific Ocean, no one will ever know what happened, so I have to be really careful.*

And I turned on the radio, and the first piece—I didn't even turn the knob, it was probably already set to a classical station—but I turned on the radio, and the first thing that came on was Mozart's bassoon concerto, which was one of my mother's practice pieces. And then the announcer came on, and then they started up with Mozart's clarinet concerto, which was my father's big practice piece. Then I went out of range of that station. So I turned the knob, and the first thing that came on was a song by the Black Crowes called "She Talks to Angels." And then, right after that, Simon & Garfunkel, "We've all come to look for America." And then "American Pie." I was not hallucinating at all. It was very real. That was an amazing . . . an amazing day.

ESBJORNSON: I say, "What are you doing here?" And he says, "I finished, Dave, it's done." It was like Moses coming down from the mountain! We went out that night to celebrate with champagne. I said, "Tomorrow we'll read *Perestroika*."

MICHAEL ORNSTEIN (Louis in San Francisco, 1991): I don't remember a hell of a lot about the rehearsal process, but I remember the day Tony brought *Perestroika* in. Holy shit, man. I remember what I was drinking! I had my coffee and Tony had on a bright purple cotton hoodie. He sat down with this gigantic phone book, and he placed it on the table, and we all realized, *Oh my God, that's the fucking script.*

ESBJORNSON: We started at 10:00, and 6:30 came and went and we were still reading it.

ORNSTEIN: It took us two days to read through the entire thing.

HARRY WATERS JR. (Belize in San Francisco, 1991): I remember we were sitting there, reading the script for the first time, and Kathy Chalfant was just weeping because it was so amazing. How could anyone write this?

KUSHNER: There's a whole subplot about Belize forming a political group. There were many, many, many more hallucinations from Harper. In this seven-hundred-page really long version, there was a lot of shit. I mean, something with a homeless kid . . . A *chauffeur* . . . ? God, there were, like, all these other characters. One of the reasons that I could write for days without stopping is I was just "Nobody ever has to know what I've done here."

ELLEN McLAUGHLIN (the Angel in San Francisco, 1991): There was no budget at all. We had about twenty dollars and fifty cents to spend on the entire set.

ESBJORNSON: I did finally just go, *Oh shit.* There was no money. It's not like you can just throw bodies and cash at it, you just have to do it.

WATERS: It was more of a San Francisco crowd. Jeff didn't do it. Lorri didn't do it.

JEFF KING (Joe in workshops and in Los Angeles, 1992): I had just moved to L.A. My son was six months old. We had just been there a few months at that point, I was just settling in, so I skipped that one. I didn't want to, but it was the thing I needed to do for my life.

LORRI HOLT (Harper in workshops): I was supposed to do the Eureka production. But my son had just been born, and I couldn't put myself through the part again right then, so I did a different show. And then I was out.

I didn't realize it was my last shot.

MICHAEL SCOTT RYAN (Joe in San Francisco, 1991): I was a company member with the American Conservatory Theater, grinding through my seventh season. Immediately after my callback, Oskar, David, and Tony spoke to me in the lobby—gave me the quick rundown of the play's complicated property-ownership issues. The upshot being that if I accepted the role, I'd need to understand that I wouldn't move on with it through its future. I was fine with that. I wasn't a very ambitious actor, much more a journeyman enjoying the private experience. I quit acting sometime after *Angels* closed.

DENNIS HARVEY (San Francisco theater critic): Even by the time it opened, people were anticipating the great new thing of American theater.

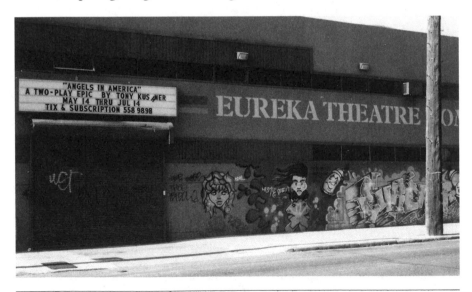

Marquee at the Eureka Theatre, 1991. (*Tony Kushner*)

ROBERT HURWITT (San Francisco theater critic): As with any theater community, there were people who were saying, "Oh my God, they are going to fall flat on their face." This thing has gotten blown all out of proportion and the second part isn't even ready yet!

KATHLEEN CHALFANT (Hannah in San Francisco, 1991): It was in some ways the most beautiful version of the play, and the most Poor Theater version of the play.

HARVEY: They basically had a giant shower curtain in front of the stage. For scene transitions they would just whip the shower curtain across, one actor at the front and one at the back, and when they got to the other side it would be a new scene.

KUSHNER: To this day, no one has ever done better with the magic. David is incredibly clever designing and building gizmos, so every magic trick in the play, David figured out a way to do it. There was no money or anything. He built all this shit—it was incredible.

DEBORAH PEIFER (San Francisco theater critic): That sense of amazement of a book popping up out of the floor in flames, all done with lighting.

KUSHNER: He did it with all these bungee cords.

ESBJORNSON: There's this rumbling from these big woofers underneath the stage and the seats, and you think, *Is this an earthquake?* Which in San Francisco is a real issue! And then simply a trap pops up from the floor. On the top of the trap is a column, maybe five feet high, and on top of that is a big book. The column lights from underneath, the book opens—we had a mechanism—the red aleph lights up, it's just backlit with a red light. And there's a bunch of smoke and all that. And then when Prior responds, like, *Did this happen??* the audience has the same response, and then there's this laughter as you realize how the effect was done.

PEIFER: In the film they actually had a book in flames, and it was like, "OK."

ESBJORNSON: Most of the things were done—not tongue-in-cheek, that's too cheesy. But I wanted to surprise them, almost to scare them. But then there would be a secondary response of laughter as you saw how the effect worked.

TOM KAMM (set designer in San Francisco, 1991): The headroom above the top of the proscenium was about three feet. That's barely enough space to mask lighting, much less fly someone in. So we cut a hole in the roof and built a little penthouse up there for the Angel to come down from into the room.

McLAUGHLIN: I was flying in the sense that I was hanging in the air. The assistant stage manager, Dede Moyse, had a rope around her waist and I had a rope around mine, and when she'd jump off a table, I'd fly up, and when she'd climb back on the table, I would land.

The Angel (Ellen McLaughlin) in San Francisco, 1991. (*Katy Raddatz/Museum of Performance + Design*)

JACK CARPENTER (co-lighting designer in San Francisco, 1991): With the Angel, Jim Cave and I knew that we needed to have something really spectacular. I had been working on using ACLs, which have tight, concentrated beams that are super-bright. Everybody was on dinner break and Jim and I were mucking about, trying to figure out how to integrate that ACL into the set, and everything was running behind, of course.

When we were working on it, one of the technicians was moving stuff around. Dust fell because they were moving around, and we saw the dust in this light. David happened to walk in at that moment and said, "Oh my God! It has to look like that!" So we had to replicate a technician kicking dust around in the grid. I think we used sawdust.

WATERS: On opening night, we decided to bring Jordan—my son—to the theater. "Oh, let's keep him backstage!" It was so tense. The whole building was just vibrating with tension over this show. At some point, because of all that tension, he just started screaming. And it wasn't a screaming that could be satisfied with a bottle. It was the tension in the air. Deb just had to bring him home.

Belize (Harry Waters Jr.) and Prior (Stephen Spinella) in San Francisco, 1991. (*Katy Raddatz/Museum of Performance + Design*)

BRIAN THORSTENSON (intern, Eureka Theatre, 1990–91): Those were incredibly difficult years for the city as a whole, not just for queer people. *Angels* really did this thing, it really did what Tony set out to do, a "Gay Fantasia on National Themes," of placing this horror that we had all been living through inside a story of America. That was really important to the city, to all of us.

MARK BRONNENBERG (Kushner's partner in the mid-'80s): I came to opening night. And I saw them have that reaction, just: *This Is Completely Amazing and Overwhelming.* The audience just went *crazy.*

PEIFER: I have never in all my life seen a situation in which people did not leave the theater during the intermission unless they had to. And I'm not talking about *Can I get a cup of coffee?* but *Can I make it through the next act without a bathroom break?* People could not bear to be out of that theater while this thing was happening.

> To call this a brilliantly realized, profoundly funny, wickedly thoughtful piece of theater is to discover the severe limitations of language. I find myself wanting to say, simply, it's more than I ever imagined. See it immediately. This is an experience in the theater you will remember for your whole life.
>
> –Deborah Peifer, *Bay Area Reporter*, May 30, 1991

JESSE GREEN (theater critic, *New York Times*): Ellen and I had gone to college together. She said, "You have got to come see this crazy thing I'm doing."

I said, "Really? I'm kinda busy, what is it?"

She said, "It's a two-part play and the first part is four hours and the second part isn't really done, but at least come to the first part and see what you think."

I really didn't want to but I went. It was like this weird thing I'm doing, to see my friend from college, who advertised it as a weird thing she was doing. Although as it turns out she knew damn well what it was. She wasn't the type to sell things that way.

When it was over I knew I had to come back and see the second part. It was the best thing I may have ever seen that was not a musical, and I say that advisedly, not so much because I'm into musical theater but because Tony is. It always seems to me that he's trying to write a musical without music, and he wants it to be Maria singing "Tonight," that's what he wants to get to, that pitch.

ORNSTEIN: Normally when you do a new play, the house isn't full every night. The *Village Voice* isn't flying out to see it. We had a line around the block every night. I got recognized. People would come up to me on the street. But it was a different way than normal. People would come up to me and hug me. And they would cry, you know? And they would say, "Thank you." They would ask *me* if *I* was OK.

ESBJORNSON: I had lived in San Francisco for four years in the late '70s. My first gay friend was from Minnesota and he came out to visit and loved it so much he stayed. He was one of the first people I knew to contract AIDS and die. That happened just as I was beginning my career, right after I graduated from NYU. I had acquaintances who I expected to come see *Angels in America*, and I looked for them, and they didn't come. They were gone.

GREEN: During Part 2, I wanted to rescind my judgment of genius.

KUSHNER: Originally, every act of the five acts of *Perestroika* started with a clown scene set in the Soviet Union. Those ended up being the first five scenes of my play *Slavs!* [1994].

ESBJORNSON: I used the five Bolsheviks as curtain raisers. I made the actors hold the scripts in hand while they moved around. And then at one point in each act, they laid down their scripts and acted out what I considered to be the central point of that act.

BRONNENBERG: I remember it going on, and on, and on. I did think, *Oh, Tony, you have got to cut this, honey.*

PEIFER: I think there might have been twenty-two acts. I'm exaggerating, but not by a lot.

GREEN: It was a mess. It was not a cute mess to me; it was not fun. It did not seem rescuable. And I said to Ellen what I'm sure everybody was saying to Ellen and to everyone else and to Tony: "Just leave the play. It will never work." Tony didn't take that in, luckily!

> The actors carry their scripts onstage. About half the scenes are staged and the rest briefly summarized. Scenery is minimal. Actors and stagehands are sometimes out of place when the curtain is flung open. . . . It remains to be seen how the playwright will make the main plot lines connect more fully to the debates of the Soviet Communists, on the verge of political extinction, gathered around a samovar. For all of "Perestroika's" unwieldiness, it's good to remember that "Millennium Approaches" was once just as sprawling before Kushner pulled it into shape.
>
> –Steven Winn, "An Epic Drama Unfolding," *San Francisco Chronicle*, June 4, 1991

THORSTENSON: It got to the scene between Hannah and Prior where Prior's in the hospital and Prior says, "I've always depended on the kindness of strangers." They finished the scene, and the audience erupted into this . . . *applause* . . . I think it lasted a good five minutes. Kathleen and Stephen looked out at the audience, like, *What is going on?*

McLAUGHLIN: I came out late into the evening as the Angel wearing the wings and the whole get-up, stood in front of the curtain, and said, "*Act 5: Heaven, I'm in Heaven.*"

And this woman in the front row said "Act FIVE?! Oh my GOD! DO YOU KNOW WHAT TIME IT IS?!"

And I said, "No." Because I honestly had no idea. It's not like I was wearing a watch.

And she said "It's MIDNIGHT, for God's sake! What's going on with this playwright? ACT FIVE? How long is it?"

And I said, "We've never done it so I don't know, maybe forty-five minutes?"

And she said, "The buses aren't even running anymore! How are we supposed to get HOME?" And she turns around to the rest of the audience and says, "Are we going to stay?" And people sort of nodded and mumbled and she says, "Well, I guess we'll stay, but I mean, really . . ."

And then she said, "But that's the end, right? There isn't an Act 6 or something?"

And I said, "Well, there's an epilogue."

And she said, "Oh my GOD, is he NUTS? An EPILOGUE? How long is THAT?"

And I said, "Well, again, we've never actually run it, but . . . ten, fifteen minutes?"

And she said, "Well, apparently we HAVE TO STAY, but this is RI-DICULOUS, TELL HIM HE HAS TO CUT!"

And then I said "Well, the longer we keep talking here . . ."

PEIFER: And people still stayed. Because people trusted him, because of that first part. So people stayed! They didn't say, like, three days later, "I have to go to work, so tell me how it ends."

BERNSTEIN: I think they would've sat through ten hours.

McLAUGHLIN: And then after the show, as the actors were basically limp-ing to the dressing rooms, Tony, looking sort of glassy-eyed, came over to us and said, "You know, a really interesting thing happens after an audience has been in the theater for a really long time, they start to lose their bearings and become very malleable. They, like, forget what they think they believe about things and what they do for a living and their names and where they live and . . ."

And we were like, "Yeah, Tony, and you really have to cut it."

KUSHNER: That was insane. Lots of people maintain that it was the greatest performance of *Perestroika* they saw, because the play was this sort of illimit-able text. You had no idea what was in all those pages, and they were being thrown all over the stage.

ESBJORNSON: The first night it came down at 12:30. So Tony wrote bridges, for things that were fun to tell but hard to show.

McLAUGHLIN: Sometimes a character would come out and say, "We don't have time to do this scene but in this scene, Joe beats up Louis and they talk about these particular court cases."

RYAN: Ultimately, the audience guided the performance with their abject hunger to find out what happens to the characters. They were now also compatriots with the company.

ESBJORNSON: It became another layer to the communication between actors, page, and audience. It was like someone stopped, became your friend, and told you what happened next. And people connected in the audience, which yelled and laughed and shouted. Kathy said it felt like a basketball game.

WATERS: Talk about *rapt*, it was like being *held* by them. We only staged around five scenes, we weren't off book. So even understanding the theatricality was really engaging. You had to imagine the whole thing.

RICHARD FELDMAN (director of Juilliard *Millennium Approaches* workshop, 1992): It was so thrilling, so exciting and immediate. It just felt like form and content were the same. *Perestroika* was reordering what was happening on the stage. I could imagine doing it every night, and you would pull out of a hat which would be seen, and described, and staged at music stands. Of course, no one does it like that.

CHALFANT: There was a wonderful scene between Joe and Louis about Thurgood Marshall that didn't move the play forward, so we took it out. But then Thurgood Marshall retired, so we put it back in.

DARRAGH: By the end of the process, Tony was like, "Oh, whatever, do what you want," so we all put back in our favorite bits.

ESBJORNSON: We got to do it in its purest form! We got to do it before everybody *fixed* it.

STEPHEN SPINELLA (Prior in San Francisco, 1991): It was the wildest ride. If this had been New York—and not to trash the Eureka Theatre, but they're hemorrhaging money, they haven't had a hit for a long time. And they have a hit with lines around the block. And they schedule another show after this show!

KAMM: It could have turned around the whole course of the Eureka Theatre.

ESBJORNSON: It could still be running today if it were still open.

KETAY: But they couldn't move it, they couldn't do anything.

ZITRIN: Board members were like, "Whaddya mean, we're closing it?" The staff did not make provisions for extending it. It was the best play in the world and people were lining up around the block and they were like, "OK, it's done!"

HARVEY: People claimed that there were two factions in the show. One faction pressured all the actors not to commit to an extension.

ZITRIN: Oh, someone has other commitments? Well, there are other actors! Oh, the space is booked? Well, there are other spaces!

HARVEY: One thing I did hear afterward is that it ended up being so expensive for the Eureka that, despite it being so successful, they lost so much money on it that the theater basically went under.

BERNSTEIN: The Eureka had a budget of about $650,000 a year. *Angels'* budget was around $250,000. That's an enormous strain to put on a company that was kind of flailing.

ZITRIN: It was catastrophic for the Eureka.

ANDY HOLTZ (business manager, Eureka Theatre, San Francisco, 1987–89): That was the end of the Eureka Theatre as a producing company. The play that cemented the Eureka's place in the history of American theater was also the play that was too epic for such a small company. It's, like, the mom died giving birth to this amazing baby.

WATERS: The Eureka is gone! We killed the theater!

VAN ALYN: *Angels* certainly gave the theater a coup de grâce.

THORSTENSON: It was *heartbreaking*. I saw *Bright Room Called Day* at the Eureka. A bunch of Caryl Churchill. They were doing work that no one else was doing, and it was this ensemble of just amazing theater artists.

KING: The biggest artistic ambition I'd had in my entire career was to be a member of a company. That's what I really wanted, have wanted, have sought, and have had.

VAN ALYN: What I said to Tony Taccone the other day was that I never would've given my life to *Angels in America*; I would've given my life to the Eureka Theatre. And did.

KUSHNER: The lawyers contacted us and said, "That didn't fulfill your contract. You have to do a production of the whole play, with *Perestroika*." So I took the first three scenes from *Perestroika*, and then the next scene was: "All of the characters of the play have assembled around the base of the Empire State Building. They look up as a dark shadow covers all of them. It is an atomic bomb falling on the Empire State Building. The bomb lands. There is a blinding light and a deafening roar. End of play." And I sent that in. And . . . I don't know how we resolved it.

ZITRIN: Would I like to have rewritten history and wish that Oskar had said, "I'll come to the Taper right after I direct this play at the Eureka"? Yes. I wish that my involvement with *Angels* was more entirely positive, that there hadn't been conflict. I feel badly about that.

ESBJORNSON: San Francisco deserved the play. There was something about it that felt absolutely right.

PEIFER: The play opened when we were still in the throes of the AIDS epidemic. But the play was filled with hope! And those were words we needed to hear. We needed to be told by these characters who matter to us: Look what we can do. Look what we can become. Look how we can *change*.

McLAUGHLIN: Not that many people saw the Eureka version of it, but it was very important to those who did. I think there was a kind of beauty to the hammer and nails and spit and Scotch tape quality of that first version. It was moving because we had nothing.

ESBJORNSON: I think that this production that wasn't supposed to happen was so important for the play and for its development.

McLAUGHLIN: What moves me about *Angels* is that it is unapologetically a play. It's passionately theatrical. You can do it with $200. You should be able to do it on the sweetest, most old-fashioned stage. There's a Christmas pageant quality to it. The tricks are not tricks, because you see the wire, you see all of the stuff as theater magic. It has *more* power. We lost hold of some of the sacredness of that experience as we went to the high theatrical effects that you can achieve with lots and lots of money.

ESBJORNSON: I don't like when people speak disparagingly about Eureka and the lack of money. We didn't let that stop us!

McLAUGHLIN: It was a 250-seat house, a warehouse, and we blew the roof off it night after night. People came in and they couldn't believe what they were seeing in there. You only get that once, the birth of a play.

SHE PREFERRED SILENCE

Hannah Pitt (and Rabbi Isidor Chemelwitz, Henry, Ethel Rosenberg, and Aleksii Antedilluvianovich Prelapsarianov)

RABBI ISIDOR CHEMELWITZ
Hello and good morning. I am Rabbi Isidor Chemelwitz of the Bronx
Home for Aged Hebrews.

–Millennium Approaches, Act 1, Scene 1

KATHLEEN CHALFANT (Hannah in workshops, San Francisco, Los Angeles, and New York, 1988–94): It was a great privilege to welcome people into the world of the plays.

BARBARA ROBERTSON (Hannah in national tour, 1994–95): Entering the stage each night was an extraordinary gift. To have those words to say to an audience, to look at them and welcome them into our story . . . it was like reading my favorite book to someone.

ANNABEL ARMOUR (Hannah in the Journeymen, Chicago, 1998): My particular nightmare as an actor is opening the show with a monologue directly to the audience.

ROBERTSON: Tony was like, "I want the rabbi to have this dialect, especially in the Hebrew." So he recorded all the Hebrew for me, so that I would have a specific dialect.

CHALFANT: Especially in New York, the rabbi was a familiar figure. You know, on Broadway, people just come. It's like a theme park: Whatever's on, people just come and see. The rabbi brought those people into the play through a portal that they knew.

SANDRA PHILLIPS (Hannah at TAAC, Sacramento, 2010 and 2014): I was very proud of myself when I made it through with no mistakes.

PEGGY EISENHAUER (associate lighting designer in New York, 1993–94): We were making a light for the rabbi's exit, and [director] George Wolfe said, "I want the light to be going off to an old, ancient place." So we brought up a shaft of warm, low light, like it was going into some distant horizon, and he said, "That's it!"

MICHAEL KRASS (costume designer of national tour, 1994–95): Can I tell you something we discovered? I'm reading this play, I'm trying to lay this fucker out, and it's torture. There's so many quick changes, wig changes, female-to-male changes. Why is it so complicated? Could the doubling be different? But by way of assignment of actor to role, it's all purposeful, because there is no straight male delivering authority. It is in fact very conscious, I think, that even the rabbi, even the doctor, even Martin, even the old Bolshevik—they're played by women. It's deeply subversive.

SUSAN BROWN (Hannah in London, 2017, and New York, 2018): I was desperately trying to find links between all these characters. When Tony arrived, I said, "I've been trying to find a link. Why do you have the actress playing Hannah play the other characters?" And he said, "Just enjoy it." That's all he said! "No, don't worry about it, just enjoy it."

ROBERTSON: Our makeup and wig designer came into my dressing room and I said, "For the doctor, just for a couple of days I'm gonna stick a sock in my pants." And he said, "No, no, I've got something." There's a thing we use in hairstyling, for turn-of-the-century hair, it's called a rat, it's a tube of netting maybe four or six inches long, and you pin it into your hair to give your hair life. He gave it to me and I stuck it into my pants. We were kind of giggling and Michael Mayer came backstage and said, "Your shirt looks a little wrinkled." And I said, "My shirt!?"

OSKAR EUSTIS (co-director in Los Angeles, 1992): There was always a threat to remove Prelapsarianov. But he stayed because he is in essence making the Angel's argument. By putting him there at the top of *Perestroika*, he is combining the politics and theology of the play in a way that is really powerful.

ARMOUR: The oldest living Bolshevik smoked cigarettes the same way [director] David Cromer did, always starting to go for a drag, but getting waylaid by what he needed to talk about, 'til it burned down to the filter.

ROBYN NEVIN (Hannah at Belvoir St Theatre, Sydney, 2013): The blind Bolshevik wore a massive coat with massive boots and a massive hat. I had a stick. I entered through an upstage curtain, by prodding the curtain from behind with my stick to locate the center split, through which I muddled. A stage manager came on to guide me to the center, where I made my rousing speech.

ANNE ALLGOOD (Hannah at Intiman Theatre, Seattle, 2014): By contrast to the Rabbi, Prelapsarianov is *still* ginned up with fervor. He's blind. He is in thrall to his radical and passionate beliefs. He is screaming his truth on a stage for who-knows-how-many listeners? He doesn't know—he can't see. He is the voice crying in the wilderness. How ballsy is that?

CRISTINE McMURDO-WALLIS (Hannah at American Conservatory Theater, San Francisco, 1994–95): On an excursion for character study, I ended up in the Richmond District at the Holy Virgin Cathedral. It was July in San Francisco and foggy and freezing and so I went across the street to a little Russian restaurant for some brandy and some soup. The owner was an older gentleman whose father had been a Cossack in the czar's army. I told him I was an actor and playing a Bolshevik. He replied, "Oh. Is easy play Bolshevik. Just act drunk and bang things," whereupon he banged the table with his fist.

JEANNE PAULSEN (Hannah at Intiman Theatre, Seattle, 1994–95): During the first preview, when I was the Oldest Living Bolshevik, I started the speech just fine, but started to panic because I couldn't remember what the next line of the speech was. I would just open my mouth *hoping* that the next line would be there. I aged thirty years during that preview performance. From that performance through closing, I carried his entire speech, typed out, in my pocket. If I got stuck, I didn't give a damn if the guy was blind, I was prepared to pull it out and read!

● ● ●

NANCY CRANE (the Angel in London, 1992–93): Hannah is a tough nut. Hannah stays like the desert, like the Great Salt Lake.

VIVIENNE BENESCH (Hannah in NYU *Perestroika* workshop, 1993): Hannah Pitt's mode of survival is: *You can hit me, but I'm gonna come back, I'm gonna come back.* I needed to harden up and buck up, because the soft inside of Hannah is gonna take care of itself. The hard part was what was hardest to locate.

CHALFANT: Hannah's basically monosyllabic. In this play in which people speak in paragraphs, Hannah is lucky if it's a ten-word sentence for most of the play. I was younger and more ambitious and worried about these things then and I thought, *Oh, I'm just disappearing.* But it wasn't true. I realize now, and wish I had then, because it would have saved me a lot of anguish, that she said exactly as much as she needed to say. Everything's going on inside, behind—there's this wonderful Greek expression, "the fence of your teeth." Hannah's fence of her teeth was a portcullis.

ARMOUR: She is one of the original badasses.

JOE
Mom. Momma. I'm a homosexual, Momma.
(He lowers the receiver and laughs quietly to himself)

Boy, did that come out awkward.

(He lifts the receiver to his ear)

Hello? Hello?
I'm a homosexual.

(Pause)

Please, Momma. Say something.

HANNAH
You're old enough to understand that your father didn't love you without
being ridiculous about it.

—Millennium Approaches, Act 2, Scene 8

ROBERTSON: Hannah thought that her love for her son was strong, clear, and unconditional, but the phone call, like an earthquake, breaks the tie of love that she thought linked her to her son.

NICK REDING (Joe in London, 1992): My stomach lurched when you mentioned that scene, I haven't thought about it for so long. There was a terrible silence when Rosemary Martin did that scene. I told her, and there was this silence, and it was horrible.

CHALFANT: I'm in my bathrobe at the telephone, completely isolated. It was the moment of greatest isolation for Hannah, for me. I felt . . . uh . . . both the connection parents have with their children and the terror when their children do something that is unfamiliar. And the knowledge that everything you said was wrong.

MERYL STREEP (Hannah on HBO, 2003): I just wanted to be awakened and be shaken. That first phone call is how people are gonna decide who she is. Like they said in drama school, the first time you come onstage you make an impression, the audience decides who you are. And then you proceed to dismantle those assumptions.

CHALFANT: And of course the next thing that Hannah does is go and see what's going on.

TONY KUSHNER: Hannah makes an insane gesture in an attempt to reestablish a connection by selling her house and moving to New York. She throws her whole world out in the wind.

Hannah (Kathleen Chalfant) and Sister Ella Chapter (Ellen McLaughlin) in the Taper Too workshop, 1990. (*Casey Cowan*)

McMURDO-WALLIS: For me, Hannah's journey begins in the scene with [her real estate agent] Ella Chapter. She's standing on the cliff and says, "There's been days when I've stood at this ledge and thought about stepping over." And that's, metaphorically, what she does: She steps off that ledge but, instead of falling to her death, she *soars*.

CHALFANT: I admired Hannah's gumption, that she came to see what happened. And I loved what happened to her, that she learned. She always seemed like an adventurer to me. A Mormon! Some of them walked across the country!

ROBERTSON: Hannah's *need* to love her son propels her on her journey and opens her eyes, and her heart. Her *need* to love God pushes her to question an unloving religious doctrine, and find her way to live with belief. Her inherent belief brings her to see and love the Angel when she appears, and guide Prior when he is afraid.

MIKELL KOBER (theater producer): Hannah embraces this new life, and this new openness to other people. I was a young Mormon who wasn't yet able to admit that I was gay, but she was the person that I could say: "That seems like something I would absolutely want for myself."

CHALFANT: When we went to Broadway, every gay Mormon in New York came up to me after the show and said, "That's my mother!"

BROWN: And if you are someone who doesn't really know, at the end of *Millennium*, which two characters are the least likely to get together, it would be Prior and Hannah. They are somehow the two characters who you're never going to see together in this play. And they are able to comfort each other! They are able to do something really positive for each other!

PRIOR
Why are you here with me.

HANNAH
Oh this is awful. I shouldn't be.
What do you call a woman who sort of feels, well some sort of strong feeling
like . . . I suppose, love, or . . . for a homosexual man?

PRIOR
Oh.
Well, it's not nice, it's called a . . . fag hag.

HANNAH
Oh, that's horrible, what a horrible, horrible . . .
Never mind, forget what I said, forget it all, I'm going.

PRIOR
Don't. I'm sorry, you scared me.

HANNAH
I am not any kind of a hag. And if you ever call me that again, sick as you are,
I will strike you.

–Cut scene from *Perestroika* (script dated April 11, 1991), Act 5, Scene 10

CHALFANT: I think she changes from the minute she gets off the plane in New York. She, like the people who see the play, spends all that time thinking things she's never thought before.

STREEP: Hannah, if you pass her on the street, you make all these decisions about her. But you can't know everything! You can't know everything in people's hearts.

PHILLIPS: I love the final scene at Bethesda Fountain, seeing how far everyone had come. I was especially happy to see the growth in Hannah. We all cried every night.

LAURA KYRO (Hannah at Stray Dog Theatre, St. Louis, 2004 and 2012): She's an intelligent, discerning woman, and adapted or evolved as she needed to. Either evolve or die, and she wasn't ready for the latter.

ROBERTSON: They made me a beautiful wig to wear at the end of the play. It moved beautifully and really told the story that Hannah had been transformed. Michael Krass especially enjoyed that movement of Hannah's hair.

KRASS: Hannah finally gets a good haircut. I remember Hannah having gray hair in a sort of chin-length bob that looked fucking good on her, after the gags about her hair.

ROBERTSON: The earlier wig consistently got a great laugh when Prior first meets Hannah and suggests she find a good hairdresser. But the second wig was so well designed and made; it looked hip and classy and moved with grace and elegance.

KRASS: A good, handsome woman who was herself, and looked good.

BENESCH: I'm in North Carolina. There are a lot of southern Hannahs down here, who, given the chance to let their hair down . . .

• • •

CHALFANT: All the scenes between Ethel Rosenberg and Roy were battle scenes, between someone who was used to winning and someone who wasn't.

BENESCH: This small woman, who was your Jewish grandmother, and everyone always thought of her as the sweetest woman but she was *ferocious*. And you only ever knew that if you hurt someone she loved or if she felt there was an injustice that she could fix.

CHALFANT: In the play, she's certainly his moral equal, and she's won. She's won the battle because in an odd way she died honorably, for the things that she believed in, and he died lying. And badly.

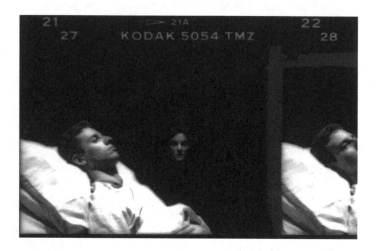

STREEP: It was great fun to lead his little willing face to the edge. I loved it.

BENESCH: The fact that she is so patient in the face of Roy's devolution, his demise: Conscience will kill you if you give it the time to.

STREEP: I wanted to be there for him in the last moments. I wanted her to be so—to smell cabbage and cooking, and really feet on the ground, absolutely palpably real and judgmental and loving. And all the things that parents are.

BROWN: Ethel has one objective, really, which is to watch Roy die as unpleasantly as possible. And she then does do a business of—because of the Jewishness—forgiving.

Roy (Ben Shenkman) and Ethel (Vivienne Benesch) in the NYU *Perestroika* workshop, 1993. (*NYU Graduate Acting Program*)

McMURDO-WALLIS: Ah, but she proves her humanity leading Louis through the Kaddish. She wins.

ANDREW GARFIELD (Prior in London, 2017, and New York, 2018): When I first heard Sue and James do the Kaddish in rehearsals, it was one of those moments where something in your soul gets woken up. That ancient language just does something, and the whole ritual, the ritual of forgiveness, the beauty of that scene—the way that Sue delivers it, it makes me want to cry thinking about it, there's so much, fuck— *(Starts to cry.)* See what I mean, it's crazy!

PHILLIPS: I was told every night that the actors backstage would all gather around the speaker to hear this part because they were so moved.

McMURDO-WALLIS: You son of a bitch.

CHAPTER 2

THRESHOLD
OF REVELATION

ROYAL NATIONAL THEATRE, LONDON, 1992

RICHARD EYRE (artistic director, Royal National Theatre, London, 1987–97): Gordon Davidson sent me the play and said, "I think you'd be interested in this." By page 2, I'd decided I wanted to do it.

TONY KUSHNER: I was visiting my father in Louisiana. I'm pretty sure my mother had died already. And I think Joyce called, my agent, and said Richard Eyre was trying to reach me and . . . I was on the phone in my parents' bedroom when we finally had the phone conversation. It felt very fancy. And really exciting.

He went right away to the question of who would direct it, and he said that he was hoping I would be willing to talk to Declan Donnellan on the phone.

DECLAN DONNELLAN (director in London, 1992): It was the first new play I'd ever done, the first time I actually worked with something where nobody else knew it. I knew it was great from the first few pages.

NICK ORMEROD (set designer in London, 1992; Donnellan's partner): We met at University of Cambridge, and we created our own company, Cheek by Jowl, in 1981. We are a classical theater company, essentially. But then when *Angels*

in America arrived on our doorstep, we thought, *This is really too good to be turned down.* There are many plays which take a sentimental view of gays, but *Angels* I think was the first one which was completely unsentimental—that we had come across at any rate.

JOSEPH MYDELL (Belize in London, 1992): That night, I sat up in bed, reading it. I said, "Oh my God, who is writing like this in America now?" I couldn't believe such a play existed.

EMILY GARSIDE (scholar of HIV/AIDS-related theater): We had—like New York and San Francisco—a hub of small companies doing plays about AIDS. Gay Sweatshop was a big one, but much of their work is lost. *The Normal Heart* had a short run at the Royal Court, and a brief run at the West End, a matter of a few weeks.

So *Angels* was pretty much the first mainstream play about AIDS in the UK. And given that it was at the National—which, at that time, was quite conservative, older, middle-class—that's quite a dynamic to drop this play into.

Director Declan Donnellan, Nick Reding (Joe), and Marcus D'Amico (Louis) in rehearsal, London, 1992. (*John Haynes/Lebrecht Music & Arts*)

MARCUS D'AMICO (Louis in London, 1992): When I read Louis's speeches, they hadn't even sent me the whole play yet, but I just felt innately like I knew what to do with Louis's speeches. But it wasn't until they sent the whole script that I was like, *Oh no. This is hard. (Laughs.)*

SEAN CHAPMAN (Prior in London, 1992): I had recently done a film called *Hellraiser*, which was big in the States. That was the territory I was in when I got the script. I remember reading the first part and just running around the room and saying, "This is one of the best things that I've ever read! This is a future classic!" And then I had to go to Declan and convince him to let me do it.

D'AMICO: The way that National productions are put together, it's so detailed that no stone gets left unturned. We had movement people. Everything got discussed about American politics.

MYDELL: Declan said something in the middle of rehearsal that I think is really important: "When people say things in America, and say things in this

---

MILLENNIUM APPROACHES AT JUILLIARD, 1992

ENID GRAHAM (Harper in Juilliard *Millennium* workshop, 1992): They announced we were doing a new play, *Angels in America*. We didn't know anything about it except that Tony was the playwright-in-residence that year.

RICHARD FELDMAN (director of Juilliard *Millennium* workshop, 1992): It's hard to remember now how risky an enterprise that might have seemed to what essentially used to be a music school. We had to call it a workshop. Tony was in London for most of that time with Declan Donnellan's production. He would pop in from time to time.

ROBBY SELLA (Prior in Juilliard *Millennium* workshop, 1992): We got this play and

it was, you know, it was typewritten pages in a notebook. We were extremely excited and frightened and worried about whether we could pull it off.

MICHAEL HAYDEN (Roy in Juilliard *Millennium* workshop, 1992): Michael Stuhlbarg played Louis, Robby Sella played Prior, Enid Graham played Harper, Hannah was played by Elizabeth Marvel, I played Roy Cohn.

FELDMAN: These were young people! Enid was probably twenty-one. She was right out of high school. Elizabeth Marvel was twenty-one, right out of high school. Stuhlbarg and Hayden were maybe twenty-four.

GRAHAM: There are no auditions at Juilliard; you're just assigned. Or another

play, whether it's about politics or religion, people take things quite personally." Declan was more interested in how we as American characters behaved with each other. That to me was more interesting than the references. These characters coming from this culture, in this play. So, by the time we all came up to the bat to do the production, we were all charged with this febrile energy of *Don't you say anything to me because fucker I will cut your throat!* You wouldn't do that in England, you'd say, "Oh, I'm terribly sorry, did you just say that?"

NANCY CRANE (the Angel in London, 1992): There were some very nice Mormons who helped us.

NICK REDING (Joe in London, 1992): They were all very clean-cut American boys. We spent a lot of time talking about being a Mormon and what it meant, how it felt, endless questions for them. I kind of avoided the issue of homosexuality until the end. And then I said, "You know the character I play is in fact gay, is a homosexual." There was just this long silence.

And one of the boys said, "We, uh, don't believe in homosexuality."

way to say it is that your entire time there is an audition. I kind of went through my years in Juilliard without getting the great parts. I was sometimes frustrated about that, so to get cast as Harper felt like a real coup.

HAYDEN: I was assigned Roy, and I read it and I said to Richard, "You're crazy!" *(Laughs.)* "You're casting me as Roy Cohn!" Of all the characters, regardless of how unlike me it was, I knew I wanted to play that part. So I was ecstatic.

GRAHAM: That's sort of a funny thing. In our little class of fourteen, a lot of us were right for those parts! I was quite suited to Harper. Obviously Beth was too young, but I would absolutely cast Beth in that role now. Michael is, like, central casting for Louis.

SELLA: I just thought, *How can I do it?* I just felt this play deserved—because it was new and because it was so important in its scope and its ambition—I really wanted to give it my all, and find a way to honor it.

FELDMAN: I went out to San Francisco to watch the Eureka production, which was *amazing* and beautiful. One thing I learned from that production—and to be frank, I stole many things—was its spareness. Fortunately for us at Juilliard, we only had the resources to do something spare, so that became a feature.

HAYDEN: Richard's idea was that it was going to be actor-driven and simple. You want a production based on the needs of the play, not just spectacle, the sound and fury signifying nothing. It was mostly

CRANE: I remember going into an operating theater to trail nurses around hospitals. Talking to a doctor who specialized in AIDS.

CHAPMAN: The cultural belief about this disease, about how it was spread, about your chances of getting it, was very different. People were putting paper down on toilet seats, things like that. Everyone was so misinformed, and so terrified.

D'AMICO: AIDS was all around me. It wasn't a mystery. I had begun to lose people when I was eighteen and I was in the West End, you know. Cast members were dying. I had had eight, nine years of all of that.

KUSHNER: I took Declan Donnellan and Nick Ormerod around on a hot summer day with a blistering sun. They wanted to see where Joe and Harper live in Brooklyn Heights. I suggested that we walk across the Brooklyn Bridge, because it's my favorite view of Manhattan.

MILLENNIUM APPROACHES AT JUILLIARD, 1992 →

lighting, movement from area to area. But the Angel flew in. We had that capacity.

FELDMAN: The Drama Theater has almost no wing space and no fly space. We found

Louis (Michael Stuhlbarg) and Prior (Robby Sella) in Juilliard's workshop of *Millennium Approaches*, 1992. (*Jessica Katz/The Juilliard School*)

a way to drop her in; it was rough rope and harness, with everything showing.

HAYDEN: I remember Tony got somewhat involved. I remember an interaction where he disagreed strongly with something I was doing, I don't remember what it was. I said to him, "Tony, I'm never going to get to play this part again, but you gotta go through Richard, he's the director." (*Laughs.*)

FELDMAN: I have an amusing story at my own expense, which I don't mind telling, since Tony has said many times how much he loved the production and I'm grateful for that. I made the mistake of inviting him to the first time we stumbled through the play. It was in a rehearsal studio, it was really dumb.

We ran it through, he was in the corner,

ORMEROD: Tony was incredibly charming and very welcoming and took us on trust, I think, basically, which was great. He took us to a friend's apartment which to some extent had inspired Prior's apartment. I remember a huge clown face hanging on the wall, and I also remember an incredibly careful constructed mosaic of different linos that the guy who owned the flat had cut up to make his living room floor.

DONNELLAN: Sometimes when you see images of New York, you think, *Oh, it's not authentic New York. It's performed New York, from movies and television.* But when you go to New York, you find that New York is performing itself. Everybody's ready for their close-up.

ORMEROD: In delis and diners and whatever, they act like New Yorkers they've seen in the movies.

furiously taking notes. We finished at, like, five in the afternoon and then he and I met. We went to a coffee shop, my memory is, down in the Village somewhere, and Tony started going over his notes.

An hour went by. Two hours, three, four . . . He had lots of notes about what wasn't working, why something was awful. Then 1:00 . . . 1:30 a.m.! We hadn't finished, so he said "Oh, let's call it a night," and he just handed me the notes to read and go over on my own.

GRAHAM: Harper's first monologue! I remember struggling with that, right up 'til the last moment, like trying something totally different the afternoon before the first show.

HARPER
People who are lonely, people left alone, sit talking nonsense to the air, imagining . . . beautiful systems dying, old fixed orders spiraling apart . . .

–Millennium Approaches, Act 1, Scene 3

FELDMAN: We struggled to make that come to life in a way where there was change, an event. God bless her, we were in a rehearsal room that afternoon. She had her sleeves rolled up and was just, "OK, we're gonna crack this." I don't think we ever totally did. I'm always grateful to Enid for how hard she worked at it. It's a worthy play to wrestle with and fail.

GRAHAM: As soon as we did the play, it was just so magical.

KUSHNER: By the time we got across the bridge, Declan had turned, like, *fuchsia*. He's very fair-skinned, Anglo-Irish. I thought he was going to die. I thought I had killed him.

DONNELLAN: It was great to be taken around by Tony.

KUSHNER: Declan's working method in part has to do with making a completely safe environment with the actors to take risks. His dramaturgy is predicated almost entirely on the actor. He wanted the actors to feel free to take chances, so I sat in on very few rehearsals.

CHAPMAN: We all explored the play together, really, with no preconceived understanding.

ORMEROD: We kind of treated it like a classic. The text was highly honed already, because he'd workshopped it a lot with Oskar Eustis. Even though at

---

MILLENNIUM APPROACHES AT JUILLIARD, 1992 →

SELLA: Nobody in New York had seen it! Most people didn't even know what this play was. A lot of people thought, *Oh, another play*, and then they saw *this* play.

GRAHAM: Hearing an audience hear a new play, you learn so much. "Oh, right, *this* is the story we're telling!" It was so exciting, because it was the story everyone wanted to hear right then.

FELDMAN: It was 1992, we were still living that history. So much had changed. What we felt like is that we were historians of ourselves.

SELLA: You could hardly get a ticket. More than it being about seeing these students

as they're about to graduate, it was about getting in on the ground floor of this play.

FELDMAN: I don't know that we've ever had crowds like that before or since, to be honest with you. It was a young audience, an audience of their peers, and it was really thrilling. It was a *moment*.

BEN SHENKMAN (Roy in NYU *Perestroika* workshop, 1993): I went to—like, at the last minute without even so much as saying, "Oh, we're going," I went to that production. It's probably the case with your first encounter with any classic play; that is the indelible production for me, that Juilliard production.

I mean I grew up in a very liberal setting in high school. And I'd been to Brown University and everything. But I did grow up in the '80s, and I guess I

first glance you thought, well, maybe it's too long or too short, whatever—probably too long—when it came to it, it worked.

HENRY GOODMAN (Roy in London, 1992): I cannot stress enough the fragility and intimacy there was in the rehearsal room. Which is key to the play, because it exists on these two levels. There's a hidden staging reality, which is big and bold and political and sweeps with imagination, but there's a tenderness and intimacy and domesticity that goes alongside it; so Declan was really concentrating on making sure that that was inviolable, and that when the audience was watching things, there was something going on between these actors. There was a lot of vulnerability and tears and insecurity and stuff.

DONNELLAN: Tony has become an extremely close friend. I adore him. He and I had a feisty relationship. We would have cheerful conversations at quite high volumes, because we are very similar and very opposite at the same time.

---

had internalized a tremendous amount of homophobia, you know, regardless of those settings. So I was genuinely shocked by the dialogue. Just seeing that stuff put onstage was absolutely incredible in a great way. It was so powerful, so funny. I mean, that first line where he says, "If I hadn't spent the last four years fellating you, I'd swear you were straight." Oh my God.

VIVIENNE BENESCH (Hannah in NYU Perestroika workshop, 1993): Beth Marvel was this sort of phenomenon. *Everyone* knew about *Beth Marvel*. Watching that production, I remember going, *Holy shit, that's a good actress*.

SELLA: You can hardly find anyone more gifted than Michael Stuhlbarg. He was someone who—in my remembrance, someone who was very bottled up about

accessing all those feelings. Not just the fear about Prior, but the bigger fear: How do we live, how do we survive. I remember this feeling in his eyes, of *Get away from me. There isn't enough love in my heart to overcome the fear.*

GRAHAM: To suddenly do a play about our time, our country, history, that we're all affected by to various degrees, and so political: It was pretty shocking. My experience at Juilliard was about *How do we make* Man and Superman *relevant to today?* It's not the same as telling a story right in the vernacular of the moment.

HAYDEN: I remember a casting director came up to me and said, "It will never get better than this." I thought, *I sure as hell hope it does, I haven't graduated yet!* ◢

KUSHNER: When you say something like "Declan, there's not going to be enough time to do this!" he responds, "Yes, but darling, there's never enough time to do anything in the theater."

REDING: Declan doesn't give blocking.

DONNELLAN: It wasn't that I disagreed with Tony about how each scene should be directed. It's just that my policy is not to direct a scene like that. I have a habit of changing things at the last minute, of cultivating a spirit of freedom in the actor. Sometimes people, like writers, think the space needs to be controlled a bit more. I remember Tony once asking, "Why is she sitting down on that line?"

And I responded, "Is she sitting down? I don't know. Sometimes she stands up."

Tony said, "You don't even know!"

"It's not directed like that!"

KUSHNER: I flew back to London and saw one of the last run-throughs in the rehearsal room before they go into tech.

GOODMAN: We were all anxious to impress him. He'd been kept out, so by the time he did come in, there was ten times more pressure.

KUSHNER: The run-through that I saw was *horrendous*.

REDING: I remember Tony Kushner sitting through a run-through, making notes continually throughout, not looking up *once*, he just took notes the whole time.

D'AMICO: It was very, very scary.

KUSHNER: I was in despair. Weeping. "I don't know who this guy *is*!" I had seen Declan's production of *As You Like It*, which was magnificent. "But I don't know what happened, because this is terrible!"

REDING: I think he might've told Richard to scrap the production. He was *profoundly* unhappy.

EYRE: Rehearsals weren't stormy. It seemed like what every new show goes through.

DONNELLAN: We went to check in on our production of *As You Like It*, because Peter Brook was coming to see it. We had to go to the Hammersmith to see him, and we gave Tony a lift to the Hammersmith and put him in a cab to Heathrow. We'd had a bad afternoon with Tony, and it really cheered me up to see Peter.

KUSHNER: I typed up my notes on the plane flying back to the United States. I spent the entire flight just typing up notes. There were, like, fifty pages of notes. I hit the send button on the fax machine as soon as I landed, not thinking about what time it was in London.

DONNELLAN: Nick and I came home, and I thought we'd been burgled because there was so much paper floating around! It turned out it was all coming from the fax machine.

ORMEROD: This unbelievable cascade of fax paper, pages and pages of his notes.

DONNELLAN: I don't blame Tony. He cares very, very much, and he has a very, very clear vision of what he wants.

KUSHNER: At first with Declan . . . it doesn't look there's anything there at all. And all of a sudden it clicks into this really remarkable shape. I don't know how he does it.

DONNELLAN: We had our rows, but they were always resolved good-naturedly.

PADDY CUNNEEN (composer and sound designer in London, 1992): Declan came to me and said, "Paddy, we need music at the top of Act 1, for the interval, after the interval, and the very end; that's all we need." But when we got to the tech . . . well, it became a bit of a thing. Declan would say, "Oh, we need music here," and "We need music there," and I would run around, write music on the fly, and give it to musicians.

CRANE: I remember at the very first preview of *Millennium* the very first time—it was just this blur of trying to remember what scene came next. That was all we could do. And when we came out, the audience all stood up. Standing ovations were much less common then. They didn't really happen. We all looked at each other and thought, *Oh my God, this is quite special.*

DAVID MILLING (stage manager in London, 1992): The staging was incredibly simple. It was a shiny blank floor and a giant American flag as the backdrop. And then in the center of the flag there were small doors for pieces of scenery to run through. Only at the end of the play did the flag split, half going left, half going right, and the Angel tracked through in a cloud of smoke.

The Angel (Nancy Crane) comes through the back wall in London, 1992. *(John Haynes/Lebrecht Music & Arts)*

DONNELLAN: I'm much happier with the unstageable than the realistic, I have to say. I don't think I was put on this world to move people around furniture.

ORMEROD: Basically, I've only ever designed one set, and that is very much the environment of an empty stage. Sometimes you think you need an American phone booth, but you don't at all, you just need a guy with a handset. As you moved on, things simplified in the interest of speed, with need being a central consideration. Removing everything you don't need.

So the environment was a distressed Stars and Stripes. It was important to me that the Angel moved forward through the main flag upstage, through the flag and into the space above the bed. So that was the main design problem. The Angel needed to make a proper entrance, not just be thrown in. And because of the three-dimensional nature of the space, she needed to move both down and forwards.

CUNNEEN: This huge *blast* of energy seemed to be coming out of America at the time. It was not long after the Gulf War, which had made CNN into an incredible news apparatus. So I persuaded Declan to put CNN on in the foyer as you came in. So the audience could surf on that American energy as they came into the space.

DONNELLAN: My production was very much about the maintenance of tension. That's why I overlapped a lot of scenes. Tony took an objection to that at the beginning. He thought that scenes followed too fluidly on from one to the other.

ORMEROD: I remember Tony at one point saying he liked the idea of scene changes, so it gave the audience the opportunity to think about what they'd just seen.

DONNELLAN: And I said, "No." I put my foot down on that one. Tony wanted to break my arm, but I kept the scenes fluid and overlapping.

KUSHNER: I was a bit nervous about it, but he made it dance.

ORMEROD: You need to keep it moving, you can't be stopping for scene changes, you need to keep the audience on its toes. It needs to be precipitous.

KUSHNER: Caryl Churchill saw one of the early performances and came up to Declan afterwards and said, "Well, congratulations, you've solved the short, choppy scene problem." When you do a play with short scenes, the scene ends, the audience has to disengage from where they've just been and open themselves up to the next thing. That's hard to do, because it involves stopping and starting over and over again. What Declan did is he dovetailed the ends of almost every scene in *Millennium*. He took the penultimate and the ultimate line, separated them, took the first line of the next scene, and put it between the two. So you'd already be in the next scene. He wove them all together.

JIM NICOLA (artistic director, New York Theatre Workshop): I thought the most confident, bold production was Declan's at the National. There's something about someone from outside the culture looking in. They can see a metaphor better than we can, because we're living it, but they're observing it.

ROBERT STANTON (actor): In London when you go to the theater you have to buy a program. I bought a program for *Angels in America, Part 1*, and there was a glossary of terms, things that people talked about in the play. The Ramble, Ethel Rosenberg, basic things, and I thought, *Isn't this quaint?*

JON MATTHEWS (Louis in Taper Too workshop, 1990): It opened with this image, there was nothing on the stage, and the furniture is on the sides, and they're sitting along the sides, and there was this balloon globe, and it had this light inside it, and they all put their hands on it, and then the play began.

> Company enter
> Rosemary & Felicity U/R
> Jeffrey Marcus
> and Henry D/R
> Nick & Zoe U/L
> Nancy & Sean D/L
> One member of the company,
> Elected each performance,

Will carry the globe.
It is held aloft, and slowly
Brought D/C & placed on
The floor. The company surround
And "refer" to it at all times

—Staging notes from the National Theatre prompt script of
Millennium Approaches

STANTON: It was about my hometown, and I was seeing it in a town several thousand miles away. I wanted to turn to everyone around me and say, "This is exactly what it's like!"

KUSHNER: Opening night in London is critics' night. It's like a stenographer's convention. Nobody laughs. Pens scribbling. It's horrible. They all go home and write their reviews and then they come out. The whole cast and Declan and I were all going to the bar. Jeffrey Chiswick played a kind of ninth character, because they didn't want Henry or the Rabbi played by a woman. So they cast Jeffrey, who was kind of a professional Jewish actor, he did a lot of Jewish characters.

GOODMAN: He went off the rails a bit emotionally. We were all being very sensitive and judicious, but he went through a late midlife crisis.

KUSHNER: He was having a nervous breakdown. He insisted that he drive me to the bar. We got into the car, and he starts looking strange, and he says, "You know what these people think? They think we're not worth anything, you and me, because we're Jews!"

Then he starts rolling down the window as we're driving around London, screaming, "Fuck you all! We're Jews! We're Jews, right! Right!" He was driving like ninety miles an hour. It was terrifying.

We go to this newsstand and I just thought, *What the fuck is he doing?* and he comes back with like this *armload* of newspapers. We go to the bar and I say, "Jeffrey, what's that?"

And he says, "Oh, the reviews, darling!"

DONNELLAN: I started opening the newspapers and reading them, and Tony was just sort of shriveling. I read all these reviews out loud, they were all total raves, and Tony was turning various colors on the other side of the table. I realized what an awful and risky thing I'd done. I was stupid. But I wasn't arrogant. It was the fact that the play was so wonderful. It just never occurred to me that anybody could say a word against it.

CHAPMAN: The reviews were explosive. The theater at that time had a top gallery. And when you'd walk out onstage, you could feel people hanging over the gallery, three-deep.

> You could say he chews off more than he can bite—giving us glimpses of Mormon morality and the mutual antipathy between many American blacks and Jews—but I infinitely prefer a play with too many themes to too few. And he is beautifully served by Declan Donnellan's direction and Nick Ormerod's design, which achieve a breathtaking fluidity: scene melts into scene, the company truck the furniture on and off and the detail feels right, down to the images of Garbo and Bette Davis that decorate the gay lovers' bedhead. . . .
>
> Sprawling and over-written as it may be, it is a play of epic energy that gets American drama not just out of the closet but, thank God, out of the living-room as well.
>
> –Michael Billington, "Nation Built on Guilt," *Guardian*, January 25, 1992

GARSIDE: The politics of it hit on the right moment. We were having our side of the conservative 1980s with Thatcher and the special relationship with Reagan. There was a kind of resentment of America, a dislike of their politics and how it intersected with our politics. And then there was an audience who hadn't seen a play about gay men and AIDS on a large scale, for whom the play was a revelation.

The big legal fight in gay rights at this time was against something called Section 28. This was the big thing. It was in effect between 1988 and 2003, and barred the "promotion" of homosexuality.

(1) A local authority shall not—
(a) intentionally promote homosexuality or publish material with the intention of promoting homosexuality;
(b) promote the teaching in any maintained school of the acceptability of homosexuality as a pretended family relationship.

—Section 28 of the Local Government Act 1988

GARSIDE: What this meant was no one was talking about it in sex education in school, in biology lessons, things like that. You couldn't say that homosexuality exists: That was viewed as promotion of it.

CUNNEEN: It seemed to come out of the theater world and come out to a wider consciousness. It was everything you want: You do something, it's important, it's timely, people see it, take notice, and want to engage with it.

It was my partner Tim Fraser who booked tickets, 25 years ago, for the first performance at the National Theatre of Tony Kushner's Angels in America Part One: Millennium Approaches. . . .

Tim arrived at the theatre on a walking stick, eyes protected by dark glasses, his cheekbones painfully sharp. And there it all was on the stage: the relationship between Kushner's Prior and Louis, pushed apart and together and apart again as Prior's illness progresses, an exact parallel of my own fractious relationship.

At the interval Tim, angry that I might be deserting him as he entered the terminal phase, threw his drink over me, the whole glass. I sat in a gin-and-tonic-sodden T-shirt for the second half.

—Mark Ravenhill, "'Angels in America' Returns to the London Stage," *Sunday Times*, May 7, 2017

JOYCE KETAY (Kushner's theatrical agent): One of the reasons we were really excited to have it in London was not to be in New York, because Frank Rich hated *Bright Room Called Day*.

An early front-runner for the most infuriating play of 1991.

—Frank Rich, *New York Times*, January 8, 1991

FRANK RICH (chief theater critic, *New York Times*, 1980–93): Look, not everyone has an auspicious beginning.

KETAY: I get a call from Alex Witchel, Frank Rich's wife, and she says, "I'm going to London and I'm going to see *Angels in America* and I want to know how long it is."

I said, "Is this going to be reviewed?"

And she says, "I'm not a critic, I'm a reporter."

If I had had any balls, I would've said, "Is your *husband* reviewing it?" But I was too scared of her! So for weeks we sat there with our hearts in our throat.

RICH: All I had to do was read the description of *Angels*, and I was very curious. The imprimatur of the National producing a play meant something.

KUSHNER: Joyce and I had this incredible moment of panic. I've written something that everybody's excited about, and he's gonna come and kill it, 'cause he hates me. I had a moment where I thought, *The night he shows up, I'm gonna get up and just go onstage and say, "This man hates my work, and he's here to destroy this play!"*

Joyce calmed me down, which is a lot of what she did back then.

RICH: The whole point of being a critic is—or the whole goal is—to go to theater with an open mind, expecting to be surprised.

KUSHNER: I got off the F train going back to Brooklyn, and I'm walking home, and there's a *New York Times* sticking out of a trash can, and there's a picture of Henry Goodman. And I walk by and go, "Oh, that's Henry!" Then I stop. Cold sweat. I glanced right below it, and it said something, there was a sentence that looked like it might be a nice sentence, so I said, "OK, I'm not going to read any more."

> Mr. Kushner has created an original theatrical world of his own, poetic and churning, that, once entered by an open-minded viewer of any political or sexual persuasion, simply cannot be escaped.
>
> –Frank Rich, "The Reaganite Ethos, with Roy Cohn as a Dark Metaphor," *New York Times*, March 5, 1992

KUSHNER: When I got back to the apartment in Brooklyn—these were the days of little cassette answering machines—I went in, and a light that I'd never seen before was flashing. The tape was empty—it had been used up. Everyone I had ever known was calling.

KETAY: Producers knew about the play, but they also knew it was long and about AIDS, so I was not getting any calls. And when that review came out, everything went nuts.

CRANE: People were flying over from the States to see it.

REDING: They'd tell you, "Meryl Streep's in the house," and you'd say, "No! Don't tell me that!" Because then you're doing the show for Meryl.

MERYL STREEP (Hannah on HBO, 2003): I've seen lots of performances that surprised me in the theater but this was on a scale—with ambition and imagination—that was unlike anything I'd ever seen.

CRANE: Richard Chamberlain was there with his boyfriend. It got really *grand*.

REDING: I had to train myself to look *between* people because otherwise you go, *Oh no! I'm staring at Paul Newman!*

DONNELLAN: Every fucking night, I'd miss the celebrities. I'd see the show every third night, and the cast would say, "Oh, Declan, you should've been here last night. You missed Marlene Dietrich. You missed Clark Gable." I thought they were going to the cemetery and digging them up.

CRANE: We were approached about transferring to the West End. The space we were in was so integral to the show, the production, that we decided not to do it. Richard Eyre—we used to have meetings with him about it—he said, "I hate talking to you, it's like talking to the amoeba, because you're all one form," we were that close.

DONNELLAN: It's a very personal thing, *Angels in America*. I am a gay man the same age as those characters, you know; you put a lot of yourself in it. But to do eight performances a week is sort of silly. You have to be able to reproduce mechanically in order to do eight performances a week, but because of the particular nerve-tearingness of *Angels*, I couldn't bear to think of it becoming in any way pat.

GOODMAN: It's not that we weren't passionate and hungry and grateful for what's going on, but I think he got it absolutely right. To make it matter that much, every night, eight shows a week. I'm a glutton for punishment, I'm known to be energetic and hungry, but you can't, in that big a theater.

DONNELLAN: Of course, it was going to fly into Broadway on a Rolls-Royce with golden wheels, you know?

A FUCKING OCTOPUS

Roy Cohn

ROY

(Hitting the hold button) Hold. *(To Joe)* I wish I was an octopus, a fucking octopus. Eight loving arms and all those suckers. Know what I mean?

–Millennium Approaches, Act 1, Scene 2

JEFF CHRISTIAN (Joe in the Journeymen, Chicago, 1998): As tough as the playwright may be on Joe, he gives him a gift right off the bat: the best seat in the house to watch Roy's "fucking octopus" aria.

RON LEIBMAN (Roy in Los Angeles and New York, 1992–94): I never saw it as an aria or anything like that. I saw it as a very specific performance for the young man, to make him laugh, so he would be ingratiated by the wonderful Roy Cohn. *(Roy Cohn voice:)* "*Cats*! It's about cats!"

HENRY GOODMAN (Roy in London, 1992): Just technically, there's no point in being coy about it, it's thrilling. It's like someone saying, "Go up on that trapeze to open the circus event, and do twenty-seven flick flacks and three double things and off you go, bye!" and can you fucking do it, or can't you?

LEIBMAN: How do you tackle that farce-like rhythm? You don't want the audience thinking this is a goofy play. It's the second scene, right after the Rabbi. You're setting everything up. It's a lot of responsibility.

MITCHELL HÉBERT (Roy at Round House/Olney, Bethesda, MD, 2016): It's a seduction scene at its heart. Roy performs the dance of power for Joe.

JOHN JUDD (Roy in the Journeymen, 1998): The "octopus" line is the first of several times Roy compares himself to subhuman creatures—one of the building blocks for the character. His finesse in communication—threatening, seducing, charming, and deceiving—are also keys to Roy. Receiving Joe while in the midst of his telephone aria reminded me of the reports that Lyndon Johnson would hold staff meetings while seated on the toilet—a crude yet cunning display of power, but also a weirdly intimate gesture.

RUSSELL TOVEY (Joe in London, 2017): Roy has no idea that Joe's a Mormon. Roy doesn't know that Joe is married. Hang on a minute! How does that work? They're slightly strangers, but they've known each other for a long time. They've never connected on a real level, but Roy's always had his eye on Joe.

Roy (Ron Leibman) performs the "fucking octopus" speech in New York, 1993. (*Joan Marcus*)

MICHAEL HAYDEN (Roy in Juilliard *Millennium* workshop, 1992): Working on a speech like that, it's like working on musical theater. You can't bang through it.

HÉBERT: There was a long learning curve: the many phone calls, the beeping and buzzing the phone makes, the checking in with Joe.

NATHAN LANE (Roy in London, 2017, and New York, 2018): The phone stuff is just technical, working the buttons, all the people, who do you have on hold, and then Baby Doll, the receptionist. I've done a lot of parts where I have to be on the phone over the years, so I'm usually good at that.

TOVEY: That is the magic of Nathan Lane. He just rides it like a perfect wave.

HAYDEN: Away from rehearsal I had to drill it and drill it and drill it, so in rehearsal I could let it fly. It was a joy. Goddamn, what a feast.

MARK WING-DAVEY (director at American Conservatory Theater, San Francisco, 1994–95): As the action begins to become more fluent, then the thrill of the technical achievement begins to bleed into the characterization itself. Both Roy and the actor playing Roy are enjoying his performance. The public face of Roy Cohn is itself a performance, as is his sexuality, et cetera. You can feel that he is himself performing, and generally I would discourage that, but not with this particular character.

HANS KESTING (Roy at Toneelgroep Amsterdam, 2007–15): It is true, part of Roy borrows parts of your personality. You never get to fully lose yourself in the character; it's always you who's giving a portrayal.

JOE MANTELLO (Louis in Los Angeles and New York, 1992–94): Roy was always going to be a star part.

BEN SHENKMAN (Roy in NYU *Perestroika* workshop, 1993): That's why you go to someone like Nathan Lane or Al Pacino. You're looking to borrow the size of their own persona, in a way, as a way of separating that character out.

F. MURRAY ABRAHAM (Roy in New York replacement cast, 1994): I was studying the play early on, and I was having trouble liking him. I don't have trouble playing characters out of literature like Mephistopheles, Richard III, Macbeth. I can understand them, I can make them as evil or as charming as I want. Charm is essential to playing evil characters. But I couldn't do that with Roy because I detested him, the real person, personally, so much.

I was doing a movie in Europe and I was studying the script on a plane to Paris. This guy sitting next to me saw the script and said, "That's a great play. You're doing Roy, aren't you?" And I said yes. And this guy said, "Oh, I knew Roy Cohn." He had a case against Roy once. And he said, "He was a son of a bitch, but I couldn't take my eyes off him." And that's when I said to myself, *I GOT IT! I GOT IT!*

That's a good story.

LANE: It's easy to find people to talk about how much they hated him. He was hated by legions of people. But I talked to people who were close to him, who were loyal to him and loved him, because that's what I wanted to know about.

ELLEN McLAUGHLIN (the Angel in workshops, San Francisco, Los Angeles, New York, 1990–94): While we were doing one of the workshops, Ron Vawter was doing his Roy Cohn one-man show. It was extraordinary. Because he was already sick too. Stephen and I went to see it. It was remarkable. This man, who was sick, was doing this extraordinary impression of Cohn, who was so important to Tony's thinking about the play.

KESTING: I'd seen the Ron Vawter monologue. He brought that monologue here. Vawter really looked like Roy Cohn! He had these big childish blue eyes. When you know he is the devil. Is there anyone who has ever tried to do it really as Roy Cohn, to imitate? That would be interesting.

SHENKMAN: I went to the Museum of Broadcasting and watched Roy Cohn and even snuck a tape recorder in there and did some recordings of his voice. I approached it as if I were playing Roy Cohn in a movie. I was kind of trying to get a documentary likeness of Roy Cohn on the stage.

LANE: I really wanted to chart the progression of the disease in *Perestroika* in a way that I hadn't seen it done before. For example, he had these tremors that came and went. He had a tremor in his right hand, then it would move to the left hand and sometimes the shoulders, and I thought that was interesting, because someone mentioned that when he had a tremor he would hold his hand and stop it from moving, because he had to control everything, even his body.

FRANK WOOD (Roy at Signature Theatre, New York, 2010): I went to the Museum of Radio and Television and I watched *Point of Order!* And Roy Cohn had his action with his tongue, poking out of his mouth. It became pronounced in the hospital room scenes. [Director] Michael Greif said he liked that, because it made him think of thrush, a symptom of dry mouth.

TERRY TEACHOUT (theater critic, *Wall Street Journal*): I was really struck by Frank Wood in the Signature production because he looked exactly like Robert Mapplethorpe's photo of Cohn.

Roy Cohn advises Senator Joseph McCarthy during the Army-McCarthy Hearings, June 1, 1954. (*Yale Joel/The* LIFE *Picture Collection/Getty Images*)

LANE: I think Tony's Roy Cohn is more fun, probably, than the real guy. If you look at that *60 Minutes* interview, the last interview he did, he makes some feeble attempts at humor and he's sort of pathetic.

LEIBMAN: Growing up in New York, you'd see Cohn in restaurants, and you'd see him at 54. You felt like you knew him but you didn't. But Donald Trump did! Birds of a feather flocked together! Sons of bitches.

BARNEY FRANK (congressman from Massachusetts, 1981–2013): One of the most despicable people in American history who did not actually kill anybody. He was just irredeemably vicious, and by the way—interesting—Donald Trump claims him as one of his mentors.

TONY KUSHNER: When I was at Tisch, I was just coming out, Michael Mayer took me to my first gay bar—not the Saint, Uncle Charlie's on Greenwich—so you'd walk around the corner and there'd be these lines of men. I probably passed Roy Cohn on several occasions.

TEACHOUT: I'm sixty. Roy Cohn is not just the guy who was in *Angels in America*. I know people who knew Roy Cohn well. I think of him not just as the demon of *Angels*, not just the pal of McCarthy, but the litigator, the Studio 54 guy. He was very much someone one knew about.

JUDD: Exposing all the things Roy Cohn strove to hide, deny, and undermine in his life was splendid justice. Hell yeah.

LEIBMAN: To work against gay rights, a man in his position at this time, it's one of the most scandalous moments in American history. What a fuckhead.

DAVID FRANCE (director and author, *How to Survive a Plague*): One of the principal doctors, one of the first people on the ground treating people with the disease well before it had a name, was paid a visit by Roy Cohn. He went to see Alvin Friedman-Kien. And he had bodyguards with him, and he said to Friedman-Kien, "If you fucking say anything about this, we are going to kill you." And then of course he went to the NHS and got onto the early AZT trials. And how he did that I don't know, and I can only imagine that it happened somehow like it did in *Angels*.

DAVID MARSHALL GRANT (Joe in New York, 1993–94): That speech, one of the most astonishing speeches in that play, to the doctor:

ROY

Now to someone who doesn't understand this, homosexual is what I am
because I have sex with men. But really this is wrong. Homosexuals
are not men who sleep with other men. Homosexuals are men who in fifteen
years of trying cannot pass a pissant discrimination bill through City Council.
Homosexuals are men who know nobody and who nobody knows.
Does this sound like me, Henry?

HENRY
No.

ROY
No. I have clout.

–Millennium Approaches, Act 1, Scene 9

GRANT: I was very taken with what seemed an honest appreciation of Cohn's point of view. I found Tony's brutally honest assessment of these people's psychologies really amazing.

WOOD: My father had served in the Johnson administration and I remember thinking, *That is a line my dad would appreciate.*

JUDD: I remember a day in the rehearsal room working on the hospital scenes with Belize. The first time I spewed the racial epithets at my scene partner, Robert Teverbaugh, and saw those words land on him and affect him—I broke down. I realized it wasn't so much fun to play the true darkness and poison in Roy. And so that day the job got more interesting.

WOOD: Billy Porter's discipline as an actor and faith in himself made me feel like I could be the son of a bitch I needed to be. And in the service of a great play, I took pleasure in that. Letting your evil hair down can be exciting and rewarding.

JUDD: I loved that there was not a beat skipped when Ethel Rosenberg appeared to Roy. They just started talking. "Aw, hell, Ethel . . ." No Scrooge and Marley theatrics.

LEIBMAN: I had a chance to meet one of the Rosenberg children. Can you imagine? I forget which one it was, I get their names mixed up. He came to my dressing room with a mutual friend, and he was smiling, and I said, "Why are you smiling?" and he said, "You *nailed* the cocksucker!" And then

Belize (Nathan Stewart-Jarrett) and Roy (Nathan Lane) in London, 2017. (*Helen Maybanks*)

we had a wonderful conversation. We had to leave, it was after midnight, they had to close the theater. He said, "I'll come back for Part 2. Because you *die!*"

WESLEY MORRIS (critic-at-large, *New York Times*): In a shitty version of this play, a cheaper, less intellectually sophisticated work of art, Roy gets AIDS but getting AIDS is the punishment. But Tony Kushner doesn't use Roy having AIDS to mock and laugh at him. It's Rosenberg and Belize—a Blatino and a dead Jewish lady—who do all the judgment and reckoning for him.

TEACHOUT: One reservation I've had about Kushner's work is his tendency to demonize characters he thinks of as enemies. He comes about as close as he can come in overcoming it in portraying Cohn. Kushner really, to an extent not usual with him when portraying villains, puts across Cohn's complexity as a human being.

GOODMAN: I think Tony goes out of his way not to just make the baddies bad and the goodies good but to make it completely credible that they coexist, that Louis can be evil and confused, that Roy can be loving and tender and fatherly.

ABRAHAM: A good trick, if you don't like a guy, is to play him in a way that appeals to you, on whatever level. When you project this positive element, his charisma, it deepens him; he almost mesmerizes you with his extraordinary talent and charm. Some people are really evil, but they're also really magnetic. You can't help but jump into bed with them. You hate yourself in the morning, but it's great the night before.

OSKAR EUSTIS (co-director in Los Angeles, 1992): At one point, [Tony and I] read Whittaker Chambers's book *Witness*, about his conversion from communism to Christianity. What began to emerge was that there were two strands in the American Right. They both believe the same thing: that people are selfish and evil. One wing says, because of that, we need to accept that we are fallen miserable sinners and throw ourselves on the mercy of Christ. That's

Joe. There's another faction that thinks that people are selfish and evil, and so let's indulge our selfishness and have as much fun as we can. That's the Cohn wing.

LEIBMAN: I had discovered that Roy Cohn had a house in Provincetown and his next-door neighbor was Norman Mailer. I knew Norman from the Actors Studio. I called him. Spoke to his wife. She said, "Oh, we were very close friends!"

I said, "Darlin', it's hard for me to conceive of Norman being friends with Roy Cohn."

And she said, "You have to remember: Roy Cohn was one of the funniest human beings who ever lived."

HAYDEN: I don't want to make him sympathetic, but I don't want him to just be evil. Only lazy actors do that.

MARCUS GRAHAM (Roy at Belvoir St Theatre, Sydney, 2013): Roy is simply having the time of his life playing with people as they make these ridiculous lunges towards power. Roy is the bringer of light, of fun and games, of seduction and freedom, and in my opinion he is a breath of fresh air.

MICHAEL RIEDEL (theater columnist, *New York Post*): Here I thought Tony was like Shaw. Often with Shaw the villain runs away with the play. And Roy is a fabulous juicy villain, and we always love the devil. And Ron Leibman had these great monologues, and you'd think, *Yeah, I wish I had the guts to be as evil as that!*

LEIBMAN: I had done *Richard III* several times. There's a lot of Richard III in Roy Cohn.

JUDD: Years later I got to play Iago, who I thought initially would be Roy-like. I found instead that Iago, a true sociopath, really had very little concern for other humans, whereas I found Roy, ultimately, to be very needy of love, human kindness, a place to call home.

SHENKMAN: You can go in and do Roy Cohn as a stand-alone star turn because he isn't connected to anybody; his main relationship is with the audience. An older, unadventurous, even politically conservative audience member could go in and not be challenged at all by the character of Roy Cohn. At all. The parts of the play that make that kind of person uncomfortable are all in the other characters, they're not in Roy Cohn. Roy Cohn is an old-fashioned kind of theatrical villain.

Roy's masculinity is never challenged. He is a masculine force. It's just as he says: "I'm not really a gay person, I'm a heterosexual man who fucks guys," and that's true, so for that reason I think he's completely unchallenging to homophobic straight audiences. Michael Corleone can play Roy Cohn, and everyone's fine. It's not like "Oh my God, we've never seen Pacino like this"; he's on a continuum with Scarface and Corleone and all those wonderful, powerful men.

VIVIENNE BENESCH (Hannah in NYU *Perestroika* workshop, 1993): There's a part of me that hopes Ben Shenkman and I get to do Roy Cohn and Ethel Rosenberg again when we're at the *right* age.

SHENKMAN: *(Laughs.)* You know what, I would not follow Nathan Lane and Al Pacino. The list is too long of geniuses who have done the part now, so I wouldn't be in a hurry to try it again.

(Pause.)

Although I will say one thing, if anyone ever said, "You *have* to play Roy Cohn," what *I'd* focus on—

STEPHEN SPINELLA (Prior in San Francisco, Los Angeles, and New York, 1988–94): What a play! I hope I get to do Roy Cohn someday.

CHAPTER 3

PREPARE
THE WAY

THE MARK TAPER FORUM, LOS ANGELES, 1992

CYNTHIA MACE (Harper in Los Angeles, 1992): The whole Taper adventure was the most extraordinary thing ever. You know, the best of times, the worst of times.

DOUG WAGER (artistic director, Arena Stage, Washington, D.C., 1991–98): Back when *Angels* was in process, before it had its first major American production, I met with Jim Nicola and Tony Kushner and JoAnne Akalaitis.

JOANNE AKALAITIS (artistic director, Public Theater, 1991–93): I have had so many discussions with Jim Nicola about shows on the East Coast that I'm sure this was one of them. *(Laughs.)*

WAGER: There was a plan for a kind for a co-production between New York Theatre Workshop and Arena to mount Part 1 in the fall of the year the Taper did both parts. It was even announced in the *Washington Post* that we were in discussions. No one had seen Part 2. I had a manuscript of the whole thing on my desk.

New York will finally see for itself when Parts 1 ("The Millennium Approaches," 3½ hours long) and 2 ("Perestroika," ditto) come to the Public Theater in February, a guaranteed hot ticket. After that, D.C.'s Arena Stage is a good possibility; discussions are underway. Kushner wants his play, subtitled "A Gay Fantasia on National Themes" and written partly with (Yo, Anne-Imelda Radice!) National Endowment for the Arts funding, to be seen in Washington. "It's the seat of a lot of what the play is railing about, or wailing about, or whatever it's doing," he says.

–Paula Span, "Tony Kushner's Railing Big Show," *Washington Post*, July 31, 1992

WAGER: When Gordon Davidson jumped the broom and offered Tony the premiere of both parts at the Taper, Gordon wanted the exclusive rights to the premiere. We were out of the loop. And once it was at the Taper, that was the beginning of the move to the Broadway production, from a rights point of view.

BRUCE WEBER (reporter, *New York Times*, 1984–2017): Gordon was the king of theater in a town where no one gave a rat's ass about theater. He felt that very acutely. The Taper is a fine theater and puts on excellent shows year over year, and at the time the tickets were bought by the big studio honchos and given to their secretaries. He was the big theater mogul in a movie town. Rightly so, he had a bit of a chip on his shoulder about that.

RON LEIBMAN (Roy in Los Angeles, 1992): I heard about it originally on a call from Gordon Davidson. They were doing this summer workshop of *Perestroika*. Just Part 2. I'd never heard of it, because it'd never been done. So I asked, "What is Part 1?" *(Laughs.)*

And he said, "Why don't I send you Part 1, it's pretty much together, it was done at the National, and I'll add to it Part 2 as it stands now."

So I read Part 1 and I thought . . . *I love this. It'll close in one night.* Just to give you an insight into my showbiz acumen. I saw that Part 2 needed an enormous amount of work. I said, "If you're ever considering doing this, give me a ring. I'd love to do Roy Cohn," but I couldn't do it that summer, I was busy.

So I guess they did that summer workshop and I got a call that they were going to do Parts 1 and 2 down at the Taper. So I read it, and I saw that he had done an enormous amount of work on Part 2. I saw that it still needed work—I didn't say that to *them (laughs)*—but Tony felt that way. Everyone thought that.

To be honest, I had qualms about playing Cohn. I loved the play. But I detested him as a human being in real life *so much*. I thought Tony had done a wonderful job creating his own version of Roy Cohn, but nevertheless I was always ashamed of him. I was ashamed of him because he was a Jew. I was ashamed of a lot of things about him. If I was going to play him, I was going to have to dig within myself to get to that level of self-hatred. I knew I was going to have to go to places that were very uncomfortable in order to make the character uncomfortable.

So they said, "Will you audition for this." And I said no.

Tony knew mostly my film work. But Oskar had seen me play Tartuffe at the Los Angeles Theatre Center, and said, "That's Roy Cohn." If you think about it, that lying, sniveling *(laughs)*, son-of-a-bitch finagler has a lot of the qualities of Cohn.

Gordon called me up and said, "Ron, you gotta audition for this." I told him you can't audition this role. He doesn't come in on any scenes with a hello, nice to see you, giving an actor a chance to warm up. He comes in doing 175 miles per hour. In an audition, it's going to be bullshit *Saturday Night Live* acting, and I don't want to do that. I don't want to fuck up the material. I don't want to do an imitation of what it should be. I'm going to do it or I'm not going to do it.

I wasn't being, *I don't audition*. I was saying this would ruin this music.

Gordon said, "We'll have to give it to someone else."

I said, "Go ahead."

And then they didn't, the fools!

JOE MANTELLO (Louis in Los Angeles, 1992): I was primarily working at Circle Rep. I was virtually unhireable. That was the startling thing of getting Louis. It wasn't a natural progression of someone who had been working a lot. It was: very few acting jobs . . . *Angels in America*.

MICHAEL ORNSTEIN (Louis in San Francisco, 1991): Joe Mantello was my buddy. I knew him from Circle Rep. I thought, if I'm not going to do this, it should be someone that I love, that I knew is good, that I knew was going to honor the part, the world of *Angels in America*. I gave Joe my script and said, "You gotta get this!"

MANTELLO: I don't think I was particularly skilled when it came to auditions. That wasn't—I just never knew how to do it. But somehow I knew when *Angels* came along that I had to do something that I had never done before, which was to kind of really up my game for that audition.

I auditioned. I got called back. I knew it had gone well, better than any audition I had ever had. There seemed to be some *mild* enthusiasm for me, but they continued, they did a biiiiig search. I remember feeling like as each week passed that it was slipping away. I remember feeling very despondent and obsessively checking in with my agent about it.

K. TODD FREEMAN (Belize in Los Angeles, 1992): I read *Millennium Approaches* and thought it was one of the best things I'd ever read in my entire life. I thought, *I gotta get in on this*.

BOB EGAN (associate artistic director, Mark Taper Forum, 1983–2003): People were aware of how special this play was. Then it gets to the Taper Too, and there

The Angel (Ellen McLaughlin) and Prior (Stephen Spinella) in Los Angeles, 1992. (© *Jay Thompson and Craig Schwartz/Center Theatre Group*)

was more buzz. Then it was going to the mainstage. Anybody would feel a certain amount of pressure to live up to all the expectations that had been flowing for two or three years. This monumental play. This great play. No one wants to fuck that up!

TONY TACCONE (co-director in Los Angeles, 1992): When we did the project in L.A., it had problems. Not the least of one was Part 2 wasn't written completely when we started rehearsals.

OSKAR EUSTIS (co-director in Los Angeles, 1992): Tony was in the unenviable position of having the *Times* say he'd written a masterpiece when he hadn't finished it.

TACCONE: All eyes were on us. It felt like Frank Rich's review said, "I'm going to make this play a success in New York on my terms." Rich is a smart guy, but of course there's a tyranny of power of the *New York Times* over theater.

FRANK RICH (chief theater critic, *New York Times*, 1980–93): Today the *Times*'s power is incredibly diminished because the nature of the game has changed, but it was always overstated. The one good part of the theory was that if you liked something in a lonely way that only a few others liked, you could at least convince producers to keep throwing money at it to make ads and keep it running. In my case, that was *Sunday in the Park with George. Sunday* didn't recoup. It never toured. I loved it as much as I loved *Angels*.

TONY KUSHNER: First was the Frank Rich review. Then Ian McKellen at the Tony Awards, getting up and saying, *(Ian McKellen voice:)* "There's a play in London, it's going to win every Tony."

> Thank you very much and good evening, everybody. Back home in London, the hottest ticket at the National Theatre is for a new American play, written by a New Yorker, Tony Kushner's *Angels in America. (Applause.)* You wait until it comes here, it's going to win every Tony.
>
> —Ian McKellen, presenting at the Tony Awards, May 31, 1992

JEFF KING (Joe in Los Angeles, 1992): When I saw Ian McKellen talking about it on the Tonys, I thought, *My God, how do you know about this?* It's this private thing we've been making and showing to our friends for years, putting everything into it, why does *he* know about it, and why are you telling everyone about it?!

KUSHNER: That plus Frank's review kicked the thing into a kind of madness.

CASEY COWAN (associate lighting designer in Los Angeles, 1992): They knew that it was going to go to New York, they knew that none of the Los Angeles design team had the chops to go to New York, so they hired a bunch of veterans to come out and do it. People out here don't think that's fair, but that's how they do it. So they hired Pat Collins. I contacted Pat and told her that I had worked on it before, and she brought me on as her associate.

MANTELLO: I remember it being somewhat bumpy when we started rehearsals.

KUSHNER: For some reason *Angels* is always terrible at the first table read. It's so long and it doesn't get its laughs, because the actors aren't going for laughs, they're just trying to figure out what's going on. I was already freaking out about *Perestroika*. After the read I went out to the plaza behind the offices. Joe Mantello was eating lunch and he said, "You seem very unhappy."

I said, "It's clear I haven't figured out this second part yet, and I feel as though I need to apologize to you."

And Joe said, "You're out of your fucking mind. You have nothing to apologize for." That meant a lot to me on that difficult day and I fed off it for many days afterward.

FREEMAN: All I remember about the table read is making sure I got my laughs.

MANTELLO: During the first week, Stephen Spinella had started to . . . he wasn't unfriendly, but he started to kind of say, "If you're over there, I can do this," that sort of thing. I let it happen a couple of times and then once, when we were on a break, I went up to Oskar Eustis and I said, "You have to stop this now or *I'm* going to stop it. And I guarantee you, you stopping it is the better option."

MARY KLINGER (stage manager in Los Angeles, 1992): We worked seven days a week, because Monday, the normal day off, we worked on the flying with Ellen. Which is fine because they were paying us. But we were getting so exhausted, I had to call the union and ask them to intervene.

MACE: As we moved into *Perestroika*, as we became more—how do I say it?— more our characters, then the collaboration got fascinating. We all ended up having interesting and fun input. Like we were all in that hot mess together.

LEIBMAN: I spoke to a lot of people who knew Cohn. I even had a meeting with [McCarthy hearings figure] G. David Schine. If he knew what the play was about, he never would've seen me. He picked the worst restaurant in Beverly Hills. He wanted to talk about his pal. I don't know if they were lovers or not; that's what the rumors were.

He just gave me boilerplate Republican stuff. I thought, *What am I gonna ask this guy that's gonna get a real answer?* So I said, "If you could name something that your friend Roy missed in his life, what would that be?"

His eyes rolled in his head. I don't think anyone had asked him that. He said, "When he would come to my house, he would always play with my kids. I think he missed being a father."

Which is an interesting thing for a stupid man to say. Suddenly it hit me: *That's* the relationship with Joe. That's what it's really about. If it's just merely about getting someone to do your bidding for you in the State Department, that's so one-dimensional. So non-human.

But I thought, *I'm not going to tell Tony or Oskar this is what I'm really working on.* I didn't know if it would work. If it would give that added emotional dimension or not. It was working for me, but then the third week of rehearsal Tony called me over and I thought, *Oh shit, they've caught me.* And Tony Kushner said, "Are you working on anything where Cohn is trying to initiate Joe to be his son?" and I said, "Do you not want me to do it?" And Tony said, "No. Thank you."

And he rewrote a lot of the second part. Do you remember in the second part when Roy finds out Joe is leaving his wife because he's gay? Cohn grabs him and says, "Go back to her, go back to her." It's like a Jewish father! And the fact that they're both gay gave it another dimension. Tony wrote that, additional scenes with the colors I had been working with.

EGAN: Tony Taccone was brought on to be co-director with Oskar. Partly that was just because of the magnitude of the undertaking. Everyone wanted to get it right.

KING: I had never, and have never since, worked with two directors. We are all still buddies, so it wasn't—it was—you had to know who to go to for certain things.

FREEMAN: Taccone was slated to be the blocking guy, and Oskar was the internal "What's your motivation?" part of the directing thing.

EUSTIS: We tried to do that. Until we couldn't.

FREEMAN: Look, it didn't really work. *(Laughs.)* It's difficult, one director says one thing, another says the other; it causes some confusion.

LEIBMAN: It was very strange. You'd have Oskar one day on a scene, and then Tony the next day. So it would be Oskar and Tony. And then Kushner came in, too, so it was Oskar and Tony and Tony. So we had three directors!

MANTELLO: There was a dynamic going on underneath the surface that we were not aware of. I don't know what that was. It always felt a little bit like being the child of divorced parents. One weekend you're with this parent, one weekend with the other.

EUSTIS: The hardest struggle was me and Tony Kushner, and our relationship. Bringing on Tony Taccone was a way of shoring up, of buttressing the cracks in my relationship with Tony Kushner. We both felt that we were suffering from being so close and being so intimate with the play and with each other. I had been there every minute with the play. There were boundary issues that we both felt. I was, in many ways, his first director. It was early in Tony's writing career. It was relatively early in my career. There was a lot that we didn't know.

KUSHNER: It was terribly fraught. The whole experience was terribly fraught. Oskar and I had a very tough time with . . . *(sighs)* the way that it was going, and so we had sort of . . . it was kind of crushing us all in a certain sense.

TACCONE: We were young. We were under pressure. We didn't know what the second part was completely so we didn't know what the design was. The designers had more experience than us. We were the rookie kids, but we were also good!

KLINGER: Without one person in charge, the designers also got more involved. So lots of people were telling me contradictory things. I think I scared them by throwing my headset and walking out one day. They were friendlier to me after that.

JONATHAN LEE (production manager in Los Angeles, 1992): It was huge. The concept of doing a two-part play was relatively new to us at the time. The Mark Taper Forum, although a lovely, moderately sized regional theater, has a thrust stage and almost no backstage space. The play takes place in thousands of different locations.

TACCONE: There was a plan for the furniture and it didn't work. We had to change the movement pattern of the play on the fly. When you're changing and trying to adapt a set that doesn't really work, go back in the middle of rehearsals and say we need more *exits*, that's hard. That's a play that needs every bit of stage trickery you can pull off. That can't stay still while you move scenery around.

LEE: Getting the furniture and the props onstage and offstage, I dunno, it was difficult. What would happen is things would get rolled out from the wings, play center stage, and get rolled off in the other direction. That was sort of a disappointment to me.

TACCONE: And the play was still in a formative stage.

KUSHNER: We made a mistake. When I wrote *Perestroika*, it was five acts long. We had this play, *Millennium Approaches*, that everybody was really loving.

Oskar and I both felt that *Perestroika* should replicate it in some way. It was inevitable that we were going to try to squeeze *Perestroika* into a three-act structure. It doesn't work in three acts.

KLINGER: It was being rewritten constantly.

STEPHEN SPINELLA (Prior in Los Angeles, 1992): It was brutal for him. It was brutal for all of us.

TACCONE: I remember being in rehearsal, blocking a scene, getting to the end, and being like, ". . . and we have no idea what happens next, so we'll have to wait to see where you go."

EUSTIS: The thing he did, and it remains the most brilliant thing I've ever seen a writer do: He took this difficulty of making these characters change and he made it the content of the play. *Angels* is about how incredibly hard and incredibly necessary it is to change. He united the form and the content. You watch *Angels*, you read *Angels*, it feels *truer* than other plays. I feel like I had a front row seat to watching Tony struggle for six years to tell the truth.

TACCONE: Our tech was a fucking nightmare—

LEE: Particularly *Perestroika*, where Ellen had to jump onto things and off of things. We didn't really know how to do the rig. Just getting her to land in the right place and be lit as she was moving—

KUSHNER: I'll never forget Ellen hanging on a wire at the Taper, and it was on some sort of pivot thing that they were trying out. And she couldn't stop spinning, and the wire caught her wig and some of her actual hair, and it was starting to scalp her. I ran up onstage, and I grabbed a broom, and we unwound her and got her off of it.

COWAN: Hanging took longer. Focusing took an extra day. There was major panic. We were supposed to be rehearsing the show and have actors on deck, and we weren't focused. So we started out behind.

KLINGER: We had gotten to a point where we had never done a run-through, but we were going to do a preview the next day.

COWAN: We were working on lighting while the actors had a meeting. Tony and Oskar and Tony weren't there. They took a vote and said they don't feel confident doing this. It's in the rules, when they vote and say they can't do it, you don't do it.

KLINGER: Stephen Spinella, who was the spokesman for the rest of the cast, said that they wouldn't do the show for an audience without a run-through. We hadn't finished teching the lights for one big section of the show. The producers agreed: They said we'll give you a run-through, and we'll do it with just basic lighting.

MANTELLO: I remember getting ready to go out for the first preview. We had to make our entrance by pushing on a park bench. It was so frightening. Right before we went on, Stephen reached over, and took my hand. We were both just shaking, and he looked at me. And then we went out. It changed from that moment on. It was like all of a sudden it dropped in. We became friends.

TACCONE: The first preview of *Angels*, just Part 1 by itself was four hours long. Ian McKellen was there, and we were just like, *Oh my God, Ian McKellen saw the worst thing ever.*

EUSTIS: It had been calamitously difficult. I hadn't even had time to stage the curtain call by the first preview. The lights went out at the end of the show, and there was a roar in the darkness. The lights came up and the audience was already standing up. I remember Jeff King's face, just looking at the audience. Oh my God, we've unleashed something.

KUSHNER: The audience had been to see *Millennium* and loved it, and so they went to the first preview of *Perestroika* ever. It was *endless* with these technical glitches.

There was a horrifying moment—I had written in the Council of Principalities scene that there was a rain of paper that falls constantly. Oskar had

decided that we would have this thing up in the flies—he found a paper sorting machine that would throw pages of paper. Where are we going to get the paper? Somebody on stage management had this great idea: There were these bins of rewrites of *Perestroika*, these recycling bins, with hundreds of thousands of sheets with all the rewrites. Let's just load it up with that.

The Taper is a thrust stage with an air-conditioning system. We had never tested it before, so we did it for the first time during first preview. And it starts sending out these things. And they don't fall down, because they're paper. They start going out into the audience. And they are rewrites of the fucking scenes. People were not having it. They were literally picking up the rewrites and passing them around and I just thought, *This is it. This is my big chance, and I've completely destroyed it.*

I fled the minute the lights went down and went to what I thought was a back staircase and took this wrong turn and I was stuck in this staircase, and the audience starts coming through after the very short and tepid curtain call. They didn't know who I was, so I was stuck with all these people saying, "What happened?! The first part was so great and this is *terrible*! This doesn't work *at all*! It's just awful!"

TACCONE: We had a notes session that ended at around 1:30 in the morning. There's this big scene in *Perestroika* that needed to be rewritten. Tony came in at seven the next morning, and he handed us this new thirty-page scene and he said, "I dreamt this last night."

MACE: God bless every molecule in Tony Kushner's brain. He would come up to the dressing room during previews and have a little paragraph, something

Tony Kushner onstage in Los Angeles, 1992. (*© Jay Thompson and Craig Schwartz/Center Theatre Group*)

new. A few new lines. By that time we were so attuned to moving that monster along that we would say, "Sure, great."

ELLEN McLAUGHLIN (the Angel in Los Angeles, 1992): Some of these were major rewrites and the preview process—when the days are spent in rehearsal putting the changes in and the nights are spent hanging on to what you did during the day—was pretty grueling.

MANTELLO: It was all very quiet, but at a certain point, once we started previews in L.A., I remember Oskar sitting in the back row of the Taper, and Tony Taccone stepping forward, and there had been some kind of regime change without any of us really being told. But I have this very vivid image of Oskar coming in and sitting in the back row.

TACCONE: This is what's fair to say. It was a traumatic experience for all of us. There was tension all around. I very much felt like I was asked to step up into more of a dominant role, and I did. I tried to do my job with Kushner's strong input as best I could. But that was a situation where the directorial pressures were sort of enormous. But you know what? The play's *really* good. The play succeeded in spite of the tension we were having.

COWAN: I'm on headset, in the back row. The acoustics in the Taper are such that if you're sitting in the back row and whisper, the audience can hear you. So we get to that scene where Roy Cohn goes to hell, and the ACLs turn on. They're really bright. We had a dozen of them in the floor in Pat's design. I see smoke rising from the deck. I'm thinking about it and I'm thinking about it, because it's against the law to cry "Fire!" in a crowded theater. I turn on the headset. I felt like a sniper, controlling my heartbeat.

"Mary," I said. "There's smoke coming from the deck."

I heard both of their chairs scrape back as they stood up to look out the window. And there was a tiny lick of flame coming out of the floor! Joe got on his headset and calmly called one of his electricians and said, "Ricky, go under the deck with a fire extinguisher and spray the ACLs." And he did.

It was a pencil burning that caused that flame. Someone had dropped a pencil. So, yeah, no more pencils onstage after that.

KING: We had to put off opening for a week because we weren't ready to do it yet. That was a radical step.

FREEMAN: Poor Ellen was slung up in that harness having to re-tech day after day that I—I—I—I scene with Prior. She had to memorize all that babble craziness, and Tony would change it every day.

McLAUGHLIN: And then came the last night before opening when I was handed a fifteen-page rewrite. That was, uh, really terrifying. It was one of those mindfucking rewrites. Not a brand-new scene, but a restructuring of what we already had. A passage that had been on page 12 was now on 4, with some new bridging text in between to make that work, so all the landmarks were down.

It was the first time Tony and I ever had a fight, and that was awful. I got the rewrite when I walked into the dressing room after the curtain call of the final preview. I had friends at the show and I wanted to go out with them but Tony wanted to read the new pages right then in the dressing room. I said "No. I just can't see straight at this point. I will read it later and decide whether I can do it."

And he said, "You have to read it now!" and I did this gesture straight out of a movie, *I showed him the door*. Which he couldn't believe. He was just furious and he stormed out. I went down to see my friends and we went to the bar, but Tony was waiting there with steam coming out of his ears and, you know, he was right, we had to read it. So we went to the corner of the bar and read it and *(laughs)* it was good, goddamn it! So what are you going to do? I had to stay up all night and memorize it. And then we spent the day of opening teching it because of the flying and all the changes in that staging that had to go in. And then that night was opening night and I had to do it in front of Frank Rich and God and everyone.

SPINELLA: Tony Kushner is an incredibly sophisticated writer who just, you know, until he gets it right he is going to put everybody through hell. He wrote, and he rewrote, and he rewrote, and he thought about it, and he struggled, and he worked through his own personal struggles with writing, and struggled with his demons and all that, and we all had to go on that journey with him.

By the time most of you read this, we will have elected a President and whatever the choice, enormous changes remain to be faced as we all move towards the millennium together. Theatre can be a courageous forum in which the major issues are confronted. In this time of reassessment and change (Perestroika, if you will), we feel particularly excited to be doing Tony Kushner's play, *Angels in America, A Gay Fantasia on National Themes*.

–Gordon Davidson, "From the Artistic Director," in the program to the Mark Taper Forum production, 1992

ROBERT HURWITT (San Francisco theater critic): The production was just gorgeous. It sealed your sense that this was the play of its age. This was a masterpiece.

EUSTIS: That incredible scene where Louis says Kaddish over Roy Cohn? The first night at the Taper, there was a disturbance in the audience, and I realized there were dozens of people saying the Kaddish along with Louis. It was so moving! People engaged on a level that I had never seen in a theater piece.

LEIBMAN: One of the things I did out there is I went to a lot—well, quite a few—hospices. The AIDS epidemic was flying. I spoke to a lot of guys who were dying. I learned a lot from listening to these guys. When we opened, the word got out. Guys with AIDS, different stages, they wanted to see the play. The theater went out of its way to make sure they got seats. But they needed to sit, a lot of them, close, because the hearing was going, the eyesight was going.

At curtain call we could see the first couple of rows. The lights would spill over. We could see the audience. The audience would generally give a standing ovation, but to see guys who could barely stand, giving us a standing ovation, you know, out of their wheelchairs.

We were doing a play, yes, but it became something else.

EGAN: There was such an explosion of response and support, gratitude, for this play.

KUSHNER: The second or third marathon performance was the day after the election of Clinton. And the next week, *Time* magazine's cover was "Overturning the Reagan Era," with a picture of Ronald Reagan upside down. On *Time* magazine! And that was back when people were still in awe of him. It was like seeing a picture of Jesus with, like, you know, bunny ears.

That performance was like a rock concert—people were just—every Reagan joke got, you know, *hours* of applause and cheering, 'cause people were so excited that this nightmare was looking like it maybe was gonna start to turn around.

> Tony Kushner's epic play about the death of the 20th century has
> arrived at the very pivot of American history, when the Republican
> ice age it depicts has begun to melt away. Yet no changes in Wash-
> ington will fade the clarity of Kushner's visions or dim the beauty
> of this staging, directed by Oskar Eustis with Tony Taccone.
>
> –Steven Mikulan, *LA Weekly*, November 13–19, 1992

EUSTIS: It was suddenly apparent that we were in a different universe, where you just hit the audience and you suddenly realize, *Oh, the appetite for this is so much bigger than we thought.*

LEIBMAN: I thought we'd have a gay audience, a Jewish audience, that would clear out in about a week. I had no idea.

EUSTIS: The run of *Angels* at the Taper was four weeks, because we didn't think anyone would want to see it. So it was followed by *An Evening with Will Rogers*. We shut down *Angels* in order to have James Whitmore play Will Rogers to half-empty houses! It was a nightmare!

LEE: I think that was part of Gordon wanting to leave them wanting more. There was a lot of buzz about it. Gordon was trying to position it in a way to set the ball to be spiked to Broadway with as much vigor as possible.

KUSHNER: It felt like the play had arrived at the right moment. And so some people said it didn't matter if *Perestroika* is a piece of garbage—this thing is going to Broadway.

> *Angels* is being presented in association with the New York
> Shakespeare Festival, which will present the play in February at
> the Public Theater in New York.
>
> —Gordon Davidson, "From the Artistic Director," in the program
> to the Mark Taper Forum production, 1992

AKALAITIS: I was there to check it out as a show for the Public. It was an event, for sure. The performance I attended, Frank Rich and Alex Witchel were there. It was like the czar and czarina of theater culture coming to check it out. I thought, *Why are they here? What are they doing here? What does this mean that they're here?*

LEIBMAN: Then I heard the Shuberts were coming, the Nederlanders were coming. I sort of got it. I realized it was going to have a life after Los Angeles. Jesus Christ, this thing is not going to close in one night!

MARGO LION (New York producer): There was this kind of flood of people going out to L.A. to see it, and I was one of them. I was at Jujamcyn at the time—I had a housekeeping deal with Rocco Landesman. So we all went out.

> But Kushner had not yet ruled out the Public, the flagship of
> the New York Shakespeare Festival, whose then-artistic director,
> JoAnne Akalaitis, made a final, fevered pitch to land the show
> that went directly to Kushner's conscience. The play is, after all, a
> proud cry on behalf of a maligned minority, and indeed it speaks
> with bruising intellect and emotion against the status quo, the
> very people whose embrace it would ask for on Broadway.
>
> —Bruce Weber, "Angels' Angels," *New York Times Magazine*, April
> 25, 1993

KUSHNER: JoAnne Akalaitis came over and made an impassioned pitch—as impassioned as JoAnne gets.

AKALAITIS: I remember that evening clearly, at Otto's Bar in the mall outside the Taper, which was, at that time, the only place we could go eat and drink and hang out. I still thought that it could come to the Public, not precluding it then moving to Broadway, but it was clear that that was not—that clearly was not part of the master plan. That someone, maybe Gordon and Tony, were envisioning a different show, a different future. I just thought, *Oh, this is how the world works*.

KUSHNER: Gordon Davidson and I had a long, long talk. He's one of the founders of the regional theater movement, and he said, "You don't have a choice. You have to take this to Broadway."

LION: There needed to be a new director, and there needed to be a commitment to do the shows in repertory.

ROCCO LANDESMAN (producer, head of Jujamcyn): We really, *really* wanted the show. Shubert went after it big time. We were at a disadvantage. They had all those great Forty-Fifth Street playhouses to offer. We had only one theater: the Walter Kerr. It was hand-to-hand combat.

WEBER: Rocco's not the typical theater guy. He's a gambler, he likes playing the ponies. He was hired to help Jujamcyn become the upstart organization in town. He was interested in plays that would challenge the Broadway establishment. It's no exaggeration to say that Jerry Schoenfeld and Bernie Jacobs, the president and the chairman of the Shubert organization at the time, were the two most powerful men in the theater.

KUSHNER: It was me, Gordon, and Joyce [Ketay]. I had a meeting with Jerry Schoenfeld and Bernie Jacobs about going to a Shubert house. Bernie Jacobs went on and on about Michael Bennett and how he was like a son to him. Michael was gay and had died of AIDS and that's why they wanted to do the play. It was all very moving.

WEBER: Tony had never been on Broadway before, and I'm sure that Jerry and Bernie brought the full weight of their authority down upon him *(laughs)* to try to persuade him to put the show in a Shubert house. If I recall, they were willing to throw one of their shows out to give *Angels* the Booth Theatre. I think the show that was in there was *Someone Who'll Watch Over Me*. They offered to either move it or close it early to let Tony do the show in the Booth, which was their nicest theater.

LANDESMAN: It was Jack Viertel and I wooing Tony Kushner. We were all in on this thing.

KUSHNER: I met Rocco and I loved him. He was so smart and so funny. He said, "I have the perfect house for this," and he took me to the Walter Kerr and said, "There it is." It wasn't like the Shubert houses, they hadn't jammed it full of so many seats you couldn't breathe. They had done a stunning job redoing it. It's a fantastic dramatic house. It's the right size for the play.

LANDESMAN: One thing I said to Tony is "This is a big and important play that anyone would want. But you will have other plays that won't be as sought after, and we are committing to you as a playwright, not just this play." As it happened, a couple of years down the road, he had *Caroline, or Change* at the Public—that was not an obvious commercial play and we put it on Broadway.

JOYCE KETAY (Kushner's theatrical agent): Tony insisted on signing his Broadway contract at the Russian Tea Room.

KUSHNER: The *original* Russian Tea Room, not the horrible mess that it became subsequently. When I was a kid and we would visit relatives in New York—that was the fanciest place I'd ever been.

KETAY: That's the only time in my entire career that the producers, writer, and agent had lunch to witness the signing of the contract.

WEBER: It took a lot of guts to turn down the Shuberts.

KUSHNER: At the Tony Awards in 1993, I went up to Jerry and Bernie—we had just won everything—and I said, "Uh, I hope you guys aren't still mad at me."

And Bernie Jacobs turned to me and said, "Tony, I forgive but I never forget."

And Jerry Schoenfeld says, "And I forget, but I never forgive!"

And I said, "Ooooookay, that's funny," and I tiptoed away.

INTERLUDE

I AM A VERY GOOD MAN

Joe Pitt

HARPER
I have something to ask you.

JOE
Then ASK! ASK! What in hell are you—

HARPER
Are you a homo?

–*Millennium Approaches*, Act 1, Scene 8

DAVID MARSHALL GRANT (Joe in New York, 1993–94): To the extent that I didn't talk about it publicly, I was still in the closet. But it's not like the media was asking me about my sexuality in countless interviews. I don't think anyone was really *(laughs)* hot on the story. I was still determined to be a movie star as my occupation of choice. So I tried to put being gay on the back burner, so to speak, and continue my work as an actor. I very much related to Joe Pitt, when first I saw that workshop at the Taper.

JEFF KING (Joe in Los Angeles, 1992): I had this image of Joe walking around with the entire Mormon Tabernacle on his shoulders. I'd look at photos of that building in Salt Lake and think of it on my back.

GRANT: Back in the day I would have "girlfriends." Joe seemed like a perfectly normal guy to me.

KATHLEEN CHALFANT (Hannah in workshops, San Francisco, Los Angeles, and New York, 1990–94): I think that George [Wolfe] always wrestled with the character of Joe. Joe is the heart of the play in many ways, and the most problematic character. As we all know, at the end, Joe is the only person who isn't redeemed. So to have someone like David who is on the hoof, a person who is universally loved, is an interesting way to kind of solve that problem.

GRANT: George was really looking for a kind of passion, a kind of anger under the surface, a kind of rage about Joe's place in the world.

GEORGE C. WOLFE (director in New York, 1993–94): He's a Negro. He's a Negro just in the sense that he is hyper-aware of how he is perceived by the "other." In my mind, the definition of a Negro is someone who is exaggeratedly aware of how they are perceived by white people, so therefore it can inhibit more organic impulses. And Joe Pitt is imprisoned in a very similar way.

GRANT: I didn't feel great in *Millennium*. I thought it took about a month to find the character, because Joe was just trying to do the right thing, and confrontation was such an anathema to him, almost a sin. Marcia [Gay Harden] was playing Harper in a—you know, she could go to a place of fury, of rage. The character felt so unprepared to be combative like that. It took a while to understand Joe's place in the world.

STEPHEN SPINELLA (Prior in workshops, San Francisco, Los Angeles, New York, 1988–94): There is something erotically beautiful about Joe Pitt. He needs to be beautiful, otherwise why would anybody put up with his shit?

PETER CROOK (Joe at Intiman Theatre, Seattle, 1994–95): That first scene is probably the last time both Roy and Joe are truly happy in the trajectory of the rest of the story. Roy with control and Joe with being promoted up the ladder . . . illusions both, they both come to learn.

PHILIP EARL JOHNSON (Joe in national tour, 1994–95): Roy was like a rabid dog. You knew to keep your hand away from the cage, but your job was to put your hand in there. It was always a little terrifying.

RUSSELL TOVEY (Joe in London, 2017): I think there's an undercurrent in the writing that's sexual. I don't think Joe realizes it. It's not like he's going to go jerk off about Roy. It's that an older man, who is powerful, is making him the favorite son, the top student, the one who is getting the good marks. He's getting singled out. That, for Joe, feels intoxicating.

HARPER
God, is my husband a—

JOE
(Scary)
Stop it. Stop it. I'm warning you.
Does it make any difference? That I might be one thing deep within, no matter how wrong or ugly that thing is, so long as I have fought, with everything
I have, to kill it.

–Millennium Approaches, Act 1, Scene 8

DENISE GOUGH (Harper in London, 2017, and New York, 2018): She loves him so much she can see he's a shell of himself, so she wants the truth and she doesn't want it, too, because of the reality of what that means. But then he says to her,

"I don't see what difference it makes," it's like: *You bastard! You don't see what difference it makes? It's a huge difference to my life!*

STEVEN CULP (Joe at American Conservatory Theater, San Francisco, 1994–95): One of the first things [director] Mark Wing-Davey said to me was "I don't want Joe struggling the whole time. It's boring if you're struggling." Now, I had been looking at this role, thinking, *What a great role for me: conflicted and tortured young man wrestling with a moral quandary.* Maybe it's my Catholic upbringing, but guilt and struggle seem to be right in my wheelhouse. So, needless to say, I was a bit flummoxed by Mark's words. I opened my script to the "Are you a homo?" scene and said, "But look, here, right up front, I say to Harper, 'I have fought with everything I have,' and so on." Mark just grinned and said, "Well, we'll just have to find a way around that, won't we?" And he was right. It took a while, but finding that level of denial—that inner mechanism by which you can move forward doing one thing and simultaneously say to yourself, *I'm not that person*—was central to playing Joe; it was central to his character.

JULIA GIBSON (Harper at American Conservatory Theater, 1994–95): I believe Harper means it—really, *really* means it—that she is willing to put his dinner back in the oven and asphyxiate the whole building in order to get him to face the truth with her. Tonight. That is a big feeling but it is not complicated.

RACHEL HANKS (Harper at Stray Dog Theatre, St. Louis, 2012): I knew that Harper's anger was frightening for them both. She had been raised to be pliant and submissive.

JEFF CHRISTIAN (Joe in the Journeymen, Chicago, 1998): I remember a number of times when I'd go off someplace alone and completely break down after working the scene—and not really know why.

TOVEY: The Harper-and-Joe scenes are forever changing, and we're forever dancing around each other. Some days we're more angry, some more loving, some more tired, sometimes she frustrates me and sometimes we feel sorry for each other. It's not a fixed performance.

CHRISTIAN: I've used this scene for years in a directing class, and it's amazing to see how many different, completely valid and interesting ways there are to play it, and how it still affects me viscerally.

TOVEY: They should have been friends. He should have been her gay best friend, and they should have been having adventures, going out, getting drunk, having a blast. But that's not what happened.

BILL HECK (Joe at Signature Theatre, New York, 2010): I think he perhaps envisions them escaping together. But of course their damage is in some ways incompatible. They can't find their answers in each other, but I think it feels more comforting to be in a sinking ship with somebody. You can bail the water a little faster.

HANKS: Harper and Joe had such a fragile relationship: In order for Joe to hide his sexuality, he needed Harper to be fragile and dependent. It gave him a cover and a convenient excuse for his behavior; it gave Harper the attention and protection she thought she needed.

TOVEY: Early on there was no physical contact with us at all besides the buddy kiss, but now there's holding of hands, there's stroking, there's tenderness. At the root of it, at the core of it, is that there's a true friendship.

GOUGH: Yeah, you're gay and I take loads of pills—fuck, what a pair. This is not gonna work, but let's just hang on to each other for a bit longer.

HECK: Zoe Kazan was so playful in rehearsal in finding ways that Harper and Joe work together. We could really connect to the lightness in their relationship. It gives you something to lose, the more precious that connection is.

GRANT: The idea of not being fully loved, not fully appreciated: It made Marcia Gay Harden and her character insane. For me, a gay guy who was with a girl, it just felt like Saturday night from long ago.

HANNAH

Have you been drinking, Joe?

JOE

(A bigger grin:)

Yes, ma'am. I'm drunk.

HANNAH

That isn't like you.

JOE

No. I mean— (Again, finding this a little funny) Who's to say?

—Millennium Approaches, Act 2, Scene 8

MICHAEL SCOTT RYAN (Joe in San Francisco, 1991): Late in rehearsals, after the scene where Joe comes out to his mother over the phone, Tony was very moved. He asked how, despite being straight, I knew what such a moment felt like. He was appreciative, not condescending. I answered that everyone has fought away unearned shame at some point, becoming a little truer to themselves.

KING: That Joe went out and actually drank, which is already a transgression, it's a subconsciously deliberate act to get me to say what I needed to say to my mother. In the big production in the Taper, the phone was miked, so I could do it as softly as I wanted to. I was regressing to the point where I was basically at my mother's breast. I could be a baby when I told her, I could go back as far as I needed to go when I told her, "Mama, I'm a homosexual."

GRANT: I did the scene for *months* and it was all very, for lack of a better word, loud. And one night it just came out very quietly: "Mom." And from that moment on, I just almost whispered it.

RYAN: It occurred to me then that Joe was a constant witness to his own slow acceptance. As he disappointed his family and faith, they grew darker to him—which is a painful truth to acknowledge, because he had been part of that darkness.

GRANT: To say that out loud, every night, the thing I tried so hard not to be, the thing I was in therapy not to be, the thing I tried to hide from my agent, it was very cathartic.

SPINELLA: You know what I'd like to see? Like a super-femme Joe. Someone who looked like Patrick Wilson from the movie, but was effeminate? He's effeminate, he's *married*, and you go, "Oh, you're *married*? . . . OK." It happens to him again and again and again in the play. Roy says, "Your *wife*?" like Roy knows he's gay. Louis says, "Oh, a gay Republican." Harper says, "I knew you were." I wanna see a Joe that can't pass for straight, that is doing it by the skin of his teeth. I don't think Tony likes that idea.

KING: You can't even entertain the thought of who you are because everything you know tells you it is wrong. Until Louis Ironson comes up to you in a bathroom and says, "Oh, a gay Republican." Louis recognizes Joe before Joe

Louis (Joe Mantello) and Joe (David Marshall Grant) in New York, 1993. (*Joan Marcus*)

recognizes himself, so he has to seek him out and say, "You know who I am? *Who am I?*"

TOVEY: Joe is so staccato, it somewhat panicked me. I felt the way everyone else was written was a lot freer and looser, rhythmically more natural. There's the scene on the steps with Louis, Joe starts telling the story about showing up for work on the wrong day, and it panicked him and made him feel exhilarated, and that thrilled him because suddenly he realized he didn't want that life. That's when it unleashed for me.

TONY KUSHNER: At the Eureka, I was watching it, and there was one scene—the courthouse steps scene—and audiences were really liking it a lot, they were loving it, but I could tell that there was something not quite landing. The scene wasn't working. And I realized it was because it was always very, very hard to get Joe to talk, and very easy to get Louis to talk, and very difficult to get Louis to shut up. And if I did make Louis shut up midway through the scene—I'm liking what Louis is saying, but Joe was just sitting there. And I thought, *What would Joe say?* And that's when I wrote that thing that he says about . . .

JOE
Yesterday was Sunday but I've felt a little unfocused recently and I thought
it was Monday. So I came here like I was going to work. And the whole place
was empty. And at first I couldn't figure out why, and I had this moment
of incredible . . . fear and also . . . It just flashed through my mind: the whole
Hall of Justice, it's empty, it's deserted, it's gone out of business. Forever.
The people that make it run have up and abandoned it.

–Millennium Approaches, Act 2, Scene 7

KUSHNER: . . . and I didn't know if that helped anything or not, but I liked it, and I gave it to the actors. And it was amazing, the reaction. I call it the "penny drop" moment: It's this thing that happens, or doesn't happen, in a play. And there's some really good plays that don't—like, I don't think *Perestroika* has one.

But every once in a while, something happens onstage, and the audience knows, all of a sudden, that while they're all individually having their own separate reactions to the thing that they're watching, they've all also been following the same trajectory, on a very deep level, very much as a community, in sync with the actors, the director, the designers, and the person that wrote the play. It's just like a chime that goes off. When it happens, if you find it, you have them for the rest of the evening. And the night that we did the courthouse steps scene, it just took off, and I didn't change anything in the play.

TOVEY: The language changes there. There's less breaks, less pauses, it's free-flowing, less edited. Once you've found that, you can see what's burning underneath.

OSKAR EUSTIS (co-director in Los Angeles, 1992): If you read that scene again, it's in Louis's voice!

JOE

I just wondered what a thing it would be . . . if overnight everything you owe
anything to, justice, or love, had really gone away. Free.
It would be . . . a heartless terror. Yes. Terrible, and . . .
Very great.

–*Millennium Approaches*, Act 2, Scene 7

EUSTIS: But what that scene is about is how Joe and Louis give each other permission to do what they want to do. So by Joe giving a speech that Louis would've said, it embodies that.

CULP: When Louis brings Joe back to his apartment and seduces him, that was a beautiful scene for Joe. It's where, if only briefly, he allows himself to bloom. As we rehearsed it, I was hit with this image of a flower blossoming, and when Joe allows himself to be kissed, I let my arms drop at my sides and my palms spread open, like a plant opening itself to the sunlight. That's how it felt.

NICK REDING (Joe in London, 1992): It's a huge moment for Joe! He's kissing a man for the first time. It's his first kiss, in a way.

TOVEY: Now he's part of this kind of movie, he's having these movie feelings like he's in *Pretty Woman*, and it could literally have been *anyone*, and Louis is the guy that it happened with, because Louis is the one who came along.

CULP: Mark Wing-Davey encouraged—nay, exhorted—Ben Shenkman and I to not hold back on the kissing, to use our tongues and explore, and I have to say that moment of the kiss, just our mouths connecting, was magic. The audience was totally still; you could hear a pin drop. I loved that Joe got to have his brief moment in the sun.

TOVEY: For Joe the relationship with Louis is all-consuming even though it's three weeks. It's *everything*. I felt that as a kid when I first started going with guys. There was this one guy I was completely obsessed with. I couldn't eat, I couldn't sleep. Joe has projected everything onto Louis, and it's only been three weeks. Louis says no, I don't want it.

Joe (Russell Tovey) and Louis (James McArdle) in London, 2017. (*Helen Maybanks*)

HECK: The scene between Louis and Joe on the beach where Joe lays himself bare before Louis and is then rejected . . . Early on I'd talked with the director, Michael Greif: I was afraid that the nudity would be distracting as opposed to keeping the audience in the story. So maybe the degree of disrobing is not complete?

But after working on the play, I remember going up to Michael and saying, "Ah, I was an idiot! What was I thinking? I *gotta* get naked. I gotta get NAKED! This guy is NAKED in every regard!" If I don't satisfy this moment, then what the fuck am I doing? It was scary but very freeing as well, to take the plunge into that more dangerous place, and know that the waters might be choppy but the play would keep me afloat.

GRANT: I always felt there was a line missing from the big fight scene between Joe and Louis. He keeps asking if I'm Roy Cohn's butt boy. "Did you fuck him?" He point-blank asks me that. And Joe doesn't answer him, but the answer is no. So there's something about—there's an accusatory moment in the play where Joe is lumped forever with Roy Cohn, but the truth is that Joe rejected that. He rejected those advances. So I always felt that there was a nobility in Joe Pitt that the audience wasn't seeing. But *(laughs)* I think I was the minority.

REDING: Tony always said he didn't judge anybody, but I had a sense there was some judgment there. Joe represents something for Tony.

TOVEY: My character gets no denouement, no happy end. His mother goes off with the other gays. Harper's going to go have adventures with loads of hippies in San Francisco. Where's Joe? He gets punished for hating himself. That's hard, that's very hard.

GRANT: As every night I would get slapped by Marcia and the audience would applaud, it would dawn on me that I was not sort of the moral hero of the play.

CHRISTIAN: Once we started running *Perestroika*, I found that I had a really hard time falling asleep after those shows—which I eventually chalked up to the feeling that I had some unfinished business as Joe.

JOHNSON: I don't think the play is cruel to Joe. He is a lost soul and his actions have consequences, which in the end are exactly what he needs even if he doesn't have the courage to reach for them on his own.

TOVEY: I just know I want one more beat for Joe that isn't there. A phone call with Hannah, Harper ringing him. Just something. It's going to be tough. He might have a shit life, but he's going to get through it.

SUSAN BROWN (Hannah in London, 2017, and New York, 2018): The only explanation that I have for it is that the relationship is too broken to be mended. And somehow, one gets the feeling that Joe just isn't going to make it somehow, that Joe is not going to shed those skins.

CHRISTIAN: After trying a number of different things in that last scene, I somewhat absentmindedly pulled off my wedding ring and stuck it in my pocket one night. Not sure if anyone ever saw me do that little bit of business, but it symbolically helped Joe move into the next phase of his life and quite literally helped me sleep.

> Michael Cunningham: Really the only character who is damned to some extent is a kind of relatively minor Republican functionary. I was wondering, is being an obedient Republican the only unforgivable sin?
>   Tony Kushner: It would certainly classify as an unforgivable sin.
>
> —Live interview, San Francisco, February 24, 1994, as quoted in Robert Vorlicky's *Tony Kushner in Conversation*

BEN SHENKMAN (Louis at American Conservatory Theater, San Francisco, 1994–95, and on HBO, 2003): A lot of the audience says, "Why is Louis welcomed back into the fold five years after, with Joe's mother of all people, and Joe's nowhere to be found?" A lot of people find that very harsh. But Tony's idea is that, despite Louis's cowardice, Louis is redeemable and Joe isn't. From Tony's perspective, Louis does not lose his soul; Joe *does* lose his soul by making peace with what he's done. The fact that Louis never makes peace with what he's done is redemption.

TOVEY: There's a scene at the end of the miniseries where Hannah and Joe have an exchange where you know that they're living together at the end.

> HANNAH
> Where's . . .
>
> *JOE shrugs.*
>
> HANNAH
> I'm sure she'll be alright.
>
> JOE (nods, then:)
> What could happen to her in New York City?
>
> *HANNAH looks around. The evangelist choir, the New Yorkers listening,*
> *rushing past.*
>
> HANNAH
> It's not what I expected. Which is the best thing you can say for it.
>
> *JOE avoids looking at her.*
>
> HANNAH (cont'd)
> Shall I make supper? Joe?
>
> *JOE doesn't look at her. He starts to lose it.*
>
> HANNAH
> I'll try to wait up. Till you get home.
>
> *She pats JOE's face. She leaves. JOE watches her go.*
> *JOE goes to the escalator and descends.*
>
> –*Angels in America* HBO miniseries, Episode 6, final shooting script

EUSTIS: Look, it is not a coincidence that that's the only scene that's added to the movie. By the time they made the movie, Tony could see that he had an unsatisfactory end for Joe.

HECK: When we were in previews and still rehearsing in the days, once we got the most technical aspects in hand, we got to do a lot more scene work, and Tony was there for that. For *Perestroika* he rewrote a good 70 percent of Joe. It was incredible to sit on the precipice with him and see how unprecious he was about his work and how newly interested he was in this man. I feel breathless about it now, thinking about it.

There were some new speeches, there were scenes that changed entirely, there was a reordering of scenes. Especially, really, the last thing that we were really digging our fingers into before we opened was the last scene where Joe's coming home and Harper leaves and the ghost of Roy shows up.

(Roy enters from the bedroom, dressed in a fabulous floor-length black velvet robe de chambre. Joe starts with terror, turns away, then looks again. Roy's still there. Joe's terrified. Roy does not move.)

JOE
What are you doing here?

ROY
Dead Joe doesn't matter.

—*Perestroika* (2017 published edition), Act 5, Scene 4

NATHAN LANE (Roy in London, 2017, and New York, 2018): That scene's an interesting one, because it's kind of Joe's resolution and it's also about his relationship with Roy, his strange father-son but slightly sexual relationship with Roy, and it's all happening in his head. Just as Ethel Rosenberg is happening in Roy's head. Joe has been in denial about who he is, to a certain degree, saying, *Roy's not like me*, and yet he lied and lied and lied, and he wants to be comforted, and they have that strange—I think the script says it's a "slightly sexual" kiss.

HECK: I seem to remember him thinking he hadn't thought much until this production about how Joe might be entering the new phase of his life. The new draft doesn't answer that question, but it breaks him apart more in a way so that somehow the possibilities are greater.

JOE MANTELLO (Louis in New York, 1993–94): One of the rumors that I always heard was that he was going to write a third play about Joe called something like *Men of Distinction*. That's not it, but it's close.

GRANT: Tony said he wanted to write a play called *A Good Man Is Hard to Find* that would be about Joe Pitt sitting in Brooklyn, eating ice cream, having gained a lot of weight thinking about how to find a good man.

KING: I have never given up on the possibility that Tony will do a third play. *(Laughs.)* I hold out hope. Not for myself—for Joe. I always thought Joe ended up teaching somewhere, some small college somewhere, something to do with the law.

KUSHNER: Of all the characters, Joe was the hardest nut to crack. He was the most resistant to *getting it*, because his whole issue is this disturbing degree of cognitive dissonance. He can look at something in the face and deny that it's right in front of him. So it made sense that of all the characters, he took the longest to admit there was even a problem.

He's kind of gotten to that place at the end of *Perestroika* and . . . good luck to him, I guess. There will not be more parts of *Angels*.

GRANT: But the character . . . a character means so much to you. Literally, to this day, I still think, *I wish the audience understood him more.*

CHAPTER 4

WHEN I OPEN MY EYES, YOU'LL BE GONE

GETTING FIRED FROM *ANGELS IN AMERICA*

MICHAEL ORNSTEIN (Louis in San Francisco, 1991): I always thought about Pete Best, the drummer for the Beatles who didn't go with them. What was his life like?

KATHLEEN CHALFANT (Hannah in workshops, San Francisco, Los Angeles, New York, 1990-94): There was, in one way or another, quite a lot of blood on the sand, as there always is in a long development process.

ELLEN McLAUGHLIN (the Angel in workshops, San Francisco, Los Angeles, New York, 1990-94): Of course I was worried. That's what it is to be an actor, but particularly on this process. I was waiting for the axe to drop. I kept on expecting to be replaced. *(Laughs.)* I think what happened was that my line of parts was so peculiar that no one was really interested in messing with whatever I was doing.

STEPHEN SPINELLA (Prior in workshops, San Francisco, Los Angeles, New York, 1988–94): I gotta say, I always felt like: Just *try* and find another actor who's 112 pounds and the right age who can do it like I do. Just try.

RICHARD SEYD (member and director, Eureka Theatre, San Francisco): I think it's really important to say that, for the most part, in terms of the ability and quality of the actors that the play was originally written for, they absolutely could have carried it. The reasons why they didn't continue, I don't think it was *talent*. I think it was dynamics.

ABIGAIL VAN ALYN (Eureka company member; Hannah in workshops): I was pissed. I was just absolutely uninterested in anyone else's point of view. I was so, so furious. I felt absolutely betrayed. I've come to see that that's a problem of my personality. *(Laughs.)*

JOE MANTELLO (Louis in Los Angeles and New York, 1992–94): Louis was the person who was always on the chopping block.

HARRY WATERS JR. (Belize in workshops and San Francisco, 1990–91): It was like a Louis merry-go-round.

MANTELLO: I don't know. I knew there were whispers that they had never been satisfied with Louis. But I think in some way, if I may, that's probably because there are things about Louis that are very close to Tony. Or at least the things that Tony was struggling with as an artist.

OSKAR EUSTIS (co-director in Los Angeles, 1992): I'm going to be completely honest because, why not, this is for the record. I think the key thing that had to happen was Tony had to admit to himself and to me that this part was modeled on him. Because he didn't want to do that for years, we had a very hard time having a clear discussion about what was necessary for Louis. Everybody kept not being quite right.

JON MATTHEWS (Louis in Taper Too Millennium workshop, 1990): In a rehearsal that Tony wasn't at, in the pickup scene in Central Park, I said: "This involves things I haven't done. I haven't picked up somebody outside and then proceeded to perform this act." So I said, "I'm happy to go off to do my own research, but if someone wants to tell me this, help me cut to the chase, I'd appreciate it." I think in Tony's mind this became that I was scared of something.

WATERS: There was also that challenge, primarily: A lot of these actors doing the role were straight. Anyone should be able to play any role, but Louis is Tony *(laughs)*, essentially, so finding that right voice was really important.

MATTHEWS: I think Oskar is a remarkable person. The most positive force in theater over the last decade at the Public. Oskar took me out to dinner in L.A. We had a wonderful fifty-five minutes of shooting the shit and talking about the production. And then he looked at his watch and said, "Oh shit, I have a meeting in Westwood in twenty minutes! Look, for various reasons, including that there's no money to put you up, we cannot ask you to come to San Francisco to do the Eureka production," and then it turned out he didn't have any cash on him, so I had to pay for the meal in which I was fired! *(Laughs.)*

ORNSTEIN: I had breakfast with Tony at Veselka. I love Tony, man. We're close friends, and we always had a kind of connection, a vibe. In the '80s, when I first became an actor, people were afraid to do roles that would peg them as gay. It was a fucked-up thing. It was not a cool scene. Most of my friends were gay but they were scared of being a gay character onstage.

Tony said to me that he felt that he needed a gay actor for Louis. Behind me, there was a table with eight people. A waiter was carrying a gigantic tray of food behind me. When he told me that, I heard him, and I took it in. We were making eye contact, we were maintaining eye contact, and that waiter dropped the plate with all the food.

And I smiled, and I said, "You need Joe Mantello."

EUSTIS: Once he was able to embrace the fact that it was based on him, modeled on him, he was able to get some distance from that so we could talk about the character, acknowledge his roots but realize he's a separate character. We knew that we had to cast someone who was incredibly charismatic, who had the equivalent attraction as an actor that Tony has as a writer and human being. Joe Mantello just walked right into that.

MANTELLO: The advice I got from my agent was "Hey, look, the pattern has been that the actor who plays this part gets replaced. It looks like it's coming to New York, so, you know, are you sure you want to go out of town? If you do, know going into it that traditionally they replace this actor in the role."

SPINELLA: It was a very long journey. With every loss of somebody, you lost something of yourself, because plays are not machines. You don't just change the cogs. They're ecological systems. One change here is going to have an effect on the whole system.

MANTELLO: Before we went into rehearsal, *Vogue* was going to do a story on Tony Kushner, so they asked if Stephen and I would do a photo. It was the first time I ever met him. They sent a car. I thought he was so chilly. It felt very, very chilly to me.

They took us out to Brooklyn and we were on a rooftop. We had to fake make out. Or, well, make out. While they photographed us.

SPINELLA: It wasn't even making out; it was . . . you know, "Put your head like this. Put your lips together, now Joe put your head like that, Stephen can you bring your chin down to seven o'clock." With our lips together. It was hilarious.

MANTELLO: It was a strange thing, meeting this person who was going to be such a pivotal part of my life for the next few years, feeling that I didn't get the warmest welcome, and then having to do this very intimate thing with him.

Looking back at it now, I completely understand where he was coming from. He probably didn't want to get too close to anybody, because nobody stuck around for more than one production. Having all this experience doing the play, he knew what he needed to do his performance, and I was starting at square one.

WATERS: It taught me to be a very generous actor. I was always engaging someone who was bringing a new thing to the character. You had to meet them where they were. You can't be like, "Well, the other person did this different." That won't work.

SPINELLA: Going from Lorri Holt to Annie, who played it at the Eureka, and then going from Annie to Cynthia at the Taper—each of those there was a loss. You got something new, but you'd built a life with an actor, and each time I had to—each time the Harper changed, Prior changed.

LORRI HOLT (Harper in workshops): When I found out that I wasn't going to do it at the Taper, I felt really betrayed.

SEYD: You know, there were very deep, complex personal relationships. Oskar's relationship with Lorri, for example.

HOLT: The role was written for me. Tony said, often, "Thank God you're doing this, because I can't imagine anyone else doing it." But then lots of people did it.

ANNE DARRAGH (Harper in San Francisco, 1991): Of course it broke my heart. *Angels* was such a lightning rod of an experience that you think your life will be transformed. And it wasn't. I couldn't get cast for a year after that. It was devastating. But Tony, to his credit, treated me really great. He said he wanted

---

Harper (Lorri Holt) and Prior (Stephen Spinella) in Taper Too workshop, 1990. (*Casey Cowan*)

to go in a different direction with the character, and I respected that. That's his right. And you know, there were already three actors involved; no director wants to take something on with a whole cast attached. It was hard, but I get it.

CYNTHIA MACE (Harper in Los Angeles, 1992): *(Long pause.)* Write down "long pause."

I said to Tony, I want to go home—meaning New York—and I trust you'll do the right thing.

No one was sleeping. We were getting ulcers. We all heard that George C. Wolfe said—and he was right—that he couldn't take the whole production if he was going to make it his own. It was like baseball: "I'll trade you the two Mormons and the black guy."

TONY KUSHNER: When I first talked to George, I said, "These people are cast: Stephen, Ellen, Kathy, Ron, and Joe. The other parts can be recast. But if you want to do the play, that's what it is."

MACE: Joe Mantello told me he called Tony at three in the morning to say "Take me!"

WATERS: Joe was gonna sue if he didn't get that role on Broadway.

KUSHNER: Joe Mantello called me on the phone right before the show opened at the Taper, before any of the decisions were being made about what happens next. He said, "I wanna ask you point-blank: Am I coming to New York?" As I recall, I said on the phone, right away, "Yes."

JEFF KING (Joe in Los Angeles, 1992): Closing night, Tony Kushner was going around, saying good-bye to everyone, "Great run," that sort of thing. We spoke in my dressing room,

Mr. Lies (K. Todd Freeman) and Harper (Cynthia Mace) in Los Angeles, 1992. (© *Jay Thompson and Craig Schwartz/Center Theatre Group*)

and I do not recall Tony saying "See you in New York." He didn't say I was continuing with the show, he didn't say I wasn't.

K. TODD FREEMAN (Belize in Los Angeles, 1992): When I got the offer to do the Taper, I was also doing my first play with Steppenwolf. I got both offers on the same day. *Song of Jacob Zulu*, the Steppenwolf show, was going to Broadway. So I was never going to go anywhere else with *Angels. Jacob Zulu* rehearsed and opened on Broadway at the same time. I got my first Tony nomination the same year. Our show was a bomb: It closed after three months. *Angels* was, well, *Angels.*

KING: It felt like my neck was stretched over a stump and I was waiting for someone to chop my head off. So I called Tony Kushner, and I left a message for him and I said, "I'm not comfortable with how this feels, so take me out of it." It was incredibly difficult, unpleasant, full of pain, but for my own sense of self-worth I didn't want to wait around for it to happen. Tony didn't like that I had left that on his machine, but we talked about it, we patched it up.

MACE: It was awful afterwards. Certainly I felt that in Los Angeles, after the casting was announced, everybody treated Jeff and me like we were the couple who had cancer. They would use that horrible tone, you know: "How *are* you."

FREEMAN: People were angry. It was really contentious. People got fired the day we closed in L.A. It was hard. I kind of pulled myself out of it because it didn't affect me.

MACE: Opening night presents are a big deal to me. Tony Taccone gave each of us a small Oscar or a small Tony with a note on it. Mine says "Damn, what a lousy vacation." I still laugh when I look at it. I had a friend who worked for the Muppets make a fur baby to give to Jeff King. I have a photo of it, with me ripped out of it. I cut myself out of it after I was "traded."

The fur baby Cynthia Mace gave to Jeff King on opening night in Los Angeles, 1992. Mace later cut herself out of the photo. (*Photographer unknown, courtesy of Cynthia Mace*)

WATERS: Jeff King, Cynthia Mace, we were in a lot of pain. To be in a production like this that's wildly successful, and you've done a lot of work and you're part of the story, but you're still disposable. There was no consoling us at some point. As I used to tell people, it was the most wonderful, horrible experience you could have, all over one production.

ORNSTEIN: Really, I was just so happy to be involved in something like *Angels in America*. Very few people have that chance, being involved in something that is truly grand and important. I never had the same joy as an actor after that. I lost my taste for doing these plays that I didn't feel were important, that I didn't feel as much for. I thought about how the gods took the life of the runner of Marathon, because they knew he would never feel that way again, after he ran to announce the victory of the battle. It wouldn't be the same if, a year later, someone was like, "Hey can you run and get me a lemon for my hummus?"

MATTHEWS: I have a conflicted relationship to that experience. But what was *never* shaken, what was difficult for me to get over, was that I was never better in anything, and I was never in anything as great, and I've been in some great shit.

KUSHNER: There were a lot of hard phone calls, but nothing compared to talking to Oskar about the fact that he wasn't going to go with it. There's very few things I've ever had to do that were harder.

> In their staging of Part 1, Mr. Eustis and Mr. Taccone have not
> departed radically from the London choreography of the overlapping
> scenes and celestial revelations. But the execution can be plodding,
> and the fabulousness of Mr. Kushner's writing, so verdant with what
> one line calls "unspeakable beauty," is sometimes dimmed.
>
> –Frank Rich, "Marching out of the Closet, into History," *New
> York Times*, November 10, 1992

KUSHNER: I needed to take care of the play. All of those decisions had been made long before Frank came and reviewed it. There was a grumbling that I took my marching orders from him. That's nonsense. I would never, ever do that.

The director switch "was not caused by Frank Rich," Eustis said, "although I hope I don't meet him in a dark alley."

–Don Shirley, "'Angels' Director Calls Split 'Amicable,'" *Los Angeles Times*, December 20, 1992

EUSTIS: The hardest struggle was me and Tony, and our relationship. That relationship was sorely tested, and the only way it survived was by not surviving. It was clear by the time we were in previews in L.A. that I was not going to continue with the project. Tony and I had articulated that to each other. That was the result of a lot of tension and disagreement and fighting between us that was incredibly painful.

It was apparent that it was a theater-changing event that would absolutely have an impact on the world, that it was having a part in changing what it meant to be gay in America. That this was the moment when our relationship was falling apart was awful. So, for me, the opening was a bittersweet experience. It was simultaneously validation and a loss.

KUSHNER: I suspect that Oskar probably still believes that it was just something in my nature: that somebody needed to be sacrificed on the altar on the way to propitiate whatever, and that that was him. That may be the case. I'm a director and I had certain ways that I liked things done, and there was a certain look for it that I wanted, a certain kind of showbiz panache that I felt that I needed, and a kind of directorial attack that I didn't feel I was going to get.

EUSTIS: When we opened and the reception was insanely rapturous, I had this moment where I thought: *Oh my God, right now, Tony is launching onward and I am staying behind, and every person with the possible exception of my mother, including my girlfriend, cares more about their relationship with Tony than they do about their relationship with me.* I had a moment in which I remember walking around the Plaza center and thinking, *Who I am now is a footnote in Tony's story.* This sounds melodramatic.

But then I thought: *That may be true in the eyes of everyone in the world, but it's not true in my eyes. I am interested in my own life. I am interested in what happens to me after this. I care. I am not ready to accept that my life is over or that I can't be the hero of my own life.* It didn't make it any less painful, but it allowed our friendship to survive and flourish.

TONY TACCONE: There was a lot of controversy about this. The union sued—the SDC sued—on our behalf. They sued the producers in New York for plagiarizing our show.

EUSTIS: That was a particularly unfortunate thing. There were enough hard feelings left behind that when SDC suggested that we should own a share of what was on Broadway, since so much of the work was from our production, we followed through on a series of meetings that were so much of a dead end, I don't know how to describe it.

TACCONE: They lost, of course, because the language was vague and George had put his stamp on it. But it's interesting: Directors don't own performances, but at what point do you say people should be compensated for their contributions to the show?

EUSTIS: I have a deep skepticism of resolving these matters this way. If writers who are talking to me are worried that I am going to legally claim to own things, they're going to stop talking to me.

TACCONE: But the union leaned on us, and we went along with it. There was a day of us being there in session. They thought it would drum up sympathy for us. It didn't.

EUSTIS: I just sat in a room thinking whatever way we're going to resolve our future, this isn't it.

TACCONE: Honestly, the thing I remember most about the mediated session for the lawsuit was sitting next to Oskar and him writing on a piece of paper "Trinity Rep is interested in me as artistic director, should I take it?" and I wrote "Yes."

It took some time for the three of us to recover. Tony went on and was acclaimed and had astonishing success with *Angels*. Oskar and I kind of circled the wagons. We dug in and we both went to different organizations and built up our own work, because we're both interested in building things, we're both good at that. But we had to, I think, both of us, redefine our meaning structures.

EUSTIS: Just looked at objectively, *Angels* was crucial to my entire career. I didn't get to direct it on Broadway. Too bad. But everything else I got in my career is from *Angels*. The comic reiteration that I am the greatest dramaturg in America—which I think is maybe a coded insult? *(laughs)*—my reputation, really, still, stems from *Angels*. I've added some other things to it but every job offer I've gotten has stemmed from that. More importantly than that, my relationship to Tony and to a few other writers is because of it.

KUSHNER: Oskar is a wonderful director, he's my best friend, we're perfectly attuned as writer and dramaturg, I can't imagine continuing to write without his input. I would never have written *Angels in America* without Oskar. He was essential. That's true of almost everything I've written, and I feel monumentally indebted to him.

TACCONE: I had a family to raise and I made choices in my life long before *Angels* came up. I didn't think my life goal was to be in New York and be on Broadway. A lot of my friends have been angry for me over the years, and my feeling is that the odds of anyone getting to work on *Angels*, and the intensity of that process, and the history of working with all of these people—they're slim. There's no price tag on that. It's wrong to even be harping on it that much.

The play was this incredible thing, and someday I'll do it again.

> Berkeley Repertory Theatre has announced the seven productions in its 2017–18 season, which will feature a world premiere musical about the Temptations, directed by Des McAnuff, and *Angels in America*, directed by artistic director Tony Taccone, who co-directed the world premiere 26 years ago.
>
> —"Berkeley Rep to Produce 'Angels in America' in 2017-18," *American Theatre*, March 21, 2017

EUSTIS: It's been an absolute blessing to me. Whatever disappointment I've had since then is divorced from my gratitude for being involved.

ACT 3

1993–1994

JANUARY
President
Bill Clinton
announces
he plans to
formally
allow gays
and lesbians
to serve in the
U.S. military

APRIL
The Concorde
Study
conclusively
proves the
ineffectiveness
of AZT

——

The third gay
rights march
on Washington
draws an
estimated
1,000,000
participants

SEPTEMBER
HBO
premieres *And
the Band Played
On*, based on
Randy Shilts's
book about the
early years of
the epidemic

1993

FEBRUARY
*Millennium
Approaches*
begins
rehearsals in
New York

MARCH
*Millennium
Approaches*
wins the
Pulitzer Prize
for Drama

APRIL
NYU
workshop of
Perestroika

——

*Millennium
Approaches*,
directed by
George C.
Wolfe, opens
on Broadway

JUNE
*Millennium
Approaches*
wins Best Play
at the Tony
Awards

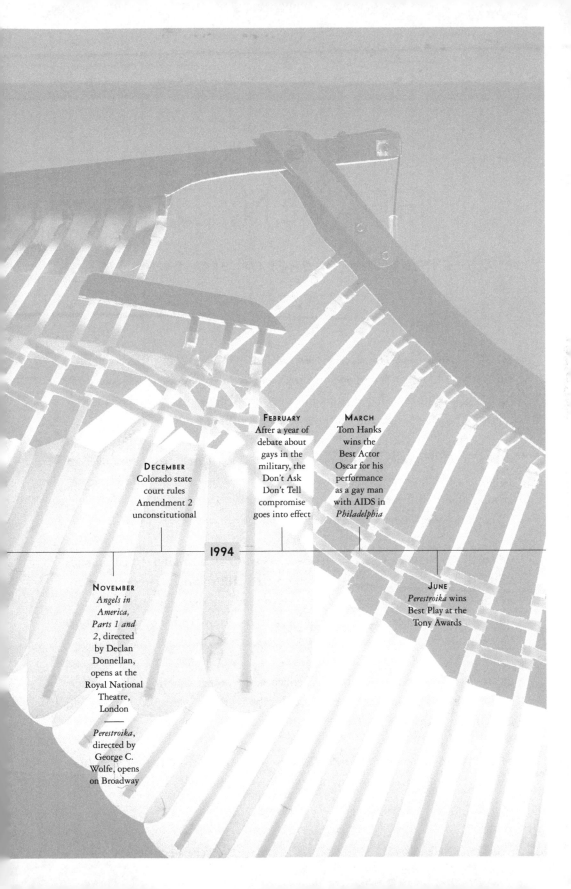

DECEMBER
Colorado state
court rules
Amendment 2
unconstitutional

FEBRUARY
After a year of
debate about
gays in the
military, the
Don't Ask
Don't Tell
compromise
goes into effect

MARCH
Tom Hanks
wins the
Best Actor
Oscar for his
performance
as a gay man
with AIDS in
Philadelphia

1994

NOVEMBER
*Angels in
America,
Parts 1 and
2*, directed
by Declan
Donnellan,
opens at the
Royal National
Theatre,
London

Perestroika,
directed by
George C.
Wolfe, opens
on Broadway

JUNE
Perestroika wins
Best Play at the
Tony Awards

CHAPTER 1

HEAVEN . . .

MILLENNIUM APPROACHES ON BROADWAY, 1993

ROCCO LANDESMAN (producer in New York, 1993–94): We committed to something that had never been done on Broadway before or since, which is to produce a play, shut that play down while you're still on Broadway, then rehearse a second play, and then run both plays in rep on Broadway.

MARGO LION (producer in New York, 1993–94): Rocco ran a great shop over at Jujamcyn. We used to gather in a room in an area by his office and bat ideas around about all kinds of things.

I said, "Well, what about George Wolfe?"

GEORGE C. WOLFE (director in New York, 1993–94): Margo Lion called up and said, "Tony Kushner would like to come to talk to you." He came up to my apartment and we talked. I had never read the play, I'd only seen it. I didn't even know the characters' names, but you know I have opinions about everything.

LION: Then there was a problem: George had a commitment to do another show. He was very honorable and felt that he couldn't do *Angels* because he had this commitment to do [*Marisol*] at Hartford.

JOSÉ RIVERA (playwright, *Marisol*): We were pretty close to starting rehearsals. George had gotten as far as having several design meetings about the play.

LION: *Angels* was being heralded as the great show of the period, he was a black director, doing this adventurous work, and we all felt like it was really important, the project was important, having an African-American direct it was important.

RIVERA: I got a call from George saying he was coming to L.A. tomorrow and he needed to talk to me. He was very upfront about it. He felt that being a black director, working on Broadway on such a seminal play that he was so connected to as a gay man felt like an opportunity he couldn't pass up. And as much as he loved my play, he felt that the challenge of directing Tony's play was so huge, he couldn't turn his back on it. I respected George a lot. If it was me, I would've done the same thing! So what could I say? I said, "You do what you need to do."

As I got home and thought about it, I was pissed off. Tony's play at that point had everything going for it. I thought, *Why did you have to take my director too?* So, by the time I talked to the *Times*, I don't think I held back very much.

> "The night George called to tell me, I was so stunned that I had to sleep on it to understand that he was abandoning our project," Rivera says. "It was the equivalent of artistic piracy. I expected more from ('Angels In America' playwright) Tony Kushner, knowing the moral tone that is set by the man and his work."
>
> –Jan Breslauer, "Wolfe Dumps 'Marisol' for 'Angels,'" *Los Angeles Times*, December 11, 1992

RIVERA: Later on, George produced *References to Salvador Dalí Make Me Hot.* We managed to reconcile during that. I remember running into Tony while we were in rehearsal. We hugged. I thought, *What can I do? I love this guy.*

> Budgeted at $2 million, the first part of the play, "Millennium Approaches," is to open on April 29 at the 945-seat Walter Kerr Theater, a relatively small house. Part II, "Perestroika," is to begin rehearsals in July, with the same cast, and is scheduled to open, in repertory with Part I, in October. . . .

The show will have a chance to recoup its investment in about 35 weeks, Mr. Landesman said.

–Bruce Weber, "The Price of 'Angels,'" *New York Times*, January 29, 1993

LION: When shows are being done that are very, you know, well reviewed previously, there's a lot of people who want to get on board. Rocco basically opened his doors to those who wanted to be participants. The whole community got behind this. It was, in some ways, a community production. The theater community had been so devastated by AIDS.

LANDESMAN: Broadway shows are a bad investment. Producing them is a bad career. If you're not going to produce plays you believe in that won't make money, why produce at all?

MICHAEL PETSHAFT (Tony Kushner's assistant, 1991–93): When they were going to do the signage for *Angels in America* on Broadway, Tony didn't even hesitate to say he wanted Milton Glaser to do that drawing. He was already famous, from the I ♥ NY sign and other things. And when that drawing of the Angel came in, the one that went on the poster and the cover of the *Playbill*, I got shivers.

 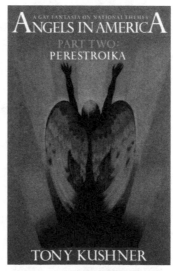

Milton Glaser's designs for the *Angels in America* posters, as seen on the Theatre Communications Group's published versions of the plays. (*Cover art and design by Milton Glaser, courtesy of Theatre Communications Group*)

BRIAN HERRERA (assistant professor of theater, Princeton University): When I went to the 1993 march on Washington, it was gay marriage and gays in the military. I was shocked. The march in 1987 was about surviving and not being erased. A different set of gay politics was arising on the national scene. There was a rise of gay visibility right as Clinton was coming in. The rise of visibility and the rise of the backlash were simultaneous.

> The agenda Clinton and Clinton would impose on America—abortion on demand, a litmus test for the Supreme Court, homosexual rights, discrimination against religious schools, women in combat—that's change, all right. But it is not the kind of change America wants. It is not the kind of change America needs. And it is not the kind of change we can tolerate in a nation that we still call God's country.
>
> –Patrick Buchanan, speech at the Republican National Convention, August 17, 1992

DAVID FRANCE (director and author, *How to Survive a Plague*): By 1993, Don't Ask Don't Tell, which was a starker redrafting of the policy against gay people in the military, had launched a conversation about gay people that was as hostile as it had ever been. And '92 was a remarkable uptick in the death rate, '93 was even worse, '94 was double that, so . . . those years were the worst in some ways.

FRANK RICH (chief theater critic, *New York Times*, 1980–93): This was before the redo of Times Square, before Disney on Broadway. No one wanted to produce plays on Broadway. Theaters literally sat there dark for months, sometimes years at a time. Now producers line up to get into these Broadway theaters, but in my day they'd give theaters away. [Legendary flop] *Moose Murders* played in the O'Neill, where *Book of Mormon* is now.

JEFFREY WRIGHT (Belize in New York, 1993–94): I was in Los Angeles. I had grown tired of struggling in New York. There was a potential film role that kept me out there, and I was auditioning over the course of weeks for this thing. I didn't get the role, I came back to New York, I was by myself at Christmas for the first time. Very disenchanted.

DAVID MARSHALL GRANT (Joe in New York, 1993–94): I was a gay actor. I was living in the Hollywood Hills, trying desperately to be in the closet. You couldn't be a gay movie star at the time. You probably still can't, really. But I was just stuck with this idea that being gay was going to get in the way of every dream I had. All I wanted was to be a famous movie star with a big family. Please put a parenthetical that says I was laughing uproariously here. *(Laughing uproariously.)* My goals were *ludicrous*, but that was me. Being gay—I thought you couldn't have a family. You weren't going to have a family being gay in 1980.

I was raised to believe in goodness as a living and breathing identity. You just did the right thing. And part of that was to do a job that helped the world. You had to succeed in that job, of course. You know, a great doctor, a civil rights attorney. You had to choose a righteous path and then you better be in the *New York Times* about it.

I related so much to Joe's need to be a good man. That's all he wanted to be.

MARCIA GAY HARDEN (Harper in New York, 1993–94): After *Miller's Crossing*, I went back to waiting tables and catering. It took a few years to get another film. I had just shot *Used People*. My agent Brian Bloom, who recently died, was so eager for me to look at this play, in a way that he wasn't usually. It was given to me with a kind of reverence for the material. He was one of many gay agents in New York, and it was clear that it spoke to him in a deeper way. I think if I had been as stupid as to say "No, I need to do some more films," I would've met with a lot of friction.

WRIGHT: Just after Christmas I got called in to audition for *Angels*. I'd heard about it, but only on the periphery. I knew the scope and the themes and I knew it was this extraordinary work of theater. I read the script; it was incredibly daunting. But also it was inclusive of all the reasons that I'd wanted to be an actor in the first pace.

HARDEN: I knew about Tony because he would come and guest speak at NYU, and was friends with Camryn Manheim, and we all looked up to him, like if we could only stand for something, like Tony Kushner, we'd be successful on some level.

MARY-LOUISE PARKER (actor): I had just come off doing over a year in *Prelude to a Kiss*, and they approached me to audition for *Angels in America*. I was excited because a friend of mine, K. Todd Freeman, was in it in Los Angeles, but it was a one-year commitment and I just wasn't ready for that. I don't want to make it sound like I was offered the part or anything; I wasn't. I'm so glad Marcia Gay Harden got it because she was wonderful in the play.

WOLFE: We saw tons of people.

CHERRY JONES (actor): I got this audition, and I was moving back to New York, and I filled this huge backpack that I had taken on a backpacking tour of Europe. And they auditioned me on a frigid, frigid day, and I came right from the train station to the Walter Kerr. Peter Frechette and Marcia Gay Harden were there. And because it was so cold, and I had walked from Penn Station, and I had this heavy backpack . . . my back froze up. I couldn't move. I was in agony. Marcia Gay sat there and—she wouldn't remember this—but she massaged my back while we were waiting to audition.

HARDEN: I want to remember that because I like that I would do that. I probably thought that she was going to get the part and that I should help her go in and get it.

JONES: Marcia Gay went in before I did.

HARDEN: From the minute I walked in the door for the audition, I forgot everything. I just couldn't stop crying. I couldn't stop being angry. I remember needing to wipe up a puddle on the floor. I had fallen over on my knees, and I had gotten the floor wet with how angry I was, how much I was crying.

WOLFE: I remember very specifically Marcia's audition. You know, before she even opened her mouth, she deeply affected me.

JONES: Of course Marcia Gay got the part!

WRIGHT: I just tried to focus on the ideas and the language. I think I went back for a callback and George hired me. After we were in rehearsal he said, "I saw a thousand Negroes. I chose you."

KATHLEEN CHALFANT (Hannah in New York, 1993–94): Marcia and Jeffrey were so clearly wonderful choices, because they were both kind of centers of anarchy. They were the clearest expression of George's aesthetic, and the kind of danger that George inserted into the process.

PETSHAFT: Marcia Gay Harden was wonderful but there was also a feeling that she was crazy. It really served the part. There were times when you felt like you couldn't walk into her dressing room! Something's incubating in there, but I don't know if I want to touch it.

PERESTROIKA AT NYU, 1993

TONY KUSHNER: The day *Millennium* won the Pulitzer, I had to go and watch a run-through of *Perestroika* at NYU.

MICHAEL MAYER (director of NYU *Perestroika* workshop, 1993): They had decided that while *Millennium* was going to be opening on Broadway, Tony wanted to do a workshop of *Perestroika* at NYU. The producers of the Broadway *Angels* weren't quite sure how to go forward with *Perestroika*, because it had been problematic in L.A. and some of the reviews didn't appreciate it as much as *Millennium*.

BEN SHENKMAN (Roy in NYU *Perestroika* workshop, 1993): Supposedly Tony was still working on it, and he would be coming in and trying rewrites out with us.

> I'm going to workshop it with some NYU graduate students. And I think that's probably all I'll do with it. I'm beginning to run out of steam, because I've been working on the play pretty much since 1988 . . . I don't want this to be the only thing that I ever write.
>
> —Tony Kushner, in conversation with Craig Lucas, *Bomb* magazine, Spring 1993

MAYER: What ended up happening was Tony couldn't come to any rehearsals. He was completely wrapped up in *Millennium Approaches* on Broadway. He didn't do any new writing at all.

SHENKMAN: We just basically did the Mark Taper version of *Perestroika*, but we did it in a black box theater, Atlas Room, over on Second Avenue. I played Roy Cohn. Michael Mayer was just starting out, and out of this black box and with, like, a ladder on wheels, he created the whole epic.

MAYER: The ceiling was, like, ten feet high. I had to have an angel flying around for a lot of it. She didn't just crash through the ceiling, she had to fly around

WOLFE: I think so much of what I did on Part 1 was keeping the hype out of the room and letting everybody play and discover. Because the hype was monumental, the hype was ridiculous.

> I think that the reason that it's gotten as much attention as it's gotten, and it's a sort of an extraordinary amount of press attention, is probably more due to the fact that it is happening coincident with a transformation in American culture and politics. This spring has seen a full public flowering of the change that's occurring in the political and cultural status of gays and lesbians in the United States.
>
> –Tony Kushner, on *Charlie Rose*, WNET-13, New York, May 10, 1993

and deliver the Epistle. I had this idea which maybe could have been stupid but it turned out really great. I just got one of those rolling stepladders and put the Angel on top of it, and I took Ben Shenkman and put a baseball hat on him and made him push the ladder around. And crew members took Fresnels down right and down left in the audience shining on her.

DEBRA MESSING (Harper in NYU *Perestroika* **workshop, 1993):** During that

Harper (Debra Messing) and Mr. Lies (Mark Douglas) in the NYU *Perestroika* workshop, 1993. (*NYU Graduate Acting Program*)

last speech where Harper's flying to San Francisco, they had me on the top of the ladder on wheels, and people just pushed me around stage on wheels to simulate that I was flying.

VIVIENNE BENESCH (Hannah in NYU *Perestroika* **workshop, 1993):** I had these earrings from my mom, these giant orange baubles. One of Michael's favorite ways to direct at that time was just to scream out, "Heeeeiinous! That's heinous!" He would wear my mom's giant orange earrings as he did it. I will never ever forget hearing him tell me choices were "heeeeiinous!"

MAYER: Mostly I was on my own with this *huge thing*. OK, but it's NYU, we're safe, it's cool, we're great. They're doing their thing up there on Broadway and we're doing our little thing downtown.

SHENKMAN: People heard that they might not have to wait all the way until September, when *Perestroika* was

WOLFE: But you can't work from hype and you can't create from hype. God knows, you can't discover anything new. And regardless of *X* number of people in the cast who had done it before, we all had to discover the play together anew.

JOE MANTELLO (Louis in New York, 1993–94): George insisted Stephen and I go back to square one. You have a brilliant director who goes back and asks a different set of questions and frames it in a different way. A director who asks you to reinvest. To not settle for things you think you know.

WOLFE: I mean, they knew what they knew. And so it was my job in some respects to contaminate what they knew.

PERESTROIKA AT NYU, 1992 →

supposed to open on Broadway, and they started coming down to see this little student production.

MAYER: We ended up having our first preview the same night *Millennium Approaches* had their first preview. They had to cancel a couple because of the set and stuff. I was walking from Astor Place and as I was walking down Seventh Street I saw this line of people, and I was like, *What the hell is this line for?* I saw a friend and said, "What are you lining up for?" and he said, "Uh, your show."

MESSING: It felt like all of New York City had exploded in celebration of Tony Kushner.

MAYER: *Angels* fever had taken over. You couldn't look at a magazine or a newspaper without seeing it. I was completely panicked that this quiet workshop had become completely public.

SHENKMAN: What I now know with hindsight, which I didn't know at the time, is how different *Perestroika* is as a theatrical animal than *Millennium*. It's not just Part 2. My memory of that just hermetic, fantastic, economic production of *Millennium* at Juilliard sort of haunted me, like: *What is this? This just feels like a mess by comparison.* I remember girding myself for those performances, kind of thinking, *OK, this is going to be sort of a disaster, you know, and so I'd better prepare myself to learn what you learn from failing.* And, you know, just from the first lines, the sense of the audience coming up to meet the piece and lifting it was incredible.

BENESCH: At our first performance, we're backstage waiting to go on after the second intermission, and the audience gave us a standing ovation before we started the last act. And we're literally crying backstage. I was with Dan Zelman [playing Prior], standing backstage, and we're hearing this applause and thinking, *This is unbelievable.*

MANTELLO: So his take on the Prior-Louis relationship, I remember his saying, it was a couple, and now—

WOLFE: All of a sudden there's a new person in the relationship, which is this disease, and what dynamic does that have on how the old relationship worked?

MANTELLO: To me, that's an amazing direction to give to actors.

GRANT: I went to New York to audition and met George. Which was like meeting a tsunami. He's just *beyond*.

CHALFANT: Meeting George for the first time is a little bit like sitting down with a whirlwind for a cup of coffee.

MAYER: They must have crammed 150 people in that place with a max capacity of 75. It remains one of the most extraordinary evenings of my life as a director. This quote-unquote imperfect play of his ended up working brilliantly.

KUSHNER: Michael did a phenomenal job with it. It was terrific. It was back before the Internet, so you could trust that these things would happen and wouldn't be written about.

MESSING: Up until then a curtain call felt like a boost to *your* ego. Like everyone is applauding your work and your interpretation and what you've done. But for the first time I had the experience of coming out and people clapping and being on their feet, and it was very clear that everybody was applauding Tony Kushner. Everyone was applauding the play, and we were just the lucky ones who were bringing it to these people.

BENESCH: It was so intimidating, because some of the Broadway cast *did* come to watch us. Not all, but some. There was a night when a number of them came. Kathy Chalfant asked if she could steal a moment from me. It was an Ethel moment, looking up to the star, the little star of her hatred. I was like, *Oh my God!*

MAYER: Over the next several weeks, all of the producers came down to see it, and they had renewed faith in the play itself, a play I loved. Oh, this play *is* good.

BENESCH: Andre Gregory came to speak to us while I was a grad student at NYU and said—I will always remember—"As an artist, if you're lucky, once every ten years in your career you will do something that actually shakes the ground of the artistic world." If you're *lucky*! "And the rest of the time we're blessed because we get to do what we love." And then the next year we did *Angels* and it was like, *Do I have to wait another ten years?*

GRANT: George is a force of nature.

MANTELLO: You know, if you've never met George Wolfe, he's got the metabolism of a hummingbird.

WOLFE: They'd gone through various directors, you know? They'd gone through a whole process which I really know nothing about. And I hadn't—I definitely had not worked with Jeffrey, I'd not worked with Marcia, I'd not worked with Stephen or Joe, or—I had no—I had no prior relationships with anyone. But I think—I remember very—I don't know, I just think they—I like—I love talking to actors, and I like actors, and I believe they—that I gained—I believe, I don't know, you could ask them—I believe I gained their trust fairly early on.

MANTELLO: He talks fast. There's a lot coming at you. If you receive it, if you open yourself up to it, it's completely fucking inspiring.

GRANT: His approach to getting more from you was just one of joy. So often, creativity comes from a place of fear that it's not going to work. George doesn't come from fear. He comes from courageous joy.

WRIGHT: I've worked with many great directors, but George is singular. Particularly when it comes to carving through social dynamics, gender dynamics, sexuality, race dynamics. From a technical standpoint, his way of shaping the timeline of storytelling is unmatched. The action, the dialogue, the silence—all has a relationship to each other in a kind of symphonic way.

WOLFE: I don't know, I had a very specific vision about the machinery of the show, of how it was going to move and how it was going to feel. I wanted

George C. Wolfe in rehearsal for *Angels in America*, 1993. (*WNET-TV*)

to find a certain sense of efficiency, so that therefore the show moved with extraordinary efficiency, so we were watching people's lives and their understanding of the world fall apart and reconfigure.

HARDEN: He's like a bass guitar. He's like a tune that can't stop playing. He moves constantly. He speaks, and moves, and directs in syncopated rhythms. I clearly remember one day, George says, "OK OK OK, Marcia Gay, I see what you're doing, I want you to come to the door more of ba da ba bamp bwow!" And I said, "I think I need to come to the door more like baaaaa, BOW!" And he said, "OK, try that."

WRIGHT: I was kind of new coming into it, while everyone was fully formed. Being the youngest in the cast, I felt to some extent that I was being observed as I rehearsed. Those were my own insecurities.

HARDEN: Jeff was new, David Marshall Grant was new, I was new. There was an initial insecurity about being as good, but there was really no time for that; there's so much to do.

WOLFE: In some respects, Part 1 was Tony and I figuring out how to work together, and sparring at times. You know, he, by that time, knew incredibly well the way to do it. But that's the antithesis of figuring out how to do it.

MARY KLINGER (stage manager in New York, 1993-94): The thing that's amazing about George is that he's mapped out the show, from page 1 to the end. All the blocking, what it's going to look like moment to moment. He doesn't tell the actors. He guides them where they need to be in a way that feels like it's their choice. It's a miracle. The actors are discovering it, but he's been able to guide them to his vision so brilliantly that he doesn't have to say, "Move downstage right." Their *impulse* is to move downstage right.

WOLFE: I mean, to be really honest with you, there are two schools of directing. You stand where you are and demand actors come to you, or you go to where they are and you charm, seduce, empower them to go on the journey in the direction that you think is correct.

RON LEIBMAN (Roy in New York, 1993–94): What I did in New York was fairly consistent with what I did in Los Angeles, because I had sculpted it properly.

GRANT: Ron Leibman was just a tour de force. Ron was just crazy on the stage. God love him, but I don't think he looked at me once!

WRIGHT: Unveiling my inner Belize was a serious challenge over the course of the rehearsal process.

WOLFE: We were working in a very methodical way, and Jeffrey was finding his way inside the material.

WRIGHT: It was very much a process of discovery and stripping away of self-consciousness and layers of biases. I can't say that I was always the most evolved when it came to issues of sexuality and sexual identity. I can't say that in the locker room of my high school football team that we were the most evolved around such matters. I remember at one point George saying, *(George Wolfe voice:)* "Jeffrey! *Drag* queens don't *drag* their feet." I said, "George, I know I'm not quite there yet. I'm not quite comfortable yet." And George said the most incisive thing to me that I still think about. He said, "I don't want your comfort. I want your talent."

WOLFE: I think everybody, all the producers involved—and I'd say Tony as well—were very panicked, I think, because he wasn't quite delivering on, for lack of a better word, the comedy. Do you know what I mean? It's unfair for me to reduce it to that, but I think a lot of that—well, a lot of it was that.

WRIGHT: There was no small degree of frustration with me by the powers that be.

WOLFE: I remember having a very difficult conversation, calling him up and saying, "Jeffrey, *today*. Bring it today." Which I'd never done to another actor, but there was really a tremendous amount of panic about whether he could deliver.

WRIGHT: George called me on a Sunday morning. He said, "Jeffrey, it's not working."

"I know George, but I have one more day."

PETSHAFT: There was always this kind of, um . . . I never thought anyone was going to be fired, but there was at times a tension in the air about doing a play like this, and there's so much riding on it.

GRANT: Joe and Jeffrey did not get along particularly, but that can happen. But also, you know, Belize *eviscerates* Louis in the Democracy in America scene, so there's some of that to it too.

WOLFE: There was a lot of tension, just personality stuff, between Joe and Jeffrey offstage, but they worked brilliantly together onstage. And I just loved that. I loved that—I love when artists, you know, find this other—respect each other, you know.

PETSHAFT: I remember a moment during rehearsal when Joe did not like something his character was saying, and I remember Jeffrey Wright being exasperated, like, can we just get on with the rehearsal? But everyone would argue about certain sections, when Tony was there. They weren't shy about questioning things. Not forcing explanations, but debate. The very nature of the play engenders debate.

ELLEN McLAUGHLIN (the Angel in New York, 1993–94): Tech went badly on Broadway. There was the flying, which in and of itself would have eaten up tech, but that wasn't the only problem. People were getting hurt. Everybody was working insane overtime, doing quick fixes and making it up as they went along because there was no time to figure everything out. The crew were just fried and the actors were scared and confused. We were putting things in during the day. Taking things out. Doing a different version every night. It was dizzying and kind of terrifying.

GRANT: The tech for *Millennium*, it . . . oh my God, it just went on *forever*. By the time previews began, you felt like you were onstage for twenty years, which made opening night a little easier.

CHALFANT: Tech was disastrous! It was terrible! There were all kinds of big set pieces. There were these giant icebergs that had been made but really didn't work. They looked like big pieces of white plastic no matter how much smoke you put around them. We spent a long time trying to integrate them into the production, because someone had spent a lot of money making them. Eventually they were abandoned backstage.

ROBIN WAGNER (set designer in New York, 1993–94): Each theater on Broadway has its own problems, but the Kerr is just small. It's hard to work in the smallest theater on Broadway. It's the shallowest, it's the tiniest stage. So to do two shows in rep on a stage that size, that was a big problem. We eventually solved it, but there were a lot of adjustments. I don't know that they made George incredibly happy.

McLAUGHLIN: Furniture and scenery had to be stored and flown on these suspended pallets, because there was no space in the wings to put anything. Things kept falling or shifting in the air and we were all having to work at such a maniacal speed that it was just a matter of when the next mistake would be made or accident happen.

KLINGER: We canceled previews because we weren't ready.

McLAUGHLIN: The stakes just kept getting higher and higher.

MANTELLO: I remember the night of the first preview. We had been in tech for a very long time. There was deafening buzz. The show had been delayed. It was scary.

WOLFE: I always say, when we are in previews, we are not the audience's victim, they are ours. We're learning and they are on the journey with us. You can't let fear of judgment stop your journey.

MANTELLO: George understood how scared we were. He said, "Oh please, please, please. Tonight is nothing. We're allowing the peasants into the castle to see what we've been up to." And we were like, "*Yeah.* We're allowing the peasants into the castle to see what we've been up to."

WOLFE: I also liken it to a hot-air balloon. It's, like, the balloon wants to lift but the basket is staying on the ground, and through the course of the preview period you find the right balance of timing and pausing and emotional moments and the way it's lit and the way it's blocked and the way it's staged before it starts to actually lift. And that to me is the journey of the preview period: The balloon is already the balloon, and hopefully the balloon is already blown up and ready to go, and you just have to figure out how to get rid of excess weight so that it can float away.

KLINGER: It was a lot of fun to call, but it was tough. There were constant cues, lots of cue lights—I want to say fifteen cue lights. It was like playing a piano with both hands.

WAGNER: The first preview, our stage manager was in the balcony.

KLINGER: They built me a booth because you really needed to see it live. Up in the gods at the Walter Kerr, they built me a booth, which is gone now. The Mary Klinger Memorial Booth.

WAGNER: When it came time for the Angel, the ceiling didn't open. Her radio system was out of whack, and I heard this voice call from the balcony to the backstage people—

WOLFE: "Open the ceiling so the Angel can come through!"

CHALFANT: "Bring in the damn Angel!"

WAGNER: "OPEN THE FUCKING CEILING!"

WOLFE: I felt at times very overwhelmed. I wouldn't say panicked. I felt very overwhelmed.

KIMBERLY FLYNN (Kushner's friend and dramaturg for *Angels*): In the early days when *Millennium* was in previews on Broadway, before the play was a known quantity, Tony and I would sit in the back of the orchestra of a packed house and take notes. The play would begin and then, once we hit Scene 4 and it was clear that Louis and Prior were a gay couple, there would emerge into the aisles people that we liked to believe were tourists, escaping the abomination. They did so politely, rustling their shopping bags from Macy's or Lord & Taylor as little as possible as they fled. We always felt kind of bad for them, for everything they were missing.

> The Committee feels that *Angels in America* is the strongest American play in many years. Although its immediate theme is the AIDS pandemic, Kushner's play ranges far beyond that: it is the first dramatic work to move the gay culture from the margins of discourse to the center, placing it strongly as an important element of American sensibility. . . . Although the Committee is submitting three plays as called for by the Pulitzer rules, it is our unanimous feeling that *Angels in America* is of a different order of magnitude than the others.
>
> –from the Pulitzer Prize Drama Jury Report, March 30, 1993

> "Angels in America: Millennium Approaches," a play by Tony Kushner that explores the AIDS epidemic as a metaphor for spiritual decay in the 1980's, won the Pulitzer Prize for drama yesterday. The play . . . will open April 29 on Broadway.
>
> –Jane Fritsch, "Pulitzer Prize to a Play on AIDS and the 1980's," *New York Times*, April 14, 1993

TONY KUSHNER: Susan Cheever, John Cheever's daughter, who's a writer, interviewed me for something, at my little apartment in Brooklyn. I'd just won the Pulitzer, and *Millennium* was about to open, and she came up to my apartment and we talked. She asked if I was gonna move, because it was a pretty miserable-looking place, and I said, "I dunno, I have to see what happens."

She said, "What do you mean?"

And I was like, "What if it fails, and I'll just be back to writing little plays for little tiny theaters downtown?"

She looked at me and said, "You *really* have no idea what's happened."

I said, "What do you mean?"

She said, "You're really never going to—even if you do fail, you'll never be one of those people again. You've gone over to the other side now. You'll always have done this thing and it's permanent."

WRIGHT: We went out for drinks after some crazy long night. Everybody was so excited, we were trembling with excitement, and George was saying, "Miracles are happening! Miracles are happening!"

CHALFANT: Everybody knew the night that the *New York Times* was gonna come. On that night George went around and talked to each of us separately. I don't know what he said to anybody else, but he said to me: "Now, just be sure to be clear." Brilliant! Because one of the things I pride myself on is clarity. And I thought, *What?? God DAMN it. You want clear, I'll give you clear.* He must have said exactly the right thing, because each of us hit the stage on fire.

HARDEN: I had a wig.

WOLFE: Oh God, the wig.

The wig. (*WNET-TV*)

HARDEN: I perceived Harper's innocence and her Mormon-ness through her hair. So I had a wig, a beautiful red wig that made me feel like her. It was thick, brownish red, it fell down past my shoulders. It felt biblical and pure. George, during previews— he should tell you why—he told me, "You need to take the wig off. We need to see you."

WOLFE: Well, I just—she had on this very sort of, like, "I am a woman of the plains" brownish wig. I knew it had to go, and then Tony was going, "It has to go, it has to go, it has to go."

HARDEN: I just felt, no, she's not me. I'm ugly, she's not, I'm not taking the wig off. And the next night George said again, "You have to take the wig off."

WOLFE: And then at one point it's like, you know, "Marcia, I'm taking the wig," and she goes, "No!"

HARDEN: Opening night, we had a tug of war with the wig.

WOLFE: Like, we're literally wrestling with the wig and I'm trying to get it out of her hands. And I said, "You're beautiful, you don't need this." And I think she smeared her makeup—I don't—it was just "Oh no, I want my wig!"

HARDEN: I was furious with myself, but I'm sure it looked like I was angry at George—you know, "I want my FUCKING WIG!"
    "Aaaaand PLACES!"
    And George is going, "Trust me, trust me," and I was weeping in the dressing room, saying, "I don't know if I can trust you, I WANT MY WIG!"

WOLFE: I mean, it was just really drama, it was really just crazy.

HARDEN: I felt that I had no protection, that I couldn't sculpt the performance, that it was too raw, that I was too exposed.

WOLFE: She was protecting herself. She was hiding. And then, with that wig removed, she had to be fully present and her vulnerability became Harper's.

HARDEN: George didn't want to hide behind any tricks. I didn't realize the wig was a trick, but when I took it off, it was like taking a veil off. The audience couldn't be distracted by anything.

WOLFE: I think she was breaking up with some boy at the time. I loved them all so dearly.

HARDEN: That night my agent came backstage, and he hugged me so hard he popped the strap on my bra. And years later, when he passed away, I understood what the play meant to him.

LION: I remember Tony wore pearls, and he went to a Chinese restaurant on opening night instead of going to the show. That was his opening-night ritual.

HARDEN: After, we were all getting dressed to walk to the after-party. And the streets of New York were like a Hopper painting. The streetlights were putting up perfect little triangles of light. When we left there were hordes of people, because they were waiting for us. And everyone was wearing long gowns and monkey suits because they had just come from the play.

We passed this one Korean fruit stand, and someone had taken one of those plastic milk crates and was standing on it, and they were in that triangle of light, and they were reading the review that had just come out. They were surrounded by a semicircle of the audience, and passersby on the street, and they were reading this paper loudly to this crowd of people. And every time they would read a good sentence, the crowd would cheer.

> What has really affected "Angels in America" during the months of its odyssey to New York, however, is not so much its change of directors as Washington's change of Administrations. When first seen a year or so ago, the play seemed defined by its anger at the reigning political establishment, which tended to reward the Roy Cohns and ignore the Prior Walters. . . . The shift in Washington has had the subliminal effect of making "Angels in America" seem more focused on what happens next than on the past.

Tony Kushner attends the *Angels in America* opening night party, May 4, 1993, Roseland Ballroom in New York City. (*Ron Galella/WireImage via Getty Images*)

This is why any debate about what this play means or does not mean for Broadway seems, in the face of the work itself, completely beside the point. "Angels in America" speaks so powerfully because something far larger and more urgent than the future of the theater is at stake. It really is history that Mr. Kushner intends to crack open.

–Frank Rich, "Embracing All Possibilities in Art and Life," *New York Times*, May 5, 1993

RICH: I had been toying with leaving the job for about a year, and had been talking to the *Times* about it. I found the theater moribund. I didn't find it interesting to write about. And then here was this great play. Not the only good play I saw that final year, but this amazing piece to write about, and it rekindled some enthusiasm in the theater itself. It was a godsend.

PARKER: Everyone was excited—what was exciting was something that was worthy of excitement. There are times when things are swept up and people get on the train of this or that, and I get kind of depressed about it. But this, much like *Hamilton*, was so worthy of it.

MERYL STREEP (actor): There was no other subject! It was all anybody was talking about. Certain writers meet their moment. They emerge with a sensibility that explains it all to us and we recognize it. I don't know why that is or how it happens. The play was the *Hamilton* of its time.

DAVID SAVRAN (distinguished professor, Graduate Center, City University of New York): So many people—theater professionals, all across the line, critics, academics, the general public—immediately recognized that this was a canonical text. It became an instant classic. That's the kind of thing that almost never happens. It's a popular success. It wins all of the big prizes. There are so many academics like me who were also taken with the philosophical and political points that the play raises. I suppose *Hamilton* is the closest, but there's no Walter Benjamin in *Hamilton*. *(Laughs.)*

• • •

MANTELLO: For a lot of us, that production was like going from zero to 100 in our careers—going from being unknown to the play everyone was coming to see.

STEPHEN SPINELLA (Prior in New York, 1993–94): It got kinda creepy. People would come up backstage, basically asking me, "Are you dying of AIDS." It was awful! The *New York Times* asked me if I was HIV-positive or not! I didn't want to set up this situation where there's a divide between those communities. But if I didn't answer the question, people would assume I was positive. Honestly, looking back, I think I did it with a little bit of cowardice.

> When Stephen Spinella takes his clothes off on stage, the murmurs in the audience are frequently audible: "He's so skinny!" "The lesions, are they real?"
>
> –Bruce Weber, "A Gay Actor's Temptation to Keep Good Health in the Closet," *New York Times*, June 5, 1993

SPINELLA: It was kind of a strange time.

Broadway cast and crew of *Angels* on a New York City Pride Parade float, 1993. (*Photographer unknown, courtesy of Tony Kushner*)

LEIBMAN: I didn't like to know who was coming. I made that request. So I used to stand next to Joe Mantello, and he would tell me at curtain call, as we were bowing, he'd say, "Fourth row. She looks a little chubby. It's Madonna." *That* was my favorite part.

PETSHAFT: I was being like Tony's blocker. People were calling me up and they wanted him and he wanted to do a million things and people wanted him to speak here and talk there. He moved from Brooklyn to a condo on the Upper West Side and I helped him get furniture. He started having friendships with really interesting people.

I was looking back at the notebooks I was keeping when I worked for him. The real heat coming from these notebooks is when we get into '93. The first couple notebooks are "Do this," "do that," "get a copy of this book." Then after *Millennium*, it's "Matthew Modine" and his phone number. "Robert Altman" and his phone number.

MANTELLO: I remember we opened and, shortly thereafter, awards season started. All of a sudden, being in the mix for awards, that changed the group dynamic. It was like . . . I certainly had no experience with them. I don't think most of the rest of the cast had, either.

GRANT: There was a term, Joe coined it, "Tony Fever." Everyone got it. Who was going to get what nomination, Jeffrey or Joe or both, was Marcia gonna win, was Kathleen going to get nominated. Of course Stephen was going to win and was a shoo-in.

> "Angels in America: Millennium Approaches" received nine [nominations], the most for any play since the Tonys began in 1947. . . .
>
> Tony Kushner, the author of "Angels," was nominated, as were five of the eight actors in the play's ensemble: Ron Leibman, Stephen Spinella, Joe Mantello, Marcia Gay Harden and Kathleen Chalfant.
>
> –Glenn Collins, "2 Musicals Each Win 11 Tony Nominations; 'Angels' Sets a Record," *New York Times*, May 11, 1993

Jessica, the love of my life—maybe we can get an apartment with a washer-dryer now.

—Ron Leibman, acceptance speech for the Tony Award for Best Actor, June 6, 1993

LEIBMAN: That was a joke between me and my wife [actor Jessica Walter]. The next day, my agent didn't get any calls for work, he got calls from washing-machine companies. Would Mr. Leibman do a spot for us and we'll give him a washing machine?

First of all, I have to thank Joe Mantello. The magnificent Joe Mantello, who is a great actor . . . and a great good friend.

—Stephen Spinella, acceptance speech for the Tony Award for Best Featured Actor, June 6, 1993

SPINELLA: Joe and I went through so much shit. We were on Broadway for the first time, and we're immediately thrust against each other for the Tony Award. We talked about it, and he was so great, he was the one who initiated that conversation. He was the one who made sure that we always stayed on an even keel.

MANTELLO: This sort of thing can be so destructive to a company. People's contributions get untangled and singled out as more valuable, more worthy of acknowledgment.

SPINELLA: When Joe was angry about something, we would talk about it, and we just . . . Joe saved me, Joe got me through so much. He was just—thank God for Joe Mantello.

MANTELLO: Then you go *back into rehearsal*!

CHAPTER 2

. . . I'M IN
HEAVEN

PERESTROIKA ON BROADWAY AND AT THE
ROYAL NATIONAL THEATRE, LONDON, 1993–1994

TONY KUSHNER: Declan *(laughs)* had had such a terrible time with me and the fax machine and all that. He told Richard Eyre he wasn't sure he wanted to do *Perestroika*. When he agreed to do *Perestroika*, he said he'd only do it if I promised not to come into the United Kingdom during rehearsals. I could come for the first rehearsal, and then I was not allowed back in the UK until second preview. I could see the preview, but I had to sit in the audience and couldn't have a pen or pencil with me. I could take notes in the *third* preview. But there were only five previews.

JOSEPH MYDELL (Belize in London, 1992–93): When we reconvened to do Part 2, with a new cast except for Nancy and myself, it was different.

NANCY CRANE (the Angel in London, 1992–93): The rest felt that it was done, and what's done was done.

SEAN CHAPMAN (Prior in London, 1992): I opted not to do *Perestroika* because I thought it wasn't as good a play. I never went to see the remounted production.

MYDELL: Marcus went on to do *Tales of the City*, so he was replaced by Jason Isaacs.

MARCUS D'AMICO (Louis in London, 1992): You know, the absolute truth is I regret making that decision. I have no excuse other than I was a stupid young guy who was constantly looking for something new. If I could go back in time, I would've done it different. I didn't realize how few those opportunities are. When you get older, you go, *Oh, I see.*

JASON ISAACS (Louis in London, 1993): When I was asked to talk to Declan, it was to play Prior. I said I didn't want to play Prior, I've just played a bunch of tough guys, I want to play the neurotic one. I flew to New York, and Tony and Joe took me around.

JOE MANTELLO (Louis in New York, 1993-94): He wanted to see the Ramble in Central Park and Bethesda Fountain. The Ramble was fairly tame, as I remember. There were, you know, mostly guys walking around, but there weren't that many people.

ISAACS: Right before I left, Tony gave me specific instructions—he said rehearsals would be difficult because the thing about Louis and Prior is that they want to make sure everyone knows they're screaming queens within a minute of meeting them. He said, "In rehearsal, if anyone asks you to play it straight, tell them to go fuck themselves."

KUSHNER: There's this thing in England—this is a generalization—they have a discomfort with queens. They immediately connect flamboyant or what's described as effeminate behavior, queen behavior—it reads to them as weak and pathetic and whiny.

ISAACS: And of course that happened. Many people told me that I was too mincing and too effeminate and no one would find that attractive in a couple. I just had to hold on to the things that Tony told me.

MANTELLO: No one ever said that to me, but I'm not Jason Isaacs.

ISAACS: I was a straight man playing a gay man. I over-intellectualized that. I was reading weighty tomes on the psychology of sexuality.

MYDELL: He went on and on, really. He was learning.

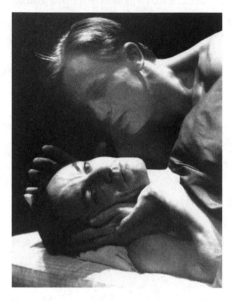

ISAACS: As soon as I kissed Daniel Craig [playing Joe], I didn't have *(laughs)* to worry about it anymore.

CRANE: The first day there's a read-through and then chitchat. I think Declan said that Nancy and Joe could go out for a while, and we went out and got drunk and we ended up calling in sick and I didn't come in for a couple of days. It just felt weird—not in a bad way, but that this cast needed to figure it out, because it's like running beside a freight train.

MYDELL: Doing it a second time was like, *Oh boy, I know what's coming.* That show tears you open emotionally.

ISAACS: Until we were running, the rehearsal period was a fractious time. Declan was a high-energy, neurotic director.

DAVID MILLING (stage manager in London, 1992–93): Jason uses his hands a lot and I remember Declan tying his hands behind his back. "OK, now play the scene."

CLARE HOLMAN (Harper in London, 1993): We would do things like improvising scenes for the angels when they all meet in heaven. It was quite wacky.

Above: Joe (Daniel Craig) and Louis (Jason Isaacs) in London, 1993. (*John Haynes-Lebrecht Music & Arts*)
Opposite: Nick Ormerod's design for the "Heaven Tower" in the National Theatre's *Perestroika*, 1993. (*Nick Ormerod/Courtesy of National Theatre Archives*)

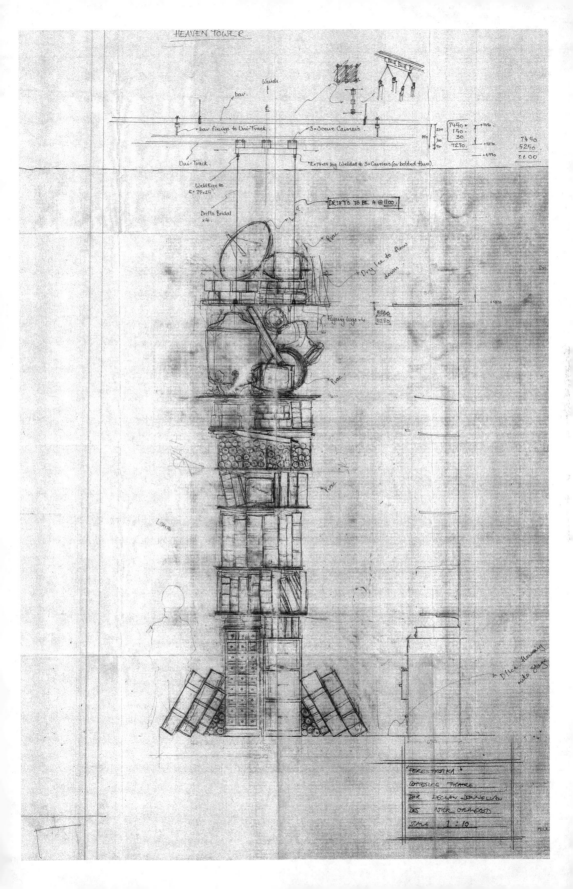

ISAACS: If you weren't *doing* something or trying to make something happen to another character, he would just yell, "Stop! You're not doing anything." It was the right direction for the play because the lines were so beautiful you could easily fall into them.

DECLAN DONNELLAN (director in London, 1992–93): It goes from being very sad to very funny and then very sad and painful to being very funny. You need quite a lot of discipline to maintain that sort of rhythm, as opposed to it going from being funny to very funny to very funny.

ISAACS: You knew you had a grenade in your hand with these laugh lines. Stephen Dillane [playing Prior] taught me an important lesson: If he got a great laugh one night, he would never do it that same way again.

PADDY CUNNEEN (composer and sound designer in London, 1992–93): The second time, I was able to say to Declan, "Declan, remember what you did last time?" So I wrote the music before tech. For the second part, we kept the music in the same vein, so that when you saw the two together on the one day, it felt like a complete arc, rather than two separate plays.

NICK ORMEROD (set designer in London, 1992–93): As soon as you start designing "stuff," it becomes less successful. I recall a lot of stuff being flown in and moved in for heaven; it was all white, a huge pile of filing cabinets and computer monitors which had to be flown and trucked in. In retrospect I think it proved two principles of stage design. First, that less is more, and second, nothing on a stage should be merely decorative. And it also proved another frustrating fact of life that often the most striking images are unexpected and ones that you have slaved over in terms of time and money somehow work out to be less successful.

DONNELLAN: I didn't want the pressure for the second one. So I said, "I'll do it, but I don't want it to open until the one on Broadway opens first!" I wanted somebody else to suffer the rewriting and all of that.

• • •

MARCIA GAY HARDEN (Harper in New York, 1993–94): I was filled by what we had to do. I felt I was in the middle of something important. Just itching with anticipation to put *Perestroika* on.

MANTELLO: It was exciting. Everyone who came to see *Millennium* in those early months, it leaves you on such a high. You could feel that anticipation of Part 2. It's a good cliff-hanger.

STEPHEN SPINELLA (Prior in New York, 1993–94): The play had gotten all of this success and the largest burden of that time really came down on George. Tony made his mark, really, with *Millennium*.

GEORGE C. WOLFE (director in New York, 1993–94): When I'd seen *Millennium* it was sacred text, it was formed, it was perfect. As a matter of fact, someone who at the time was running a major studio said, "Well, everybody knows that Part 1 is perfect, so if it screws up, it's your fault." So, that was—yeah, that was the lightbulb.

Stephen Spinella (Prior) and Tony Kushner in rehearsal for *Perestroika* on Broadway, 1993. (*Joan Marcus*)

KUSHNER: George is astonishing. His combination of tenderness and toughness.

WOLFE: We're working, we're working. Tony was panicked. He said, "Everybody's pressuring me about Part 2." I said, "Go just write it. You discover it as you discover it."

KUSHNER: We had to go into rehearsals for *Perestroika* and I didn't have a new draft. I was just, like, blocked.

MICHAEL PETSHAFT (Tony Kushner's assistant, 1991–93): He was very nervous about not hitting the magic he'd already established.

SPINELLA: He got very mad at me at his birthday party. We went to Union Square Cafe for his birthday in July. We'd all been waiting to start rehearsals for the second play for like a week and a half, and I said something like "How's the play going, did you finish the play?" He threw a napkin at me and yelled, "You ruined it! You ruined my birthday!"

MANTELLO: We ran *Millennium* I want to say three months, eight performances a week, then we went back to rehearsals for *Perestroika*, so we reduced the number of performances of *Millennium* to four a week and rehearsed every day.

ROCCO LANDESMAN (producer in New York, 1993–94): That's crazy. That's crazy! But we committed to doing it, and we did it.

WOLFE: The big problem was I had to design much of Part 2 working with Robin Wagner before I basically knew what it was going to be. It was very important to Tony that Part 1 and Part 2 look and feel very different. And so I tried to have a very—a very sort of "sleek" for lack of a better word—that Part 1 moved with extraordinary efficiency, as I think the writing does. And then Part 2 was something messier and rawer.

SPINELLA: Tony had originally written *Perestroika* with a five-act structure, and he tried a three-act structure in L.A. And he felt it was a failure, it didn't allow the play to breathe. So he went back to the five-act structure.

PETSHAFT: I got him a little office in a building on Fourteenth Street by Union Square. Little, I mean, it could fit two people. He would lock himself in there and work on *Perestroika*. He had deadlines, he would blow by deadlines, he would lock himself in this room and just do whatever he did there. I remember the amount of errands I was running was, like, triple. But he was also working on so many other things at the same time! He was giving speeches and writing essays. He was stressed out, but from my point of view he knew how to handle stress better than anyone I've ever seen.

KUSHNER: María Irene Fornés said to me, "Oh, nobody's going to fix this play for you. You don't need a dramaturg. You're the only one alive who can fix it, so go and fix it." So I . . . *(Pause.)* I think I did. I rewrote and rewrote and rewrote the Anti-Migratory Epistle in seventy-five thousand different ways. I got rid of about five scenes that were in *Perestroika* at the Taper. And then, uh, I don't know.

ELLEN McLAUGHLIN (the Angel in New York, 1993–94): When it came to *Perestroika*, to putting it up in connection with *Millennium*, everything would sort of fall apart.

HARDEN: If you said today, "Oh, we're going to do a three-hour play, and then another three-hour play, and it's not written yet, and we're going to be rehearsing the second play while doing the first," people would say, "*Absolutely not.*" But at the time it just seemed like that's what you do, if that's what it takes to push that boulder up the hill.

JEFFREY WRIGHT (Belize in New York, 1993–94): We were a well-muscled organism by then.

KATHLEEN CHALFANT (Hannah in New York, 1993–94): From the point of view of the workers on the line: We worked all day long on this one play, and then all night long on this other one. And then we had a regular six-out-of-eight rehearsal day. That's a lot of work!

RON LEIBMAN (Roy in New York, 1993–94): *(Laughs.)* I've managed to forget that. It was brutal. It was exhausting. I'm fifty-five years old at the time, you're working from ten in the morning to midnight. Jesus Christ.

HARDEN: You know, when you look back on something that requires such a herculean effort, you think, *Huh, why does it only seem herculean now?* At the moment it just seemed like this is what we were doing. I would get up, ride my bike to the theater. Go to rehearsal, go to dinner, do a three-and-a-half-hour show. I don't remember if I was exhausted. I really don't think I was. I think I was exhilarated.

KUSHNER: George didn't dramaturg in the sense of going through the script line by line, talking about serious structural things. We would just have these conversations here and there. We'd have dinner. I'd go to his place after a day's rehearsal.

WOLFE: There were all these beds that were around—Prior's bed, Roy's bed—and so Tony and I would, like, lie in bed and we'd talk about the script.

KUSHNER: And he just talks. He throws out little remarks that are completely brilliant and push you in one direction or another.

SPINELLA: Because Tony was so deeply in the weeds, George had more influence on how the second play developed.

WOLFE: You know, I was in the room.

CHALFANT: *Perestroika* was exciting to George because it was the one he got to shape.

WOLFE: In true Mr. Kushner form, I think I got five acts five days before we went into rehearsal, and I would probably say 60 percent to 70 percent of that changed.

LEIBMAN: When I see George Wolfe now, I ask him "Hey, you have the rewrites for the second act?"

MANTELLO: I remember George saying early on: "It's a new play, we're going to continue working on it, and as we chip away at it, every single day, one day the seesaw will tip and it will start to feel smooth. But it won't feel that way at first." When someone describes the context like that, you can breathe a little, you can relax.

WOLFE: I'm in heaven in that world. I understand that world, I know how to protect that world, I know how to nurture that world. Because every day something gets better. That's the rule of that world: Every day something must get better.

WRIGHT: *Perestroika* is the more difficult half of the play. Because it is a world that's been built up that's now burst open and has to be reshaped.

KUSHNER: We had to cancel a week of sold-out performances. George insisted, so that I could have another week to work.

LANDESMAN: Each day you don't play, you're another $40,000 away from recouping.

> It's the most expensive writer's block in history, maybe.
>
> —Tony Kushner on *City Arts*, WNET-TV, December 9, 1995, as quoted in Robert Vorlicky's *Tony Kushner in Conversation*

CHALFANT: We had many, many producers walking around the theater, mumbling to themselves. George would sit in the middle of the house protected by people from the Public, and he was the bulwark between us on the stage and the producers in the audience. If you were ever in a war and you needed a general, George would get you through.

KUSHNER: George protected me like nobody's business. Nobody was allowed to give me notes, not even Rocco.

WOLFE: If there are twenty-seven different producers—which I think there were on *Angels*—I said, "Y'all talk amongst each other, figure out what your concerns are, and then one person talks to me. I'm not talking to twenty-seven people." Sometimes that can happen if the rules aren't clear. And it's not because anybody is a bad or horrible person, it's that, you know, there's money on the line and there are reputations on the line. People can allow anxiety to take hold.

LANDESMAN: We weren't panicking. But anxiety was really high. Money was going out the window. We wanted them to get on with it. George wants to get it right. He's not necessarily in a hurry to get it right, and we were to a certain extent held hostage. We didn't have a choice: You have to support the artistic team.

DAVID MARSHALL GRANT (Joe in New York, 1993–94): There was nearly an unfortunate accident involving Stephen at the tech rehearsal.

SPINELLA: At one point I needed to walk offstage in a blackout. And the blackout happened and I couldn't see. I walked off the stage in the direction that I thought would be fine.

Robin Wagner's set had these poles that these flaps would swing on in *Millennium* and they took the flaps off the poles for *Perestroika* and I just walked smack into one of these poles. It was like 11:00. I was bleeding. I had to have stitches in my forehead. After that, there was a company meeting

The Angel (Ellen McLaughlin) and Prior (Stephen Spinella) in *Perestroika* on Broadway, 1993. (*Joan Marcus*)

and *(laughs)*, you know *(grandly)*: The Tony-winning actor is bleeding on the stage. It made an impression, let's just say that.

GRANT: There was a meeting of the cast, led by me, because I was the Equity Deputy, and then I had to alert Rocco Landesman to the fact that the actors were not comfortable going on.

MARY KLINGER (stage manager in New York, 1993–94): The first time we canceled it, it was because George said we weren't ready. Which we weren't. The second time, it was Tony saying it. The third time, George went to the cast and said, "I can't cancel it again, you say you're not ready," and they did. The fourth time, he came to me, and said, "I can't do it again, you tell the producers we have to cancel it." But I work for the producers—they're the ones who pay me. So I told the producers that we could do it, but we'd have to stop for about forty-five minutes to tech the fourth act.

McLAUGHLIN: Technicians come up with nicknames for shows, and ours was called "the Money Store" because they got so much overtime.

KUSHNER: The first preview was *fucking horrendous*. It was like ninety hours long.

KLINGER: We had an hour's worth of intermissions while we figured stuff out.

McLAUGHLIN: The most moving thing for me was, the first preview, at the curtain call, as we were waiting in the wings to go out, we looked around and all of the tech staff was onstage clapping for us. That's never happened in my entire life. That undid me. The tech staff were *heroic* on this show, and I adored every single one of them.

KLINGER: Afterwards, we went to McHale's. The company went to the back room. I was so exhausted, I just stayed at the bar. And then someone came and got me and brought me back and they applauded me. Which was nice.

HARDEN: And then cuts would come in.

KLINGER: We cut Roy Cohn in hell.

> ROY
> Yes, I will represent you, King of the Universe, yes I will sing and eviscerate.
> I will bully and seduce, I will win for you and make the plaintiffs, those traitors,
> wish they had never heard the name of . . .
>
> *(Huge thunderclap.)*
>
> –*Perestroika* (original published edition), Act 5, Scene 7

LEIBMAN: I didn't want to agree to the cut, believe me. It's a brilliant, funny speech. Hustling God! *(Laughs.)* I said, "Is this going to help the play?" I swear to God, I asked that, being the good Boy Scout that I am—and I'm not, I'm not a good Boy Scout, I'm a bad Boy Scout—"Is this gonna help the play?"
George said, "Yes."

IS *PERESTROIKA* A LETDOWN?

ELLEN McLAUGHLIN (the Angel in workshops, San Francisco, Los Angeles, New York, 1990–94): At some point in San Francisco, Tony was talking about what he was going to do with *Perestroika*. The Angel was going to come down and do this prophecy. Prior would have to return to heaven, but first he would wrestle like Jacob. And I said, "Yeah, right. You're never going to be able to do that."

TONY KUSHNER: The first great two-part play is *Faust*. *Faust, One* is an absolutely perfectly made play—it's like this great little folk play. *Faust, Two*, which Goethe wrote over fifty years, releasing acts as they were finished, was not really meant to be performed.

TONY TACCONE (co-director in Los Angeles, 1992): Obviously *Millennium* is like a perfect play.

SEAN CHAPMAN (Prior in London, 1992): The first play, despite the openness of its ending, works tremendously well on its own.

KIMBERLY FLYNN (Kushner's friend and dramaturg for Angels): *Millennium*, as a play, it's indestructible. You could hand it to the most inept high school drama teacher imaginable and it would still work. It's like this bow and arrow. You pull back and pull back and pull back and then you let go and it always hits its target.

So I said, "Cut it."

I shoulda said no. Ach! Too late! Oh well, I did OK.

KLINGER: Part of the problem was, *Perestroika* had like three distinct endings: Roy Cohn in hell, night flight to San Francisco, and the Bethesda Fountain. Cutting Roy Cohn in hell helped us move to the others in a more concise, clear way.

WOLFE: I was sitting there going, "He's dead! He almost died three times!"

KLINGER: I think George was instrumental in making that more succinct.

WOLFE: "LET HIM BE DEAD!"

DONNELLAN: The Broadway opening *(laughs)* started getting delayed and delayed and delayed. It was like one of those ancient Russian folk tales— avoiding some terrible fate in which you tie everything up and in fact, lo and behold, we were opening it again.

KUSHNER: That play—it just is a machine. It's very hard to fuck it up.

MICHAEL RIEDEL (theater columnist, *New York Post*): Part 1 is much better than Part 2. If I were running a theater, I'd just do *Millennium* and ignore *Perestroika*.

JOYCE KETAY (Kushner's theatrical agent): *Angels* still gets done, but sometimes they only do *Millennium*. I think that would be so frustrating! They'll have plans to do the second part the next year, but it doesn't happen.

TINA SHACKLEFORD (stage manager at Dallas Theater Center, 1996): Part 2 is far more difficult. You have a different kind of buy-in to produce Part 2.

CHAPMAN: *Perestroika*, it seemed to me, was a much more indulgent and less disciplined piece of work.

JOANNE AKALAITIS (founder, Mabou Mines; artistic director, Public Theater, 1991–93): I read your thing in *Slate*, and I enjoyed it, but I thought it was hyperbolically reverential. I think the first part of *Angels in America* is a good, solid, conventional play about something that was—is—crucial. Frankly, I liked the second part much better. I think it was more experimental and adventuresome. More poetic. The fantastical kind of writing that I liked.

KUSHNER: Robert Altman said after he saw *Perestroika*, "Really, I think it's the better play of the two." And I thought,

KUSHNER: Declan was hoping there wouldn't be many rewrites, but there were thousands of them. I was sending them over day after day after day.

DONNELLAN: We'd be getting new characters while we're rehearsing. I remember the whole Mormon family and so on coming to life. They'd be coming through on the fax, and I remember being on a telephone in a corridor at the National and people hurrying past me while I was yelling at Tony. And he's yelling back at me down the phone.

RICHARD EYRE (artistic director, National Theatre, 1987–98): Tony's not somebody you edit. You ask and then he writes. He's not like a screenwriter. He's not writing to order. He says what he wants to say in the way he wants to say it.

KUSHNER: At some point Declan said, "We're not going to do any more rewrites. We're going to do what we have now." I was so caught between the two productions, I just said, "OK."

DONNELLAN: There was already quite enough for an evening's entertainment.

IS *PERESTROIKA* A LETDOWN? →

Well, that's nuts. Then when I met George to talk about doing it on Broadway, he said, "I love *Millennium*, but I really love *Perestroika* more." *(Pause.)* I wasn't sure why they were saying that.

GEORGE C. WOLFE (director in New York, 1993–94): *Perestroika* went through all of these changes and grew, and kept growing and growing in, I think, depth and complexity and expansiveness. That was astonishing to me. Part 1 is astonishingly ambitious, but I consider Part 2 to be messier and more human and more political and a thrilling, thrilling, thrilling masterpiece.

DALE PECK (literary critic, author of *Martin and John*): I went in resistant to *Perestroika*. I just thought there was no way that the second part of the play could balance the really heavy themes with the commercial impulses. But I completely—I was entertained by it, I was moved by it, but I was also provoked by it. That magical mixture of it working on every level.

OSKAR EUSTIS (co-director in Los Angeles, 1992): The structure of *Perestroika* is what Tony's called a calamitous synthesis: to throw completely opposite characters together—Prior and Hannah, Joe and Louis, Belize and Roy—and see what happens when these characters come together.

KUSHNER: God, that was all so tough.

McLAUGHLIN: I, as a playwright, do not have that ability. I couldn't do good rewrites under that circumstance. We were putting entire scenes in and taking entire scenes out the next day.

LANDESMAN: Personally, I think the show is a bit long, particularly in *Perestroika*. I was lobbying for cuts and got none of them. Tony was very gracious. He would hear me out politely and do what he wanted to do, which was not cut. It was like a conversation with August Wilson but worse.

McLAUGHLIN: After the fifteen-page rewrite Tony gave me the night after the last preview in L.A., I thought, *Well, at least I'll never have to do it again.* And then on Broadway HE DID IT AGAIN! But it was a twenty-five-page rewrite.

This time we did it right. George and Tony and the stage manager and I all went out and we talked through it and Tony did some tinkering and then we worked it the next day. And it was good, but it was unbelievable pressure.

VINSON CUNNINGHAM (culture critic, New Yorker): It seems so big and messy and shaggy and loose, but when you really look at it it's just this incredible arrangement of these dialectics between not just gay and straight but Jew and Goyim, Belize and Cohn. It's these series of minute encounters, and things are worked out piece by piece. People give *Perestroika* a bad rap, but these things *have* to be worked out piece by piece. You gotta have that.

KUSHNER: It's also, you know, *Sgt. Pepper's Lonely Hearts Club Band* and the *White Album*, or *London Calling* and *Sandinista!*—you know. You discipline yourself to write something that's tight. And then you just let your brain splatter all over the page.

VIVIENNE BENESCH (Hannah in NYU *Perestroika* workshop, 1993): I love a cosmic mess!

RIEDEL: *Perestroika* felt to me like "I'm reaching for the mantle of epic dramatist!"

ANGUS MacLACHLAN (Louis at Charlotte Rep, 1996): Even its bagginess is so great. So many people talk about not liking *Perestroika*. Like Michael Riedel, who has his head up his ass. But if you read a great novel, there are parts that are difficult; that's part of what makes it great. Especially having done film where you have to distill and distill and distill, I'll read part of *Angels* and think, *Well, that maybe could be cut a little bit*, but its elephantine aspect adds to its greatness.

At some point I asked Tony, "Why did you do that to me?" And he said, "Because I know you can do it." That was a compliment, but it was a little maddening.

SPINELLA: Frank Rich was leaving the *New York Times* position of chief drama critic. He was gonna come review it on a certain day. And we pushed back the opening, and he was gonna come, and we pushed it back again. And it ended up being the very last play Frank Rich reviewed in his tenure at the *New York Times*.

> People no longer build cathedrals, as they did a thousand years ago, to greet the next millennium, but *Angels in America* both spins forward and spirals upward in its own way, for its own time.
>
> –Frank Rich, "Following an Angel for a Healing Vision of Heaven on Earth," *New York Times*, November 24, 1993

MYDELL: So we opened at the National, and you could see Part 1 and Part 2 in one day. That was seven and a half hours. People did it! We did it, and

IS *PERESTROIKA* A LETDOWN? →

Perestroika has just changed and changed and changed and changed, and it's still changing, and that's appropriate, because that's what the play's about.

–Tony Kushner, in conversation with Craig Lucas, *Bomb* magazine, Spring 1993

TACCONE: Tony's rewritten *Perestroika* quite a bit over the last twenty-five years.

STEPHEN SPINELLA (Prior in workshops, San Francisco, Los Angeles, New York, 1988–94): 'Til the day he dies, I think he'll do rewrites.

KUSHNER: I know I haven't gotten it right yet. I'm not saying I don't think

it's good—I think it's always been a good play, *Perestroika*—but it's never been a finished play and it never ever will be completely finished. When you're writing something, there is nothing quite as hideous as the feeling that you've run up to the limits of your powers as a writer and you know that the thing you're after is somewhere beyond that, and you're not gonna get it. You start to say to yourself, *If I was* this *kind of writer*, this *kind of poet, I'd be able to get it*. That's a hard place to go.

TACCONE: There's a deeper soul in *Perestroika*. There's an artist who is grappling with the deepest parts of himself. The scene in heaven where God has abandoned them, the brilliant monologue the Angel has that's a

people came to see it! It didn't seem like—it felt like it was an *event* more than a play.

> When the National finally premiered Part Two: Perestroika in November 1993, I booked the ticket myself. Just the one. Tim had died six months before. . . .
>
> . . . In the second part, Prior Walter—fevered and fighting for breath—is heralded by an angel as a prophet and climbs a burning ladder to heaven, asserting humanity's need to progress and his will to survive. He lives.
>
> It was difficult to reconcile the fantastical portrayal of those with Aids as visionaries of a new metaphysics with my own reality of signing a death certificate, administering a will, clearing Tim's flat.
>
> –Mark Ravenhill, "'Angels in America' Returns to the London Stage" *Sunday Times*, May 7, 2017

CHALFANT: When we were doing both parts, that was when we became a cultural phenomenon. People used to bring their parents to the marathon

description of the world, and Harper's Night Flight to San Francisco speech—these are things that *live on inside you*.

KUSHNER: At the end of the show, audiences are usually transported into some kind of a communal sense—not just because you've been sitting next to the same person for a long time, but because the play itself feels like an epic journey. And it needs to be its kind of slightly overstuffed self to make that happen. I really have come around to believe that *Perestroika* does something that *Millennium*—as good as I think *Millennium* is—doesn't do. It's every bit as good a play as *Millennium Approaches*.

KARL MILLER (Prior at Forum Theatre, Silver Spring, MD, 2007): I sometimes hear a sad contest to rank the two halves and I don't know why people bother themselves with this kind of bullshit. *Perestroika* has the task of exploring, and then answering, what exactly happens on the day *after* revelation. And, for that matter, the day after the *revolution*! That it manages to answer both is a far grander miracle, in my book, than *Millennium*'s giddy Death Star explosion of an ending.

You need both plays, is what I'm saying.

NATHAN LANE (Roy in London, 2017, and New York, 2018): It's one phenomenal scene after another. It's like a movie.

McLAUGHLIN: He pulled it off! ✎

and take them out to dinner between the shows and say, "Oh, by the way, I'm gay," and then come back.

GRANT: The things that people would say when they would come back-stage. This lady took her clearly straight sixteen-year-old son to see *Angels in America*, the double-header, on a Saturday. During the first act of *Millennium*, he's squirming, looking down, and then in the second act he's paying attention, and by the third act he's riveted, staring at the stage. So then they get Chinese food and see *Perestroika*. He's at the edge of his seat, apparently. It's all over, and she turns to him and says, "What do you think?" and he says, "That was amazing. I just never realized it before. Gay people are just assholes like everybody else!"

HARDEN: I'd walk through the West Village and people would come up to me and say, "I took my parents to see the play and then I told them I was gay." Or "I took my parents to see it and then I told them I was dying." And we would cry on the street. That happened once every couple of weeks.

GRANT: Joe said to me one day—we were exhausted, eating in between shows, we were just quiet—and he said, "You know, you are experiencing this, right? Every moment?"

And I said, "Every moment."

And he said, "Good, because we'll never experience something like this again."

We all knew that.

ISAACS: I remember near the end of the run I was sitting despondently in the wings. Harry Towb and Susan Engel, who played the older characters, walked by, and they could see I was a bit down in the dumps. They said, "You all right, Jase?"

I said, "I'm worried nothing I do in my career will ever touch this."

And instead of doing what I hope I would do now and saying, "Oh, I'm sure that's not true," they said, "Oh yeah, we were just saying we're glad this came toward the ends of our careers."

• • •

F. MURRAY ABRAHAM (Roy in New York replacement cast, 1994): It was late in the run, but the original cast was doing it. My wife and I were blown away at a matinee. The house manager said that there was a role that I might be interested in replacing, the wonderful role that Ron created. And I said right away, "I don't replace."

That evening I thought, *What am I, crazy? This is one of the great plays of the twentieth century!* So I called back and said I was interested and they gave me the role, and just, what can I tell ya, it's one of the best performances of my life. I had only two and a half weeks' rehearsal for the whole seven hours, but I decided the only way to really learn it was to take the risk and get onstage.

> This is a time of both celebration and concern for the producers of "Angels in America." On one hand, Tony Kushner's two-part AIDS epic at the Walter Kerr Theater is an unqualified smash; receipts during the week ending last Sunday totaled $400,931, a Broadway record for a straight play . . .
>
> On the other hand, the show has entered a time of transition. Ron Leibman, who won a Tony Award last year for his portrayal of Roy Cohn, is leaving. . . .
>
> Mr. Leibman is leaving without acrimony; his contract is up. He is to be replaced, eventually, by F. Murray Abraham, but Mr. Abraham does not begin rehearsing until Feb. 1. . . .
>
> Also leaving the cast is Marcia Gay Harden, who plays Harper, the Mormon woman whose faith is turned to cynicism by her marriage to a self-denying homosexual. Her contract expires Feb. 4; her understudy, Susan Bruce, is to step in.
>
> –Bruce Weber, "Highs and Lows," *New York Times*, January 7, 1994

SPINELLA: They were lowballing us for the next contract and they were trying to split us off from each other. When they gave us the lowball contract, Marcia Gay was so disgusted she just walked away.

HARDEN: We had been in it for a year, and we were negotiating for raises, and I didn't like the language of the negotiations, what we were being told.

I didn't like it. I thought we were—I thought it was not honest. And that made me feel like it wasn't the spirit of the show. So I left.

MANTELLO: She's a very proud person. I wonder if the producers now would say that they handled it in the right way.

LANDESMAN: I don't remember that. The general manager would know, they did the contracts.

HARDEN: I loved doing it, but I quit on a principle. Which is an odd thing to say. I look back on it and I think *Why did you do that? You should've just stayed with it.*

WRIGHT: We all sensed that we were doing good work and we deserved what we deserved. I don't recall it being this Norma Rae moment. We were a very close family, for lack of a better word. I was kind of the bad boy at times, but I was ultimately forgiven for my transgressions.

MANTELLO: It was that feeling of . . . *Oh, I'm no longer useful to you. My contributions, my hard work, my investment in getting this material there is no longer required.* I'm sure that was an incredibly expensive production. On the other hand, I don't remember us getting much pay.

SPINELLA: We were getting $2,000 a week, which in 1993 was about a thousand dollars a week above scale. And I was just—wow, two thousand *dollars?* And then I got my first paycheck, and I realized, two hundred immediately goes to my agent, and the taxes and union dues and all of that stuff, and you end up seeing a third of your money. It was still more than I'd ever been paid in my life.

MANTELLO: They played hardball. They contacted all of our agents. Eventually we got a raise. It wasn't much.

GRANT: Having been nominated for a Tony Award, in the anticipation that I would have some unexpected victory—not to laugh at myself *again*, but, please, *huge* parenthetical laughing uproariously here *(laughing uproariously)*—I sent my notoriously gay agent a letter via FedEx telling him the Tonys are coming up and I am bringing my boyfriend, just so you know what's going to happen. His response was "You didn't really need to tell me that, David."

> It's very important for me to remember four friends who I lost this year. Four men of the theater. Keith Jones, Alan Perry, Paul Walker, and Ron Vawter. I think we all lost them this year. I feel as a stage actor, I depend so much on people's memories to give my work life after I'm done, this remembrance is appropriate tonight.
>
> –Stephen Spinella's acceptance speech for the Tony for Best Actor, June 12, 1994

> Twenty-five years ago on June 27—the night that Judy Garland was laid to rest—was the Stonewall uprising, which marked the official beginning of the gay and lesbian liberation movement. I'd like to dedicate this award tonight to my gay and lesbian brothers the world over who are fighting for both a cure and for citizenship.
>
> –Tony Kushner's acceptance speech for the Tony for Best Play, June 12, 1994

JONATHAN LEE (production manager in Los Angeles, 1992): I think my favorite experience of the whole thing was watching Gordon Davidson time his sprint to the podium at the Tonys when *Millennium* won so that he got to talk. That was one of Gordon's great achievements. And then he tried to do it on *Perestroika* and they were ready for him then. Somebody threw an elbow or something.

SPINELLA: We were all going to leave right after Stonewall [June 28]. And then—they came to me individually and they offered to have me alone— they asked me if I would stay just to get through the hump of the summer. I think Joe felt betrayed by that, that I should have said, "Are you gonna offer everyone this?"

MANTELLO: There were certain pieces that were essential to it continuing. Ron and Stephen. Or if Ron wasn't there, F. Murray Abraham. So long as they had them, they would've been OK. As long as they had Stephen. The rest of us felt, you know, replaceable.

WRIGHT: Three of us decided together that we were gonna leave. Joe, and David, and myself. It seemed like the right time. About six months before, I had gone through an experience that was difficult for me—my roommate died one night and I came home after the show to find him. There was a lot happening in my life at this time, and so I moved on to the next thing.

> I share this with an actor who never got to stand here. His name was Ascanio Sharpe. I know you're watching, brother.
>
> –Jeffrey Wright's acceptance speech for the Tony for Best Featured Actor, June 12, 1994

SPINELLA: The one time I ever made a lot of money on Broadway was when the rest of the cast left and I was alone with Kathy and Ellen. They gave me points with the box office, and I've never seen anything like that. There was a week where I got $10,000. That was mind-blowing that I got that much money. I was reading about people who were in the original workshop company of *Hamilton*, and they got points. I realized: The original workshop cast of *Angels* was me, Kathy, and Ellen. What if we had gotten a point on that?

CHERRY JONES (the Angel in New York replacement cast, 1994): They were getting ready to close. They wanted to offer me the Angel. I was in between jobs, and I knew that it was in the dog days of *Angels*. But I thought, *How great to be part of it for any length of time.* I don't think I saw Tony until the closing night of the production; I don't think I ever saw George. I thought Kathy Chalfant would still be in it, and then as soon as I said yes, I found out that Ellen and Kathy had made this blood pact that they would leave together.

To be worked in like a new tool in a toolbox was so strange. It was like coming into this wildly creative factory job. Everybody knew their moves in their sleep. I'm not talking about the acting onstage; all of those replacements were superb. Everyone backstage, the crew, it was a factory job, the way things moved.

ABRAHAM: Usually, in a long-run show, the backstage crew shifts. They do it for a while, they get bored, a replacement comes in. With this show, the crew never changed. Shall I tell you why? Because there is a set change three times a week. You gotta change the set from one of the plays to the other. They get paid minimum four hours for the changeover, but they figured out how to do it in less than an hour! Downstairs, it was like a rabbit warren. They had beds, they had cable TV, it was all the comforts of home.

JONES: I think I was doing it for two or three weeks when we got the closing notice. So it was starting to dwindle. It seemed like half of the audience was international: You didn't hear that much English in the audience. That was fantastic.

LANDESMAN: It barely recouped. It would've been a great moneymaker if we had just done *Millennium*. But it became a riskier thing because we did both parts. But the worst thing in the theater is to aim low and miss. That's the most miserable feeling. If you aim high and miss, you don't feel so bad. With *Angels*, we aimed high, and we got away with it.

FRANK RICH (chief theater critic, New York Times, 1980–93): It was a phenomenon but it barely recouped. That's what I'm saying. This was a terrible period economically and creatively for the theater.

TERRY TEACHOUT (theater critic, Wall Street Journal): The fact that it made it to Broadway, was commercially successful, had such a long run, is important. People knew about AIDS. They knew a lot about it. But it mainstreamed it as a topic, at least in the broader cultural conversation.

MICHAEL RIEDEL (theater columnist, New York Post): There was a sense then that the straight play, the nonmusical play, on Broadway was dead. And then comes this epic American play, not a British import, that suddenly became a cultural event.

LANDESMAN: It was unusual to have a running play on Broadway discussed in the intellectual press, the *New York Review of Books*, things like that. After that, we were taken seriously as a Broadway player, and we never had to bow and scrape. We had cred. We had respect.

GRANT: I stopped acting after *Angels in America*. I didn't think there was anywhere else to go. I felt like it touched me—I'm getting emotional, I'm sorry. *(Cries.)* It touched me very deeply. My mother, who only wanted me to be famous by doing the right thing, finally got her wish. I felt a part of something that was way beyond me. But the world only spins forward, and I wanted to see if I could find a second chapter in my life. Being an actor was so filled with the shame of being gay and my whole journey, refusing to be who I was, that had all gotten mixed up with acting. I wanted to be myself.

Ellen McLaughlin (the Angel) and Tony Kushner, outside the Walter Kerr Theatre, 1993. Kushner keeps this Polaroid, framed, in his New York apartment. (*Annie Leibovitz*)

I'M AMBIVALENT. THE CHECKS BOUNCED.

Louis Ironson

Louis and Belize facing one another at a table in a coffee shop. Louis, responding to something Belize has said, is pursuing an idea as he always does, by thinking aloud.

LOUIS

Why has democracy succeeded in America? Of course by succeeded I mean comparatively, not literally, but . . .

–Millennium Approaches, Act 3, Scene 2

TONY KUSHNER: I got sort of stuck after I finished the second act. The characters were not . . . In *A Bright Room Called Day*, all the characters had behaved and obeyed the outline that I had written. I didn't know what to do next, and for the first time ever I asked one of the characters to explain to me what the play was about, and I picked Louis because he was sort of the most like me—

JON MATTHEWS (Louis in Taper Too workshop, 1990): Louis is Tony if Tony is anybody.

JASON ISAACS (Louis in London, 1993): Tony was clearly the model for Louis.

JAMES McARDLE (Louis in London, 2017, and New York, 2018): Once I heard Tony's voice, and saw him move, I was like, *"Ah."*

KUSHNER: —at least demographically. And I sat down at the writing table on Clinton Street, and said to Louis, "What is this play about?" and then just started writing. And the first thing he said to me was "Why is democracy succeeding in America?" Then I realized he was nervous, and he was talking to somebody, and then I realized it was Belize, and that scene took place.

PETER BIRKENHEAD (Louis in national tour, 1994–95): I mean, where to begin with the Democracy in America scene? The size of it? The dozens of ideas packed into it? The velocity with which they zip through Louis's brain? The fuel that keeps them zipping: the fierce dread Louis feels at the prospect of opening his eyes to himself and his behavior? It was like every acting challenge in the world all balled into one.

OSKAR EUSTIS (co-director in Los Angeles, 1992): For audiences who are following every word Louis says, it's rich and dense and gives them a great understanding of the play. But for audiences who have no idea what Louis is saying, it's still riveting because they get the dramatic situation: a character running his mouth off, filled with guilt.

ADAM DRIVER (Louis at Signature Theatre, New York, 2010): My initial connection to Louis was guilt. Guilt is something I think we can all get on board with. Then needing to feel justified for having your guilt. Then being surprised by how strong the nerve is to self-preserve. Then the self-loathing.

MARCUS D'AMICO (Louis in London, 1992): He knows instinctively that he's absolutely, miserably failing to be the partner that he needs to be. He *knows* it. So his defense mechanism is just to intellectually vent. He cannot afford at that point to allow this to be a normal dialogue, a normal exchange with Belize, because he knows that it's no surprise that Belize is going to call him on it.

JOE MANTELLO (Louis in Los Angeles and New York, 1992–94): In rehearsal, when we got up to that scene, people would leave the room. It's incredibly boring to watch an actor work through it.

MARY KLINGER (stage manager in Los Angeles and New York, 1992–94): The Democracy in America scene was a nice break, because they just talk for, like, forty-five minutes. I'd say, "Oh, thank God, I'm going to get some tea."

MANTELLO: The volume of words was overwhelming.

BIRKENHEAD: One of the scariest things about that monologue is that it doesn't emerge from a scene the way most do. It's just lights up and *bam* you're on the train. A runaway train if you're not fully present.

DAVID CROMER (director and Louis in the Journeymen, Chicago, 1998; director at Kansas City Rep, 2015): When you're vamping to justify your position—which I'm probably doing in this interview—one tends to hold their position very passionately. He's walking very dangerously in this minefield with the best friend of the person he's wronged, trying to justify himself intellectually. So I can definitely identify with how he just keeps going, and doesn't let go of the talking stick.

BEN SHENKMAN (Louis at American Conservatory Theater, San Francisco, 1994–95, and on HBO, 2003): There is a huge tangent that begins two lines in. The speech says "Why has democracy succeeded in America?" And immediately it goes into a tangent!—
(Delivers two pages of the Democracy in America speech from memory on his cell phone while walking down a New York City street.)
—which is a departure from this thesis thing about America having a functioning democracy. He just runs to the end of it, and then Belize just goes, "Mm-hm." And he goes, "Don't you think it's true," and Belize goes, "Uh huh, it is." "But I mean in spite of this—" and *then* he continues with the initial thought.

MARK WING-DAVEY (director at American Conservatory Theater, San Francisco, 1994–95): You need to understand the ideas. They're not just verbal diarrhea. They're real ideas. They can't just simply be the verbal component to let you see the emotions underneath. No. We need to understand what you're saying.

BIRKENHEAD: It was incredibly important to me that it not be just a torrent of words from Louis, that the audience not tune it out and chalk it up to ol' blabbermouth running his mouth again. I cared more about that than anything else I did in the play.

JONATHAN BOCK (Louis at Round House/Olney, Bethesda, MD, 2016): He's really making a convincing argument about what stops progress from taking hold in American politics. It's just that Louis is so damn quick, he is always stopping himself and anticipating arguments before they happen.

McARDLE: I often think about previous casts; I wonder if these ideas were still up for discussion. Now I think it's just assumed that we all know Louis is wrong.

WING-DAVEY: Louis is not wrong. Nor is Belize. It's certainly possible to have Louis's views and be unconsciously racist. That is absolutely true, but it's not to say that his beliefs are not well held and well expressed.

BIRKENHEAD: Louis's great gift, and his curse, is his ability to perceive the sorts of connections and nuances that he articulates in the Democracy monologue. Ironic, of course. To the tenth power. That this emotionally crippled commitment-phobe should possess this facility.

MANTELLO: I did one smart thing with it. I pulled Tony aside one day, when I was going between rooms, and said, "Would you read this out loud for me the way you hear it?"

And he said, "No no no, I don't want to give you line readings."

I said, "No, not line readings, I just want to hear the rhythm of it, the rhythm that you hear in your head. I can make it my own but right now I'm overwhelmed. It's chaos to me. If I hear how you hear it musically, purely musically, there will be an impact."

I'm not a musician. I don't know how I thought to do that. I think that's a pretty sophisticated idea, really. (*Laughs.*) Then Tony read it, and it started to make sense. I could hear, even in his way of not-acting it, how he put thoughts together. I heard him play through all the ideas.

ISAACS: Of course that monologue is all about Belize. For twenty minutes I'm talking, but for twenty minutes you're thinking, *When is Belize going to say something to him?*

MARK BRONNENBERG (Kushner's partner, 1982–86): He's talking on and on and on about political theory and you're sort of listening to it, you know it's interesting, you're getting annoyed at him. And then Belize pipes up and he says *exactly* what you're thinking, what you're feeling.

GREGORY WALLACE (Belize at American Conservatory Theater, San Francisco, 1994–95): There are few things more pleasurable than being onstage and listening to an audience quietly turn against another character.

BRONNENBERG: The audience's experience gets *named* in a way that's really profound. I'd rarely experienced that in theater before.

MICHAEL MAYER (director of national tour, 1994–95): The hardest thing at first was: How do we keep Belize quiet? How do we keep him from interrupting? That became a real challenge.

JOSEPH MYDELL (Belize in London, 1992–93): You have to know how to listen. You really do.

JEFFREY WRIGHT (Belize in New York, 1993–94, and on HBO, 2003): I like listening to other actors go on! So I kind of enjoyed the act of listening.

HARRY WATERS (Belize in San Francisco, 1991): I thought, *OK, that's the choice that he's making, so let's make sure that the fact that I am not speaking has some power.*

MYDELL: You are sitting here, talking to me, black in America, and you're talking about democracy? OK, sure, go ahead.

OBI ABILI (Belize at Headlong, United Kingdom tour, 2007): I've learned the hard way that for a black body to be in a space is a statement. And the words, as much as they're brilliantly written, almost become irrelevant. It doesn't become about the words so much but the physical effort of what is happening and how we are occupying this space with the guilt and the shame of what is going on.

NATHAN STEWART-JARRETT (Belize in London, 2017, and New York, 2018): I understand the idea of allies, I understand the idea of discourse, of doing something through conversation, through argument. But you are using my oppression as social currency, and it kills me. And for that conversation to happen onstage, I don't even have the words to describe how frightening and awful that is.

WATERS: I always loved this moment. I got to smoke the cigarette. All I have to do is listen to him rant and smoke a cigarette. And how you get to use

Louis (Jon Matthews) and Belize (Harry Waters Jr.) in Taper Too workshop, 1990. (*Casey Cowan*)

that as a tool, how you shape that action, how you are effective without saying anything—that was great. Now I know when to blow the smoke. Now I know when to flick the ash. It's a dance.

K. TODD FREEMAN (Belize in Los Angeles, 1992): Once I said that first "Uh huh," and the audience broke out, we looked at each other just like *"Oh, it's on."*

MANTELLO: K. Todd and I were old friends. That was fun. That tennis match with him was fun. It brought out my competitive spirit. We're not going to turn this into the Belize Undercutting Louis Show! I was able to protect Louis, in all of his foolishness. All of his loss. I wasn't going to let him be made a fool of.

ISAACS: Joe Mydell was an absolute genius with an eyebrow or an "Mm-hmm," and the audience was going wild—and I was drowning.

SHENKMAN: Tony is smart enough to put certain entertaining safeguards into that incredible piece of text, to make sure it functions as a piece of theater and as a memorable audience experience.

PAUL OAKLEY STOVALL (Belize at Kansas City Rep, 2015): The biggest mistake Belize can make is to make faces or outwardly react to everything Louis is going on about. To simmer effectively was a challenge and a thrill. It's a bit like edging while having sex. The more you're able to hold back, hold back, hold back, the better the release when it's time to let loose.

MYDELL: When Belize finally starts talking, when he gives that speech, you have to go for the jugular. You have to just wipe. Him. Out.

WRIGHT: He really expresses his intellectual and moral clarity in that scene, respective to his place in the struggle and Louis's place on the periphery of it.

GEORGE C. WOLFE (director in New York, 1993–94): Belize has read *Democracy in America*. He's not bored because he's stupid, he's bored because Louis's take on it is that it's all legitimizing his own smallness.

WRIGHT: It's Democracy in America, that's the name of that scene. These things aren't happening outside the room, they're happening right here at this table. And we're bringing these things together to collide at this table. Race and gender and responsibility and citizenship. Your responsibility to those you love and those who are of your community.

CROMER: Often in a play, you always know when it's your turn. People in plays talk slower because they know they have the floor. That scene is perfectly constructed to not let you do that.

STEWART-JARRETT: Tony said, "If it doesn't feel like it's going too fast, you're not doing it right."

SHENKMAN: I haven't seen a production yet that's really devoted to explicating that speech, and—even more brilliantly—explicating what's *driving* this speech emotionally, what he's saying, a white privileged person talking to a person of color, floating this huge target by giving short shrift to the incredible compromise of racial discrimination. Louis knows what he's doing on an unconscious level. He knows Belize well enough to know what the moral makeup of the man is, what his temperament is, so he's kind of cruising for a bruising.

CHRISTOPHER SHINN (playwright, *Four* and *Dying City*): The attempt to stage difference, in a really meaningful way that doesn't resolve the difference—that to me is so profound. Right now we as a culture seem unable to explore difference without lapsing into attack.

STEWART-JARRETT: I find that scene so fundamentally depressing. It's too real.

IRA MADISON III (culture critic, *Daily Beast*): I see that conversation happening on Twitter every day.

WRIGHT: Once after the show there was this older Jewish woman who said to me, "That scene, a Jew and a black at a coffee table—that's New York!"

. . .

PRIOR
I couldn't tell you.

LOUIS
Why?

PRIOR
I was scared, Lou.

LOUIS
Of what?

PRIOR
That you'll leave me.

LOUIS
Oh.

(Little pause.)

—Millennium Approaches, Act 1, Scene 4

McARDLE: As soon as I pause, you feel the audience go *(winces)* "Ohhhh." And you feel like: *Buckle down, it's only gonna get worse from here.*

STEPHEN SPINELLA (Prior in workshops, San Francisco, Los Angeles, New York, 1988– 94): It's established in the very first scene that Louis is a chickenshit.

> I think Louis carries the biggest burden of the play. One of the things it's about is that it's incredibly hard to take care of someone

who is catastrophically ill. I think this is going to become an issue that is inescapable, because people are getting sicker all the time.

–Tony Kushner, August 1992 talkback at the National Theatre, quoted in Robert Vorlicky's *Tony Kushner in Conversation*

KIMBERLY FLYNN (Kushner's friend and dramaturg for *Angels*): People used to say things to me like "Are you Harper?" *(Laughs.)* If I'm any one person in this play, I'm *Prior*. The articulation of crisis followed by outrage, and the sense of "Can I get a witness" that you hear in Prior, was in part fueled by something I was experiencing, and that Tony was hearing on a daily basis, because he *was . . .* well, he was my witness.

> "'Millennium' is completely infused with dealing with the consequences of [Flynn's] accident," Kushner says. "There's a certain injustice in it. Not being the injured one gives me the physical freedom it takes to sustain a long writing project. You have a strange relationship with calamity when you're a writer: you write about it; as an artist, you objectify and fetishize it. You render life into material, and that's a creepy thing to do."
>
> –Arthur Lubow, "Tony Kushner's Paradise Lost," *New Yorker*, November 30, 1992

FLYNN: When you hear Prior tell Louis that he, Louis, needs to bang his head up against the hard wall of biological fact, it's pretty close to something I actually said to Tony. Prior's fury has a tenor and energy that is all too familiar to me.

> Since the accident Kimberly has struggled with her health, and I have struggled to help her, sometimes succeeding, sometimes failing; and it doesn't take much more than a passing familiarity with *Angels* to see how my life and my plays match up. It's always been easier talking about the way in which I used what we've lived through to write *Angels*, even though I sometimes question the morality of the act (while at the same time considering it unavoidable if I was to write at all), than it has been acknowledging the

intellectual debt. . . . *Angels* is more the result of our intellectual friendship than it is autobiography. Her contribution was as contributor, teacher, editor, adviser, not muse.

–Tony Kushner, "With a Little Help from My Friends," *New York Times*, November 21, 1993

BIRKENHEAD: Louis loves the very things about Prior that come back to bite him so ferociously after he leaves him, and that he himself so profoundly lacks. Prior is as clear-eyed as Louis is abstracted, as brave as Louis is afraid. Louis hides from his life. He takes refuge in his head, but Prior lives in the world—the big, mysterious, infinitely terrifying world.

JOE
What's wrong?

LOUIS
Run in my nylons.

JOE
Sorry . . . ?

LOUIS
Forget it. Look, thanks for asking.

JOE
Well . . .

LOUIS
I mean it really is nice of you.
(He starts crying again.)
Sorry, sorry. Sick friend . . .

–*Millennium Approaches*, Act 1, Scene 6

ANGUS MacLACHLAN (Louis at Charlotte Rep, 1996): That scene Louis has in the bathroom with Joe Pitt had everything you want in a scene. When I became a playwright and a screenwriter, I thought about this: It's funny, it's serious, it's political, it moves the plot, it tells you a lot about the characters, and it is four and a half minutes. It's unbelievable. It felt like waterskiing. If you just got on it and rode it, it would take you.

D'AMICO: I remember Tony saying that he hadn't originally envisioned Louis played as emotionally as I did it. In England at that time—and this was said to me by other people, so I hope it's OK to say—young *male* actors in the theater hadn't really exposed that kind of range of emotion before. In a certain kind of way, because Louis is gay, I gave myself permission to completely open up emotionally.

MANTELLO: I remember, very early on in L.A., Tony said, "May I give you a bit of advice? I think that you should, when you rehearse this scene, go full out. By that I mean fake sobbing, so that it's too big, too much. Let it be as phony as you want it to be, but throw yourself on the floor. Don't worry if you're not feeling it, just do it. Until you understand the emotional level of the scene, which has to start very heightened, you won't find the scene."

So if you approach it like an American actor, you know, *My mother, I have to dredge up something about sadness and all that, oh God, I'm not really crying, everyone knows I'm not crying*—he was saying don't do that. Until you understand the scope of it. The greatest advice I've ever gotten. Just fake it. And if you are a good enough actor, you'll fill it in later.

More than anything that happened to me on *Angels*, that conversation was life-changing. It changes my approach to actors today. I want to release them from the pressure of reality. American actors have been fed this line that if you're not feeling it, it's not good. I don't agree.

> Audience Member: I wondered why you chose to make Louis such a miserable individual . . .
> Tony Kushner: Oh God *I* don't think he's miserable. He's certainly miserable in the sense that he's incredibly unhappy.

—August 1992 talkback at the National Theatre, quoted in *Tony Kushner in Conversation*

MYDELL: That incredible scene in Central Park where Louis goes and meets the man in leather [who's played by the actor playing Prior], when we did it, they didn't touch.

SEAN CHAPMAN (Prior in London, 1992): We couldn't stage the sex scene literally. At that time, you couldn't do that, because if you depicted actual homosexual sex onstage, there were all sorts of legal issues around it, and there was a chance you could go to prison. That was how we developed the staging of having myself stage right and Marcus stage left, facing out, having a conversation through the audience. And we then worked out this mimed sequence. I would undo my trousers, he would kneel down, looking out. And then we mimed having sex, the condom splitting.

MYDELL: The dialogue is so highly charged, it was shocking for lots of people who saw it. Lots of our audience knew nothing about gay sex.

Cottlesloe Theatre
Stage Manager's Show Notes
25 Jan 1992

A member of the audience fainted and fell down the steps during Act 2. He was looked after backstage (without the action stopping) whilst a fireman and then the nurse was sent for. Apparently he was overwhelmed by the scene in Central Park, finding it all too much.

DAVID MILLING

MANTELLO: We were on two different sides of the stage in L.A. It was very abstract. It was very concrete in New York. I sort of . . . I disagreed with George's choice and then I really admired it. I thought there was something about taking it out of the abstract which made it difficult for the audience to really watch. Then I thought, *Oh right, that's actually the point.* The safety of that abstraction was titilating, but it wasn't shocking. To actually see it was different.

CROMER: You don't want to torture the audience but this is what it's about. If you don't want to do that, you should do another play.

BOCK: In the rehearsal room at first there was some giggling. It's not easy to bend over and do the deed with all these coworkers in a fluorescent room watching you. But it gets easier.

McARDLE: Whenever we're finished in rehearsal, I hear Nathan Lane saying, "Oh my Gaaaaaaad."

MANTELLO: Uh . . . the only other thing I remember about it was when my parents came to see it on Broadway. I heard them laugh and was just like, *Oh fuck, I am going to be fucked right in front of my mother.*

GARRET DILLAHUNT (Prior at American Conservatory Theater, San Francisco, 1994–95): Whenever Ben Shenkman would have family there, I would go extra long. That's the kind of guy I am. He would look back at me like *You fucker.*

SHENKMAN: Louis is effeminate. He's campy. Louis has sex onstage, has anal sex. Louis is penetrated. And so, as an actor, all the internalized homophobia—when I began to work on Louis, when we started to work on the park scene, I was, like, depressed afterwards. I actually felt like I had done something shameful. And in my mind I think the shape that it took was *Oh my God, you know, my parents or whatever are going to come and see me in this play, and they're going to be subjected to this ugly, ugly thing, this ugly, ugly, embarrassing, shameful thing.*

And yet, you know, ultimately it became, you know, a scene I looked forward to. It's just such a good scene. Instinctively or by calculation, somehow Tony understands that he's going to take the audience to that place where they're going to come up against that taboo thing. And then that dialogue between him and the guy in the park, it's just one of the best—it's one of the best things in the whole play. So, you know, the audience is rewarded, the actor is rewarded, and yet everything that happens in that scene is still . . . it still happens.

• • •

EMILY NUSSBAUM (television critic, *New Yorker*): Louis's chatty, self-centered, obsessive Jewishness, and his kind of sexual charisma with which he seduces Joe—those were very familiar dynamics that were exciting to see on stage.

LOUIS
You smell nice.

JOE
So do you.

LOUIS
Smell is . . . an incredibly complex and underappreciated physical phenomenon.
Inextricably bound up with sex.

–Perestroika, Act 1, Scene 2

NUSSBAUM: One thing that was great about it was that the relationship between Louis and Joe was incredibly hot! And that was weird, because they were doing something wrong, but it was driven by sex in a dirty romantic way. That was thrilling to see.

Joe (Patrick Wilson) and Louis (Ben Shenkman) in the HBO miniseries, 2003. (*HBO/Stephen Goldblatt*)

JONATHAN SILVERSTEIN (director at Yale Dramatic Association, 2008): I was in the closet when I first saw *Angels*. I was so into the love story of Joe and Louis that I really wanted them to get together. Years later, as an out gay man, I directed the play, and I realized, *Oh, that's really not cool, you're not supposed to have that thought.*

NUSSBAUM: We watched *Melrose Place* every week because we were so absurdly grateful there was a gay character. But of course he was just a cookie-cutter dignified best-friend neighbor. And then it was in the news for weeks that he was going to kiss someone, and when he did, it was filmed as though the cameras were panicked birds spinning around their heads.

BIRKENHEAD: It really is vile, the choice Louis makes, to not only leave Prior but to leave him for this closeted, Ayn Rand–loving, self-loathing Reaganite. But that's the point of it, I guess.

MANTELLO: The audience had sympathy with Louis through the end of *Millennium* and then that ran out very quickly in *Perestroika*. The only way I can describe it is that they were willing to go down the road with him a certain distance and allow for terror, allow for contradiction. But I'll tell you, once *Perestroika* started, it was like a cold shower. I felt their impatience. I felt their anger.

BIRKENHEAD: I think I would have been failing if audiences had not had a hard time liking Louis, and also if they'd not felt some small amount of something like forgiveness for him. I wanted both. I remember once, in a restaurant in Los Angeles, as I was getting up to leave my table, someone called out, "We're rooting for you, Louis!" And, I mean, my heart just lifted. It was the perfect thing to hear. Much more so than "We love you" or "We hate you" would have been.

MANTELLO: I remember coming out of the stage door one day, and this woman was fawning all over Stephen. Then she turned to me and said, "I hated you!" That was hard.

JOSEPH HAJ (Louis at Alley Theatre, Houston, 1995): I remember audience members asking me, "How could Louis leave Prior when he is dying of AIDS?" And I remember saying, and maybe I got it from Kushner: "There are people who leave their lover because their partner has gained fifteen pounds."

CROMER: You know, it's a club, the guys who have done Louis. When I meet actors and they're going to play Louis, I say, "I have to tell you, they're going to hate you."

MacLACHLAN: I kinda felt like I was his defending attorney sometimes.

MANTELLO: It felt that a verdict was reached on Louis, and it wasn't good, and it was guilty.

SCOTT PARKINSON (Prior in the Journeymen, Chicago, 1998): None of us knows how we would deal with what gets placed in Louis's lap. I don't think the play ever asks us to sit in judgment of him but to try and understand, maybe even sympathize, with someone who makes such a seemingly egregious moral decision.

JESSE GREEN (theater critic, *New York Times*): When I saw *Perestroika* in San Francisco, the key thing of the play was not there and wouldn't be there for quite some time: the scene where Tony figured out what to do about Louis. Louis, despite being despicable in some ways, he was the audience guy. He was the person who brought you into this material. And as bad as what he does in the play is, when performed well, he sort of makes you feel like *Maybe I would do that terrible thing too.* Then he disappears!

I know it sounds like a small thing, but the real core is, a man walks out on his dying lover, he doesn't come back. He nevertheless is allowed to live. But he wasn't yet allowed to live.

EUSTIS: What I remember more than anything is the day that Tony brought in the scene when Louis comes back to Prior in the hospital room, after Prior comes back from heaven. That was, to me, the key to the entire play. The play cannot end until Louis comes back to visit Prior. The thing that made the process of the play last for five years was Tony trying to figure out what Louis could say. And when he finally did figure it out, the play was over.

When he brought that in, my response was to cry, and cry, and cry. Because what it meant to me was that *Angels* had fulfilled its promise. He had done exactly what we want from an artist. He had asked an incredibly difficult question: What do we do when we fail ourselves, our beliefs, and someone we love? How do we go on?

LOUIS
I really failed you. But . . . This is hard. Failing in love isn't the same as not loving. It doesn't let you off the hook, it doesn't mean . . . you're free not to love.

–Perestroika, Act 5, Scene 7

EUSTIS: That last speech of Louis's, it's human brilliance. He's figured out something as deep as *Angels* promised. What he's doing in an astonishing way is forgiving himself. He's forgiving himself by saying, "I still have to demand this from myself. I don't get to damn myself and thus release myself from responsibility." In doing that, Tony is putting together the great theme of the piece: what we owe to others, and what we owe to ourselves.

NUSSBAUM: The little bit of pushback the play got was about Louis leaving Prior, that no one would ever do such a thing.

> That almost never happened in real life. And then he has the Reaganite Mormon who heroically takes the poor, abandoned gay man to the emergency room because there's no gay people there to help him. . . . I remember feeling this at the time, that what it was describing was not the truth. The truth was that people with AIDS were abandoned by their families and they joined together and they forced this country to change against its will.
>
> –Sarah Schulman, interview with *Vulture*, June 2014

NUSSBAUM: Look, no one rejected *Angels*, really, but the quest for positive role models can be the death of art. The richness of the drama was that these characters were real, that gay characters could act badly onstage.

> I think what Louis does is shocking. Realistic? Well, yes, I know two people who walked out on people who were sick. They weren't like Louis—they were actually kind of trashy.
>
> –Tony Kushner, interview with *Body Positive* magazine, September 1993

DALE PECK (literary critic; author of *Martin and John*): I'm sure it happened. Whether it happened a lot is something for a historian to tell you. Was it politically helpful? I think it actually was. Whether or not lots of people were doing it, lots of people *thought about it*. And not just one partner leaving the other, but people breaking off friendships when friends got sick. Consciously or unconsciously building walls to shield yourself.

McARDLE: It's hard not being a hero! You're not the one that people are behind. You're not the noble one. You're not the gay man dying of AIDS in the '80s. But I think Louis is the person that most of the audience would be like in this situation.

KIM RUBINSTEIN (associate director of national tour): Louis, he's amazing, because he's a part of all of us, and audiences don't want to see that part of themselves that much.

CROMER: Here's what I believe about that play: We all want to believe that we are Harper and Prior, these magical wounded heroes who, despite cannons being fired at us, find in our weakness, our madness, our sickness, all this miraculous strength. We even want to believe that if we're a bad guy we're Roy, the bad guy who says the cool shit.

Most people are Joe and Louis. We are all Joe and Louis: We are weak and liars. And I love those characters for that.

ACT 4

1994–2003

DECEMBER
The FDA
approves
saquinavir, the
first protease
inhibitor. That,
together with
two reverse
transcriptase
inhibitors—the
so-called Triple
Cocktail—
transforms
AIDS
treatment.

MAY
The Supreme
Court rules
Colorado's
Amendment 2
unconstitutional

1994 ———————————————— 1995 ———— 1996

MAY
Fine Line
announces
Robert Altman
will direct
two *Angels
in America*
movies, with
planned
theatrical
release in 1995

SEPTEMBER
The national
tour of *Angels
in America*,
directed by
Michael Mayer,
begins in
Chicago. It will
run for over a
year around the
country.

DECEMBER
The Broadway
production
of *Angels in
America* closes

AUGUST
Fine Line
places Altman's
films of *Angels
in America* into
turnaround

MARCH
*Angels in
America* opens
at Charlotte
Rep

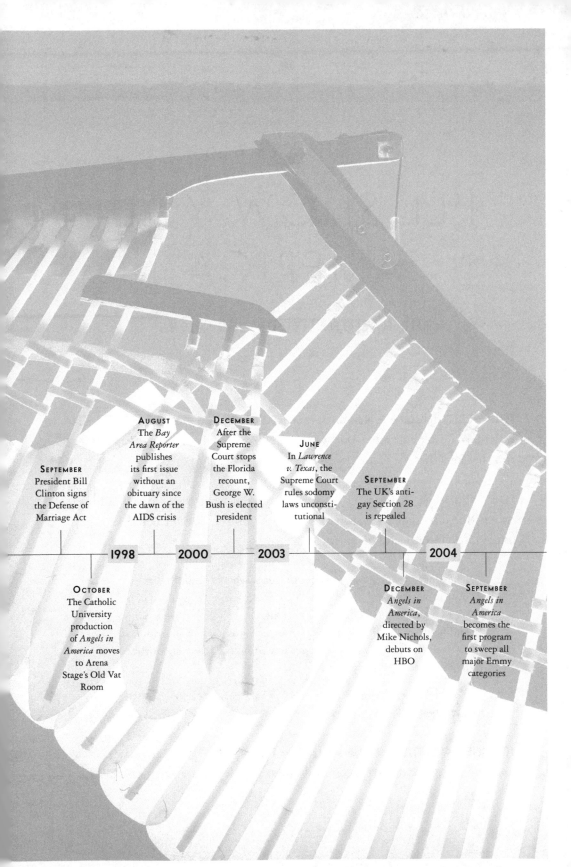

SEPTEMBER
President Bill
Clinton signs
the Defense of
Marriage Act

AUGUST
The *Bay
Area Reporter*
publishes
its first issue
without an
obituary since
the dawn of the
AIDS crisis

DECEMBER
After the
Supreme
Court stops
the Florida
recount,
George W.
Bush is elected
president

JUNE
In *Lawrence
v. Texas*, the
Supreme Court
rules sodomy
laws unconsti-
tutional

SEPTEMBER
The UK's anti-
gay Section 28
is repealed

1998 — 2000 — 2003 — 2004

OCTOBER
The Catholic
University
production
of *Angels in
America* moves
to Arena
Stage's Old Vat
Room

DECEMBER
*Angels in
America*,
directed by
Mike Nichols,
debuts on
HBO

SEPTEMBER
*Angels in
America*
becomes the
first program
to sweep all
major Emmy
categories

CHAPTER I

I'LL SHOW YOU AMERICA

THE NATIONAL TOUR, 1994–1995

TOM VIERTEL (producer in New York and of national tour, 1993–95): Touring Broadway plays wasn't common. But we knew when *Millennium* won the Pulitzer and the Tony that we had a chance.

TONY KUSHNER: Right after George Wolfe and I had agreed he would do *Angels*, JoAnne Akalaitis was removed by the Public Theater board and they offered it to George and he accepted it.

> The other big loser was JoAnne Akalaitis, who last month was ousted by the board of the New York Shakespeare Festival, in large part because projects that cause this kind of excitement were not ending up at the Public Theater. Akalaitis was slow in warming to "Angels," or at least she didn't get heated up over the play until it looked as though she'd lose it.
>
> –Bruce Weber, "Angels' Angels," *New York Times Magazine*, April 25, 1993

JOANNE AKALAITIS (artistic director, Public Theater, 1991–93): Gee whiz. There's so many things that have been said about my departure from the Public, including that I was too pro-Palestinian, which is probably the most accurate thing said about me at the time. I could come up with anything. There was a blizzard that year. An unusual thunderstorm. Alchemists in Brooklyn. There were plenty of reasons that I got fired. That may have been one of them.

KUSHNER: So it was pretty clear: George was gonna spend the year he took directing *Angels*, but after that he was gonna go and run the Public Theater, which is a very, very, very big job. And he said, "I'm not gonna do a national tour, I can't do it."

VIERTEL: It couldn't be a tour that presented the Broadway production, which was very grand and quite expensive. It would never recoup.

KUSHNER: I had loved Michael's production of *Perestroika* that he'd done at NYU, and Michael is one of my closest friends, so I asked Margo Lion to go see that production of *Perestroika*.

MARGO LION (producer in New York and of national tour, 1993–95): I loved it. I loved it because it was Poor Theater: It didn't have the bells and whistles of the Broadway show.

VIERTEL: Here's a young person of great talent who has the ability to make something different and smaller.

MICHAEL MAYER (director of national tour, 1994–95): She was offering me the best job in the world at the time, to take that play to America. I actually couldn't believe what she was saying. I remember leaving the office at Jujamcyn, and thinking, you know, *That was really sweet of her to say*. I really never thought it was going to happen.

VIERTEL: It was pretty clear as we talked to presenting organizations around the country that there would only be *some* interest. So many of the touring venues were exclusively presenting musicals. Their audience wasn't really attuned to plays, they didn't really book plays, they didn't think it was part of their mission.

REG FLOWERS (Belize in national tour, 1994–95): I thought America was going to reject *Angels in America*. There were definitely places where it would be well received, like going back to San Francisco, maybe in L.A., maybe D.C., maybe Chicago. But would it play anywhere else?

VIERTEL: I didn't hear that people were rejecting the show on the basis of content, though that doesn't mean they weren't thinking it.

MICHAEL KRASS (costume designer of national tour, 1994–95): Most of the South did not book the tour.

VIERTEL: We knew we wanted to mount the play in a small venue where we could play for a while, which was the Royal George Theatre in Chicago. That gave us the opportunity to get our sea legs under us. We'd play six months at the Royal George and then go out on tour.

> The Chicago production, with a price tag of just under $1 million, is expected to be cast almost entirely in Chicago. It will be directed by New York-based Michael Mayer under the supervision of the show's Broadway director, George C. Wolfe.
>
> –Lewis Lazare, "The New Royal George: Chicago's Next Big Theater?," *Chicago Reader*, April 7, 1994

MAYER: The deal would have to be that George Wolfe would be given the bottom line credit as "production supervised by George C. Wolfe." Honestly, at the time I was too naïve to know that this was just a way to keep his name on the show in some way, so that when they were selling it to venues across the country they could say it was related to the Broadway production.

I was intrigued at the idea of being in communication with George! He's a very smart man and a wonderful director, and I thought it couldn't hurt to have him on the line. But that never happened. I never had another conversation at all with George from that point on. He had less than nothing to do with the tour.

VIERTEL: You do no midweek matinees. To replace those, you do a 6:00 or 6:30 performance on Sunday night. Once that's over you have to load out the show, get it into the trucks, move it to the next city, get it out of the trucks, set it up, and do a sound check at 4:00 or 4:30 on Tuesday. Our brief to Michael and David Gallo, who designed the set—we said, it's gotta be able to fit that profile. It's gotta be able to get out Sunday night and get back in by Tuesday afternoon. They designed to that set of restrictions.

KRASS: The Broadway show had a fucking expensive set. It was a big set with big pieces gliding on. We thought we were doing something more political and authentic.

PETER BIRKENHEAD (Louis in national tour, 1994–95): The set was spectacular, especially for *Perestroika*, a 3-D collage of earthly junk against the upstage wall.

MAYER: I wanted to bring the feeling that this was America's attic, you know? The repository for twentieth-century American cultural iconography. So it was a series of wings that were three-dimensional storage shelving units that could move on and off, and inside all of them were the props and iconography. There was a section of an old broken marquee for *Judy Garland: A Star Is Born.*

KRASS: Perhaps our mission was pragmatic, but immediately Michael Mayer turned it more positively into a more human-driven production. We absolutely, from the very beginning, made the choice that objects and furniture would be moved by actors on purpose.

KUSHNER: The play is not really about the scenery and the machinery, it's about the actors.

MAYER: The only thing that I didn't have the clout . . . *(Pause.)* It became clear that there was no situation in which the Angel was *not* going to be flying across America. But I missed my Angel on the rolling ladder. I felt that to be a little more magical than using wires and a harness.

ROBBY SELLA (Prior in national tour, 1994–95): Now, I can only speak to what I heard from agents and other industry people, but initially the tour was just going to cast with actors based in Chicago. I thought, *That makes sense, that's a strong theater community.*

KRASS: They have a chip on their shoulder there, so half the cast had to be from Chicago and we had to go live there.

SELLA: But a while later I got a call and they said Tony felt like there were certain things he was looking for in the characters that they hadn't found in Chicago, and they asked me if I would audition.

BIRKENHEAD: They were casting two or three companies at once. Replacing Louis on Broadway, and the tour, and casting the Alliance in Atlanta. I auditioned for three companies over the course of a few weeks. I wore this lucky outfit to every audition. I probably didn't even wash it. This pair of green pants. I can't explain it, I won't defend it. I think now that's the exact thing Louis would never wear. But it was the '90s.

FLOWERS: There were a *lot* of people I knew who were auditioning for the play.

BIRKENHEAD: It was *the thing* happening that month, so everyone was there. It was a surprisingly collegial, fun atmosphere.

FLOWERS: I'm six foot eight, and at the time was this really lank, leggy, caramel-colored, not-easily-cast actor. I usually walked into auditions and either they would say, "We *have* to cast him," or they wouldn't even take me seriously. In my first audition [casting director] Jay Binder asked, "Where do you think they're gonna find high heels to fit you?"

BIRKENHEAD: The table of people was incredibly overpopulated. Usually there are four or five people but I remember it being like twenty people, an enormous group, including Tony and Michael and Margo Lion.

CAROLYN SWIFT (the Angel in national tour, 1994–95): I met Ellen McLaughlin the day before I auditioned. I asked for her blessing, and she put her hands on my head and blessed me.

KATE GOEHRING (Harper in national tour, 1994–95): Carolyn Swift is unbelievable! She herself will just change your life.

MAYER: At her audition, we just thought, *She doesn't even need wings to fly, she is so extraordinary.*

BIRKENHEAD: Carolyn Swift is a force of nature.

SWIFT: During auditions I just had a feeling, I just had a connection with the Angel that I couldn't describe. I locked eyes with the reader and I saw that I changed him in the scene and I realized, *Oh, this is a huge part.* I saw that I was going to have to fall in love with Prior and hate him at the same time.

> The news is in from auditions for the long-awaited Chicago production of Tony Kushner's Angels in America, and it isn't heartening. Only three Chicago actors—Barbara Robertson, Philip Johnson, and Kate Goehring—wound up in the cast of eight. The remaining five actors were selected from among those who auditioned in New York: Peter Birkenhead, Reg Flowers, Jonathan Hadary, Robert Sella, and Carolyn Swift. . . . Earlier this week one longstanding local casting agent said several Chicago actors who seemed ideal for certain roles in the show weren't even called in for a first audition.
>
> –Lewis Lazare, "The Decline of the International Theatre Festival/ Casting for Angels," *Chicago Reader*, June 23, 1994

SELLA: They have a wonderful, insular community in Chicago; they're so proud and very protective of their own. I got there a few days early, because I had to find a place to live. I was meeting a real estate agent. She was showing me an apartment. And at one point she asked, "Well, what do you do?" and I said, "I'm an actor." She said, "Oh, do you know we're getting *Angels in America* here in Chicago?" And I was just about to say, "Yes, I'm in it!" and she said, "And you know what else, they're bringing all these actors in from *New York* to do it. As if we don't have enough people here in Chicago who could blow it out of the water." And I was like, "Umm, how many bedrooms does it have?"

SWIFT: There was this weird dynamic with Steppenwolf, across the street.

SELLA: There was a pub on Halsted where everyone would go, and Peter went there with some of the guys from the show, and it almost turned into a fistfight!

SWIFT: I thought we would all meet there after our shows and have a jolly time. I would say "Hi, I'm from *Angels*," and they just wanted nothing to do with us. They're the truth tellers and we're the hacks, that's how they felt.

GOEHRING: I know there was a little preoccupation about: Is this a Chicago show or what? I just thought, *Well, I'm a Chicago actor, it's a Chicago show.*

FLOWERS: Peter Birkenhead ended up writing an editorial that got published in the paper.

> I have been hearing unasked-for opinions about New York and New York theater since I've been here. I've read countless reviews and articles that share an embarrassingly parochial point of view, never failing to single out the hometowners in our cast, implying some sort of connection between geography and talent . . . and am generally aware of a constant hum of resentment in what I now refer to as The City of (a Huge Chip on Their) Big Shoulders.
>
> –Peter Birkenhead, op-ed in the *Chicago Tribune*, November 6, 1994

BIRKENHEAD: I was a hotheaded young man with too much time on his hands, and what can I tell you? I got all ranty about it. I mean, I wasn't cast as Louis for nothing.

• • •

VIERTEL: I told everybody when we started rehearsals, I gave a little talk, I said: "This is America's *Angels in America. That* was New York's. But this one belongs to everyone in America."

SELLA: There was a lot of concern about would this play around the country. You get your flyer for Cedar Rapids, Iowa, the theater there, and it's *Cats*, and

Arsenic and Old Lace, and there isn't always room for things that are different and difficult and challenging.

FLOWERS: I was a little bit apprehensive about it. Who was this Michael Mayer person? I didn't know him at all. He was brilliant enough to cast me in the play, but what if that was his only stroke of brilliance?

KUSHNER: Michael was *born* out. He's a fantastic singer and has a really amazing voice. Few people know that but he has a beautiful voice, he can really sing.

KRASS: Performative. Dramatic. Hilarious. Impassioned. Pained. He's very happy to throw himself on the ground and say, "You guys, this sucks, what do we do?" He was an actor in grad school, so he performs pain and need and thereby involves his collaborators on an emotional level, which I have enormous respect for.

BIRKENHEAD: I remember Michael saying—I don't want to put words in his mouth, but it was something like he wanted this to be the *gay* version.

MAYER: It's a *gay fantasia on national themes*. So you would get the feeling of the history that gay people had lived through the years—it was important that it be gay history, not just American history. It needed to be through that lens. It started with the overture to *Wizard of Oz*, and at the end of *Perestroika* it ended with the end of *Judy at Carnegie Hall*, the end of "Over the Rainbow."

KRASS: Michael often said, "You guys, it's *Wizard of Oz*." So my little hospital gown on Robby Sella was blue and white gingham to look like Dorothy's dress.

KUSHNER: One of our big bonding moments was Judy Garland. We take our Judy-ism very seriously.

KRASS: We were very aware that we were doing a very gay, what would now be called queer, production. The girly production in the butchest of cities, Chicago. At the same time, Mark Wing-Davey was doing the butch version

in the gayest of cities, San Francisco. Tony was going back and forth, and I believe he was doing rewrites for both.

FLOWERS: Tony Kushner was in the room. He was still writing! This was a play that had just won two Tony Awards. I think the day before we started rehearsal *Perestroika* won the Tony for Best Play.

BARBARA ROBERTSON (Hannah in national tour, 1994–95): We were rehearsing it at the Germania Club in Chicago, which was this big, huge, cavernous—it must have been, like, a ballroom.

SWIFT: We rehearsed for four months.

BIRKENHEAD: We were rehearsing both *Millennium* and *Perestroika* together at the same time.

KRASS: That was definitely the intention, to do the whole motherfuck right away. It was crazy. *(Laughs.)* Nobody over forty would do that ever.

Prior (Robby Sella) and Harper (Kate Goehring) in the national tour, 1994. (*Joan Marcus*)

KIM RUBINSTEIN (associate director of national tour, 1994–95): It was a huge thing for Michael! In terms of his career and the launching of it, there was a lot of understandable anxiety. I remember a couple of nights when he was like, "You have to sleep over." I'd stay over on his couch and we'd listen to Joni Mitchell and try to go to sleep.

KRASS: We teched twenty-three days—it was absolute torture. Michael had a God mic and sang Judy Garland for twenty-three days. We wanted to kill each other.

GOEHRING: We got a joke from Steppenwolf. The cast of *Clockwork Orange* sent us a congratulations card and it was this big piece of poster board that said, "While you were in tech," and it had all these world events that had taken place.

KRASS: So we did a run-through and everybody in all those days of tech had forgotten that it was a funny play. It was OK, they got through it, but it was boring. Michael in notes was like, "Guys, it's funny, c'mon!" So the next night, Tony comes, they really played up the laughs. That's how it works: You do it different ways, find the balance. But unfortunately Tony saw the campy night.

RUBINSTEIN: Michael was on my right and Tony was on my left. And literally after the run I had scratch marks on my arms from both of them! Scratching me with their nails!

KRASS: I was sitting in the balcony above him because we were all afraid of him. He filled a notepad. *Filled.*

SWIFT: Afterwards he was waiting for us backstage and it was terrifying, because he was not pleased with what we had done. The dressing rooms in the Royal George were down below and kind of across from each other with a little hallway between them. He was in the hallway and every single actor that came offstage to the hallway he went *(beckons with finger)* "Come here."

To me he said, "Why did you throw away all your original instincts as the Angel? Those were the instincts I cast you for. You have to go back to that."

MAYER: Oh boy. I just remember being in the hotel room with Tony getting his notes until well into the morning. It was well past 3:00, it might have been 5:00 a.m. It was an entire legal pad full of notes.

KUSHNER: I just remember him sitting there in some hotel room in Chicago looking completely catatonic and not able at some point to respond anymore.

MAYER: There was not a single area that was not addressed fully—from every design department, lights, sound, the flying, the costumes, the staging, the acting, my interpretation of a moment or something.

SWIFT: The next morning, a very brave Michael Mayer stood in front of us. He said, "Guys, it's my fault, I led you astray, we have to go back to our original instincts. It's my bad." It was so brave! We all loved Michael anyhow, but that day he became our hero.

TONY HAS NOTES

TONY KUSHNER: I usually write my notes out so they don't get too hideous. If I'm giving them orally I tend to get very emphatic.

TONY TACCONE (co-director in Los Angeles, 1992): Tony—he would cop to this—he's legendarily tough on the directors he's worked with over the years.

RICHARD FELDMAN (director of Juilliard *Millennium* workshop, 1992): I remember one page, and all it said on it was "Ugh." (*Laughs.*) It didn't refer to anything.

NICK ORMEROD (designer in London, 1992–93): You can see Tony taking notes, he's just writing, he's not actually looking at the stage, he's just writing, and you think, *How is that possible?* He's

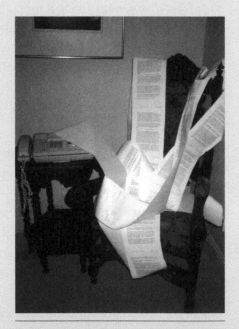

Tony Kushner's notes, Declan Donnellan and Nick Ormerod's fax machine, 1992. (*Declan Donnellan and Nick Ormerod/Cheek by Jowl*)

MAYER: Oh, that's incredibly sweet. I just realized, this has to be done. It was my work that needed to be addressed, not theirs.

SWIFT: Michael doing that saved the show.

KRASS: It was horrible, horrible, a horrible weekend. Tony was reacting as Tony should, with deep specificity, but kind of to a false event. So I think some of the camp, and I use that word reservedly—maybe *fun*, silliness—some of that was cut before it had really been tried. Michael had more joy in his mind than what wound up on stage a couple of weeks later.

GOEHRING: I needed to make a big adjustment to let go of the humor. It's not about the humor, it's about this individual's very real pain and concerns.

KRASS: I had Harper in Antarctica dressed in a Sonja Henie ice-skating outfit, a coat with fur trim, stuff like that. Tony was offended? Mad? It was simply

not seeing anything, he's just writing all the time.

DECLAN DONNELLAN (director in London, 1992–93): I mean, I don't blame Tony. He cares very, very much. He's just got a very, very clear vision of what he wants. And we have laughed about it and drunk about it.

TACCONE: I've definitely had moments where I've said, "I can't hear this anymore, I can't hear what you're saying." So we'll go to our corners and take a time-out.

MICHAEL MAYER (director of national tour, 1994–95): I had not had the Tony Kushner Note Experience until the tour. I lost my virginity after the first preview of *Millennium* at the Royal George.

PETER BIRKENHEAD (Louis in national tour, 1994–95): I remember his yellow notepad

out in the house, those yellow pages flipping like a fan, and me thinking, *Oh God, what is he writing?*

KIM RUBINSTEIN (associate director of national tour, 1994–95): That night Tony was on a rampage and Michael was cowering in a corner.

MAYER: I've never, in all of my years, I haven't had note sessions like that with any other writer. Never.

RUBINSTEIN: We went to Tony's hotel room and put on robes, I think we were there all night, and ordered room service, and Tony talked about all these things that needed to be different.

MAYER: There were some big things. "I hate that"—"I hate the staging"—"Change it all." I realized very quickly

gone. He thought, I believe, that it did not take her or that moment seriously. That was cut without discussion.

SWIFT: Michael wanted me to be a lot funnier as the Angel, and I could never do it. So for me to be able to go back to instinct, to play her as a broken-hearted woman, that was a huge relief.

KRASS: He was Tony's girlfriend—those guys were, at least, best friends, in the silliest, most fun ways. We knew they went shopping together. They laughed together. They had, you know, silliness as their intimacy.

KUSHNER: But we had to work out a different kind of relationship, that was sort of complicated, and it was my baby. It's hard, playwrights and directors, it's just a very hard relationship.

• • •

TONY HAS NOTES →

that there was nothing worth fighting for, because he had his position pretty set.

KUSHNER: I'm not proud of that. I was very hard on Michael.

RUBINSTEIN: I remember thinking, *I cannot believe this man who is being so mean wrote* Angels in America*!*

And then in the course of the evening, talking about it, he transformed, he became, like, a rabbi in front of our eyes. He started talking in this much larger way. To me it was a great revelation of what the play is about. We are our human selves struggling on the earth, and there is this part of us that is part of God, divine, and we struggle with the finite and the infinite. I remember him talking about the Hebrew tree of life, and that some people

are born at one of the higher Sephirot, a higher level, higher on the tree, and that sometimes they are given more exquisite and extraordinary challenges because they are higher up towards the face of God.

Look, it's possible he didn't use any of these exact words, but I remember his whole demeanor changed. We were all wearing these white robes. And all of a sudden there was this light coming out of him. It was really quite extraordinary.

TACCONE: Sometimes it's overwhelming, you know, for actors. An actor will ask a question, Tony will give a brilliant three-minute answer, I'll just say, "Uh, do it faster." *(Laughs.)* And then the actor says, "OK!"

JAMES McARDLE (Louis in London, 2017, and New York, 2018): You can bounce a question off him, but be ready for a

KRASS: We knew from the beginning that doing a national tour of that play was hugely important. We were very aware that we were bringing a story and a set of political thinking to people who had not heard it. Who had not seen it represented, had not seen two boys kissing onstage or off-.

TODD WEEKS (Prior in national tour replacement cast): We had a bus! We rode the bus from town to town.

VIERTEL: Those first few weeks are a matter of figuring out how to fit what you have inside the trucks. Each truck costs about $20,000 a week. You don't want to find yourself in four *and a half* trucks.

SWIFT: At every new theater we would have a new flying rehearsal. It was dicey, to be honest. We were in different theaters, and there were a couple times when we tried sharing that responsibility with someone on the local crew, and that's when I got thrown into some walls and things. That's when we realized the fliers had to be members of our own crew.

tsunami of an answer. You pitch him a tennis ball and he sends back a ten-page email.

ZOE KAZAN (Harper at Signature Theatre, New York, 2010): One morning before a preview matinee Tony asked, "Can I take you out to brunch?" I was so excited he wanted to sit down with me and talk, I treasured every moment like that. And we sat down in the restaurant and he talked me through every line of the play. He was still going through it two hours later on my way into the theater. I was like, "OK, Tony, I gotta go get my makeup on."

FRANK WOOD (Roy at Signature Theatre, New York, 2010): I got $20 for taking a note from Tony Kushner. He said, "If you try this note, I'll give you $20," and I still have the $20 bill.

TACCONE: He and I figured out a way to do it, but it took ten years. It's drama-free and relatively easy, but that took hard work. I include him in every stage of the process in a way that I don't with other writers. He—it's really important that he understands what the intentions are from the beginning.

OSKAR EUSTIS (co-director in Los Angeles, 1992): Tony and I had a discussion about this three days ago, before he left for London. The way Tony gives notes on his shows is incredibly difficult for every director he's ever worked with. There's a few directors who have essentially turned the room over to Tony and let him do the line-by-line work with the actors. There are directors who have barred Tony from the room and forced him to accept it. But there's never been the "normal" relationship between playwright and director with Tony. It doesn't exist.

WEEKS: I remember we went to Schenectady. I'm doing the last moment of *Millennium*, on the bed and looking up. And where I usually see Carolyn Swift hovering over me on wires, ready to descend—she's not there. I look in the wings and she's just standing there holding a portable mic, wearing her full angel costume. And she just shrugs at me. And I realize, *Oh God, we don't have the fly space for her to come down*. So we had all the sound effects and lights and everything but she didn't even come out, she just delivered her line from the wings.

I was so upset and so was she! As soon as the show was over, we ran out to the lobby and we gathered a makeshift audience, whoever was still there. We found a table in the lobby and I laid down on it as if it was a bed. She was in full costume and we did the entire scene for everyone who was there, just so they could see it.

BIRKENHEAD: In so many cities we were surprised at the incredibly warm reaction we got, which says a lot about our own prejudices as sophisticated New York artists.

TONY HAS NOTES →

KUSHNER: Y'know, Marianne [Elliott, director of the 2017 National Theatre production] has worked—I've never seen a director work as long or as hard on a production, a year of preparation. And I don't want to go in and become this nightmare figure for her. So I sort of decided that I'm gonna try something I've never tried before, which is to not drown everybody with notes and let them find it on their own terms. It's hard, it's really hard, because I know one way at least to make every moment in the play work, and to sit and watch people going through moments that clearly aren't working . . . But there may be other ways to make them work, or other ways to arrive at the same place.

MAYER: That's what he told me about London, too, but then he also told me he got a gigantic list of questions over email, and that he ended up writing tons in response. Maybe he didn't send the email.

KUSHNER: I mean it's great in another way—twenty-five years of thinking about this play and giving notes. I've written volumes, literally volumes, of notes about *Angels in America*. It feels great to not have to do that. So we'll see; it's gonna be an interesting experience.

MARIANNE ELLIOTT (director in London, 2017, and New York, 2018): Yeah, he gave a lot of notes. *(Laughs.)*

McARDLE: Did he give notes? Did he? *(Deadpan:)* Yeah.

SWIFT: So many mothers would come to us backstage after the show and say, "My son is dying," or "I just lost my son." We were still in the middle of the epidemic, and we were in places where those losses hadn't been recognized. They needed to be hugged, and they needed to cry.

GOEHRING: We'd have strangers come up to us on the street and do something better than compliment the piece; they'd tell us their stories. This person was living with AIDS, this person's heart had been broken, this person is a Mormon or Jewish or believes in angels. This person's a Democrat, a Republican, knew Roy Cohn, survived the Holocaust . . . They'd launch into the story, and you knew they were in the process of giving themselves permission to live in a bigger world. And they'd totally teach you—audiences will teach you—especially if you hang out together for eight hours.

FLOWERS: We were like the gay Dallas Cowboys coming to town. We were walking through the country, sprinkling this magic dust that made it OK to celebrate your identity.

NATHAN STEWART-JARRETT (Belize in London, 2017, and New York, 2018): There was one point, he was like, "I want to talk to you about Mr. Lies." We went out for dinner, and he's just so sweet and so warm and loving and encouraging, and he was like "Do it how you do it." And I was like "Now? At dinner?" And he was like "Do it now, speak some lines," and I did a version of the character. And he was like, "Yeah!" and I was basically doing my lines in my chicken. It was the weirdest thing!

ELLIOTT: Tony doesn't do anything by half. If he decides to get involved, he's not going to leave any stone unturned. But he did say to me: "These are my notes, it's up to you which ones you take." There was a moment when I realized that this was my production, it's my interpretation, and

I therefore have to make a choice about which notes I was going to use, and he was very generous about that.

ELLEN McLAUGHLIN (the Angel in workshops, San Francisco, Los Angeles, New York, 1990–94): The thing about Tony's notes is . . . you have to take them. What are you going to do? *Not* take that man's notes? Nobody works harder than he does. And look what he's done. You're always going to want to hear what the man has to say.

MAYER: Getting Tony's notes was tough, but now I feel I'm a member of a really awesome club.

FELDMAN: To be engaged with that mind and heart was a privilege. *(Laughs.)* But I can still see that *Ugh* written on a piece of notepaper.

GOEHRING: We had a few places where there were people outside protesting. Not nearly as many as I would have thought. We did have a few, which was very exciting!

WEEKS: We were in Clearwater, Florida, and we were told we had to go in under police escort. There had been threats. I was of two minds: (A), Oh my God, theater used to cause riots, this is what theater is about. The other side: I didn't sign up for this!

SWIFT: They had weapons checkpoints set up. One of the security guards said, "We're here to protect the fucking faggots," and someone on the crew overheard that, and that guard was immediately fired by our very gay company manager.

WEEKS: Someone was protesting in the bitter cold, I think in Lincoln, Nebraska. I want to say it was the Phelps family, but I don't quite remember.

SWIFT: Yeah, it was [Fred] Phelps. It was Lawrence, Kansas. We arrived for our sound check, and it was about ten degrees below, and he had his little children with him, and they were bundled in their snowsuits and shivering and had their little signs reading, "Faggots Burn in Hell."

WEEKS: Carolyn Swift went out with soup. There was no irony in that, she truly was an angel. She was concerned they were freezing out there.

SWIFT: I asked him, "Won't you let your kids come in and warm up in the lobby?" I have never seen such a face of hatred as he showed me.

SELLA: One day when Prior revealed his Kaposi's sarcoma lesion to Louis, someone stood up—in the Kennedy Center!—and yelled, "Why don't you die already?" And someone else yells, "Why don't you shut up?" And there was a kerfuffle and he was escorted out. Imagine!

BIRKENHEAD: D.C. felt less like a negative reaction than an emotionally stunted one. At the party at the Kennedy Center, Donna Shalala and Ted Koppel talked to me. Usually the reaction we'd get was quite emotional.

People would come up to us and grab us by the hand and tell us their life stories. But Koppel asked me, (*Ted Koppel voice:*) "So how do you feel about gays in the military?" and I'm like, "Did you see the play?!"

FLOWERS: I met my husband on the tour. My husband had seen the show in Chicago and had only recently come out to his parents. My husband is from Columbus, Ohio, which happened to be one of the last stops on the tour. By the time we got to Columbus, he had graduated from the University of Chicago and was back home. He was a teacher, as vanilla ice cream as they come, and he brought his mother to see the show. A few days later I was sitting in a coffee shop in the gay neighborhood, the Short North—we found the little tiny gay neighborhoods in every town we visited—it was a snowy day, and this man walked in and his face *lit up*. It was so beautiful.

BIRKENHEAD: I do remember a kind of weariness set in. Eight people is a pretty small cast; it's not like a musical. We all really felt like we loved each other, but there was a feeling, like, well, *Here* he *is again*.

RUBINSTEIN: It's a hard play to do even for a regular run. It requires everything you have: stamina in voice, in body, in the spirit, in the heart, in the mind. You have to be stable but you have to fall apart every night. It was pretty intense sometimes, people were losing their minds about little things.

FLOWERS: Clearly it's not like there was never a fight, but I would say hands down that it was an amazingly loving group of people. Across the board.

BIRKENHEAD: We were in an elevator in the Kennedy Center, going up to the rooftop restaurant, and the doors closed and it was just the eight of us. And we hadn't been together in that configuration for a really long time. And

Louis (Peter Birkenhead) in the national tour, 1994. (*Photographer unknown, courtesy of Peter Birkenhead*)

Carolyn just said, "Oh look, it's us!" And we had the *Mary Tyler Moore Show* group hug.

RUBINSTEIN: Some of them, it broke them. I get it.

PHILIP EARL JOHNSON (Joe in national tour, 1993–94): I love this play even though it was an excruciatingly difficult time in my life. It took me many years to heal from the emotional toll that play took on me, and yet I am deeply proud to have been part of that production and to have survived 379 performances in 351 days.

SWIFT: It kind of ruined me in a sense. When it was over and I went back to auditioning, I knew that it would never ever be the same for me. And I kind of began plotting my departure from the theater after that. It was like having a brilliant lover, and after that lover goes, you just *know*.

INTERLUDE

THE MESSENGER HAS ARRIVED

The Angel (and Emily, Sister Ella Chapter, and the Homeless Woman)

ANGEL
Greetings, Prophet!
The Great Work Begins.
The Messenger has arrived.

(*Blackout.*)

–*Millennium Approaches*, Act 3, Scene 7

KATE GOEHRING (Harper in national tour, 1994–95): In *Millennium Approaches*, when the Angel burst through the ceiling at the end of the show and said "Greetings, Prophet!" and the music soared and the lights went out—I remember literally thinking, *NO WAY! You can't end a play that way!*

DEBORAH PEIFER (San Francisco theater critic): How funny is that! It's an angel, you'd think they could just float through somehow, but of course she doesn't, she crashes through the ceiling. *That's* how change will come, not slipping through.

ROBERT HURWITT (San Francisco theater critic): You almost feel that image of the Angel breaking through the ceiling was the play itself breaking through the confines of the theater.

JOSEPH MYDELL (Belize in London, 1992–93): Growing up in the South, I have a great sense of religious imagination. I mean, it's America! Everyone knows someone who has had a revelation! Tony takes that and adds into it a kind of redemptive grace, a kind of transcendental scope. It's like everything to do with Walt Whitman, Emerson, right down to the Holy Roller churches, the snake handlers. It's so American, and Tony just made it very, very particular and specific to this gay man. It's a gay man having this experience! This religious experience! Get your head around that one!

KATHLEEN DENNEHY (Harper at Dallas Theater Center, 1996): Ellen McLaughlin's Angel was one of the most revolutionary things I've ever seen in my life. She

Ellen McLaughlin (the Angel) backstage at the Mark Taper Forum, 1992. (*Photographer unknown, courtesy of Ellen McLaughlin*)

was vicious. She was a vicious angel. I went to Catholic school for twelve years. God was tough, he was a balls-out dude, you know. But I never had the experience of an angel being so fierce and defiant and scary.

CHERRY JONES (the Angel in New York replacement cast, 1994): Ellen is a little otherworldly. And she has those long, beautiful fingers that she used to such great effect as that Angel. It seemed like she could stop the earth spinning with those two fingers. I can see it right now.

TONY KUSHNER: When I wrote *A Bright Room Called Day* and the devil appears, the devil is specifically meant to be a literary device borrowed from *Faust*, from the Dublin Trilogy, from *Doctor Faustus*. The Angel is different. I at first thought she wouldn't be, but then she got away from me. I never realized I was capitalizing when I said "She" or "Her"—I just for years have been in the habit of capitalizing, and I don't like to fuck around with it. I have this, like, slightly weird feeling that there's something there.

MARK WING-DAVEY (director at American Conservatory Theater, San Francisco, 1994–95): She's not the sort of soft, nurturing angel. It's a more Old Testament version of an angel.

ROBIN WEIGERT (the Angel at Signature Theatre, New York, 2010): She's the most fantastical. She's a pure creation of the imagination in every sense.

ELLEN McLAUGHLIN (the Angel in workshops, San Francisco, Los Angeles, New York, 1990–94): How do you embody an idea? A philosophy? A *process*? And not so much make it human but animate it?

ELIZABETH LAIDLAW (the Angel in the Journeymen, Chicago, 1998): We really invested in the image of the Angel as a bird of prey, "the Bald Eagle." She was not a human being. She was powerful, and animal, and her mind didn't work like a person's.

McLAUGHLIN: The lack of human psychology is what makes her so fun. It's what makes her scenes both comic and terrifying. She has no means of understanding the human. I think about it a lot because I do so much work with the Greeks. Divinity isn't cozy to the Greeks. The gods are terrifying. They don't understand human beings, they don't *want* to understand human beings. They don't love us. They don't see every sparrow's fall. On some level, they loathe us, or at the very least they are *indifferent* to us, which is much more chilly.

SARAJANE ALVERSON (the Angel at Stray Dog Theatre, St. Louis, 2012): I re-watched a fair amount of Amy Acker as Illyria in the television series *Angel* for inspiration.

NANCY CRANE (the Angel in London, 1992–93): This is going to sound weird, but I thought about Jessye Norman. She's a diva, that character.

CAROLYN SWIFT (the Angel in national tour, 1994–95): I really got her torment. Her conflict, and the sense of being bereft, of having this love relationship with the divine that was kind of old-fashioned. There was a real resonance for me about being disillusioned by men, disillusioned by relationships, and my whole spiritual life was changing. God, as a guy in the sky, was gone.

• • •

MICHAEL MAYER (director of NYU *Perestroika* workshop, 1993, and national tour, 1994–95): The fucking Epistle. We probably spent more stage hours on that goddamn thing than anything else.

JENNIFER ENGSTROM (the Angel at Kansas City Rep, 2015): My experience performing the Epistle was like what I imagine childbirth to be: terrifying, exhilarating, physically exacting, possibly dangerous, and truly divine—and I don't know how the fuck I did it.

KERRIE SEYMOUR (the Angel at Warehouse Theatre, Greenville, SC, 2013): You first see it and think . . . um, a ten-page orgasm? Seriously?

DAWN URSULA (the Angel at Round House/Olney, Bethesda, MD, 2016): It was like working on a classical text. Heightened, poetic, often obscure.

ALVERSON: How to make sense of these beautiful words written in stanzas like poetry without sounding like I was reading poetry? How to convey the glory and beauty and utter terror this creature evokes? How to exit the scene walking regally but completely backwards, up a ramp, barefoot, without tripping?

CRANE: I was at balcony level, and I was looking down at the audience. When you say, "Stop moving," you'd see them react. Like, *Oh, what does that mean?*

ANGEL
(With great passion and force:)
YOU MUST STOP MOVING!

PRIOR
(Quiet, frightened:)
Stop moving.

–*Perestroika*, Act 2, Scene 2

CRANE: It was a powerful moment. The mystery around the Angel was very satisfying to audiences.

JONES: With the Epistle, it was really joyful. Even though you had a lot to do, the other scenes, the other parts were so brief. Here you had a real arc to the scene, and it was *so* physical, you had these physical obligations.

SEYMOUR: This was certainly a moment when I think some audience members checked out a bit. We are smack-dab in the Bible Belt, so an angel fornicating with the prophet while he is getting intimate with a book . . . well, it's not the typical Greenville fare.

MARY BETH FISHER (the Angel at Court Theatre, Chicago, 2012): The Epistle is incredibly hard. To understand the dynamics of the scene between Prior and the Angel, and Prior and Belize separately, and then as a triangle.

KIMBERLY FLYNN (Kushner's friend and dramaturg for *Angels*): Belize repeatedly interrupts Prior's dialogue with the Angel, drawing Prior to re-enter a dialogue where he, Belize, not only challenges Prior's assertion that the Angel is real, but critically interrogates the Angel's pronouncements, directives, and origins. The effect of this Brechtian arrangement is that both the seduction and the interrogation are kept in play for the audience, as in a well-paced debate.

McLAUGHLIN: If you only play power, if you only play certainty, the audience can't hear anything. It has to be a specific vision of truth. Otherwise, it's just a rant by a crazy lady and it becomes dull.

I mean, angels *are* dull. Because they don't have the specificity or particularity of human characters. What I think is built into the part, which is smart of Tony, is that she is fallible. She makes mistakes. Things don't go according to plan for her. It's *that* that makes the Epistle so comic. It's one of the funniest things I've ever done.

Stephen and I did the first public reading of that scene in San Francisco. I have *never* cracked up onstage. But I couldn't hold it together.

ANGEL:
Now.
Remove from their hiding place the Sacred Prophetic Instruments.

(Little pause.)

PRIOR:

The *what?*

–Perestroika, Act 2, Scene 2

GEORGE C. WOLFE (director in New York, 1993–94): The audience is thinking that they must be stupid. And then at the end of that long speech, Prior indicates he didn't understand it, either. It got a *huge* laugh, and the audience relaxed: *I'm not an idiot, oh, I can laugh.*

McLAUGHLIN: There is just nothing like seeing a character like the Angel undermined by this skinny, spiky gay guy in pajamas who won't put up with her nonsense. Finally, in frustration, I create an explosion and he comes back with the suitcase and yells at me for breaking his refrigerator. He's so outraged. "You cracked the refrigerator, you probably released a whole cloud of fluorocarbons, that's bad for the, the environment." *(Laughs.)* It's one of the funniest things I've ever been part of. But it's because of that fallibility, which is comic, when things aren't going the way she expected them to go and she gets flustered, that she overcompensates, if anything, and becomes more and more terrifying towards the end.

The angels have so much riding on Prior. As far as they're concerned, the fate of the cosmos is riding on this and they have no choice but to try to make him their messenger. That's what I think makes her so funny, that the stakes are just ludicrously high, but it's also what makes her so disturbing, because she is of course right, there is something terribly wrong, the fragile ecological balance has been imperiled by human life and there is no simple solution . . . and perhaps no solution at all. We may have broken the planet irreparably.

If the Angel isn't funny, the play doesn't work, but if the Angel isn't terrifying, it doesn't work, either. You have to do both of those things. *That* is the job.

ENGSTROM: I met Tony Kushner and told him I was the Angel and he signed my script, "Sorry the Epistle is so hard."

KUSHNER: I made a terrible mistake with the flying.

> If you are mounting a production of the play, and you plan to have an airborne angel, which is a good thing, be warned: It's incredibly hard to make the flying work. Add a week to tech time.
>
> –Playwright's Notes, first (1994) published edition of *Perestroika*

KUSHNER: I was nervous about the Epistle. So I thought, *OK, you're going to have somebody really doing these amazing acrobatics and flying around in the air.* George Wolfe agreed, we got the Foy brothers, they went down to Philadelphia with Ellen and George, and they did all this flying and somersaulting and things like that.

SWIFT: I got flown into a lot of walls.

Prior (Garret Dillahunt) and the Angel (Lise Bruneau) rehearsing the midair fight in ACT's production, 1994–95. (*Photographer unknown, courtesy of Garret Dillahunt*)

CRANE: I got dropped once. I could see the flash of a stage manager's hand and I just thought, *I'm aiming for that*, and I hit him and it was okay.

FISHER: Unfortunately, on my first tech, the track snapped and I was dropped about ten feet. I had injuries and it was very traumatic physically and psychologically. Later, once we closed, I was deeply depressed about it.

JONES: One night, when I went to lay the kiss on Hannah, I did a somersault, and I got down in a batlike place with those wings and I couldn't get back up. I couldn't right myself. I had to take my legs, with my robe over my head, and wrap them around the wires, and pull myself up. It was not a graceful move.

NICK ORMEROD (set designer in London, 1992–93): I remember there was one performance when the Angel ended up upside down, which wasn't great.

CRANE: One of the wires came dislodged, and as it clicked out of place it caught the wig. It was the wire that kept me stable, and I felt it take the wig off, and then I went back and forth because I wasn't stable, and the wig was hanging from the wire.

DECLAN DONNELLAN (director in London, 1992–93): This American academic came to see the show one night when we'd gone to see something else. And he called and said, "Oh, Mr. Donnellan, I need to leave a message. It was incredible! The most extraordinary thing of the evening was the meta-theater moment when the Angel flew over the audience's heads, and it appeared that a cord snapped and she turned upside down, screaming. Her wings fell into the audience, and the stage manager came on. And it was incredible because it looked so real, but I knew you'd rehearsed it!"

CRANE: And everyone thought it was hilarious, you know: *Oh, ha ha ha.*

DONNELLAN: I opened a bottle of very good red wine.

Cottlesloe Theatre
Stage Manager's Show Notes
7 Nov 1992

As the Angel came through the wall, the line that pulls her forward came off, and she swung back up stage. The snap hook had got tangled up in her wig, and when she tipped her head forward the wig had released the pin and so came away. Miss Crane was unhurt. The wig remained dangling over the stage for the curtain calls.

   Otherwise a good show.

DAVID MILLING

CRANE: I do associate that scene a bit with thinking I was going to die.

KUSHNER: It's like having a swordfight in the play. It will eat up all the rehearsal time. It's very difficult to do.

McLAUGHLIN: My experience of tech was hours after hours of me helplessly spinning away up there while a whole lot of techies stood below me looking up my dress and shaking their heads. "Yup, she's spinning again."

JONATHAN LEE (production manager in Los Angeles, 1992): We made the decision to fly the Angel with a single-point harness, which was a very big problem. You can't maintain the orientation of which way they are facing if they're stationary. We had to have guide-wires that we attached to Ellen's costume to hold her stationary on the floor, and then as soon as the wall opened up, the lines dropped and the stagehands scurried offstage so they weren't visible. It was really a nightmare. When the Angel was revealed at the end of *Millennium*, she had this tendency to spin slowly and face the wrong way. *(Laughs.)* You know, "Greetings prophet! The great—" *(Uncontrollable laughter.)*

TONY TACCONE (co-director in Los Angeles, 1992): Who doesn't want to see an angel move forty feet in seconds? But there's a question of how much you wanted this. There's brilliant language here; at what point does the flying subvert the language?

KUSHNER: It took me until—the thing that taught me what it was, was Ivo van Hove's production in Amsterdam, when all they did for the entire Migratory epistle was: The guy who played the Angel—it wasn't a woman—the actor playing Belize, the actor playing Prior, they sat on the ground and they just did the lines. It was like watching a Talmudic study group. It was the best version of it I'd ever seen. I just thought, *There it is*.

EELCO SMITS (Prior at Toneelgroep Amsterdam, 2007–15): We decided to let it be weird. And just be a sick person communicating about how he is losing his mind. And his best friend going, "Don't do it, because if you go crazy I'm going to lose you." It became about that friendship between Prior and Belize.

KUSHNER: It's a scene. Between three people. It's not an angel doing somersaults. It's not a circus act. I put it in the script.

> I've come to the conviction that attempting extensive flying is not only unwise, because it lies beyond the technical and temporal means of most theaters, it's a distraction from the real business at hand.
>
> –Notes About Staging, 2017 published edition of *Perestroika*

KUSHNER: Because if you try to do the flying thing, in addition to the fact that it won't help the scene at all, because there's nothing that motivates her giving an aerobatics display, it'll eat up all of your rehearsal time, and you'll never get it good. I mean, *Spider-Man* had five and a half years. And five or six people were smashed into pillars and things.

WOLFE: I used to say that Ellen was more comfortable in the air than she was on the ground. She felt dazzlingly comfortable there.

JONES: Ellen was like a bat. She would hang for hours during tech rehearsals. The blood would drain from her head to her ankles, and so she would flip upside down.

McLAUGHLIN: I had a human being on the line with me, and I got to choose my fliers. Bernie did horizontal flying, Doug did the up and down. He's the one who had my life in his hands. I knew that he was steadfast and strong and calm and utterly, utterly reliable. We spent a lot of time learning how to dance together, basically. It convinced me I was really flying. It was like those dreams you have where you suddenly realize you can fly. It felt effortless for me. I adored him.

SWIFT: That relationship got very, very deep. Because they did the Epistle with me. It wasn't just that they were hitting their marks. They got to know the text so well that they could sense if I was making a subtle adjustment. There was a line of communication—those wires to the ropes to their hands.

McLAUGHLIN: A few months into the run, the woman who gave me my massage on Fridays before the show said, "It's the weirdest thing. You seem to be developing wing muscles." Because there were these ridges of muscle I'd developed alongside my spine where I flexed the wings, opening and closing them. She said she'd never seen anything like it. It was as if there were some residual muscles that humans didn't have anymore that I had reawakened.

JONES: The very first night, once I was in position above center stage, I noticed all these little fingerprints. And then I noticed all these little black pastilles, the little throat lozenges? They were resting on top of this baton. They were all Ellen's. It was like going to the moon and seeing what Neil Armstrong left behind.

SWIFT: In rehearsals I emailed Ellen McLaughlin. I had some flying issues. I didn't know it would be so painful! She kept reminding me, "Just remember, you're *flying*!"

• • •

CRANE: Did Tony tell you Sister Ella Chapter's backstory? The reason she wears a wig is that she's bald, because she's in love with Hannah, and she and her husband had sex, and it upset Sister Ella Chapter and she went downstairs and fell asleep smoking on the sofa, and it burned her house down. So from that day to this, I feel protective of Sister Ella Chapter because of her horrible accident and unrequited love for Hannah Pitt.

McLAUGHLIN: In the first draft of *Perestroika*, which we couldn't manage to read in a six-hour rehearsal day, there was a whole play that Tony was circling around writing that involved Emily, the nurse, because it was the AIDS nurses who began ACT UP.

CRANE: She was gay and her lover had been HIV-positive and she became politicized. That gets realized now with Belize swiping the AZT. I found that character really interesting. It was like a whole one-act play.

McLAUGHLIN: I loved the character. I would've loved to have played that. But there simply wasn't time for that play in the midst of *Angels*.

CRANE: I remember reading the first draft of *Perestroika* and I loved it. And I stayed on [for the second year of *Angels* at the National] for reasons that had to do with that draft. Of course, then those things weren't part of the final script.

KUSHNER: (Alarmed:) Nooooo. Nancy never saw—no. She's misremembering, she has to be. That thing got cut—
    (Sighs.) I think they were called Pink Underpants, the group that these AIDS nurses were forming to steal drugs. But . . . I'm amazed anybody remembers that.

McLAUGHLIN: An audience can really only follow, in the sense of *care for*, a limited number of characters, even in a play of that length.

KUSHNER: Emily is a great character. There's a real arc for her from *Millennium* all the way to the end in terms of her connection to Prior. You get a nice little sense of what working with that population was like in the mid-'80s, but I don't think that anybody should grieve the loss of that particular plot.

McLAUGHLIN: It's such a weird group of satellites, that line of characters. They're outliers, most of them, odd characters—some, like the Angel and the Mormon Mother in the diorama, not even human—who enter briefly in order to speak prophecies or make sweeping ideological statements.

AMANDA LAWRENCE (the Angel in London, 2017, and New York, 2018): They all say, "Stay put."

WEIGERT: They all speak with a reactionary voice.

McLAUGHLIN: My job as an actor is very different from anyone else's in the play. I do a series of three- to four-minute scenes with quick changes in between. You have to go with very specific, clear choices that make the character vivid, get the dramaturgical work done that the character needs to do in order to support the play's structure, and get off cleanly.

JONES: Normally you think about the character's posture, the character's way of speaking. But here it wasn't like I was understudying anybody—I was understudying Ellen McLaughlin, who has all these idiosyncrasies that make you want to watch her. I practically had to crush on her watching her doing it.

McLAUGHLIN: Each one is not so much a character as an idea, and in the case of the Angel, as Tony puts it, an idea with wings.

ENGSTROM: Oh, the wings! They were magnificent. Looked like steel and swayed like feather. They were designed to seem almost like an extension of my arms—I could gesture with them, almost point, using the feathers as fingers. They were incredibly sexy.

McLAUGHLIN: My balsa-wood wings at the Eureka were made by a wonderful local artist. They looked like something off of a Renaissance angel in the corner of some Annunciation scene or a Dürer sketch.

URSULA: Gorgeous. Pure white and the material was slightly opaque and shimmery so the lights would sparkle and bounce off them.

FISHER: My wings were stylized, long pieces of white fabric. They were probably easier on my back than bearing the weight of more realistic wings, but were tricky to control.

SWIFT: It took two people to lift them up and put them into my corset, and two people to lift them off. They needed a lot of "grooming" as I was always losing feathers here and there, and the wire framing would bend out of alignment. They caught the light beautifully.

CRANE: I could put my feet on this stirrup that would make the wings flap.

McLAUGHLIN: John Deary, who made the wings for Broadway, had AIDS. He was quite sick while he was making those wings. They were gorgeous, an incredible accomplishment, because they were enormous, but they were light enough for me to wear—something like twenty-five pounds of aluminum and feathers—and I could close and open them with the movements of my back muscles. They were the last thing he created. He made it to opening night, he got to see them, and he died soon thereafter. I felt like I carried him on my back after he died and I was always grateful for the extraordinary care he expended on them. They were something to behold.

CHAPTER 2

IT'S A PROMISED LAND, BUT *WHAT* A DISAPPOINTING PROMISE!

ANGELS AND THE CULTURE WARS: CATHOLIC UNIVERSITY AND CHARLOTTE REP

TONY KUSHNER: The thing at Catholic University was a horrible experience.

DOUG WAGER (artistic director, Arena Stage, Washington, D.C., 1991–98): Right when I became artistic director was the peak of the culture wars that broke out with the assault on the NEA.

BRIAN HERRERA (assistant professor of theater, Princeton University): The culture wars were a tipping point. Up until then, even though there was contestation with the NEA, there wasn't a sense that it was going to go away.

WAGER: The NEA imprimatur is the thing that gives the foundations their incentive. So the absence of that imprimatur gave funders some really good reasons to avoid anything too sticky or controversial, in general.

HERRERA: Queer people and people of color became poster children for what conservative America doesn't represent, like Robert Mapplethorpe and *Piss Christ*. It was a way of using particular artists to mark a line in the sand and say we therefore do not support the arts. And using the shock of the artists and their work and their identities as proof that they were corrupt and thus unworthy of funding and, by extension, not good Americans.

WAGER: All of that was giving politicians—putting them into a cold sweat—and giving them a justification for suppressing, diverting, or cutting federal funding for the arts.

GREG REINER (director, theater and musical theater, National Endowment for the Arts): In 1992 we had $172 million. And then in '96 that's when we lost 40 percent of our funding. This year our funding is $150 million, which is close to what it was in pure dollars, not counting inflation, in the mid-'90s.

GARY WILLIAMS (professor emeritus, drama, Catholic University, Washington, D.C.): We were aware of the gay community, of gay culture. The NEA controversy around Mapplethorpe at the National Gallery in Washington, right at the steps of the White House.

We had a bright, thoughtful, modest, gay MFA student in the drama department. And this bright young man says to the faculty, "I'd like to direct *Angels in America* for my final project." Ooooookay. Here we are. *Angels in America* at Catholic University.

CHRISTOPHER BELLIS (MFA student at Catholic University, 1996): Catholic University isn't going to do a Gay Fantasia on National Themes! But the administration said to me, "If it's what you're most passionate about, this show should be on your list." I just thought, *Yeah, right, they're gonna pick* Angels in America. *Suuuuure.*

But they did.

GITTA HONEGGER (chair, department of drama, Catholic University, 1993–2001): Obviously, we knew from the start that it could be problematic, given the whole university, the religious ethics, and so on. We didn't do that on purpose, we just wanted to deal with contemporary art.

WILLIAMS: The chancellor of Catholic U. was also the bishop of Washington; that's mandated in its charter. It stands in a very special role within the Church in that way, and feels itself very visible, you know, a light on the hill for Catholicism.

HONEGGER: It was a time when fundamentalist religion was becoming stronger in this country. I'm not sure in an earlier decade it would've been a problem.

BELLIS: So we cast everything. Everyone was excited. I asked if the administration was OK; I was told they had asked and hadn't heard anything back. It was going to be done on the mainstage of the Hartke Theatre, a five-hundred-seat theater with a proscenium arch. Sometime around the first day of classes, late August, [Professors] Jackson Phippin and Bill Foeller showed up at rehearsal and said something to the effect of "The administration has expressed some reservations about this show being done at Catholic University."

Say wha? They'd known about this since April. It's late August. Why are we only hearing about this now?

GAIL BEACH (professor of costume design, Catholic University): We didn't get a reaction back from the university until right literally as school was starting. So that's part of what created the absolute maelstrom. It was so late. You know, this student's production is going up in six or eight weeks and you're telling us no.

HONEGGER: The dean was very suspicious of our activities.

WILLIAMS: The dean had made it pretty clear that the play dealt sympathetically with the homosexual lifestyle and therefore was inappropriate for the university.

BEACH: The then president, Brother Patrick Ellis, had written a four-page letter explaining why the answer was no. It was this rather rambling thing where he kept praising it as a play, so it wasn't really, it didn't make total sense.

HONEGGER: It was very hard. They were not willing to enter that discussion. But of course there were priests on campus who had great understanding and were supportive of the project.

KUSHNER: They had a lot of gay priests. Four or five guys who taught there, closeted, and they all came to tell me. This one guy had a membership at the Saint, and he somehow managed to bill the Jesuits for his membership!

BELLIS: I felt at that point that things were going to go sideways, that I needed to be more proactive about talking to people about what the hell was going on. That was what led to the original article in the *Washington Blade*.

> Christopher L. Bellis, the student who is director of the production, said he was assigned *Angels in America* as his graduate thesis project by a panel of drama department faculty.
>
> "At the time of narrowing down a thesis, the faculty unanimously approved [*Angels*] and found it to be acceptable," he said.
>
> There was earlier talk of banning the show altogether, said Glen Johnson, a tenured English professor who teaches at Catholic University.
>
> –Leah Wynn, "University Forbids Ads for Angels in America," *Washington Blade*, September 20, 1996

WILLIAMS: The controversy about our production was widely reported in the press, and in our profession. I knew that would happen. The size of this production, taking place within the campus community . . . probably, rather than suppress it, you want to avoid that attention. I tried to go to the president and warn him about that. I couldn't even get into his office.

HONEGGER: I thought that, since I had built so much trust, I could make an argument that theater was an important tool that reflects society, but it was a non-starter.

BEACH: That little loophole came in the conversations: You know, we could move it off campus.

WAGER: Gitta called and basically asked if it would be possible.

BELLIS: Moving it allowed them to fulfill the educational obligation to me while making it not *quite* a Catholic University production. By the end of that week, the administration had decided to allow the production to go off-campus.

KUSHNER: Before I even got involved, Doug called and said, "Come do it at the Arena Stage," so it was solved instantly. The ugly thing for me was an exchange I had with the dean, who was a priest.

ANGELS IN SCHOOL

CHRISTOPHER SHINN (playwright, *Dying City* and *Against*): Tony was my playwriting teacher at NYU in I think '94 or '95. The thing that was really remarkable about it was how little playwriting was the subject of the class. He had us read *What Is History?* by E. H. Carr. He talked a lot about Freud and Marx. He was really teaching us how to think, and pretty explicitly communicating that being a playwright was less about self-expression and more about engagement with the world.

Even at that time he saw a disturbing trend toward solipsism in the university. He was suspicious of identity politics. He was suspicious of arguments against the canon. He was conveying over and over as young artists the most important thing we had to do was engage with the great minds that came before us. Other teachers are asking, "What's your protagonist's objective?" and here's a guy saying, "There's a thousand years of thought out there and your job is to engage with it."

KATE GAUDET (has taught *Angels* at University of New Hampshire, 2013–present): It's never been obvious to me how to teach this play. What makes this play great is the complex interplay between humor, anger, grief, hope, truth—the aesthetic experience is built on harmonies among contradictions and conflicts. Students tend to look for simpler "themes" and "meanings" as they are taught in high school, which doesn't work well with this one, or any really good literature.

DEBORAH GEIS (has taught *Angels* at University of Tennessee, Knoxville; Oberlin; DePauw; 1994–present): In '94 or so, I was teaching *Angels* in an upper-level modern drama class at a much more

Dean Suziedelis replied with a letter in which he questioned Bellis's judgement in choosing a play such as *Angels*. "It would be poor judgment," Suziedelis wrote, "for a student of art at a Yeshiva to propose a garden of swastika sculptures as a thesis project. It was not," he continued, "a prudent choice to state *Angels in America* as a thesis project for Catholic University."

–Stephen Nunns, "No 'Angels' on Catholic Campus," *American Theatre*, December 1996

KUSHNER: I wrote to him. I sent him a copy of a photograph, the last image of my great-grandparents in Kaunus in Lithuania, 1939. It was sent over to their sons who had already immigrated. They were never heard from again, they were murdered by the Nazis. I sent it to him, I said, "I want you to stop for a minute, whatever your feelings are about homosexuals, and think about what you're saying. Really, is there a comparison between the LGBT rights

conservative southern school. There was a pivotal moment in that class where they did a scene in which there was a male-male kiss, and it was like . . . you could see jaws dropping as the students did it. That, at the time, was like breaking a taboo. I will always treasure that moment because I was so proud of the students doing that scene.

MICHAEL KRASS (costume designer of national tour, 1994–95): I taught for many years at NYU undergrad. Over and over the students would do scenes or projects from *Angels* through the late '90s all the way until four years ago. Increasingly, they were humorless and reverent, as though they were doing a scene about Dr. Martin Luther King. *(Laughs.)*

GEIS: Now it's kind of a period piece. Your typical college student was born in '97 or so. They know less than nothing about the history of the Reagan era.

MONICA MURRAY (has taught *Angels* at Cambridge Rindge and Latin School, Cambridge, MA, 2006–present): What can often be a challenge for modern young people, who are much bolder and willing to speak their truth, is to get them to understand that, in the past, people could not come out. We talk a lot about how times have changed and what it meant for these characters or people in my generation to hide their identity.

LOURDES TRAMMELL (has taught *Angels* at University of Arizona, Phoenix College, Pima Community College, 2002–present): The real opposition came in the form of challenges like "Why do gays think they're the only ones who get AIDS?" And we had to go right back to History of AIDS 101.

GEIS: Even the references to things like *The Wizard of Oz, Streetcar, My Fair Lady*, all those, they didn't get those. That was a surprise. You know when you teach

movement and the Nazis, or for that matter the Catholic Church—which is immensely powerful, especially on its own turf—and the Jews of Germany and Europe?"

I said, "I think that you should really apologize to me for this and I think that you should retract or clarify that statement, whatever else you may feel." And he wrote back some unbelievably loathsome—he obviously had just the most barren, misshapen moral landscape.

BEACH: The school would've had a much stronger case had this not been a student's thesis show. But even the School of Theology and Religious Studies wound up supporting us on the grounds of academic freedom.

BELLIS: Catholic University spent like thirty or forty thousand dollars to move the production off-campus. Our set for the first production was halfway built, and it had to scrapped and we had to do a new one. It was really pared down.

ANGELS IN SCHOOL →

Austen or Shakespeare or something like that, you get an annotated version of the text? We're almost at that point with *Angels*. *(Laughs.)*

MICHELE VOLANSKY (has taught *Angels* at Washington College, Chestertown, MD, 2001–present): The very best thing about teaching the play is exploring the sociopolitical landscape. Current students are so far removed from the AIDS crisis, from Ronald Reagan, from the emerging gay rights movement, that when they learn and discover the backstories behind the characters, they become politicized.

MONICA MILLER (taught *Angels* at Georgia Tech, 2017): Students were completely unaware of Roy Cohn as a historical figure. They looked him up and were a bit shocked to learn that his portrayal in the play had a historical foundation.

Cohn's role as Donald Trump's mentor was something that several students noted. I wanted to be careful not to let class devolve into Trump-bashing, but I did try to guide students into looking at parallels between now and then, and how the 1980s setting speaks to today.

KEITH MARTIN (producing director, Charlotte Rep, 1996): I failed my background check when I first applied for my job at Appalachian State because of the lawsuits [over the 1996 Charlotte Rep production]. I tell my students that they must discover their activist potential and make themselves heard. They can't let themselves be marginalized. When the board of elections denied the voting precinct on campus, my students sued and got it put back. I'm very proud of that.

KERRIE SEYMOUR (has taught *Angels* at Clemson and University of South Carolina Upstate, 2006–present): I teach in the

WAGER: Our best option for them was the Old Vat Room, which wasn't at the time much of a theater. I think we had the Capitol Steps there once.

BELLIS: The Angel had these huge wings. They were, like, twenty feet wide, made out of corrugated steel! We were trying to fill a huge space when we designed them. So we had one big-ass angel for the finale.

BEACH: They were going to be up in the cherry picker in the middle of the space. But the Vat Room has, what, ten-foot ceilings? So they created a rolling stand with the wings on it and the actor stood in front of it.

BELLIS: Our Angel was afraid of heights, so I think she was relieved to go to Arena Stage in the end.

conservative South, so it can be very challenging to talk about the major themes of the show, be it Reagan-era politics or homosexuality. I have noticed that the openness to the show and its characters and themes has become greater over the years.

ANNE DENNIS (taught *Angels* at Mohave Community College, Lake Havasu City, AZ, 2004–07): Oh, yes, there are always a few students who hear the topic, cross their arms, lean back in the chair, and tune it all out, or even become nearly hostile.

JAYCE TROMSNESS (has taught *Angels* at South Carolina Governor's School for the Arts and Humanities, Greenville, 2001–present): The challenge is, with students this age, their knee-jerk, dogma-based reactions to what they've been told about the play and its themes. They assume it's a "gay" play and that it's immoral. I try to teach them it's a play about love and humanity and the quest for spirituality.

GAUDET: The play treats sexual orientation as a fixed truth; discovering and coming to terms with that truth is the only right path. But students, and I, have some sympathy for the idea that a person can choose his lifestyle and social orientation independent of sexual orientation, though they wouldn't necessarily articulate it in those terms. So I think that the meaning of the play is changing as understandings of sexuality change.

TRAMMELL: In Queer Studies courses, naturally, the response was enthusiastic. However, these students were already in camp and actually rejected any critical inquiry or discourse about the work. I think they've decided it's "sanctified" and can't be subjected to scrutiny by anyone, even—and especially—themselves. In one class, gay students shut down a straight peer so viciously for attempting a critical inquiry that she dropped the class.

WAGER: The play does very well from very little. I think probably, in the end, necessity being the mother of invention, my guess is the production turned out better than it probably would have.

HONEGGER: The Catholics will kill me, but they were worried about how to stage the scene in the park. We knew where the nuns would likely be sitting, so we staged it so they wouldn't have to see it close up.

BELLIS: It solidified, for me, the importance of the themes of the play. You have to stand up. You have to be heard on the issues that you care about. You have to be prepared. You have to do the right thing.

• • •

ANGELS IN SCHOOL →

KRASS: Unfortunately, it's taught as an Important Document of Liberation. That loses the fact that it's a *play* on a whole lot of levels, including the visceral, the subversive, the hilarious, the cheaply theatrical—I mean that positively. On the simplest possible level, it really is shaped to get an audience to root for two boys to kiss, which I find fabulous.

VOLANSKY: I think that the longer the distance between the initial production and today, students believe that some of the issues have been resolved. The reignition of the culture wars will, I suspect, change some things.

KIM RUBINSTEIN (associate director of national tour, 1994–95; now professor at University of California San Diego): I had not visited it for a couple of years and then this year, because of the way the

world is, I said, "We need to do *Angels in America*." The relevance and resonance of the struggles, the conflicts, the language, the revelations—it's remarkable. I can't even tell you how much it changed my students. They were able to put language to so much chaos that was going on inside of them and in the world around us.

GAUDET: This semester, the first of the Trump era, I found that I let my politics fly far more openly than in the past, so students made more political connections than they have in the past.

MURRAY: Of all the plays I teach, *Angels in America* evokes the most passion in the students. I have never had a play that a class hurries to class for like *Angels*.

TIM CARMODY (taught *Angels* at University of the Arts, Philadelphia, 2009): It's a very smart play, but a very accessible one. It treats its audience like

TOM VIERTEL (producer of national tour, 1994–95): We intended to tour in Charlotte and the Charlotte Rep *begged* us not to come, to let them do it themselves. It was very inconvenient to us: We had a route that went right from Atlanta through Greenville, South Carolina, through Charlotte and then north. It really fit our economic model and it was a big inconvenience to change.

STEVE UMBERGER (director at Charlotte Rep, 1996): We were growing. We had done some challenging work, we had just started doing collaborations with the Charlotte Symphony: *Midsummer*, *Romeo and Juliet*, *The Tempest*, full text, with orchestra, working on a big canvas. Expanding our audiences.

KEITH MARTIN (producing and managing director, Charlotte Rep, 1990–2001): We got the rights to *Angels in America* in 1994, but we produced it in 1996.

adults. For my eighteen- and nineteen-year-olds, I felt that was important.

GAUDET: Because it is such a pleasure, I have moved it to nearly the end of the semester so that we end on a high note and I get good evaluations. That's a half joke.

MURRAY: This year I made the decision to perform a one-act version of *Millennium Approaches* as our winter festival show. This was only the third time this show has ever been performed publicly in a high school in the U.S. We knew our toughest and most challenging audience would be the student population. As much as we like to think we are a tolerant community in Cambridge, the high school crowd can be tough.

The theater was full to capacity and, after getting the crowd to be quiet, the show began with Roy on the phone. They hadn't heard swearing allowed officially in school, and they went crazy! After they

got past it, they were completely in the show. It got uncomfortable at times as one could hear, especially at the moment of Joe and Louis's kiss. But the audience was engaged. Later that day one of the teachers overheard these two kids talking to each other. They're kids who would never do theater—he thinks they were athletes—and one said he could never do anything like that. "Maybe I'd kiss on the cheek but not on the mouth."

GAUDET: I teach in the humanities department, so the subtext of everything is always: Why do we need art, literature, the humanities? I think teaching *Angels* is the best I do at providing an answer to that.

MURRAY: They have so much more courage, insight, and understanding on these issues than previous generations. I can't help but feel it will someday lead us to a better way of life. 🖋

PERRY TANNENBAUM (founder and editor, *Creative Loafing Charlotte*): There were only six theaters in the United States that were being allowed to do the show that near to the Broadway production. It was a *big deal*.

VIERTEL: They were so passionate about this that we agreed to let them do it. And they did it, and they were all fired. They literally dissolved Charlotte Rep.

UMBERGER: We didn't do it to create any sort of political sensation. I think Tony Kushner felt . . . we were the smallest of the companies, and I think he had some sympathy for that. He was also certainly aware of the political climate, and Jesse Helms.

KEVIN R. FREE (Belize at Charlotte Rep, 1996): There were all these discussions about the New South versus the Old South. Charlotte was supposed to be the New South. The New South was supposedly progressive, more inclusive of gay inhabitants, people of color. The attitudes were supposed to have changed.

UMBERGER: Charlotte is the largest city in either Carolina. So you have this strange tension between an aspiration to be a "world-class place," a phrase that's

---

The cast of the Charlotte Rep production, 1996. Front: Mary Lucy Bivins (Hannah), Alan Poindexter (Prior); Back: Tamara Scott (Harper), Angus MacLachlan (Louis), Graham Smith (Roy), Kevin R. Free (Belize), Barbi VanSchaick (the Angel), Scott Helm (Joe). (*Charlotte Rep publicity, courtesy of Steve Umberger*)

been thrown around a lot in Charlotte, and a very small-town way of thinking that's always been at the core: a southern, conservative, church-going sensibility.

LAWRENCE TOPPMAN (arts reporter, *Charlotte Observer*, 1980–2017): The boosterish talk about "a world-class city" didn't reflect reality then or now. Even more than Atlanta, a city Charlotte leaders alternately mocked and emulated, Charlotte was an odd conglomeration of northern transplants seeking warmer climates, workers imported by banks from other cities, and natives who still thought of it as an overgrown small town.

MARTIN: It was our due diligence that got us into trouble.

TANNENBAUM: Part of what had been recommended was this sort of community outreach.

MARTIN: We created a series of community-wide education and outreach activities in hopes of shedding light on the difficult issues of the play, rather than heat.

UMBERGER: All of the events happened so quickly, a week or less.

MARTIN: The *Charlotte Observer* went page A1 with the following headline: "Theater Aims to Avert Storm over 'Angels' Drama."

> Tony Kushner's seven-hour epic, which Charlotte Repertory Theatre opens March 20 in the North Carolina Blumenthal Performing Arts Center, has been hailed as the play of the decade, the winner of one Pulitzer Prize and two Tony Awards as best drama.
>
> It also contains nudity, a simulated homosexual act and adult language—elements that have caused trouble for Charlotte's cultural organizations in the past.
>
> In one scene, a young man with AIDS takes off his shirt so a nurse can check his lesions. "Only six. That's good," she pronounces. "Pants." The young man drops his trousers so she can continue. He is as naked as the day he was born.
>
> —Tony Brown, "Theater Aims to Avert Storm over 'Angels' Drama," *Charlotte Observer*, March 6, 1996

TANNENBAUM: The head of the so-called Concerned Charlottians, the Reverend Joe Chambers, sent a fax to city council asking for a roll call about who supported this homosexual event and who didn't.

KUSHNER: Reverend Chambers was nuts. He had declared Barney the Dinosaur an agent of the devil. I mean, he was a hideous person.

> The popular PBS kids' show character is "straight out of the New Age and the world of demons and devils," warns Rev. Joseph Chambers, who runs a four-state radio ministry based in North Carolina.
>
> Barney, adored by millions of toddlers and preschoolers, is yet another sign that "America is under siege from the powers of darkness," adds the politically active Chambers.
>
> And for a donation to his 25-year-old Paw Creek Ministries in Charlotte, Chambers will send you a booklet explaining it all: "Barney the New Age Demon," recently retitled "Barney the Purple Messiah."
>
> —*Cox News Service*, November 25, 1993

TANNENBAUM: After the fax was sent out, the Blumenthal Performing Arts Center, the city council, the local attorney general, all enjoined the Rep from opening.

SCOTT BELFORD (director of public relations, Arts & Science Council, Charlotte, 1995–2000): It became a rallying point to question freedom in the arts.

MARTIN: Their lawyers tried to shut us down using the North Carolina obscenity law. But they couldn't. Works of "intrinsic artistic and literary merit" were excluded from the law. The only legal option they had was North Carolina's indecent exposure statute, because of the roughly eight seconds of full frontal male nudity.

The cease-and-desist order constituted prior restraint, because we had yet to break any laws. It also constituted an imminent threat, because I was named personally. That allowed me to seek judicial relief from the court in the form of a restraining order, which later was made into a permanent injunction. In six hours I had to find a lawyer, file a formal request, find precedent, a sympathetic judge, request a court hearing, deal with my staff, my board, the cast, the crew, the media, and get process servers.

UMBERGER: We all knew there was a chance the show wouldn't open. There we were, at 5:00 in the green room before first preview, wondering, *"What's going to happen next?"* We had worked for a year—were we going to be able to do the play?

MARTIN: At 4:58 p.m., two minutes before the clerk's office closed, the judge's order was signed and filed with the clerk, and process servers fanned out across the county to serve notice.

UMBERGER: At 5:15 or something, we found out we were doing it. The show was at 7:30, I think. So it was close!

MARTIN: We served the Performing Arts Center board and senior staff, the police chief, city police department, the county sheriff, the sheriff's department, the DA and all of his magistrates, even the local and state alcohol and beverage control board, because we had a full bar at the theater and you can't serve alcohol at a premises with full nudity. Anyone who had the legal authority to shut us down, we got an order against them. We were painting with a shotgun, not a rifle.

ANGUS MacLACHLAN (Louis at Charlotte Rep, 1996): We were warned there might be bomb threats, or that during the nude scene people might try to stop the show.

TANNENBAUM: It turns out that the Concerned Charlottians showing up en masse to protest the opening numbered 15 or thereabouts. And the number of people picketing in favor of *Angels* numbered between 150 and 200!

MacLACHLAN: It felt like two different factions, like what's happening now in America. What Trump is doing, what the conservatives in America are doing, but most people didn't vote for him. We had tremendous support from the community.

KUSHNER: They tried this direct assault, actually stopping it, and ran right into the First Amendment. I mean, it didn't work, and in fact made it a huge thing, and everybody with a conscience in Charlotte felt they had to go and see it.

MARTIN: Opening night, I said, "Good evening, ladies and gentlemen, and welcome to *Angels in America*," and there was a standing ovation. We hadn't even done the show yet!

> Be splendid tonight, be focused, have fun, make theater: That's
> our way of repudiating the bullies, the killjoys, the busybodies
> and blowhards. We know the secret of making art, while they only
> know the minor secret of making mischief. We proceed from joy;
> they only have their misery.
>
> –fax from Tony Kushner to Charlotte Rep, March 20, 1996

MacLACHLAN: That night was so electric, and so supportive, it was really about what you wanted it to be about: Kushner's words, the events onstage. The feeling, the connection from the audience, was everything you want in a theater. That's what was happening, not the little noises from outside.

MARTIN: The headline in the papers next day was "Judge: Let 'Angels' Play." It was a bigger typeface than Kennedy's assassination.

Supporters of the Charlotte Rep production counterprotest on the night of the show's first performance, March 20, 1996. (*Donna Bise*)

A last-minute court order Wednesday secured opening night for the tense cast and crew of the Pulitzer Prize-winning epic, which played without protest in city after city until it reached Charlotte. A group of Christian conservatives tried blocking the show over scenes of nudity, profanity and simulated sex.

Even after the legal victory, some expected an outburst during the nude scene, but when Charlotte actor Alan Poindexter dropped his blue slacks and for seven seconds faced the audience naked, no one said or did a thing.

–Tony Brown, Gary L. Wright, and Paige Williams, "Judge: Let 'Angels' Play," *Charlotte Observer*, March 21, 1996

BELFORD: The show sold out and extended because it was in the headlines every day and there was so much discussion around it. A lot of people felt they had to see it to see what the fuss was all about.

TOPPMAN: Charlotte Repertory Theatre never did a more accomplished show.

MacLACHLAN: Tony Kushner came down and saw it. I remember him saying this play has been done all over the world, in very conservative countries, and nothing like this had ever happened.

KUSHNER: They stopped the plane on the runway and suddenly all these policemen came on, and the stewardess asked me if I was me, and they helped me off the plane because they were worried about a death threat or something. It was nonsense, but it was exciting.

MARTIN: They picketed every one of the play's thirty performances. They even showed up Monday nights. The first time that happened, they told the media they had successfully stopped the show. The police had to tell them we were dark on Mondays.

TANNENBAUM: We were all very euphoric at the time. It remained, until the company folded, the most staggering hit they had. Eleven thousand people saw that show in Charlotte.

UMBERGER: The next season, we had a 20 percent increase in subscriptions, and when we polled people they said it was because of *Angels*.

TANNENBAUM: There was a tremendous feeling that this was a huge opportunity for Charlotte theater to expand. This is *(laughs)* obviously not the scenario that played out.

FREE: I can't talk about *Angels* without talking about *Six Degrees*.

UMBERGER: We had chosen [John Guare's] *Six Degrees of Separation* for the next season. Joe Chambers or someone seized upon that as proof that we were continuing to violate standards, that it was bigger than *Angels*. We tried to defuse that, say that wasn't what the play was about.

FREE: It wasn't nearly as good, but it became "Why is Charlotte Rep doing all these gay plays?" *Six Degrees* isn't even really a gay play.

MARTIN: It's available in the comedy section at Blockbuster.

KUSHNER: They did what these people always do: The next year they realized a full frontal assault on civil liberties and freedom of speech wasn't gonna work, so they defunded the Rep.

MARTIN: In November of 1996, the Mecklenburg County Commission became dominated by Republicans who had a stealth mission to defund the arts. The "Gang of Five," led by Hoyle Martin.

UMBERGER: I think it was on April first. April Fools' Day. It was a vote to defund the $2.5 million Arts and Science Council. It was funny, because they wanted to defund us because of *Angels*. But they wouldn't say "Well, we can't give money to organizations that do gay material," so they had to defund the whole thing, the thirty-odd groups that got money from the council.

That meeting started at 6:00 in the afternoon and went until 2:00 in the morning. There was an overflow crowd. It was a very tense and raucous seven or eight hours that had many speakers for and against. The head of the commission was not part of the Gang of Five. He voted against. Right before the vote he said, "Watch us, and forgive us."

BELFORD: It was a five-to-four vote.

UMBERGER: That was two and half million out the door.

BELFORD: The Arts Council funded programs for kids. The symphony. The opera. Just because this one group funded by the council did one play with a gay character in it.

MARTIN: Hoyle Martin went so far as saying we should ban all works that include the word *homosexual*, works created by artists who were homosexual. One minister railed from the pulpit about the works of Leonard Bernstein. One said they should ban *The Nutcracker* because Tchaikovsky was gay. I was "outed" myself, by Republican county commissioner Bill James, the only one of the Gang of Five who is still in office. This was a surprise to my wife and teenage daughter.

BELFORD: It was a real wake-up call to the community. A black eye to Charlotte. We're trying to be a very progressive, forward-thinking city.

MARTIN: Four of the Gang did not survive the next election cycle.

BELFORD: After the elections, the funding was returned and increased.

TANNENBAUM: There was a dampening effect. It ushered in an era of extreme caution. They actually convened—the Arts and Sciences Council—convened a task force where all sides would be represented and would issue guidelines for arts events in Charlotte. And of course any compromise would preclude events like *Angels in America*.

UMBERGER: I was on the task force. Also on that task force was Joe Chambers. Everyone had been invited to the table. All sides.

TANNENBAUM: The appeasement from beginning to end of these wackos is really just startling.

TOPPMAN: Charlotte Rep fomented controversy, wittingly or unwittingly, by responding clumsily to the negative comments. Self-righteousness, even when one *is* righteous, doesn't convert or engage enraged people. Cowardly, confused politicians didn't help.

TANNENBAUM: It pretty much reaffirms what we're seeing today in Charlotte. Some little thing, like a bathroom and who is supposed to go in it, stirs up a national furor.

UMBERGER: A lot of people assume that *Angels* is the reason Charlotte Rep closed. That wasn't the reason. It was a supporting factor. People were tired. The theater staff was tired. The city was tired from all of the fighting. I was gone in 2002, and it lasted until 2005, but it happened when the economy was beginning to fail. Charlotte Rep needed another million bucks to keep healthy, but that money was nowhere to be found.

TOPPMAN: No one came out of this mess covered with glory, except the actors and technicians.

MARTIN: I have almost one and a half file drawers from *Angels*. Of the thousands of articles, there's one that's my favorite, an editorial from March 24, 1996, in the *Charlotte Observer*. The headline is "Bravo Charlotte Rep." "In this conservative city, on this matter, that took guts. Bravo."

I'M JUST THE SHADOW ON YOUR GRAVE

Belize

ROY

What's it like? After?

BELIZE

After . . . ?

ROY

This misery ends.

BELIZE

Hell or Heaven?

ROY

Aw, come on . . . Jesus Christ, who has time for these . . . games . . .

BELIZE

Like San Francisco.

ROY
A city. Good. I was worried . . . it'd be a garden. I hate that shit.

–Perestroika, Act 4, Scene 3

GEORGE C. WOLFE (director in New York, 1993–94): It was very important to believe that Belize was as smart and had just as aggressive a degree of intellectual rigor as Louis did. That was very, very important to me, because I didn't just want a black gay clown.

JEFFREY WRIGHT (Belize in New York, 1993–94, and on HBO, 2003): Belize's place there is not comic relief, although he's witty and all of that.

ADAM NEWBORN (Belize in Civic Theatre of Allentown, PA, 2017): To just play him sassy or shady or whatever is an insult to his intelligence.

JOSEPH MYDELL (Belize in London, 1993–94): I discussed this with Declan at some point: I just can't see him reacting to everything and just doing this kind of black charm. And Declan said, "Yes, you don't have to do black acting here." And I thought, *Oh, thank God*, because I want Belize to feel *real*, and not to put characters at ease by making jokes at his own expense. Tony didn't write it that way, but you could play it that way, and miss how challenging he is.

K. TODD FREEMAN (Belize in Los Angeles, 1992): Belize came quite naturally to me. Belize was just me. What I brought to it was me. I loved his sarcasm, the way he cut through bullshit with Roy and Louis. That's very much how I am as a person.

NATHAN STEWART-JARRETT (Belize in London, 2017, and New York, 2018): He's kind in ways that I couldn't be. Belize is so much more gracious. I haven't got that amount of grace at all.

DR. VERONICA ADES (director of global women's health, NYU School of Medicine): Belize is that intense because he's working at a time when the epidemic requires you to work at the top of your skills. There's certain kinds of nursing that aren't that intense. But he's on the forefront and he's facing the patient all the time.

OSKAR EUSTIS (co-director in Los Angeles, 1992): That first appearance of Belize in Prior's hospital room, Belize is a kind of angel himself. He is one of the real people in the play who will most turn out to be heavenly in his associations. I think that sense of mercy and kindness was at the heart of Belize from the beginning. What was hardest really was defending his edge.

STEWART-JARRETT: I'm not from New York but seeing black gay men walk around New York, they're very self-possessed. I think you kind of have to be, don't you? You have to say, "This is who I am," because it's going to be very difficult being that person, so you have to make it out quite clearly.

HARRY WATERS JR. (Belize in workshops and in San Francisco, 1989–91): Some of the funniest and most vicious people on earth are black drag queens! They can make you laugh and they can *e-vis-cer-ate* you. But that was about survival. You were always a target. If you weren't shooting at someone else, it was going to come at you.

CALDWELL TIDICUE (Bob the Drag Queen, *RuPaul's Drag Race*; Belize at Berkeley Rep, 2018): When you're a drag queen, you tend to have this sass that can't be defeated. You're always in the room, you're the one under good lighting, you're holding the microphone. Drag queens are superheroes and everyone else are mere mortals, and you carry that outside of your drag as well.

MYDELL: The physicality has to click. For me, it was when I got the sort of sashay walk that says: "I don't give a shit, take me or leave me, this is me." It's what we'd say in Savannah, Georgia, where I'm from: *There they go, switching down the street.* When you switch, your hips go from side to side, and it's like you just don't care.

KEVIN R. FREE (Belize at Charlotte Rep, 1996): I demanded hair extensions to play the role. I loved having this hair so much! I was constantly flipping my head.

I would answer a question and flip my hair. It was longer and braided, small braids, think cornrows. Think Bo Derek, but not a perfect 10.

WRIGHT: The breakthrough for me was when I stopped thinking about mannerism and affectation and the externals, and started to focus more on the internal qualities of the man. The humanity and compassion and fierceness and wit of the man were really vehicles for the glitter and the boas and the flamboyance. It wasn't the opposite. And so when I got that, then I got it, you know.

REG FLOWERS (Belize in national tour, 1994–95): There had been *Paris Is Burning*, right? A particular version of black queerness had become iconic. Madonna wrote "Vogue." That character seemed to me as though it had already been stamped on the world. So my feeling about Belize was: *Of course that character has to be in that play!*

TIDICUE: You never really get to quit drag. Drag always makes it back to you.

VINSON CUNNINGHAM (culture writer, *New Yorker*): Belize is weirdly not a token because even the white people are highly differentiated. There is a Jewish guy, and part of his deal is that he's *very* Jewish. There's a Mormon guy, and part of *his* deal is that he's Mormon and clueless. Even the white people are playing types. So you feel like he is part of this tapestry of types. There's that commonplace thing people say when discussing representation in art, that blackness is not a monolith. The play is a kind of argument that whiteness isn't a monolith, either.

IRA MADISON III (culture writer, *Daily Beast*): Belize did always feel like a black person written by a white person. Which is hard to get away from! I like that he confronts Louis about his ignorance. It's a good conversation to have. But, in a way, Belize exists in the play to sort of point out these things.

CUNNINGHAM: He does do a lot of checking people, which these days might play the falsest.

TIDICUE: As a black actor, in college, I think we've all done Belize's monologue about the national anthem for a character study.

WATERS: It was a gay epidemic, but the black character was peripheral. But here was a process where it was being rewritten and worked on. I remember this workshop we did. That had to be '90, '91? Several friends of mine came to the show. They gave me the charge that if you're going to play the role in this piece, there's a lot of responsibility. Even though it's written by this white Jewish guy, he's writing this character that represents us, and nobody else is giving us this opportunity.

There's a consciousness you have to have as an actor, with a story this bold and this broad, about what your participation is. I was aware that there was a community that I was a part of and that I was responsible to. I'm not sure the other actors would've felt that. But in New York in the '70s and '80s when AIDS hit, what was disturbing for me even then was that the voices of the black gay community were erased by the white voices screaming and

Belize (Jeffrey Wright) and Louis (Joe Mantello) on Broadway, 1993. (*Joan Marcus*)

hollering. I was losing so many friends during that period, who weren't getting the celebration, the notoriety, that white gays were getting.

Now, in *Perestroika*, there's much more. I think it was apparent, the focus that needed to be put on this other relationship, so Tony did more writing for Belize.

FREEMAN: I'm sure there are lines in *Perestroika* that I kind of came up with that are still there. Tony was great about that. He's very collaborative. He would say, "This is what this scene is about. How can I help you, what about what I've written is not helpful to you?" It's very rare for a playwright and very smart of him as well. He's kind of egoless when it comes to that. If he doesn't agree, he'll say absolutely not. But if you're stuck, he definitely wants to hear.

> The issue of a white writer writing a black character is so loaded. And I made mistakes when I started the play in 1988 and if I were doing it over again I probably wouldn't make him a nurse; having read Toni Morrison's *Playing in the Dark*, I would have avoided that. I didn't feel tremendously comfortable with the fact that I was writing a contemporary black character and I think some of that discomfort is embedded in the text of the play.
>
> –Tony Kushner, interview with the *Iowa Journal of Cultural Studies*, Spring 1995

MYDELL: I remember very distinctly that just as we got to Part 2, I had a conversation with him about Belize, saying, "Why is it that a black character's always an attendant to a white character? Why don't we know anything about Belize other than his relationship with Prior? Does he have a life outside being a nurse?" Then he wrote this incredible scene between Louis and Belize.

BELIZE

Just so's the record's straight. I love Prior but I was never in love with him.
I have a man, uptown, and I have since long before I first laid my eyes on the
sorry-ass sight of you.

LOUIS
I . . . I didn't know that you—

BELIZE
No 'cause you never bothered to ask.

—Perestroika, Act 4, Scene 5

WRIGHT: It was a fully collaborative process—not that we as actors were driving the writing process, obviously, but the work that we were doing informed the process, as it should.

WOLFE: I think we were working on something—I think I was working on something with Jeffrey and he was working on something that I think was much more complicated, and then as a result of what he did, I think it significantly informed rewrites that were done for the character in Part 2.

Nathan Stewart-Jarrett (Belize) and Andrew Garfield (Prior) in rehearsal, London, 2017. (*Helen Maybanks*)

WRIGHT: I can tell you the most memorable part of that experience was when Tony came in one day and said, "I've written a scene for you." And it was the heaven scene with Roy. There was a gap that I kind of had recognized, and he recognized, for that relationship between Belize and Roy, and he filled it with this incredible piece of poetry that was, like, an actor's perfect gift, you know?

BELIZE
Mmmm.
Big city, overgrown with weeds, but flowering weeds.

(Roy smiles and nods. Belize sits on the bed, next to Roy.)

BELIZE
On every corner a wrecking crew and something new and crooked going up catty-corner to that. Windows missing in every edifice like broken teeth, fierce gusts of gritty wind, and a gray, high sky full of ravens.

ROY
Isaiah.

BELIZE
Prophet birds, Roy.

–Perestroika, Act 4, Scene 3

STEWART-JARRETT: Oh yeah, the scene that no one understands. It's the scene where everyone changed their mind weekly about what it meant, and I, weirdly, started being like, "No, I know this." I don't really go on those huge emotional journeys that Harper goes on or Prior goes on, so there are certain moments that I call leakage, because I feel that Belize has a shell, and I think those moments are where the truth comes out, the heart is showing, you can see the cost.

NEWBORN: And I find that by the end of Belize's description of heaven I'm almost in tears. There's a vulnerability that Tony Kushner injects in that moment for Belize.

PAUL OAKLEY STOVALL (Belize at Kansas City Rep, 2015): This scene was very physical and erotic for me. Belize, to my mind, needed to be experiencing this heaven in order to relay it to Roy, and to juxtapose this complete physical ecstasy with Roy's physical state. There was a great love affair between Belize and Roy. This was a very delicate page in their journey together.

MARK WING-DAVEY (director at American Conservatory Theater, San Francisco, 1994–95): Belize is enjoying the irresponsibility of playing with someone's mind when they are—as Tony explains—on a morphine high, and their defenses are down. Roy behaves in a way that is—not kind, but unprotected. Put it that way.

NATHAN LANE (Roy in London, 2017, and New York, 2018): It's one of the few vulnerable moments he has. He just wants it to end, and because of the pain and the morphine he's like a child, and it's slightly flirtatious and also emotional.

MITCHELL HÉBERT (Roy at Round House/Olney in Bethesda, MD, 2016): Roy finally surrenders.

WRIGHT: That scene is the essence of who Belize is. Throughout, his actions are clear. He's clearly the compassionate heart of the play. But he's not there just for comfort. He represents, in this case, an enlightened humanity that is considerate and loving in spite of all the reasons not to be.

EUSTIS: I remember one of the complaints that Tony had sometimes about actors playing Belize was that in that first scene with Roy, they wouldn't always understand how deeply Belize hates Roy. It's not a catty dislike over a heart of gold. It's *hatred*.

FLOWERS: For my final callback I did the Roy Cohn scene, and it was really important to them that the actor playing Belize could do that scene. A lot of actors could do the fun, snappy stuff, but they were worried that the Belize they cast couldn't do that kind of venomous scene with Roy.

LANE: Nathan Stewart-Jarrett was saying, "I'm the only one in the play who's honest with him." It's not like they become friends, but there is a respect, a growing respect for one another, in the way they handle each other, that's really interesting and moving. And we have a moment: After the seizures and I pull the IV out of my arm and there's blood, and I'm back in the bed and he must bandage me, it's embarrassing and he knows it's not getting better and we just look at each other for a second. It's just one of my favorite things in the play.

EUSTIS: If Belize really is an angel of mercy, as he first appears, what would be his biggest challenge? How do you actually feel humanity towards Roy Cohn? Tony set this up to force Belize to come to terms with it. Belize has to believe that Roy is a bully and a traitor, but also see him as a victim.

> I wanted him to be the ideological counterweight to Roy, that there were two people in the play who were not lost and inert and swimming around deeply confused. I wanted there to be two people, one of the Left, and one of the Right, who had a very clear moral compass and knew exactly where they were in the universe at all times, and who were not in theoretical, ethical crisis.
>
> –Tony Kushner, interview with the *Iowa Journal of Cultural Studies*, Spring 1995

GREGORY WALLACE (Belize at American Conservatory Theater, San Francisco, 1994– 95): I think what is most striking about Belize is his capacity for empathy. It is a brittle and irreverent empathy that he's somehow able to maintain in the face of unbelievable malevolence and depravity. The fact that Belize has the grace to assemble an impromptu Kaddish, a final prayer and blessing, on behalf of one of the most despicable humans ever has always fascinated me.

EUSTIS: That Kaddish scene is really important to Louis, but it's essential to Belize. It's Belize's moment.

WALLACE: Belize is not always very friendly but he is generous, often begrudgingly so. As our country goes off the rails, more and more so each day, I find myself asking if I am capable of that sort of generosity with the people I so vehemently disagree with. I'm not so sure, but I do think Belize is onto something when he says,

BELIZE

Maybe . . . a queen can forgive her vanquished foe. It isn't easy, it doesn't count if it's easy, it's the hardest thing. Forgiveness.

–Perestroika, Act 5, Scene 3

CHAPTER 3

VERY STEVEN SPIELBERG

THE *ANGELS* FILM, 1991–2003

TONY KUSHNER: Cary Brokaw made contact fairly early on.

CARY BROKAW (producer at HBO, 2003): I courted him—not too forcefully. In 1991 we had dinner at the Greenwich Bar and Grill. I felt that he was beginning to trust my motives. "In an ideal world," I said, "who's the film-maker you'd want to direct this?" He said, "It's going to surprise you: Robert Altman."

STEPHEN SPINELLA (Prior in workshops, San Francisco, Los Angeles, New York, 1988–94): Tony had an enormous admiration for Altman. We all did. In the '70s, he was The Guy.

> It's not only structured like a movie—it's literally structured like an Altman movie. Quite literally, the form is stolen from "Nashville."
>
> –Tony Kushner, quoted in "Anxious in America," *New Yorker* Talk of the Town, December 26, 1994

KUSHNER: *Nashville* is one of the greatest films ever. It redefined the notion of an epic. It doesn't travel over a great distance temporally or geographically.

It takes a couple of days for *Nashville* to unfold, but it's this crazy quilt of all these intersecting lives.

MATTHEW SEIG (Robert Altman's employee; executor of the Altman estate): The '80s were a real low point in Bob's career. He was doing small television projects for which he'd receive no money. His self-image didn't seem to change any, though. Even though objectively you might say, "Wow, what a failure," he didn't look at it that way and neither did the people around him. There was no difference between making *Streamers* or making *Nashville*.

BROKAW: At that point I was in post-production with *The Player* and preparing *Short Cuts* with Bob. I had Bob go to a preview at the Taper and he, too, was knocked out.

SEIG: It was the kind of sprawling multi-character, multi-plot story that he was one of the originators of, and he loved the politics of it.

LIZ MANNE (co-founder and executive vice president, marketing, Fine Line Features, 1990–97): Bob rides back in with *The Player*, it's hugely successful, and I can't remember how many Academy nominations it got. We won critics' prize after critics' prize, the press coverage was unbelievable, in the independent film sector that year it was considered *the* critical and commercial success story.

IRA DEUTCHMAN (co-founder and president, Fine Line Features, 1990–94): Everybody wanted to do business with him. He was very clever, Bob, along with his agent Johnnie Planco, in trying to make sure that he wasn't going to have another lull. So they went to Cannes with two projects they wanted to get made back to back, *Short Cuts* and *Prêt-à-Porter*. They sold me on one without telling me about the other, and sold Miramax on the other without telling

Robert Altman at the Cannes Film Festival, May 18, 1992. Altman won Best Director for *The Player*. (*Gerard Julien/AFP/Getty Images*)

them about the one. So they walked away with two deals. *Short Cuts* at Fine Line and *Prêt-à-Porter* at Miramax. Of course they sold that one to Miramax. It was filled with models and sex.

KUSHNER: I called Chris Durang, because Altman filmed *Beyond Therapy*, just to see how he was treated. Chris said that Bob treated him nicely.

MICHAEL PETSHAFT (Tony Kushner's assistant, 1991–93): I went with Tony to a screening of *Short Cuts*. I don't remember if it was the Brill Building, it was some famous building, but we go into the elevator and go up and the elevator doors open and there Robert Altman is, smoking a joint. Altman looks at everybody in the audience, maybe twenty people, and he says, "I want you to watch this film, but I don't want you to tell me what you think."

BROKAW: We were working with Fine Line and New Line—we went to them first with *Angels* and they agreed to develop it as two movies.

DEUTCHMAN: We wanted to work with Bob again, even though *Short Cuts* wasn't hugely successful. It did OK. It was a *succès d'estime* rather than a *succès de moné*.

> After months of wrangling, Fine Line Features has nailed down its plan to produce back-to-back pix based on Tony Kushner's "Angels in America." Robert Altman will direct and Cary Brokaw will produce the pix, which will be released some time in 1995.
>
> —*Variety* Cannes Daily, May 13, 1994

KUSHNER: I was thrilled. I was really excited. When he was doing *Prêt-à-Porter* he said, "Come, you can follow me around Paris while I do location scouting and we can talk about *Angels in America*." We did not talk about *Angels in America*. At all. We did smoke pot in his hotel room with Annie Ross and Anouk Aimée. That was—I was happy!

BROKAW: Tony wrote two screenplays that somewhat condensed the plays but were largely quite true.

KUSHNER: I did, I sat down and I wrote a screenplay that I have not looked at since. We came up with some fun things. Bob didn't give me a great deal of guidance about what the film should be but I thought I needed to make it different from the play. There were things that I had wanted to try in the play, and this felt like an opportunity to explore some of those things.

Belize and Donald kiss.

BELIZE
(Doing Madeline Kahn in YOUNG FRANKENSTEIN:)
Careful, careful, the hair, the lips . . .

They start to kiss more passionately, smearing the make-up, and
Donald pulls Belize to the floor.

BELIZE
Taffeta, darling! TAFFETA! *TAFFETA!!!!*

–*Perestroika* screenplay, 1st draft, July 4, 1995

KUSHNER: I guess I felt: *OK, I don't know exactly what we're doing with this idea making a movie, but it should do things that it couldn't do onstage.* Prior's climb to heaven: He kept going from one floor of the hospital to another and things just kept getting weirder and weirder.

Then he comes to a floor on which there is an exact repeat of the
operating theater of the previous floor. This time the attending surgeons and
nurses turn to face Prior. They are surgically-masked, robed and gloved,
but their flesh is like marble and their eyes are flames. Great opalescent wings
suddenly spread out behind them.

–*Perestroika* screenplay, 1st draft, July 4, 1995

SPINELLA: I read a screenplay of it. I thought it was weird. It just went in this weird place, and I didn't understand why it wasn't more like the play. I never really understood why he went so far afield of what was happening in the play.

KUSHNER: I think it's OK to say this: Bob was obsessed with the idea of the Angel's penis. He loved that she's a hermaphrodite. He had seen two productions, the Taper and Broadway, and he was frustrated—he said, "Why doesn't she ever have a dick! She says she has one!" Every time I talked to him, he wanted to know! He had some idea for this weird multi-pronged penis that she'd . . . I wasn't sure why that was of such great interest to him.

> I mean it will have breasts and probably a little penis tucked away like David, and I think it will have feathers, down, instead of pubic hair, and I think it will be kind of beat-up and naked.
>
> –Robert Altman, interviewed winter 1996, in Deborah R. Geis and Steven F. Kruger's *Approaching the Millennium: Essays on Angels in America*

MANNE: We were planning on it being two movies. You have to remember the first cut we saw of *Short Cuts* was five hours long, which I swear was better than the final cut, which was still two and half or three hours long. And we had released *Hoop Dreams* at two hours and fifty minutes. If you think about it in the current world of quality television drama, now all of those would be miniseries.

DEUTCHMAN: Altman was insisting it was going to be two movies, financed as one movie, meaning he'd shoot it like one movie, release it like two movies. I am attracted to things like that and always have been. I'm not sure I would've released them a year apart, I might have done something more radical. Released them a month apart, kept them released. It differentiates it from the marketplace and makes it feel like an event.

BROKAW: We budgeted the movie and started casting.

The budget is based on the text of the play but, per our discussion, it does not include the portions of the text that are not in the New York production of Perestroika:

Council Room of the Continental Principalities (expanded)
The Streets of Heaven
A Smouldering Pit

—*Angels in America* budget memo from Nellie Nugiel to Cary Brokaw, April 20, 1994

BROKAW: That was when I approached Al Pacino about playing Roy Cohn. There was at least a preliminary conversation with Meryl and her representatives about playing Hannah.

MERYL STREEP (Hannah on HBO, 2003): I never even knew about it! I don't think I even knew it was happening. I saw the London production. I don't usually go to things and watch in a covetous way. I usually sit there and think, *How did they do that? I could never do that!*

BEN SHENKMAN (Louis at American Conservatory Theater, San Francisco, 1994–95, and on HBO, 2003): At some point, in the middle of the '90s, there was some idea about Robert Altman doing the movie. And I remember sitting around with somebody just sort of thinking about a cast for that movie, just, you know, like Daniel Day-Lewis as Prior and Meryl Streep as Hannah, you know?

KUSHNER: He wanted Robert Downey Jr. to play Louis. Not sure he ever asked him about that.

SPINELLA: I did meet Robert Altman. He came to the opening of *Angels* on Broadway. That was fun. I had no idea—I was hoping they would put me in the movie but there were no guarantees about anything.

BROKAW: We figured we could make two movies with Al, Meryl, and the rest of the cast to be determined for roughly $25 million. And New Line balked. They thought because it was about AIDS, it was so controversial, and they passed.

MANNE: I suspect the project just got bigger and bigger, and the money just didn't match, and Ira left, and New Line changed everything they were doing, and they were not risk-tolerant.

DEUTCHMAN: I don't remember the chronology that well, but somewhere in there I was fired. Maybe if I had still been there it would've happened.

> Tony Kushner's two-part "Angels in America" is headed for turn-around after disagreements between Kushner and Fine Line Features over whether to produce two separate pictures, as Kushner and director Robert Altman wanted, or a single one that encompasses the plays' combined seven hours of material.
>
> –Gary Levin, "High-Profile Gay-Themed Pix Hit Roadblocks," *Variety*, August 28, 1995

BROKAW: We shopped it around to every other studio twice. We cut the budget down to $20 million and had no takers.

> We're sitting there with a pair of gloves in a world that sells shoes.
>
> –Robert Altman, winter 1996, in *Approaching the Millennium: Essays on* Angels in America

MANNE: After Bob had a failure or two, *Prêt-à-Porter* and *Kansas City*, he no longer had the leverage he may have had after the combination of *The Player* and *Short Cuts*.

BROKAW: We talked to Colin Callender at HBO. Colin was a huge advocate of *Angels* even then. We cut the budget down to about $12 million but [president of HBO Pictures] Bob Cooper wasn't ready to take the leap.

KUSHNER: It was getting harder and harder to find Bob and get him pinned down to working on it. When we worked on it, he would throw out more and more ideas, it was never about refining what was there. I was beginning to get very, very nervous.

BROKAW: A while later Tony and Altman and I decided to part ways. Mostly amicably.

KUSHNER: Warren Beatty called me to ask me if I wanted to write *Bulworth*. He said, "I wonder if right now you're beginning to feel that Bob is not preparing for the film and you're being asked to solve a lot of things that you'd assume the director should solve."

And I said, "I am beginning to feel like that a little bit."

And he said, "You should really listen to that. You're going to wind up on the set with him, and holding this thing together is going to fall into your lap. Because he doesn't do that. He does other things." Then he told me this story: Altman had convinced him to convince Julie Christie to make *McCabe & Mrs. Miller* even though there was no script, just a vague idea and a location. Beatty said, "I'll convince her to do it, but you have to promise me there's going to be a script." Bob promised. Warren convinced Julie to do it. The day before she arrived in British Columbia to start filming there was no script. Warren said that he and Julie Christie's hairdresser went in a trailer and wrote the script for *McCabe & Mrs. Miller* so that when she landed they'd have something to show her.

I love the panache. The daredevil attitude on one level is so thrilling. But also I was like, *Holy shit, this guy's crazy. (Laughs.)* This was the mid-'90s, so I'd spent six or seven years structuring the plot of *Perestroika*, figuring all that shit out.

> If you decide to stick with the project, and I hope you do, we need to proceed to a discussion immediately on how exactly the screenplays are to develop. I really don't know how to make these films. I don't think I'm going to come up with any great ideas; I think the screenplays are good and they certainly represent my best shot. I can work on editing them and polishing them and giving you rewrites, but I don't want to reinvent this wheel a third time. A great deal of my slowness around this project has to do with a desperate need on my part to work on things other than *Angels*. I intend to spend most of this year writing a new play. So you'd need to take over in a big way, and make this your film. This may not be the kind of process you'd envisioned. I'd love to collaborate closely with you on some original film, but in the long run you're Robert Altman and I've never even been on a movie set, and I

asked you to immerse yourself in this morass all those years ago because I believe in your great vision and talent. . . .

I'm writing rather than calling because, frankly, you intimidate me—not because you've ever been anything other than generous and wonderful when we meet, but . . . you're too much of a daddy-introject for a wimp like me to feel pushy around. So excuse the letter. These are urgent matters and this is my best way of handling them.

—Letter from Kushner to Altman, February 13, 1996

KUSHNER: So I was in Cafe Flore in San Francisco and I just took a deep breath and called him up and said, "Listen, you know, I don't think we're doing this." And I could tell he was a little surprised.

BROKAW: P. J. Hogan attached himself for a period of time. He took a whack at the script and tried to condense it into one two-hour movie and it didn't work out. We still couldn't get anyone to bite. They would be delicate and tactful. (*Delicate and tactful voice:*) "It's a very *controversial*, *bold* movie about AIDS." And even with the cast, even with the pedigree—the consensus was that it was not gonna cross over to a mainstream audience.

MANNE: My guess is that it would have failed as a theatrical release. So, for example, if you looked at the ratings on HBO's *Angels in America*, and let's pretend that for every eyeball that watched it, you calculated a $15 or $13 ticket sale, I bet those grosses would not be $4 million. It would not be enough. And then the rule of thumb is marketing and distribution in the U.S. alone is equal to the production times two. So a $50 million P&L, then you've got $100 million that somehow you have to get back. It's absolutely impossible that those films would have made the money back.

BROKAW: And so it kind of went into a kind of somnolent state of waiting and seeing if something would change.

KUSHNER: Neil LaBute and I talked for quite a while about it.

NEIL LaBUTE (playwright and film director): It was primarily in 2001. I had kids who were Mormons, and that was gonna be a really tricky world for me to navigate. People within the church judged the play, often without seeing it, because of the combination of the religion and the poor choices that many of those characters made. I knew it would be a powder keg, although that didn't make me shy away as much as I don't think I was the right person. Like many projects, you end up being the person who watches it rather than the person who makes it.

KUSHNER: And then I really decided to give up. I would meet with Cary once or twice a year and say, "Go forth." He had this card in his pocket with names, you know, Martin Scorsese, every famous film director.

• • •

BROKAW: I was making *Wit* for HBO with Mike Nichols and Emma Thompson.

MARK HARRIS (journalist and Mike Nichols's biographer; Tony Kushner's husband): Mike said at one point: "Whenever you have a big noisy public failure"—I'm paraphrasing—"the next thing you do should be something you feel strongly about that you're just doing because you want to do it." The last theatrical movie that Mike had made was *What Planet Are You From?*, which was a huge bomb. He was already close to seventy, and one bomb when you're that age can make it a little harder to get a studio to give you a green light for a theatrical movie. So he made *Wit* for HBO.

BROKAW: We were staying in London, shooting at Pinewood Studios, and all through pre-production we would drive to and from set together every day. I had signed copies of *Angels* DHLed to my hotel in London and I gave them to Mike on Thursday or Friday. Diane Sawyer was supposed to come for the weekend, but then came down with the flu. It was a typical rainy weekend in London. Monday morning Mike has this huge Cheshire grin on his face: "I read all of *Angels*."

KUSHNER: I put down the phone and I said to Mark—it was like our first or second year together—"Should I let Mike Nichols direct *Angels in America?* He's a great filmmaker, but I don't know."

And Mark said, "Are you fucking kidding? Call him *immediately*."

HARRIS: When Mike became the wunderkind of Broadway, it was almost entirely by directing Neil Simon comedies and other lighter plays. As early as 1969 or 1970 one criticism he faced from his detractors was "Oh, you only direct fluff." Which I think was really unfair, but you can see his appetite to counter that right from the first movie he directed, *Who's Afraid of Virginia Woolf?* My theory is that later in his career Mike got attracted to taking bigger swings. *Death of a Salesman*. Pinter. Even Beckett in the '80s with *Godot* at Lincoln Center. He wanted to hit some of the theatrical benchmarks. And *Angels* had been one. I think he wanted to put his mark on some really big plays that people knew.

COMING OUT WITH ANGELS

SCOTT COHEN (law student): I tell my friends that the story is a conservative's worst nightmare. You know: BOOK TURNS KID GAY!

R. KURT OSENLUND (managing editor, *Out* magazine): *Angels in America* changed my life.

KRIS VIRE (theater editor, *Time Out Chicago*): It was a direct result of performing in *Angels* that I finally came out to my family.

MIKELL KOBER (theater producer): At the time I was not out to myself yet. I was very devout in the Church. I was the oldest of six. I had a wonderful family, wonderful parents. But homosexuality was not . . . I couldn't imagine myself as

lesbian any more than I could imagine myself an astronaut.

KYLE AARONS (actor): I'd known I was bisexual since I was a kid. I had a boyfriend in high school who was very physically abusive. In college, I was raped. So I just shut that side of me off. I focused on women. *Angels* helped me understand why I needed to come out.

OSENLUND: The film came out in 2003, right around the time I was coming out. I had that moment, you know, would my father rather have a gay son or a dead son? That was a real feeling.

AARONS: My junior year, I took a class, and my final scene was the "Are you a homo?" scene. And I had to leave the class, I was so upset. It just hit me: If I kept ignoring that part of myself, I was going to turn into Joe.

BROKAW: At this point Bob Cooper had left, and Chris Albrecht was running HBO with Colin Callender, the head of movies and miniseries. Three days later Colin came to visit us on the set. We told him we wanted to do *Angels* next, and he said, "Well, what's the budget?" And we gave him a number. It was a little bit out of the air.

COLIN CALLENDER (president of HBO Films, 1999–2008): There was no director in my mind better suited for *Angels in America*. Mike's background was as a theater director and as a film director. But also Mike's own personal journey, coming to America at the age of nine, not speaking any English. That opening speech with the rabbi saying "there are no more journeys like this"—talking about the journey from the shtetl to New York—that was Mike's personal journey.

BROKAW: We called Al, we called Meryl, we enlisted Emma. Colin greenlit it: 37 million and change. It was so fast.

VIRE: Summer of 1994 was the summer between my junior and senior years of high school. I was attending Arkansas Governor's School, on the campus of Hendrix College in Conway, Arkansas. One day at school, I was in the library, looking for some monologues or something. I ended up sitting there on the floor, in the stacks at the college library, for about three hours, reading both *Millennium Approaches* and *Perestroika*. It was as if a whole new world had opened up to me.

COHEN: It was taught to me as a high schooler. On some level, I knew that I was gay. I was beginning to realize it, and then this play landed at that time. I'm sure that's one reason why the teacher taught it to seventeen-year-olds, to help them figure this out.

KOBER: I was in a charter school for the performing and visual arts and we had a really, really wonderful head of the theater department. He had this massive book collection. I saw the book on the shelf and I read *"Gay Fantasia on National Themes"* and thought, *I don't know what that means but it sounds exciting*.

He knew I was Mormon and he was like, "Uh . . . are you sure you want to read that?" And when you're seventeen and a teacher says, "Maybe you should reconsider reading that," of *course* you're going to read it.

KEV BERRY (playwright): It was the first thing with real characters that I had come across who were gay. The more and more I read it, the more I felt the humanity of the gay characters in the play and saw them as real people, and appreciated that Tony Kushner saw them as real people, wrote them as real

DEUTCHMAN: The business model at HBO doesn't require that they be blockbusters. It just requires that people talk about them.

MANNE: HBO ultimately becomes the perfect, possibly the only place for it.

CALLENDER: You have to remember, in those days, the A-plus-level household name movie star still wouldn't do television. But Al Pacino said that he wasn't convinced that it would work in the cinema given the realities of independent filmmaking. He thought that HBO was a great place to do it because we wouldn't have to worry about opening weekend grosses.

HARRIS: In 2001, doing things for HBO was much less done by A-list directors or actors than it is now. By then it was clear there was not going to be any way to adapt *Angels* for a theatrical movie. So if he wanted to do *Angels*, it was pretty clear HBO was the option. Altman was never going to do it any

COMING OUT WITH *ANGELS* →

people with full political opinions and everything. It helped me make sense of the process of coming out.

KOBER: It was the first time I had seen myself as a Mormon, as someone who is part of this national dialogue. Because I was in Orlando, I felt invisible as a Mormon and invisible to myself as a lesbian. Having Mormon characters on stage with Jews and angels and prophets and gay people, it absolutely blew my mind. It told me that I played a part in this national progress, this gay fantasia. That was so empowering, and so powerful, that I would read the play over and over.

VIRE: Five years later I'm in college at the University of Arkansas, and we are doing *Millennium Approaches* and I am cast as

Joe. I'm, like, twenty-one at this point, and had been in the process of coming out for a couple of years. In the middle of a rehearsal for *Millennium*, I got on the phone to my dad, during a *break*. They were going to come see the show. I was going to—we were going through the scene where Joe was on the phone with Hannah, and I just thought, *I can't ask my parents to come see me play this scene without actually coming out to them first.*

OSENLUND: It taught me cultural references and helped me build my personal canon. I had never seen *Come Back, Little Sheba*, for example.

TRAVIS FOSTER (assistant professor of English, Villanova University): The play really changed my understanding of coming out. What it means to come out is not to be in this sort of individual project of self-affirmation; it is to be in a

way but in a theatrical movie. But the difference between HBO in 1995 and in 2001 was, in short, *The Sopranos*.

MARY-LOUISE PARKER (Harper on HBO, 2003): When a friend told me Mike Nichols was doing the movie, I said, "I'm so angry that you even told me

that, because I'm never gonna get that part, so I wish in the future you wouldn't give me that kind of news flash that is going to ruin my entire life."

STREEP: Mike asked me if I wanted to play three parts in *Angels in America*, and I said, "Yes!" And

Roy (Al Pacino) and Ethel (Meryl Streep) in the HBO miniseries, 2003. (*HBO/Stephen Goldblatt*)

really *political* project that is profoundly interconnected.

KEN URBAN (playwright): That play taught me that being gay is about more than who you sleep with. It's about a whole host of other things. I had never seen it dramatized before, but the relationship between economics, religion, sexual identity, and gender stuff.

OSENLUND: There was something great about "an angel is a belief that has arms that carry you." If it's just a belief in something that's greater than my Philadelphia suburban town, then maybe that's enough to give me hope. You can feel really hopeless when you're coming out. It gave me a kind of temporary religion.

I would walk out of my parents' basement and they'd say, "Why are you crying? What happened?" and I'd be

crying, saying, "Everything's fine! It's great!"

TONY KUSHNER: For gay kids, it's—it's so much easier now than it used to be, but it's still difficult. Feeling that you're fitting in, feeling that you're accepted, not feeling threatened, not feeling that you're going to be rejected by your own family, is still a struggle for gay kids and queer kids and trans kids. The play is saying that you're not immediately marginalized, you're not irrelevant. There's a national conversation, a conversation within your own community. Claims can be made for your centrality in that conversation. If the play serves as a touchstone of some sort, I think that's exciting. 🍃

then we signed the contract and he said, "Would you play a fourth part for free?" They hadn't included the Angel in the second part. He got me four for the price of three! He was a sly one.

PARKER: It was right around the time where I made this rule for myself that I was not gonna audition ever again. I had spent years auditioning all the time and I never got anything. I'm not a very good salesperson. Am I really gonna wash my hair and go to midtown for blah blah blah? And literally the next week they were like, "Mike Nichols is doing *Angels in America*, would you like to audition for it?" and I was like, "Ugh, I guess I can come out of retirement for that one."

SHENKMAN: It was in the casting breakdowns. I was like, yeah, but, you know, it's Meryl Streep and Al Pacino and Emma Thompson. It's all going to be household names. And then I heard that Mike Nichols had decided that, for the young men, that they didn't want household names, he would prefer guys that had some connection to the theater.

Louis (Ben Shenkman), Hannah (Meryl Streep), Prior (Justin Kirk), and Belize (Jeffrey Wright) in the HBO miniseries, 2003. (*HBO/Stephen Goldblatt*)

JUSTIN KIRK (Prior on HBO, 2003): I guess Mike Nichols had seen me in plays in New York. I don't think he was a big *Jack & Jill* aficionado.

SHENKMAN: When I heard that, I started to realize that I was sort of the exact right age and I fit that description pretty well. I'd been doing theater. And, you know, the guy had to be recognizably, iconically Jewish in a certain way. And on top of that, I had the whole history with it, and I was going to be able to audition with a certain knowledge of the character that not a lot of other actors were going to have.

So then I got scared, because I realized I was trapped. I wanted to go in and do this great audition, but I didn't want to get the part, because, on some deep level, I felt like I really wasn't up to it, not on that level, not on the Meryl Streep level. So I was sort of stuck. I didn't want to blow the audition, but I didn't want to get the part. Honestly, it was, like, terrifying.

KIRK: They flew me out to New York. I read with various Louises, including Ben. My agent said, "It was great, you couldn't have done better, you killed it." A week goes by, weeks go by, a month goes by. And then I got a call one day from fucking Mike Nichols on my cell phone.

PARKER: I went in and read almost every single scene in the play so I not only auditioned but pretty much performed the play. I still can't believe he gave me that part.

JEFFREY WRIGHT (Belize in New York, 1993–94; on HBO, 2003): I heard whispers about the movie. My thought was that no one was going to play Belize other than me, and if they tried to bring that into being, some sets might mysteriously burn to the ground.

BROKAW: Jeffrey was so brilliant onstage, there was no reason not to cast him. We struggled a lot with Stephen Spinella, who was also so brilliant onstage.

SPINELLA: Tony said, "Well, he wants you to do the movie," and I was like, "Tony, I'm in my forties! The guy is thirty! It's in the script!"

BROKAW: We agonized over it, but we realized he would just be too old.

WRIGHT: Mike came to a play that I was in at the time to see another actor who was in the play—names redacted to protect all involved. He came to the play with the intent of hiring another actor for Belize. And then, after seeing the show, he realized that he was mistaken, and so he *wisely (laughs)* asked me to be in the movie.

SHENKMAN: I confessed to a lot of my apprehensions the first time I met Mike Nichols. Right in the audition. The idea of getting the part just based on one audition or a second audition felt so terrifying that right away I said, "So I'm not exactly sure how that happened, and I'm not exactly sure how to do it again and again and again." And he was so wonderful. He essentially said, "That's movie acting. That's what all actors deal with."

ROBIN WEIGERT (the Mormon Mother on HBO, 2003): Emma Thompson wasn't available for the table read so I got to read the Angel with all those remarkable actors. Ben and I have known each other since we were little kids at school at Sidwell. I remember at the table read we both looked at each other like *Can you believe??*

PARKER: So often with scripts I'm just trying to make it sound like a human being is saying it. But with *Angels* it's like I'm just trying not to ruin it. It felt sacred.

KIRK: We had a long rehearsal process that mostly consisted of sitting around a table—minus the big three, Emma, Meryl, and Al—for a few weeks and we mostly talked, including stories from Mike.

SHENKMAN: They weren't Sidney Lumet rehearsals where you're doing your blocking.

PARKER: He directs anecdotally sometimes; he'll tell a story about his brother, rather than poring over the text.

TRIP CULLMAN (theater director, Nichols's assistant during Angels filming): I remember thinking, *Oh my God, when are we going to get to work? What the hell? This* *is so off topic!* And yet what it did was bond everyone together, create family, create trust and intimacy. It was rehearsing without rehearsing.

SHENKMAN: I had this sort of premonition that some of the stuff that helped redeem Louis onstage wouldn't work in the movie. I think two things redeem characters onstage that don't necessarily redeem them in the movies. One is funny lines, jokes. And the other is being the mouthpiece for the politics. The fact that this guy's rattling on and saying these witty putdowns of Ronald Reagan and stuff, that would bring the house down in the theater. But in the movie, it just made him a guy who very clearly had, you know, kind of channeled all his self-loathing into his politics.

And so that meant to me that the thing that would hold the audience was his soul. *(Laughs.)* What he was feeling. Which meant that I had to be emotionally transparent. And if I was even a little bit not emotionally transparent, the audience wouldn't connect to him.

WRIGHT: I was so looking forward to playing Belize on film, because the technical requirements are very different. There's an opportunity to distill everything down and refine the language that's unavailable to you onstage simply because you've gotta speak louder.

SHENKMAN: The first scene we shot was the diner scene, Democracy in America, and it was April Fools' Day 2002. *(Laughs.)* I remember that. I remember them thinking, *Oh man, have you seen how many pages we're supposed to shoot? We're going to be here a whole week.* And then, you know, we got it in one or two days. They weren't used to that dense theater level of dialogue, bang, bang, bang, bang, bang, bang, bang.

CULLMAN: My job was *(laughs)* not in any kind of official capacity, but I served a very specific purpose for the film indeed. Honestly, I was the only gay person on the entire creative team, including the actors. So basically I tried to help Mike with verisimilitude in terms of, like, the Central Park cruising sequence and what it looks like when gay guys cruise each other. Justin Kirk would ask me, you know, about effeminacy and how to get it as realistically as possible, because his character is more femme than some of the others.

KIRK: I'm sure lots of people more famous than me wanted that part, so I wanted to make Mike feel as though he'd made the right decision. I went home every night thinking, *Oh God, you didn't hit it.* I felt bad a lot of the time. Emma Thompson was very comforting to me during that whole process. She was actually my guardian angel, to be disgustingly corny about it.

CULLMAN: The vibe on the set was extremely joyful, creative—especially since he cast everyone and doubled them the way they are in the play, which I think is an unusual thing for film: You don't expect the same actor to play all these roles.

STREEP: I mean, how they could not do that! I mean, look at what it wants you to believe! Of course we doubled.

CULLMAN: Every time Meryl Streep would emerge from her dressing room, it was like, *Who the fuck is that?!*

BROKAW: We shot in spring and broke at the end of July. And then we ramped up again in September and finished shooting in the fall. Mike was seventy-four years old; it was important to him to have a break.

Emma Thompson (the Angel) and Mike Nichols on the set of the HBO miniseries, 2003. (*HBO/Stephen Goldblatt*)

KIRK: I did a play during our break, at Playwrights Horizons. And my entrance in the play, I came down off the catwalk and jumped onto the stage from the ladder. I remember I had a friend there and I wanted to impress him with a badass jump and I hurt myself, I fucked up my foot. I had to go to the emergency room, and I returned to the show on crutches. When I returned to *Angels* in the fall, I had been faking a limp for Prior's neuropathy, and now I had a real limp. But if it had been the other foot, we would have been fucked.

BROKAW: We shot heaven at Hadrian's Villa outside of Rome, which was incredibly expensive.

KIRK: It was cold and I was wearing a hospital gown and pretty much nothing else. You can only imagine! In many ways it was like the actor's nightmare.

FRANK RICH (chief theater critic, *New York Times*, 1980–93): It's one of the very, very few successful film adaptations of a major American play. Maybe one of three: Kazan's *Streetcar*, and Nichols's *Virginia Woolf*. Both Nichols and Kazan came out of the theater. They were able to shepherd these works to a new medium more successfully than—I mean, we could sit all day and talk about the embarrassingly bad movies of terrific plays.

SPINELLA: I thought one of the smartest things Mike Nichols did was, he just filmed the play. That's all you need to do.

ROCCO LANDESMAN (producer in New York, 1993–94): I'll never forget, we all came to the opening of the HBO movie. I thought it was a really good film. I go out, and I see Tony right after, and he has this sheepish look on his face, and I said to him, "You son of a bitch, you gave all those cuts to Mike Nichols that you wouldn't give to me!"

LaBUTE: It really sparked a career renaissance for Nichols. He had made some very forgettable movies in the years before that. But *Angels* was the beginning of a series of really great projects for him.

BROKAW: With all due respect to Bob Altman, I feel that he was a little too cynical for *Angels*.

DALE PECK (literary critic): That play, when it was written, was aimed at the Bush years, at the second decade of the AIDS epidemic. It was kind of a referendum on the Reagan presidency, and it reflected several years of very intensive and reasonably successful AIDS activism that changed how the disease was seen in America and the amount of political power and visibility the gay community had. It was a decade later when it appeared on TV, and the film version of the play didn't acknowledge that. It sort of treated it as timeless, like: "It's a story of the triumph of the human spirit" and blah blah blah.

MONICA PEARL (professor of English and American Studies, University of Manchester): The fact that the subtitle—*"A Gay Fantasia on National Themes"*—did not make it to the title of the film suggests on the one hand something about wanting to pander to a mainstream audience. But it also suggests that the country had become more aware—not more open to but more aware of—to the ways that homosexuality was important to the American landscape and American history.

CALLENDER: You know the final lines of the play, that gay people will survive and be citizens. When the play came out, that was a call to arms. That was aspirational, and defiant, so to speak. By the time we made it, it was a statement of fact. And the speech took on a completely different cast, as did much of the rest of the play. It was "we *are* going to survive." Through the determination and the commitment of so many people along the way.

> "Angels in America," the adaptation of Tony Kushner's two-part fantasy, set in the Reagan era, about AIDS, tolerance for gays and political hypocrisy, was the big winner at the awards show. The elaborately filmed epic cost about $60 million, one of television's most expensive series. . . .
> In all, "Angels in America" won 11 Emmys.
>
> –Bernard Weinraub, "HBO Is Big Winner at Emmy Awards," *New York Times*, September 20, 2004

SHENKMAN: (A) It was going to be probably the biggest audience the play had ever had; and (B) it was going to be the permanent record. And I'll tell you, it was so easy to imagine people saying, as is true of other plays, "Oh, one of the best plays I ever saw. Isn't it a shame about the movie?" Or it was even easier to imagine, like, "Isn't it a shame about the movie? I mean, Meryl Streep was great, but who were *those* guys?" But, yeah, to my great relief, it was not received in that sort of head-shaking way.

PARKER: I just wanted Tony and Mike to be happy. I'll never be happy with what I did in that movie, but as long as they were satisfied, I was OK.

KUSHNER: I remember this: Mike and I would watch scenes that he had filmed, together, and if Mike liked them, he used to say, *(Mike Nichols voice:)* "Well, that's what I meant."

ACT 5

1998–2018

SEPTEMBER
Don't Ask
Don't Tell
ends, allowing
LGBT people
to serve openly
in the U.S.
Armed Forces

MARCH
The first same-
sex marriage
takes place in
the United
Kingdom

NOVEMBER
Barack Obama
elected
president

1998 ——— **2004** ——— **2008** ——— **2010** ——— **2011** ——— **2013** ——— **2014** ———

JUNE
The
Journeymen
production
of *Angels
in America*,
directed by
David Cromer,
opens in
Chicago

NOVEMBER
Peter Eötvös's
opera of *Angels
in America*
premieres at
the Théâtre
du Châtelet in
Paris

MARCH
The Toneel-
groep Amster-
dam produc-
tion of *Angels
in America*,
directed by
Ivo van Hove,
premieres at
the Stadss-
chouwburg
Amsterdam

OCTOBER
*Angels in
America*
receives its first
major New
York revival at
the Signature
Theatre,
directed by
Michael Greif

JULY
Tony Kushner
awarded the
National Medal
of Arts and
Humanities

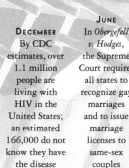

DECEMBER
By CDC estimates, over 1.1 million people are living with HIV in the United States; an estimated 166,000 do not know they have the disease

JUNE
In *Obergefell v. Hodges*, the Supreme Court requires all states to recognize gay marriages and to issue marriage licenses to same-sex couples

JUNE
The United Kingdom votes via referendum to leave the European Union

NOVEMBER
Donald Trump elected president

JULY
Donald Trump announces a ban on transgender people in the U.S. Armed Forces

2015   **2016**   **2017**   **2018**

OCTOBER
The Toneelgroep Amsterdam production of *Angels in America* performs at the Brooklyn Academy of Music

MAY
Angels in America opens in London at the Royal National Theatre, directed by Marianne Elliott

MARCH
The Royal National Theatre production of *Angels in America* transfers to the Neil Simon Theatre on Broadway for an eighteen-week run

APRIL
Angels in America opens at Berkeley Rep, directed by Tony Taccone

CHAPTER I

IT'S WHAT LIVING THINGS DO

ANGELS TRANSFORMED: THE JOURNEYMEN, CHICAGO, 1998; THE OPERA, 2004; TONEELGROEP AMSTERDAM, 2008–2015

DAVID CROMER (director and Louis in the Journeymen, Chicago, 1998): Here's what I think might be the thing about *Angels in America*. It's never been defined by a single production, and I don't think it can be. Lesser works, there might be a production that defines it. It's like *The Cherry Orchard*. It's not conquerable. It's a mountain you can never totally climb.

ELIZABETH LAIDLAW (the Angel in the Journeymen, 1998): David Cromer was at the beginning of honing his stripped-down style of this period, and he started with assembling his dream cast for this show in a reading.

CROMER: I started to feel that the idea that the play is gigantic wasn't totally true. People say it has to be done like a musical, you have to do something dazzling with it; but when I read it, I realized most of the whole thing is, like, two-person scenes on things like park benches.

ANNABEL ARMOUR (Hannah in the Journeymen, 1998): David brought together a group of people who devoted themselves to the play on next to no money, because it is a piece of genius.

CROMER: We did these readings over the course of a year, a year and a half. And then we rehearsed for four months. We met every night and kept working on it.

SCOTT PARKINSON (Prior in the Journeymen, 1998): We rehearsed whenever we could for months on end without the certainty of a theater to open in or even an opening date, to the point where I think many of us wondered whether or not the production would happen at all.

CROMER: Of course, no matter what, by the time you get to the end of the second play you're just *(laughs)* throwing shit up to get it done in time.

LAIDLAW: This production was *very* "Chicago storefront."

PARKINSON: It was a true all-hands-on-deck experience, with everyone pitching in on everything, even down to building props and prepping the theater space before we opened.

CROMER: We settled on saying it was directed by David Cromer and the Company. There were tons of ideas from everyone. I would kind of make the initial decision and the final decision at the end of what we had discussed.

PARKINSON: I think the whole thing eventually came in at under twenty grand or something.

CROMER: We did it in an alley configuration in an eighty-seat theater, two banks of audience on either side. Let's say when you went to the first bench scene, the bench would be on one extreme side. The audience would watch that, and you'd sneak on the Pitt apartment on the other end, so when that scene began, you'd look over there, and it had appeared.

JOHN JUDD (Roy in the Journeymen, 1998): Half the house was facing the other half with us in the middle. I think it was one of the ways we kept a communal spirit in our production. We could all see each other.

PARKINSON: The effects were done using the cheapest of theater magic combined with sheer imagination.

CROMER: We saved the magic for big gestures like the Angel.

LAIDLAW: There happened to be a rolling utility stair, like you might find in a warehouse, in the rehearsal space we were using. David asked me to climb up to the top, and he and one of our interns just pushed me around.

PARKINSON: We couldn't bring the Angel in from the ceiling in that space, but we absolutely wanted the effect of her crashing in directly above Prior's bed.

CROMER: We were in a bar one night, and we came up with this idea that we could shift the audience's perspective.

PARKINSON: With earsplitting sounds of a meteor hurtling towards the room, the lights momentarily blacked out, and in the blackout the bed that I was in was propped up from horizontal to vertical. Meanwhile, Elizabeth Laidlaw came in on a moving ladder unit from the opposite side of the stage.

The Angel (Elizabeth Laidlaw) and Prior (Scott Parkinson) in the Journeymen production, Chicago, 1998. (*Michael Brosilow*)

LAIDLAW: The stair ladder was painted the same stone gray as my gown, and it became an extension of the Angel, of my body—

CROMER: She was on a six-foot ladder, she is six feet tall, the wings came three feet over on either side, so she was twelve by twelve—

PARKINSON: Blindingly bright white lights suddenly came on from behind her, lights that momentarily disoriented the audience—

CROMER: And she unfurled—

PARKINSON: As their eyes adjusted they could see that it was now as if the Angel was hanging above me, although with the scene having been turned on a 90-degree angle.

LAIDLAW: I'm one-quarter Seminole-Creek, and I look it, and one of David's thoughts about the Angel of America is that she looked . . . American. Rather than blond and Anglican.

CROMER: When we were talking about the Continental Principalities, we thought maybe the American Angel isn't the Bethesda Angel.

JUDD: We performed the play in an un–air-conditioned church in June, July, and August of a very hot summer in Chicago.

CROMER: You were so happy when you got to a naked scene.

JUDD: On Saturdays we would do both parts with a two-hour dinner break. I loved and admired those Saturday audiences especially, as they sweltered and laughed and cried with us through the whole story.

JEFF CHRISTIAN (Joe in the Journeymen, 1998): For some reason, we scheduled both parts to be performed on the Fourth of July. We all chipped in and we ran down to a nearby hardware store to buy all the standing oscillating fans they had in stock. We all unpacked them together, plugged them in, and pointed them toward the area where the audience members would be spending their Independence Day. As funny as it sounds, it was a perfectly fitting way to celebrate being Americans.

> The Journeymen's beautifully acted, low-budget production offers even stronger proof that less is more. Eschewing almost any hint of large-scale spectacle, this black-box staging comes closer to the heart of Kushner's moving, funny work than either the New York or national version.
>
> –Albert Williams, "No-Frills Thrills," *Chicago Reader*, June 18, 1998

CHRISTIAN: One of the many benefits of playing in a small venue was that after almost every show I was able to make eye contact with someone in the house. I really did feel a tangible bond between individuals onstage and in the audience.

PARKINSON: They would sit in the aisles if there were no seats left, fanning themselves and always leaning forward, engaging with the material.

CROMER: In 1998, the triple cocktail had been invented, so you had to say in 1998: Do you think the play is dated now that the cocktail is out? The response to that is simple: It isn't different for Prior. Prior doesn't have a cocktail.

PARKINSON: I feel like I hear people calling the play "dated" a lot, or opining about whether or not it will stand the test of time. First of all, who cares? Its importance remains undisturbed by whether or not it will be read and studied in schools one day. But I suspect that it will in fact still be done in a hundred years. It taps into something so fundamental about our struggle with how to change, about how to progress forward as a citizenry and as a species, and I suspect it will remain relevant to us for as long as those things are relevant.

● ● ●

The world premiere opera of *Angels in America* as composed by
Peter Eötvös will debut at the Théâtre du Châtelet in Paris, France
Nov. 23-29. Philippe Calvario directs.

Featuring a libretto by Mari Mezei based on Kushner's plays,
Angels in America is an opera in two parts. The Théâtre du Châtelet commission is compressed into a roughly 2½-hour work to be
sung in English.

–Ernio Hernandez, "Roy Cohn Sings! Tony Kushner's *Angels in
America* to Debut as Opera in Paris; Julia Migenes Is Harper,"
Playbill, November 17, 2004

PETER EÖTVÖS (composer, *Angels in America* opera): Upon reading *Angels in
America* I could immediately hear what my opera will sound like, and I knew
I have found the perfect subject to my "American opera."

DANIEL BELCHER (Prior in *Angels in America* opera, Théâtre du Châtelet, Paris, 2004): I
was auditioning—oof, this is probably 2001—a general audition. At the end of
the audition, the head of the company came up to me and said, "I have a project
in mind but I need you to meet the composer. Do you know *Angels in America?*"

And I said, "Yes."

So they said, "Can you go to Amsterdam tomorrow?"

So they sent me from Paris to Amsterdam to meet the composer. I sang
Billy Budd's soliloquy for him. We talked a bit; he said, "You'll be perfect."
And I said, "Uh, Maestro, what role will I be playing?" And he said, "Prior
Walter," and I just about fell over.

> I had one conversation with Mr. Eotvos, and he asked if I'd be inter-
> ested in organizing a libretto. And I said: "No [expletive] way, it's
> seven hours of text. I really recommend you find one string of scenes
> or just do Prior's story or just do Roy and Joe, and boil it down."
>
> –Tony Kushner, interview with Zachary Woolfe in "Don't Talk
> Too Much: Tony Kushner on an Operatic 'Angels in America,'"
> *New York Times*, June 9, 2017

SAM HELFRICH (director of *Angels in America* opera, City Opera, New York, 2017):
It's not so much an adaptation of the play as a distillation of the play. I don't
think one precludes the other.

EÖTVÖS: The profoundly human story of imagination's power over everyday suffering is what moved me the most.

BELCHER: Peter's wife, Mari [Mezei], adapted—well, truncated—the text of the plays to about one-tenth of the text. Peter really wanted to tell the whole story from the aspect of Prior. So some of the roles, like Roy Cohn, weren't nearly as thoroughly drawn as in the play. It was much more focused on the fantastical, on why the angels are choosing this man, and his journey.

HELFRICH: It's not an AIDS play anymore. When we saw the play on Broadway, there was no other lens to see it through. But the play is a quarter of a century old now. The AIDS epidemic has totally changed. The opera cuts out the background political stuff. What you're left with is a four-way relationship, Harper and Joe and Prior and Louis.

EÖTVÖS: In my distilled and—because of the music—elevated version on Kushner's original play, everything timeless and generally human matters way more than the play's take on America in the '80s. I find that Roy Cohn being himself on my opera stage is just enough historical allusion in itself.

Prior Walter (Andrew Garland) and the rest of the cast in the Bethesda Fountain scene, New York City Opera production of *Angels in America*, 2017. (*Sarah Shatz*)

BELCHER: A moment can be very extended in opera. In *Angels*, a lot of the text was spoken on pitch, so it was a lot more idiomatic in terms of its delivery.

EÖTVÖS: I am attracted to two voice types the most: mezzo-soprano and baritone. I find these two voice types the closest to the natural human voice range. Prior is a baritone. He is human. The Angel is a high soprano, which is a kind of a surreal voice type. There is your scale from real to imaginary.

BELCHER: I remember at some point saying to Peter, "You know, my part starts out very low, and by the end I'm at the top of my range." And he said "Danny, that mirrors your ascent to heaven. By the end you're at the top."

HELFRICH: There's this phenomenal musical touch in the opera, an offstage trio that sings almost constantly from the pit. They keep singing echoes of what the characters are seeing and thinking. It's fascinating. It's like the voice of the pit is the psychology of the characters. One of them sings in a high, chirpy voice, the other voice on the end of the phone of the Roy Cohn scene.

> Every time I do a new production of "Perestroika," the thing
> that has tormented me the most is the angel's epistle with Prior.
> And Eotvos's setting of it, the kind of blood-freezing, apocalyptic
> chiming of it, the warmth of parts of it, I found electrifying.
>
> –Tony Kushner in "Don't Talk Too Much: Tony Kushner on an
> Operatic 'Angels in America,'" *New York Times*, June 9, 2017

HELFRICH: The biggest challenge was to get the singers to—not to ask them to be theater actors, but to get them to let go of some of their assumptions about what acting is in an opera. Most three-year vocal conservatories, you get one semester of acting training, and it's focused on movement so you can walk across the stage gracefully and do *Marriage of Figaro* in a ball gown. I pushed this cast to play against those instincts.

BELCHER: My daughter was born a few weeks before we premiered. When I was asking for more life—you know, "What do you want?" "More life"—we were navigating my daughter's health. She had just had surgery to remove part of her lung because of a congenital illness. So it took on this extra meaning for me.

> If you don't know the story at all, I'm not entirely sure you can follow it. But I chose to sort of relax about that a third of the way through the first time and look at it as a meditation on people in the middle of a modern plague. I thought it was a wonderful distillation of at least part of the spirit of the play, and, in a way, who cares? It's its own work of art.
>
> –Kushner in "Don't Talk Too Much: Tony Kushner on an Operatic 'Angels in America,'" *New York Times*, June 9, 2017

HELFRICH: Harper's story disappears. Louis's. Joe's. Roy Cohn's. They all disappear, and they never get resolved in the opera. The play ties up all these threads, the opera instead gives you this cross section of humanity in crisis.

Music is structure, and structure is freeing. You can take a pause in a play to have a set change, but you can't in the opera. The heaven scene and Bethesda Fountain cross over, musically. You can't stop in between them. And it's not an accident.

BELCHER: Now New York City Opera's doing it, and a buddy of mine is doing the role of Prior. He asked me if I had any advice. I said, "Do what Peter put on the page, it makes sense, it heightens the text, and you're in for the ride of a lifetime."

• • •

HANS KESTING (Roy in Toneelgroep Amsterdam, 2008–15): I saw the first Dutch production of *Angels* in 1995 in Rotterdam.

IVO VAN HOVE (director of Toneelgroep Amsterdam, 2008–15): My good luck, I wanted to do it already in the beginning of the '90s, but someone had the rights already. And Holland is such a small country you cannot do the same play, it's not possible.

KESTING: I went on a Saturday afternoon for both parts. It was in Dutch. I was completely riveted. I had an amazing afternoon. I was really, really moved. It had all these theatricalities, the Angel coming at you. Little did I know I would be in an *Angels* production with no stagecraft of that kind!

VAN HOVE: We had the design of a huge set. I'm not gonna say what it was exactly. *(Pause.)* It was a hospital-like situation.

KESTING: They first had an idea of an enormous staircase spiraling up to the roof of the theater. And hospital beds.

EELCO SMITS (Prior in Toneelgroep Amsterdam, 2008–15): Complete hospital scene.

JAN VERSWEYVELD (designer, Toneelgroep Amsterdam, 2008–15; van Hove's partner): It was also a womb. It had a kind of liver/skin color, and it was completely closed on all sides. It only had a big spiral staircase, like a DNA helix, like an umbilical cord.

We were, in our analysis, looking for a space where transition is the most important thing. Transition in a society. Transition in various areas

Roy (Hans Kesting) and Belize (Roeland Fernhout) in Toneelgroep Amsterdam's production, 2007. (*Jan Versweyveld*)

of a human's life. An emergency room or a hospital is a place of transition, especially from life to death.

VAN HOVE: Suddenly, I was so annoyed that we were going for such a big, large-scale set design. And I called Jan from home, and I said, "I have this strange—something that hounds me. I feel that it's too much." And he said, "What would you want?" I said, "I think . . . I . . . I don't need anything!"

VERSWEYVELD: So then we said, "Yeah, OK, what space is a better space for transition than the stage of a theater? Everything is possible there."

KESTING: That's very typical in Dutch theater, a bare stage. Everyone has experience with saying, "Look at the horse coming!" and there is no horse.

SMITS: The audience can imagine the horse.

VAN HOVE: I say an empty stage but it's a light design. The light situation is quite complicated.

VERSWEYVELD: I added a few little things which created a space in which Ivo could work: some hanging fluorescent fixtures, laterally from the back of the stage to the front. We created projection screens, because video was going to be an important issue, but we created it in a way that you could hardly distinguish them from the theater itself.

TAL YARDEN (video designer, Toneelgroep Amsterdam, 2008–15): It's something Jan really excels at. It's really about creating a theatrical space, but it doesn't have theatrical intention in it. It's like an installation, like walking into a gallery.

VAN HOVE: Video was also an important element but very subdued. So sometimes New York, but sometimes a video image was there for half an hour.

VERSWEYVELD: They were not intended to explain.

YARDEN: I had lived through the '80s in New York City, I had friends who had died of AIDS, so there were places that to me were very important that I added in. There's a very abstract projection of a brick wall with windows, and one window has a red curtain hanging out. That was an image that I found when I went over to St. Vincent's [Hospital]. To me, that was the epicenter of AIDS care back then, where the first AIDS wards were, where I first visited people. I went over there to film the emergency entry, but then, looking at the nurses' quarters across the street, I saw that image.

VERSWEYVELD: We had a record player and vinyls on the stage.

VAN HOVE: I had decided immediately to use David Bowie's music because I wanted the era of the end of the '70s, beginning of the '80s to be there, and to me that's David Bowie. It's a very impulsive, emotional, simple thing.

MARIEKE HEEBINK (Hannah in Toneelgroep Amsterdam, 2008–15): We heard the stage would be naked for this and we couldn't imagine how that would happen.

VAN HOVE: I started rehearsal and of course this empty stage was a burden, because to have nothing is really hard.

KESTING: My first scene, I got terribly frustrated, very irritated. Not having a switchboard, a telephone. I have to talk to this woman, that man, Baby Doll. Ivo said just use your thumb and finger as a phone! And switch hands when you change calls. I thought, *How can this work?* And this is my introduction!

VERSWEYVELD: Ivo as a director is extremely well prepared. He has numerous sessions with the dramaturg, ten, twelve sessions, two hours each, where they really analyze each word. He has that in his backpack when he enters the rehearsal room, then he can watch the actors, let them be free. It's only when something happens where we need a prepared idea because it's not working out that Ivo says, "OK, we can do it this way or that way."

VAN HOVE: We discover the play together. It's really an exchange, like trial and error.

KESTING: But having worked with Ivo a long time, you know these moments are always there. He comes up, or Jan comes up, with solutions, or we come up with solutions because Ivo trusts our impulses, that are sometimes risqué or not the safe thing to do.

SMITS: But you'd never say no.

KESTING: So Ivo would say, *(steps back, Ivo van Hove voice:)* "Something has to happen." You have to come up with some—

HEEBINK: Super-solution.

KESTING: You have to create! "Something has to happen." He is always saying that.

VERSWEYVELD: We ended up, with Roy Cohn, in the end, when he's in his final stage, he's like a bag lady dragging a whole bunch of machinery with him, a breathing machine, drips, blood, urine, so your whole body gets taken outside, in a way. And in the final stage, Roy was in a big diaper, and a hospital gown, open in the back.

VAN HOVE: It's a private story. Jan, who is also my partner, was in a hospital for a thing. He wasn't in his room and I saw him in a corridor walking very far away with his IV stand. He didn't have a diaper but he had this little, this very simple gown. And I saw him walking slowly. That was the image for me.

> He starts walking across the stage, and he farted. I don't know how he did it—this long, horrible sound, and it was so humiliating and hideous.
>
> –Tony Kushner, quoted in Rosemarie Tichler and Barry Jay Kaplan's *The Playwright at Work*

KESTING: The idea was when I meet Ethel, and I say to her, "I'm still a member of the bar," and she says, "No, you've been disbarred." And then all the diarrhea I had been holding all pours out.

SMITS: We did it with actual "diarrhea" first.

KESTING: Yes. But it didn't work, and anyway that was a breach of the contract not to use any stagecraft like that.

SMITS: So we kept the sound.

VAN HOVE: He just—*(blows a raspberry)*—with his mouth. He turned his head. It was all self-contained what the actors did! There was no trick.

> It's the first time I realized that this is a play about AIDS, but it's also really a play about illness. . . . It really was a play about watching a body die.
>
> –Kushner, quoted in *The Playwright at Work*

VAN HOVE: The last week was hell because I made a lot of changes. One of them was a whole day of work just for entrances and exits.

VERSWEYVELD: We were in a very small rehearsal room, and then suddenly, of course, we came on the big stage in Amsterdam.

KESTING: The big theater at the Stadsschouwburg—very illustrious, lots of decorations, but then a bare stage.

VERSWEYVELD: The space was five or six times—maybe more—the surface of the rehearsal room.

KESTING: It was a complete liberation. From the first moment on, it felt that everything worked. And so each scene finally found its form in the actual space where we're going to play.

VAN HOVE: The day before opening night, the ending of Part 1 I wasn't happy with.

SMITS: When we rehearsed it, Ivo had the Angel, who was just an actor dressed as a hospital nurse, simply enter, and we listened to music together. And it was really not enough. I could feel it was not enough.

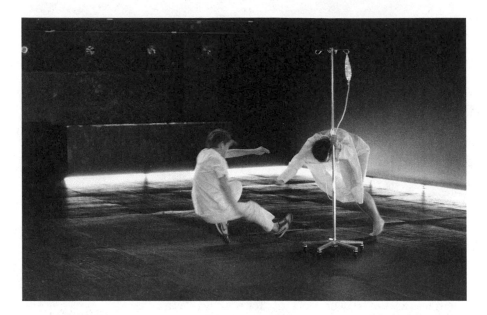

VAN HOVE: I came up with this idea that the Angel should spin him around, like getting him out of his comfort zone. It's almost like a voodoo ritual.

SMITS: At the last moment he made this character grabbing me and swirling me around. Which felt good, but also very dangerous and very frightening. I felt that was what it needed, that it became physical and hurtful. It's all about pain.

VAN HOVE: Eelco, who played Prior, it was his first really big main part. So he was also afraid. And tired and exhausted and so many things were at stake for him in his mind.

VERSWEYVELD: He was just, already, he was filled up. Eelco had to fall on the floor like six or seven times, and he just couldn't cope with that extra challenge anymore, on top of doing the show for a few hours.

SMITS: I actually had a little bit of a fight with him.

VERSWEYVELD: It was really confrontational between Ivo and Eelco at that time. He just didn't want to do it.

The Angel (Alwin Pulinckx) and Prior (Eelco Smits) in Toneelgroep Amsterdam's production, 2007. (*Jan Versweyveld*)

SMITS: It felt stupid.

VERSWEYVELD: Ivo said something like "OK, then maybe it's not good to play Prior if you cannot do this, it's a part of him, to embrace everything." And I think the next day it was solved and we just did it.

SMITS: We first did the show for people from the AIDS foundation, and this one man came up to me and said, being thrown around, that's what that disease is.

VERSWEYVELD: For me, it was like he was trying to get him either to die or to live, the pivotal moment between life and death, but physically it was an *enormous* challenge.

> Kushner first saw van Hove's rendering of "Angels" in 2009, and wept at the scene. "It was shattering," he told me. "By the sixth time you watch this guy get thrown and land on his butt, your butt starts to hurt. The playfulness of it made the cruelty of it so much more sharp and disturbing: you are dying, with this very silly, undignified thing going on."
>
> –Rebecca Mead, "Theatre Laid Bare," *New Yorker*, October 26, 2015

VAN HOVE: I cut the whole ending, the epilogue.

SMITS: I didn't miss it.

KESTING: I saw it in the production in Rotterdam. I found it very redundant somehow. I didn't like it at all.

VAN HOVE: The epilogue is really, like, so feel-good. *(Whispers:)* It's very American.

JIM NICOLA (artistic director, New York Theatre Workshop): The last image of the play was this extraordinary sequence of light and sound with the body of Roy Cohn wrapped in a white sheet, and upstage was a black-and-white film of waves crashing on a shoreline, and then lights slowly receding upstage, like the sun was setting, or shadows were consuming the space.

YARDEN: I had gone out to the end of Rockaway Beach, which is referenced in the play as a cruising area. I went there and filmed the empty beach, it might have been late fall. There was something very significant and emotional about filming out there, this idea of a kind of quiet, clandestine, anonymous space in which to engage in sexual activity and be released from the world in that moment.

VERSWEYVELD: The light physically shrinks onstage, on him; Roy becomes in the shadow, and you see the sea.

NICOLA: And then it extinguished the imagery of the sea, leaving us with the sound of the waves. And then out. It had this amazing sense of the frailness, the littleness of the human life in the spectrum of the universe. There were some people who had a more direct experience of the plague years here who found that hard to take.

VAN HOVE: They have a beautiful French word, *tristesse*. It's, like, this is life. You can cry with it and laugh a little bit with that. Of course life has an end. It's not sad in a tragic way. It's not a tragedy.

It's not the end of the world. It's the acceptance of the continuation of the world, whatever happens.

It felt cosmic, this ending, to me.

KESTING: What was most important was what Kushner thought.

HEEBINK: When he came to see the play, they didn't tell us. Only he comes onstage at the end.

KESTING: During the curtain call. They announced, "This is a special moment, we have the writer here." And we were like, "What?"

HEEBINK: It was good they didn't tell us he was coming. Tony said, "It is always the case that actors hear I am coming, they have a bad night, and then they feel bad, and I have to make them feel better, and I'm so bored by that."

KESTING: You could really feel that he had gone through something he had not gone through before.

VERSWEYVELD: We were very excited and very . . . unsure . . . that it was going to work OK in New York in 2014. It's like going into the fire with it. OK, this is not going to work at all, the American public is going to hate it.

HEEBINK: Right before I went on, Ivo came to me backstage, said, "Come on girl, give it big energy!" Usually he doesn't do that.

KESTING: In Holland, when the play started with the rabbi, it was very quiet. Maybe a bit of giggling, but it was mostly a nonevent. Is that fair?

HEEBINK: Yes. A nonevent.

KESTING: But in New York, there was huge laughter immediately! At first we thought they are laughing at us, the actors, but no, this is their play, these are their characters, this is their world. It was so . . . gave us wings, you know.

HEEBINK: Immediately there was enormous laughter! I came off, Ivo said, "Bring it down! Slow it down!"

VERSWEYVELD: We were very happy. *Angels in America* ignited something where we could also work on Broadway, things like that. It was a big success.

NICOLA: What I saw was something you see in a great play. Like Shakespeare. The people who do it make their own metaphor, their own mythology of it. I felt, *Well, this is a play that will have many different meanings as it moves on to the future.*

I SAW SOMETHING ONLY I COULD SEE

Harper Pitt (and Martin)

HARPER
Night flight to San Francisco. Chase the moon across America. God!
It's been years since I was on a plane!

–Perestroika, Act 5, Scene 8

I do love the character that Tony has written for me, Harper Amity Pitt. Lapsed Mormon, bad girl, Valium addict, an incredibly pained but beautifully sensitive woman. Married to someone who turned out to be a gay Republican.

–from Lorri Holt's journals, December 1988

TONY KUSHNER: I wrote the part of Harper for Lorri Holt.

LORRI HOLT (Harper in workshops, 1988–90): I remember Tony being frustrated by the character of Harper. He used to say to me, "So, I don't know what to do with Harper." And then I just would say some—I would make some comments.

RICHARD SEYD (Eureka Theatre company member, 1980–88): By this point Tony Kushner had a real idea of actors. The advantage of writing for actors is you write within their range, you write to their strengths. The role and the actor tend to fit like a hand in a glove.

HOLT: And he would go away and write these scenes and come right back. And I would say, "This is great." And then I would read them, and then he would say, "You made it work. How did you do that?" He just knew what to do. I think it was, like, this magic—he's really skilled at getting into the minds of other people. And he worries about it all the time.

SEYD: I think she would've been a remarkable Harper.

HOLT: When it was eventually done at ACT, in San Francisco, I was asked to understudy it. And then I finally, finally got to do the second part in a production. Julia Gibson—who played Harper—went back to New York for a few days and I got to do *Perestroika* for three nights. For me, it was, at least I get to do this monologue that I—I really wanted to do. And it felt like bringing something full circle. I wish Tony would have been there. I wish somebody would have been there who was part of the original thing to see me do it.

DEBORAH GEIS (co-editor, *Approaching the Millennium: Essays on Angels in America*): Harper is someone who is at times marginalized in discussions about the play. So much focus goes towards Joe or Louis. Poor Harper is there on the margins. She's struggling.

OSKAR EUSTIS (co-director in Los Angeles, 1992): Harper's a hard part. Tony would occasionally refer to her as the character from hell.

ELLEN McLAUGHLIN (the Angel in workshops, San Francisco, Los Angeles, New York, 1990–94): She is, in some ways, as remarkable an achievement as the character of Prior is. That nuanced prophetess that she is. It's unique in American literature, I think.

EUSTIS: Harper suffers and doesn't do much until the end of *Perestroika*. To find somebody who can play that character, keep her alive and sympathetic through several hours of passivity, is very hard. Couple with that the fact that from the very beginning Harper is a poet. What's tended to work the best for Harper is that you get somebody who absolutely has the imagination and poetry so that you believe in them as an artist, as a poet, but also is tough enough and has enough of an edge that the character doesn't become droopy and self-pitying.

HEIDI KETTENRING (Harper at Court Theatre, Chicago, 2012): Oh, Harper was fun to play. And hard to play. And exciting to play. And wretched to play.

ZOE KAZAN (Harper at Signature Theatre, New York, 2010): The material was *tough* in the way a person is tough: It has a background and a history and internal rules and logic, and you can be doing a great job but not the right great job for the play.

MARCIA GAY HARDEN (Harper in New York, 1993–94): In acting, one is demanded to make it personal. If it's not personal, it's boring. It's painful to remember it. And yet, I think everyone going through that play went to those places.

McLAUGHLIN: She's a very hard character to get right, but she's one of the great characters. I've watched a lot of people work on it.

KAZAN: To prep me to play the part I think, after the audition, Tony dropped off a Laurie Anderson mixtape he had made for me.

CYNTHIA MACE (Harper in Los Angeles, 1992): She's not sad. She's a fighter. In her own way.

KAZAN: There are a lot of ways of looking at that character from the outside: She's crazy; she's not crazy; she just has an active imagination; she's using; she's not using; she just needs something to change her.

ANNE DARRAGH (Harper in San Francisco, 1991): I think Harper is really smart. And she's trapped in this very limited palette of looking at the world that she's been taught. She knows it doesn't fit but she doesn't have anything else. The tension between those two things is driving her crazy.

GRETCHEN KLINEDINST FURST (Harper at Civic Theatre of Allentown, PA, 2017): I hate when people say she's crazy. If that's all they see, they don't get it.

CLARE HOLMAN (Harper in London, 1992): Well, she's kind of crazy! But very, very funny.

MACE: Oskar would say, "You're too funny," and I would say, "Oh, darling, I'm in more pain than anyone you know, but humor is the best defense."

KAZAN: She's a seer, the way Harold Bloom talks about Juliet being a seer. She's a visionary, she has visions, connected to science and the real world, connected to something greater—but that something greater is our humanity rather than an externalized God.

ENID GRAHAM (Harper in Juilliard *Millennium* workshop, 1992): There's really a red herring in the role about her being addicted to Valium. There's a trap there. The reason she takes Valium is to stop her mind from running away.

KATE GOEHRING (Harper in national tour, 1994–95): You're meeting her on the first day that the Valium did *not* work.

HOLMAN: All those instincts that sometimes women have, when they're being wronged, and people tell them they're being hysterical—they were all encapsulated in Harper. Her instincts were right! She *was* being betrayed.

HARDEN: There was an incredibly emotional journey that she was going on, and she was *angry*.

DENISE GOUGH (Harper in London, 2017, and New York, 2018): One of the reviews said that I had chosen to play her as a sad depressive and that made her tedious company. Why should she be charming company?

HARDEN: Desperately seeking a way to connect with her true self, with God, and with her husband, whom she loved. But she knew that something was not clicking.

GOUGH: I don't want my girl to be like *(baby voice:)* "I'm so so out of my mind that I'm just gonna burn everything because I'm so so sad that you're not here." *(Shakes head.)* It's like the Ophelia effect, I can't bear it. So often they're kind of wheeled out and when the men let them down they just go mad. I don't know any women for whom that happens. The women I know get angry, get mad, get bitter, get—*(growls)*!

DARRAGH: She deeply loves Joe. She really doesn't want him to be miserable even though he's making her miserable.

Harper (Denise Gough) in London, 2017. *(Frank Herholdt)*

KATHLEEN DENNEHY (Harper at Dallas Theater Center, 1996): They married as young naïve children, and then, through their separate crimes and omissions, adulted the fuck out of each other. They forced each other to grow up and apart.

KETTENRING: Joe protects her. Joe keeps her safe. Joe got her out of Utah.

DENNEHY: He got her the fuck out of Utah and he has health insurance.

JULIA GIBSON (Harper at American Conservatory Theater, San Francisco, 1994–95): We each had created extensive bios for ourselves, then came in front of the cast and told a little about ourselves and answered questions. The day I was interviewed as Harper, Tony Kushner was there. Afterwards he told me that I got everything wrong. Our version was more stereotypical pure, innocent, clean-cut Mormon—and his was darker. He told me that Harper was an unhappy misfit in her community who wore acid rock T-shirts and had dirty hair.

JOE

I don't have any sexual feelings for you, Harper. And I don't think I ever did.

(Little pause.)

HARPER

I think you should go.

–Millennium Approaches, Act 2, Scene 9

HARDEN: I vaguely remember, in a rehearsal, David saying the "no sexual feeling" line to me and I remember my responding with anger, and George saying, "Wait wait wait wait Marcia Gay, what did he just say to you?" And then I really heard what he said. What's so devastating there is the "I don't think I ever did." He could just say "I don't." Everything between us has been a lie.

DENNEHY: They trap each other in a very convenient web of stasis until they can't bear it anymore.

HOLT: I just felt like I didn't ever not understand the character.

DARRAGH: This may sound weird—I didn't find Harper difficult. She made total sense to me.

MARY-LOUISE PARKER (Harper on HBO, 2003): I understood Harper the first time I read it.

KAZAN: It was so much harder than I thought it would be.

• • •

HARDEN: You know that part, Martin, the D.C. fixer? Harper gets to play that part. I had this toupee and strands of hair and big glasses like my dad.

Harper (Zoe Kazan) performs Night Flight to San Francisco at Signature Theatre, New York, 2010. (*Joan Marcus*)

JESSIEE DATINO (Harper at Kansas City Rep, 2015): Our costume designer, Alison Siple, was so fun, and handed me undies with balls to play around with.

HARDEN: I had grown up in the Pentagon environment, those civil servants, and how they jingle their change in their pockets irritatingly.

RACHEL HANKS (Harper at Stray Dog Theatre, St. Louis, 2012): I approached Martin like he was one of the flashy sycophants from *American Psycho*.

GIBSON: I *loved* playing Martin! In our production I ate a complete meal in the course of the relatively short scene, and I wore a horrendous comb-over wig that I also loved. I was not very *good* at playing Martin, however.

KAZAN: I found that scene incredibly hard. I wanted to be a big man but I am a small girl and I never felt like I bridged that gap.

DENNEHY: I did feel inadequate as a man, but I figured lots of men feel inadequate as men.

KAZAN: Tony asked me to do it like Jimmy Stewart—he was like, "How's your Jimmy Stewart impression?" Oh my God, Tony.

HARDEN: There's a moment when Harper comes upstairs and has to take off everything and get changed. And Joe and David would come upstairs and speak to me as Martin, Martin in character. And it turned out that Martin deeply loved David.

DAVID MARSHALL GRANT (Joe in New York, 1993–94): So I would leave the stage, and Joe was offstage at the time, too, and we would go into Marcia's dressing room, where she was getting out of her Martin makeup. She would be in the character of the actor who played Martin. And "he" would endlessly talk about "the girl," who was, of course, Marcia.

GEORGE C. WOLFE (director in New York, 1993–94): Marcia created a personality for the actor playing Martin, and then Joe Mantello filmed all of these documentaries, all of these little shorts of Marcia talking as the actor who played Martin.

HARDEN: It was like Martin and David and Joe were all these buddies, these lines were blurred between these characters and ourselves.

GOUGH: I play Martin and I have to make this speech, and this speech basically says what's going to happen, word for word: By 1992 we'll get the Senate back and in ten years the South is gonna give us the House, we've got the White House packed—

FURST: Now Martin's speech is eerie. Nobody laughs. It's too true to what's happening now. His world now is no longer something of the past.

• • •

HARPER
The plane leapt the tropopause, the safe air, and attained the outer rim,
the ozone, which was ragged and torn, patches of it threadbare as old
cheesecloth, and that was frightening . . .
But I saw something only I could see, because of my astonishing ability
to see such things.

–*Perestroika*, Act 5, Scene 8

KUSHNER: It's the most beautiful thing I've ever written.

GOUGH: Night Flight for me is her victory. She sits back in her seat. I'm going to San Francisco, a city, like heaven, of unspeakable beauty.

KUSHNER: Marcia Gay Harden said, when I told her everyone worried about where Joe was at the end, "Why aren't they worried about Harper? She's still lost."

I said, "No, she's going to San Francisco."

And Marcia Gay said, "Right. She's leaving her gay husband and she flies to San Francisco. She still doesn't quite get it."

MACE: She's out of the fire and into the fire. That, to me, is a life lesson.

GOEHRING: How great to play someone who gets broadsided by the mandate to be brave. Who wants that? Tony's writing asks you to risk it and reminds you that it's more expensive to be a coward.

DENNEHY: My very own marriage—to Todd Weeks, who was my Prior—was crumbling. So the monologue of describing a newly single woman's exodus from a painful marriage into the less frightening unknown was not that hard for me to prepare for.

DARRAGH: I love that scene so much. It was such a gift to have Harper end up *there*. You could easily drop that character in so many ways, to just say, *Oh, there goes the looney tunes wife,* and instead you get this great, great scene. I always ended *Perestroika* feeling very good, like *Why is everyone so sad?*

GIBSON: I believe that Night Flight helped to keep me sane throughout our run. After going through the anger and heartbreak, living through her belief that she is the crazy one, the one to blame for the sadness of her marriage, the one to blame for Joe's lack of attention, the bad girl . . . if I had to go home each night without Night Flight, the run of the production would have been a much more exhausting experience.

KETTENRING: I would truly feel my insides spool out into calm while doing this monologue. Six hours–plus of stress coming undone. It felt like a gigantic exhale.

PARKER: It's a speech I could do for the rest of my life and not be satisfied with. The goal is to make it sound like a person talking who speaks poetically. You really need to let the audience hear it and get out of its way. There's a danger of acting it and letting the audience be impressed by your acting. But that's not what an actor playing Harper should do.

HARDEN: I'm tingling right now thinking about it. The synchronicity of the immune system of the earth, and that can be healed by the people who are suffering with the holes in their own immune system, the tragedy of the souls of those who have been hurt forming a web of protection around the earth. It's one of the most beautiful things I've ever said—or read—in my life.

PARKER: We shot it in an airplane hangar and I was really trying to rein in my emotion, I didn't want to hijack the audience's experience. I was trying to hold back so you could really hear the words. I just didn't feel I quite reached it. I went to lunch and I was so distraught and I went to Mike and said, "Can I do it again?" They were literally taking down the wall and he said, "Oh, my child," and turned to the crew and yelled, "OK, put the wall back up!"

KAZAN: I don't wanna sound like a dick, and I struggled with a lot of things in that play, but not that speech. It was one of the only things Tony didn't give me notes on. It was my polestar. It connects up deeply to what I believe

Harper (Mary-Louise Parker) in the HBO miniseries, 2003. (*HBO/Stephen Goldblatt*)

about the universe. But also it's a real distillation of her character. It's a perfect speech. I felt every night I just had to open my mouth and let Tony's voice take me.

DEBRA MESSING (Harper in NYU *Perestroika* workshop, 1993): One of our teachers, our improvisation teacher, his name was Paul Walker. He was, at the time, he had AIDS. And was very sick. It was very raw for all of us, watching him slowly get sicker and working on this play and that speech—you know, it's so stunning. Just the idea that these people who were not appreciated and celebrated on earth, the way they should be, were the agents of healing up in heaven.

DARRAGH: When we would do the whole thing, it was a much harder journey for some of the other characters, but she ends in a hopeful place. Her marriage has failed, but she's on her way, she's figuring it out.

MACE: What will happen to her? Is she equipped to start a new life? I was convinced that if she wasn't by the time she strapped in, she is by the time she lands.

PARKER: She's a bit of a philosopher and a bit of a poet. That's what she went on to do.

GOEHRING: Maybe she becomes an ecologist in San Francisco!

KAZAN: I'm not a religious person, but I get nervous flying, and I say Harper's entire speech whenever a plane takes off and whenever it lands.

CHAPTER 2

MORE LIFE

ROYAL NATIONAL THEATRE, LONDON, 2017

ANDREW GARFIELD (Prior in London, 2017, and New York, 2018): How am I doing? I don't know. It's, um, you know, it makes you bigger, it makes you grow, doesn't it? It kind of breaks you open. Most of the foundational feeling is gratitude, to be honest.

• • •

EMILY GARSIDE (scholar of HIV/AIDS-related theater): For Britain there's been an even bigger gap for *Angels in America*. There was a small tour in 2007, but that's been the only revival. Some people only really know it's a famous play you should see. It's on the list of American canonical theater.

MARIANNE ELLIOTT (director in London, 2017): I've never seen it in production, although I saw the HBO one.

JAMES McARDLE (Louis in London, 2017): I'd read bits of it at drama school. Louis's Democracy in America speech for example.

GARFIELD: I had seen Mike Nichols's HBO two-parter, when I was studying in drama school. It was one of those things that was just on loop, on repeat in our shared actor house. There were a few DVDs we would watch over and

over and that was one. Uta Hagen's acting class was another, *Eddie Murphy Delirious* was the third, *Labyrinth* was the fourth.

DENISE GOUGH (Harper in London, 2017): I did it in drama school and I played Hannah Pitt. And I was desperate to play Harper; I remember being so jealous of the girl who played Harper, but she was so brilliant.

SUSAN BROWN (Hannah in London, 2017): I saw the original production in London, in the '90s. And I remember being absolutely blown away by it.

NATHAN LANE (Roy in London, 2017): I saw the original Broadway production and loved it. I thought it was one of the great plays of the twentieth century, a masterpiece.

RUSSELL TOVEY (Joe in London, 2017): I saw the TV show when I was about seventeen, and from that moment onwards, it became my—where I set the bar for quality.

GARSIDE: People have also been very hostile to it: Why are we doing this old huge American play? Why is it still relevant? Where does it still fit in now?

LANE: Being in rehearsal with all these young people and referring to this play set in the '80s as a period piece, asking about the St. Marks Baths? (*Grandly:*)

Tony Kushner talks to Andrew Garfield during rehearsal in London, 2017. (*Helen Maybanks*)

I had sex at the St. Marks Baths, I can tell you. I'm a living artifact of that period, I lived through the whole thing. But the play is as relevant and as resonant as ever.

RUFUS NORRIS (artistic director, National Theatre): When it was first put on in 1993, there was a sense that it was a great anthem to gay rights and really illuminating a whole movement and a whole deeply personal and political period in American and international history. But now the universality of it has grown immeasurably. That has really surprised me, being closely involved: how undated it is, how it speaks to today.

ELLIOTT: When we started rehearsals back in January, it was Donald Trump's first day in office. Our press night was the day when, in Chechnya, the government began cracking down on homosexuals.

A GENERATION OF PLAYWRIGHTS ON *ANGELS IN AMERICA*

STEVEN LEVENSON (*Dear Evan Hansen* and *If I Forget*): My *Angels* origin story was my freshman year of college.

TRACEY SCOTT WILSON (*The Good Negro* and *Buzzer*): I had just started writing plays, I was living with my mother, I didn't have any money.

YOUNG JEAN LEE (*Lear* and *Straight White Men*): It was right after I'd decided to drop out of grad school to become a playwright.

SAMUEL HUNTER (*A Bright New Boise* and *The Whale*): When I was about seventeen, I came out of the closet and left the fundamentalist Christian high school I was attending.

STEPHEN KARAM (*Sons of the Prophet* and *The Humans*): I was eighteen or nineteen, a freshman in college at Brown. I was having a rough time coming out of the closet.

MAC ROGERS (*The Message* and *The Honeycomb Trilogy*): I was visiting New York from North Carolina with my mother and sister.

ITAMAR MOSES (*The Band's Visit* and *The Fortress of Solitude*): Towards the end of my junior year of high school, I was visiting colleges. I stayed with a friend at Wesleyan and he was reading the script for class.

CHRISTOPHER SHINN (*Dying City* and *Against*): I remember driving with my mom to see it. I was eighteen and we were, you know, listening to Nirvana.

LIN-MANUEL MIRANDA (*Hamilton* and *In the Heights*): *Angels* was the first *play*

TONY KUSHNER: It was weird: When I went to London, they were doing Act 2 of *Perestroika*, and it absolutely hadn't occurred to me how different something called "the anti-migratory epistle" was going to sound—I mean, I just have not thought, with all the endless talk of the travel bans and stuff, that suddenly there's gonna be huge impact when those words are spoken. "Stop moving," specifically about not migrating.

AMANDA LAWRENCE (the Angel in London, 2017): This whole anti-migratory kind of thing is just fantastic to say. Marianne said in rehearsal, "The Angel and Roy Cohn are very similar. This disgust, this racism, this disgust."

ELLIOTT: It felt like a much bigger deal for us that Trump got into office, no matter how heinous Brexit was, but it felt really imperative that we were always going to be looking for pieces of work that could make a statement about the political climate.

I saw on Broadway. I'm, you know, a musicals guy. Dan Futterman was on Louis. And the late great David Margulies was on Roy Cohn. It was 1994, so I'm fourteen years old.

JORDAN HARRISON (*Marjorie Prime* and *Maple and Vine*): I was sixteen and my grandparents bought us tickets to the national tour in Boston.

TAYLOR MAC (*A 24-Decade History of Popular Music*): When I moved to New York both parts were playing on Broadway and, after paying for the full version, I would second-act both parts multiple times a week. That way I could see them for free.

ANNE WASHBURN (*Mr. Burns: A Post-Electric Play* and *10 Out of 12*): I first saw a touring production in Portland, Oregon. I think I left at intermission of *Millennium* only because it was a hopelessly remote

experience, but I got the books and really first came to the play that way.

HUNTER: The University of Idaho was mounting a production of *Millennium Approaches*, and I saw it at least four or five times.

ZAKIYYAH ALEXANDER (*10 Things to Do Before I Die* and *Sick?*): I went to LaGuardia High School of the Performing Arts. My best friend performed the scene in acting class where Prior puts on makeup and joins Harper's hallucination.

KARA LEE CORTHRON (*Welcome to Fear City* and *AliceGraceAnon*): I was assigned to read *Millennium Approaches* for a script analysis class.

KARAM: They were holding auditions for a production on campus. I remember buying Part 1 at College Hill Bookstore,

IAN MacNEIL (set designer in London, 2017): Tony has this phrase, the "bloody opulence" of American history, and I thought, *That's it.* America is a Jacobean tragedy but all done in steel. You know, you're doing Jacobean but setting it in the Chrysler Building.

BEN POWER (deputy artistic director, National Theatre): It feels like the disease becomes metaphorical now for other kinds of threat and uncertainty, external and internal. Threats that we can recognize. Certainly in this country, since the crash, there's been this feeling of instability rather than stability in our political and social institutions. That sense of a shuddering, a juddering, which is manifest in the disease in the play.

ELLIOTT: I knew that the rights were with the Old Vic and that Kevin Spacey was possibly going to do it in his last year there. But the minute I heard

A GENERATION OF PLAYWRIGHTS ON *ANGELS IN AMERICA* →

and then rolling off my twin bed and speed-walking down Thayer Street to buy *Perestroika*.

ZOE KAZAN (*We Live Here* and *After the Blast*): I read *Angels* in three different classes. In playwriting, in a Brecht class, and an intro-to-theater class.

MASHUQ MUSHTAQ DEEN (*Draw the Circle*): It was years before I ever saw a production of it, but I knew exactly what the Angel breaking through the ceiling looked like, knew exactly how the snow fell around Harper.

MAC: I kept returning to the plays because they were a balm, shedding all the years I was told to be less than when expressing my queerness. Seeing the Angel fly—metaphorically, literally,

theatrically, and literarily—felt like activism. It was taking a country empty of angels and inserting a queer mythology in its place. I freaking loved it.

CORTHRON: What struck me most powerfully was the fact that I laughed! It was my first encounter with a dramatic work that was universally considered important, life-changing, trailblazing, that made me laugh.

WASHBURN: There are delightfully cheap jokes in *Angels*, which are really important, as well as the sublimity.

SHEILA CALLAGHAN (*Bed* and *Women Laughing Alone with Salad*): It was so exciting to hear people talk about theater like that, to describe it with such rapture—and these were kids who did theater in high school and left it behind for more sensible pursuits. They weren't freaking out about a monologue

through a little bird that that wasn't going to happen, I basically begged the National to get on the phone and get the rights, because I really wanted to do it.

NORRIS: Marianne expressed interest in it, and in a way, from our viewpoint, that was that. We bent the rules around budget and rehearsal time and whatever.

KUSHNER: I had just seen *The Curious Incident of the Dog in the Night-Time* on Broadway, and what I really adored about it—apart from just the superabundance of directorial invention—was that she created a giant machine but that it was an entirely actor-driven machine. Everything that could be done by hand was done by hand and by human muscle. And also I knew a lot of the actors who had been cast, and they were all doing what I thought was the best work they'd ever done onstage.

---

from *Hamlet*, they were talking about a contemporary play.

MIRANDA: It just blew my mind. I mean, it was the first time I'd ever seen a play with, on a pure surface level, the production design and scope of a musical. And the way it moved! I sort of thought a play—this was my own prejudice, of course—a play happens in single-set locations, it's small. I'd never seen anything that moved the way George's production of *Angels* moved. The seamless transitions, and a tempo and a rhythm—it felt like a musical to me. From a very naturalistic scene, to a scene in Antarctica, to the scene where Louis is spinning out pages and pages of liberal guilt and Belize just sits there. It had room for all of the tempos! It had room for all of the things at once.

CALLAGHAN: It wasn't realistic, but it somehow communicated heightened

emotions in a way that made sense to me. It felt akin to all the high school musicals I'd grown up with, like when people launch into arias when emotions become too great.

WILSON: In terms of pure theatricality, the scene where Harper is in the Mormon center, and she's looking at the mannequin and it becomes Joe—the theatricality of those scenes, the way it brought everything together . . . I just read it over and over, amazed at how he got away with it.

HARRISON: Maybe *miracles* is the right word, rather than *magic*. The human mingled with the divine. These were rules that I didn't know you could break until I saw *Angels*.

ALEXANDER: Just from the page it was clear that this play broke all the rules I had learned—so, were there no rules at all?

ELLIOTT: I said to Tony the first time that I met him, "I can't tell you logically why I want to do this. I'm not gay. I'm not American. I'm not Jewish. But I feel an absolute imperative to do this play. It's absolutely about me."

NORRIS: I employed myself as Marianne's casting assistant. I went to have dinner with Nathan and never mentioned the play. He's nobody's fool, so he had to have known what was up.

LANE: I was asked to have a dinner with Rufus Norris, who they told me wanted to have more of an exchange with American actors. And he mentioned the play in passing and then we talked about a lot of other things. When they asked me to do it, I was surprised. I told Marianne, "He was very discreet about it, he just sort of mentioned that you were doing it." And she said, "That's why I sent him! To get you!"

A GENERATION OF PLAYWRIGHTS ON *ANGELS IN AMERICA* →

LEVENSON: And the audacity of it, the scope of writing a play that was about History with a capital *H*, and about Politics with a capital *P*. And the Universe. It was such an unapologetically *big* play. Bigger than anything else I had read.

MIRANDA: When's the last play you saw that you can quote lines from like you quote tunes from your favorite musical? "History is about to crack wide open." "More life." "I wish I was an octopus, a fucking octopus." That's just a greatest-hits reel of shit off the top of my head, and they're all these unforgettable character-defining moments.

MOSES: After I went to see Part 1, I literally started writing my first play the next day.

HUNTER: After seeing the production of *Angels* at the University of Idaho, I wrote my very first play. It was nearly three hours long, and it was called *Sixth Armageddon*. It was, in many ways, an *Angels* knockoff.

LEVENSON: The first real play I wrote had Bill Clinton as a character.

KAZAN: When I was in college I did *Angels in America*, Part 1. I played the Angel. It was very scrappy: We had a budget of like $200 or something. We had the confidence of nineteen-year-olds.

MIRANDA: I was not a big speech-and-debate kid. But in high school Veronica Ades and I did a Joe-and-Harper scene. I remember doing that in some weird carpeted room in front of judges and not making it very far. We didn't get all the complexities, I guess.

GARFIELD: My connection to the play came through Mike [Nichols], who directed *Death of a Salesman* in New York, and I got to know Tony through Mike, just a little bit, just vaguely, from afar, and I think it was that connection that warmed Tony to me. That fact that Mike saw something in me probably made Tony go, "Oh, maybe."

LANE: And it was a hard decision for me, because it meant leaving home for seven months, leaving my husband and my dog and my life. And yet you think, *Well, when is this gonna come around again?* And then Tony wrote me an email, a very persuasive email, so I said yes.

GARFIELD: It was Tony who emailed me first about playing Prior. I've only had this reaction twice in my life, when Mike called me to play Biff and Tony asked me to play Prior. When every cell in my body just spoke and screamed yes.

VERONICA ADES (Lin-Manuel Miranda's classmate): It's high school! What was fun about it was that Lin was so into it, and so was I, and it was so great to completely nerd out on this amazing theater. Of course you're gonna pick a scene from *Angels in America*.

MIRANDA: That's how big that play is! It was one of the only plays I knew, and I could probably have recited all of *Man of La Mancha* for you at that age. I guess that underscores what a benchmark play *Angels* was for our generation. The way *Who's Afraid of Virginia Woolf?* or Tennessee Williams was for previous generations. That was *it*.

LEE: I had to kind of avoid thinking about it when I took my first steps into playwriting. I found it incredibly intimidating.

MIRANDA: Kushner's ambition in writing

Angels was something that both armed and scared every playwright since. It leaves a big wake.

ROGERS: The problem with *Angels in America* is keeping it *out* of my work, not letting it in. It so dominated the theater conversation right at the time I was beginning to treat playwriting as a lifelong discipline that it basically bonded with my playwriting molecules just as they were forming. I wrote a play in *2010* with a larger-than-life political operative in it, and making him *not* be Roy Cohn was a line-by-line struggle, one I probably lost on a third of the lines.

WILSON: The first play I had produced at the Public, *The Story*, the entire structure of the play was based on the quartet—the overlapping scenes with Prior and Louis and Harper and Joe. I was rereading it and just thought, *Wouldn't it be cool to base a whole play on this?*

KUSHNER: I've never seen a director work as long or as hard on a production. A year of preparation. And you can see that degree—the depth of involvement, it's reflected in the design and in many of the choices she's made.

ELLIOTT: We spent about a year and a half on the design. Not every day, but we touched in a lot. And I wished that I had longer!

POWER: There is no doubt that there is pressure when you announce that a director as celebrated as Marianne is doing a play as celebrated as this with this company. There'd still be huge pressure had there been eight actors no one had heard of. Every time someone was added to it an expectation developed. Marianne was very good at getting that stuff out of the room, but still, vibrating at the door of the rehearsal room were the expectations around the show.

ELLIOTT: We had eleven weeks, longer than anyone else had had.

A GENERATION OF PLAYWRIGHTS ON *ANGELS IN AMERICA* →

LEE: I'm actually revisiting it now as research for a play I'm writing, looking for tricks to steal.

WILSON: I remember before I met Christopher Shinn, I read *Four* and thought, *Oh, this rhythm is the rhythm of* Angels.

SHINN: I think every play I've written has my version of the Democracy in America scene in it.

CATHERINE TRIESCHMANN (*How the World Began* and *One House Over***):** Before I wrote my thesis play in college, I wanted to remind myself how to write a good play, so I reread *Angels* over and over. I memorized speeches. I outlined scenes. And this is what I learned: Despite the perspicacious mind at work, the vast ambition at play, and vivid theatrical

spectacle on display, the action of any given scene is really quite simple. One character wants love from somebody else who is reluctant to give it. I remind myself of this axiom every time I start a new play.

HARRISON: Whenever I write cast doubling into my plays, which is often, there are two works I'm always talking to: *The Wizard of Oz* and *Angels in America*. The way Kushner uses that ensemble to make an entire universe—these indelible characters who slide into other skins but are still always partly themselves. When Louis fucks the anonymous man in the park, he's played by the Prior actor, and the effect is that Louis can't block out the man he's running from.

MAC: The size of *Angels*, the unabashed queerness of it, and the intellectual pursuit mixed with its delicious camp humor are all things I've been spinning off of through the entirety of my adult artistry.

KUSHNER: In a way it's the first adequate rehearsal period we've had for these plays.

ELLIOTT: And all the actors came in with high stakes. They're leading actors having to be in an ensemble. No day was a cruise, shall I say.

GARSIDE: And now it turns out it will be her swan song.

NORRIS: Marianne has left us as an associate, she's set up her own company. I only wish her completely the best.

ELLIOTT: (*Laughs.*) Yeah, exactly. So there were pressures all over the place.

GARFIELD: She's very smart, she never ever dictates, it's all very question-marky and leading and guiding. And when she doesn't know, she'll say, "I

MIRANDA: I know that in writing *Hamilton*, the approach to storytelling is similarly all-hands-on-deck. We don't make a choice of Oh, there's one narrator—whoever's closest to the events of the story, he tells the story. If Burr's the closest, he tells it. If it's Eliza or Angelica, she does. *Angels* is freeing in that respect. It doesn't just have to be a naturalistic play, it can go from here to here to here as you need to.

ROGERS: I feel a need to make my characters' conflicts and traumas reverberate throughout the globe and cosmos, and that likely wouldn't have even occurred to me without *Angels in America*.

MOSES: If you want to know how to structure a play that actually wants to be a mess, you can't do much better than to look at *Perestroika*, which consciously rejects the orderliness of Part 1 in order

to excavate an aesthetic space that would be otherwise unreachable.

KARAM: *Angels* inspires simply by being incredibly fucking entertaining! Kushner is fiercely political but he's also a showman. It's empowering to know the two things can coexist. They have to, really, for a play to succeed.

LEE: It's still ahead of the curve. It's the most interesting kind of political play—one that comes from a place not of knowing but of unknowing. Of finding the available truths intolerably inadequate, and trying, through all the means available to theater, to figure out what an adequate truth could be.

WASHBURN: *Angels* made it clear that it was possible to talk about politics in a way which was entertaining, and personal, and intemperate—the latter being the part which might be most

don't know about this yet." She's truly a humble human being, or maybe it's a tactic. *(Pause.)* It could always be a tactic, but it's a fucking good one.

TOVEY: It was the longest rehearsal process I've ever done. It was insane,  and all-consuming. I found rehearsals personally very tough. I love Marianne, her energy is incredible. I don't know how she's done it, kept this play in her head.

ELLIOTT: It's a *grueling* amount of time to be working on

Director Marianne Elliott during rehearsal in London, 2017. *(Helen Maybanks)*

A GENERATION OF PLAYWRIGHTS ON *ANGELS IN AMERICA* →

important. I feel—to be hideously general—that a lot of political theater before *Angels* was about carefully drawing up an argument or dramatizing a particular point or issue and also sometimes about making it appear to be evenhanded even while it was clearly not. The characters in *Angels* are passionate political beasts who come to their politics not from reasoned understanding but as part of the whole of who they are. The play itself is full of convictions, and those ring through, but those convictions are animated by imperfect searching people.

HUNTER: The play is not afraid of talking openly about the nature of justice and democracy and God and history, and it feels to me twenty-six years later that this is the resonating effect the play has had

on American playwrights. It gave us all permission to say something bold.

MOSES: If you were between the ages of fifteen and twenty-six when that play was on Broadway, it's the reason you started writing plays.

HARRISON: There's a generation of playwrights, maybe thirty-five to forty-five years old now, who I think were pulled into the profession because they were inspired by what was grand and unwieldy and ambitious about *Angels*. And I'm not sure we found that theater always welcomes this kind of work.

SHINN: I really thought when I saw that play, *You can be really deep and be on Broadway!* I thought that would happen all the time. *(Laughs.)* If I had known it was really that rare, I maybe would have chosen another field.

something so intensively, and to be working on something that goes so deep into exploring existential angst and requires incredible specificity on every level.

GARFIELD: She treats it like Shakespeare. It *is* like Shakespeare to me.

McARDLE: It helped me not be nervous because there was just so much work to do. People say stuff about the cultural importance of the play, and I'm like, "I've got twenty pages to memorize tonight, fuck off."

TOVEY: Her attention to detail is incredible. It can make you, uh, panic. *(Laughs.)*

GOUGH: She had to let me go through all sorts of variations, the cutesy Harper and the really high Harper, and then it was overworked, three and a

DEEN: If anything, and this is the cynical part of me now, I would say as groundbreaking as *Angels* was, it hasn't changed the American theater *enough*. I don't place the responsibility for that with Kushner but with us. There is no shortage of injustice in the world. So I place the responsibility with writers when we don't push ourselves to engage the world in which we live. With producers who don't take the risk of leading their audiences, instead of being led by them. With audiences for not demanding better from their artistic institutions.

ALEXANDER: Over the years I've read many unproduced or workshopped plays that break form, are epic, bold, theatrically challenging, plus politically relevant, that have not yet made it to the stage. I'm not sure how *Angels* changed the *produced* plays we see.

ROGERS: Look, *all* of us have people

telling us "Write three characters in a room for eighty-one minutes" all the time.

HARRISON: We're living in a time that seems to be screaming for a vast canvas and bold strokes and newly minted language. I think in addition to the brilliance of Tony and his collaborators, the play was made great by the cultural and historical moment that it rose to meet. So here, again, is our opportunity to rise to the occasion.

DEEN: The point is to be inspired by *Angels* and to take those same risks with new plays that engage the injustice and the complexity of the world we live in now.

ROGERS: I'm pretty sure no one my age or younger writes a play without *Angels in America* lurking quietly in the corner. It's a feeling of: That's what it looks like when you go ALL THE WAY. Someday *I'm* gonna go ALL THE WAY too. ✒

half months in. I said, "Now you have to leave me alone." Because Marianne will never stop, she'll go, "What about this little thing I found over there, what about that?" and at a certain point you have to go, "OK, the stew is all there, now we need to let it simmer."

LANE: Maybe rehearsal was a little too long, because then people start to second-guess.

TOVEY: The journey, as Prior 2 says, has been rocky, dark, and steep.

GARFIELD: One of my concerns is, in reality, in my life, I—as far as I know—am a heterosexual male in a heterosexual male's body. And I'm not confused about that, right now. That was a big, big concern, that tricky balance, as a heterosexual male, to attempt to portray that and live that and offer that in a way that's totally authentic, totally honest, and not shy; those were the main choppy waters for me. I knew deep down it was gonna be fine, but just above that deep down was a fucking layer of terror.

Andrew Garfield's gay comments stir backlash - CNN.com
www.cnn.com/2017/07/06/entertainment/andrew-garfield-gay-drag.../index.html ▾
6 days ago - (CNN)**Andrew Garfield's** reported remarks about how he prepared to play a gay man aren't going over well. ... **Andrew Garfield** is "**gay** without the physical act" because he watches RuPaul. ... Hey did you know that if you marathon Drag Race you are a **gay** man?

Andrew Garfield Comes Out as Gay 'Just Without the Physical Act ...
https://www.out.com/.../7/.../andrew-garfield-comes-out-gay-just-without-physical-act ▾
Jul 5, 2017 - Hollywood heartthrob **Andrew Garfield** has come out of the closet—sort of. The English actor currently stars in Tony Kushner's Angels in ...

Andrew Garfield Said He's "A Gay Man Right Now, Just Without The ...
https://www.buzzfeed.com/.../andrew-garfield-said-hes-a-gay-man-right-now-just-wit... ▾
6 days ago - So, **Andrew Garfield** is currently starring in Tony Kushner's theater production Angels in America, where he plays Prior Walters, a **gay** man in ...

Andrew Garfield Faces Backlash for Gay Reference | Variety
variety.com/.../andrew-garfield-backlash-gay-without-the-physical-act-1202489140/ ▾
6 days ago - The internet and the LGBTQ community are not too pleased with **Andrew Garfield** after he said that he's "a **gay** man right now just without the ...

Andrew Garfield: I Am a Gay Man Without the Physical Act - Rolling ...
www.rollingstone.com/.../andrew-garfield-i-am-a-gay-man-without-physical-act-w49... ▾
6 days ago - **Andrew Garfield** has claimed to be "a **gay** man right now just without the physical act" while performing in a London production of 'Angels in ...

A Google News search for "Andrew Garfield," July 2017.

KUSHNER: I can't say enough about how much I admire what Andrew has done. He's a straight guy and he just dug so deeply into the spirit of this 1980s queen that you—it feels so absolutely, authentically *gay* to me, and I think that that's extraordinary.

ELLIOTT: He went on a big journey, but he never ever stopped working. He was hungry for more work. We had a drag . . . advisor, should we call it? Who has his own drag company. He took Andrew out on drag nights. He and Nathan Stewart-Jarrett dressed up in drag and did drag improvisations.

NATHAN STEWART-JARRETT (Belize in London, 2017): We did a drag workshop, which was hilarious in so many different ways—hilarious because it's amazing how vulnerable I felt in that situation, and it's amazing what it took to get me not to. Also, we had wonderful people working with us. They were named Harry and Hugh. They were like, "So. This is *shade* . . ." and I was like, "I can't be hearing about shade from two white English boys."

ELLIOTT: Prior reminded me in some ways of some women I know, and of parts of me. So we talked about that.

GARFIELD: Marianne would say, "You remind me of my best friend from school," and I'd go, "What was his name?" And she'd say, "No no no no, her name is Ruthie." So it was all this kind of subconscious *Come out come out come out.*

His physical elegance, and that performative drag aesthetic that Tony would always say "is totally sincere, it's totally fucking serious, even though it's artifice." He believes so totally in artifice. That took me a minute to comprehend.

ELLIOTT: I spoke to Tony early on and he said he was quite surprised how many productions dressed the Angel in white feathers and a flowing Roman robe. I went away and thought, *Great! Great! If she doesn't have to be that, what can she be?*

POWER: Prior's standing on his bed, as in other productions. The lights are changing. The sound of the approaching object is getting louder and louder.

It's extremely loud in the auditorium. The lights change around him and he says, *"Very* Steven Spielberg."

Everyone's eyes are on him, and they're also going up to the flies. We know what's going to happen. They're going to fly in a woman with wings. As we're looking, as it's all building to a point of climax, at that point of climax there is the sense of a drop and a full blackout, which is very disorienting.

The lights come up. Everyone's eyes are up, looking for what object is coming in through the broken roof. Andrew's looking up there. And there's nothing there. As his eye line comes down, there, strewn on the floor, among the rubble, is this *thing*. It's a sort of creature mess in browns and blacks. And then it rises from the floor—it's clearly been dropped from a great height—and coalesces into one body.

KUSHNER: When she first told me about it, I loved the kind of shock. It had always been very important to me that the Angel breaks the ceiling, but then I assumed that she would put the brakes on and that she would stop, midair. Marianne is the first person who has actually had her smash into the floor and then have to kind of reemerge. I thought that was beautiful, and broken, and scary.

GARSIDE: I was aware they were going for some kind of different interpretation, and that they'd enlisted a puppetry team. But it wasn't until actually seeing the production that I knew she wouldn't really "fly."

ELLIOTT: Every image you see of this play involves a lovely angel in a white dress on a wire. I didn't want that.

FINN CALDWELL (puppetry designer in London, 2017): Sometimes when I watch wirework it seems like the amount of possibilities has shut down. You see the wire and you go, *OK,* you can't go left or right or up or down very easily. I don't think she could trash the room or knock Prior over. We always felt like we wanted the Angel to have a real power. She was filled with possibility. She was capable of anything.

POWER: Amanda Lawrence plays the Angel, and there are these shadow figures who puppeteer these giant wings and puppeteer her.

KUSHNER: Marianne said, "We're going to call them 'familiars,'" and I wrote back and said, "You absolutely cannot call them that." As far as I'm aware, "familiars" are devils; that's just not angelic. And then I thought of "If we shadows have offended, think but this, and all is mended"—the ending of *Midsummer Night's Dream*. Shakespeare's use of *shadow* as a metaphor, as a word for actor. And so I suggested "shadows" instead, and she liked that.

GARFIELD: Because Mandy's being puppeteered, there was a whole separate rehearsal process going on.

CALDWELL: Whenever we're developing a new movement language, you have a period of work where you're just working on the technique.

LAWRENCE: We had a puppeteer choreographer in the room, these six other people onstage, constantly moving, and the wings going, and I hadn't even gotten into the room really with Marianne. I just remember stopping the rehearsal four weeks in and going, "Stop, stop, no one is gonna hear this very complicated dialogue."

GARFIELD: There was choreography being created, very beautiful choreography, with dancers playing the shadows, totally separate to the main rehearsal room, without some context of actually unpacking the scene in a deep way.

LAWRENCE: So then Andrew brilliantly said he just needed one to one, me and Marianne. We just stripped it away and brought it back down to basics in two or three rehearsals.

CALDWELL: We sat around a table, broke the scene apart, figuring out what everyone is doing at every moment. The shadows are part of the Angel's personality, so they need to know what the Angel is thinking and feeling at any given moment. Then we put it on its feet.

GARFIELD: Basically, we're able to cut down and reinvent the choreography according to the discoveries that were made in the main rehearsal room. It was a very disjointed process for that particular scene.

GARSIDE: On one hand it's brilliant, it's one of the things I love most—that Elliott managed to genuinely surprise me with a play I know backwards. On the other, as someone so familiar with the play, it's so hard to let go of those expectations and ingrained ideas. But ultimately I'd much rather a revival that challenged audiences and their expectations than just gave me the classic Xerox revival.

ELLIOTT: We realized slowly that we wanted to go from a relatively realistic place to a rather abstract, Brechtian place by the end of *Perestroika*. So the weirder the play gets, the stranger, more abstract, the more we wanted to engage the audience's imagination.

MacNEIL: We knew that we would go from a set that felt more normal to something that was more spare and empty. We had three turntables, and the idea is that the set would fail the characters. So the revolves go completely away. *Perestroika* is in a large black void.

ELLIOTT: When the Angel lands, we called it infesting the earth. She had contagiously infested the world and was trying to manipulate Prior and what was going on in the world. So the shadows, who puppeteer her, could also puppeteer the furniture and the world around them.

CALDWELL: They should be insectoid, non-human, without will. Servants of will, but without will of their own. They're like cells, really, of Prior's illness, these infected cells moving through the space.

GARFIELD: When we were first rehearsing, I was treating the shadows like they were creatures, and that was not right. So I made the decision that they are an energy, some mystical otherworldly energy, that surrounds the Angel, and that opened it up for me, and I can acknowledge the energy without being distracted by what Mandy as the Angel was saying to me as Prior.

ELLIOTT: After Prior rejects the prophecy, the shadows help him go down to earth, but then they disappear. He has made a choice to be in control of his own life, so they're not relevant anymore.

LAWRENCE: When we first did it, it was like six hours long, *Perestroika*; we were visibly aging. Tony was there watching, we all had beards coming out of our butts.

POWER: Tony came in and was lovely, but there was obviously this nervousness. I said to Tony, "When did you last see a run of this?" He looked at me with the whites of his eyes burning and said, "It was five or six years ago that I was in a rehearsal room seeing one of these plays, and I'm not sure I can do it again in my lifetime."

GOUGH: We had to stop because we ran out of time in the day. And then we all had to go to dinner together afterwards because it was unfinished and we'd been so deeply affected by this thing.

LAWRENCE: We were drenched in tears.

GOUGH: If that's what we're getting in a rehearsal room with a pretend set and no effects or anything, no huge audience, then oh my God, this is gonna be a thing.

NORRIS: It's so intimate. Nobody's got any makeup. They're in jeans and a T-shirt doing all that amazing stuff, so your imagination is working overtime. What you get then is the truth or nothing. If I get to spend another three days like those days in my career, I'll be very happy.

Of course, it also made me insanely jealous, because it wasn't my rehearsal room. *(Laughs.)*

ELLIOTT: We had the shortest tech period anyone's had on this piece. The first play, we teched it in two and a half days. The second play we teched in four and a half days. They each had six previews only.

LANE: It's crazy here! You rehearse for over three months and then they give you fifteen minutes to tech it. *(British accent:)* "Oh, get on with it."

GARFIELD: They didn't have much time to tech two incredibly technical shows, with a bunch of actors who are freaking out about feeling like they lost contact with the play. Because now we're in this strange theater away from the intimacy of the rehearsal room, and now there are revolves turning, and music and lights and a rake, and velvet ninjas walking around backstage. You're bumping into pieces and tripping over sets.

ELLIOTT: The first preview of *Perestroika* came in at quarter to twelve.

NORRIS: The front-of-house manager said, "The key moment is five minutes past eleven, that's when people are going to miss the last train at Waterloo. Everyone relying on a train at Waterloo knows that, so wherever we've got to at that point, we'll have to brace ourselves for people leaving." So we all knew we had to work to get it so the show was done by five to eleven. But tonight, we'll have to deal with people leaving.

GARFIELD: We had a couple of show stops.

ELLIOTT: The moment where the Angel and Prior are wrestling for the blessing and she goes up on the wire—the wire didn't attach.

LAWRENCE: We've got this huge harness on the base of me, then Andrew's got a harness on him because he's gonna go up. We're doing this dance in huge metal diapers, basically, and then we have to really fight and we get hooked without the audience seeing and then we fly.

GARFIELD: In the middle of wrestling the Angel, oh no! One of the shadows, Lewis [Wilkins], said, "Stop stop no fly no fly no fly"—

LAWRENCE: My pants got tangled in the harness hook.

GARFIELD: I think my ass is facing the audience, my head is under Mandy's shoulder, and there's Lewis sitting there on the floor going, "No fly no fly no fly," and I'm like, *OK, what do I do?*

LAWRENCE: They had to bring the curtain down.

GARFIELD: Sure enough, we had a five-minute break while they figure why the wires didn't come down, the wires do come down, we all get clipped up, I resume the position, I stick my ass towards the audience, the black comes up, we resume wrestling, and then we go into the air and we carry on.

LAWRENCE: The audience loved it.

NORRIS: When it was over and quarter to twelve, it was an instant standing ovation.

GOUGH: You saw them run for their trains, but even as they're running they're clapping.

KUSHNER: And the *Times of London*, that piece of shit, and you may quote me on that, tripped over itself to run an article saying, you know, "Oh my God, this dreadful thing at the National is going for nine hundred hours, it's terrible and nobody's staying."

> In four hours and 45 minutes one could fly to Baghdad from London. You could even get halfway to the moon.
> Or you could see just one half of a play at the National Theatre.
> Audience members were finally able to troop out of the theatre at 11.45pm this week after a performance of its highly anticipated production of *Angels in America*.
>
> –David Sanderson, "National's 285-Minute Test of Patience," *Times of London*, April 27, 2017

KUSHNER: Anyway, there was a lot of angst at the National about why is this thing so long and oh my God, oh my God, oh my God, and I said, "It's what happens in early previews, it's going to go away." And I was mostly right.

McARDLE: About two weeks prior to opening, I had the biggest meltdown I've ever had in my career. *Do they think I'm shit? Are they with me?* When you get an audience, you get noise back, about what people think about Louis, and I didn't really have to face that in rehearsals. And suddenly everyone's giving me their opinion on Louis.

GOUGH: And then when the audience came in—I was like, "Oh my God, they hate Harper."

McARDLE: I just didn't want go on. I've never had that! I heard other actors do that, say they suddenly have stage fright, and I'm always like, *What bullshit, get over yourself.* But then I'd sit up here and think, *I don't want to go on and do this.*

TOVEY: By the time we opened we were buckled with exhaustion.

> The entire run has sold out in advance—apart from day seats and ballot tickets—for the National Theatre's most anticipated show of the year. And that feels like no more than justice as Marianne Elliott's mighty, cast-to-the-hilt production sweeps you through.
>
> –Paul Taylor, "This Production Sweeps You Through the Seven-and-a-Half Hour Experience," *Independent,* May 9, 2017

McARDLE: The marathons are amazing. I hate just doing *Millennium.* By the end of *Millennium* you're just getting ready to rock! When you just do one show you feel like *(announcer voice:)* "Next time, on *Angels in America,*" or "Previously, on *Angels in America.*"

GOUGH: A lot of people see *Perestroika* before they see *Millennium,* because they can't get tickets any other way. So their first introduction to Harper is her dragging a tree across Antarctica, saying, "I chewed this tree down with my teeth, like a beaver."

McARDLE: I think I'm the only one who loves two-show days.

TOVEY: The only way I can describe it is: When you go out drinking and the next morning you remember something terrible you've said and you wake up with guilt. That's how I feel the morning after a two-show day.

GARFIELD: I do love them, I really, really do. I absolutely adore them in the sense that it's impossible and you know it's impossible. There's something beautiful about that, reaching beyond what you are capable of doing. *(Pause.)* Of course, it goes without saying that you kind of feel like you're gonna die.

STEWART-JARRETT: The audience is like, "Oh my God, well done, how do you do it?" and I'm like, "How do *you* do it?" It's a union at that point: You ask someone to sit down for seven hours of theater, no matter how hard you're working onstage they are doing something as well.

BROWN: When it's seven and a half hours, you can't, personally, in every scene, all be good or all be bad.

McARDLE: At the end you're like, I have done a great show, an average show, a shit show, a show where I forgot lines, I did every kind of show you can do. You kind of just have to surrender to it.

GARFIELD: There are some nights where, ugh, I can't almost die of AIDS tonight. But something fucking weird happens every single time, as soon as I'm walking out of this dressing room down for my call, where suddenly you feel like an army joins you and it's magical.

LANE: It's one of the most incredible parts I've ever played. It's up there with Hickey in *The Iceman Cometh*, in terms of complexity . . . and *length*. Five hours is a walk in the park compared to this. But you see why people keep talking about it, why it keeps coming back, and why he's so protective of it.

McARDLE: It's truly a privilege to do this play. I really mean that, it's not just me being a wanker.

GARFIELD: You know, Prior is the perfect inspiration. Whenever I'm feeling too pathetic to go on, all I have to do is put myself back into Prior, and it's just: "More life, more life, more life," and that's it.

YOU ARE FABULOUS CREATURES, EACH AND EVERY ONE

Prior Walter

STEPHEN SPINELLA (Prior in workshops, San Francisco, Los Angeles, New York, 1988–94): There really weren't gay roles like this. Gay roles were either queens we could laugh at, or some kind of disturbed person. Prior was a serious queen. He was very funny; he was going through hell. He wasn't a butch guy. He was a bottom. You just don't see those guys.

ELLEN McLAUGHLIN (the Angel in workshops, San Francisco, Los Angeles, New York, 1990–94): Tony took an unapologetically gay character, severely ill with AIDS, and he made him an Everyman. Prior is absolutely, unabashedly the hero of the play. If you feel anything about the play, what you'll feel is an identification with that character. You can't experience the play otherwise. It's impossible.

EMILY NUSSBAUM (TV critic, *New Yorker*): Stephen Spinella was playing a very familiar type of funny queeny guy, and expressing rage and sadness, and not being a clown, but being a tragic romantic hero.

TONY KUSHNER: Prior was written for him, for his incredible elegance and wit and grace. It's Judy Garland and Bette Davis, it's not a wilting flower. It's modeled on Joan Crawford, although I don't think Prior would be a Crawford queen.

ROBBY SELLA (Prior in Juilliard *Millennium* workshop, 1992, and in national tour, 1994–95): What I loved about Prior from that first table read was how witty and intelligent he was. There was a fierceness that—if he hadn't had the experiences he had, if he hadn't had to live with this disease, that ferocity might never have come to the fore.

SPINELLA: Every time I played him he got more confident. I think Tony constructed the perfect guy to go through all that. He became more tenacious the sicker he got. And he just got stronger and more confident the sicker he got. He begins the play terrified. The terror never really goes away—it's the way he deals with the terror.

ANDREW GARFIELD (Prior in London, 2017, and New York, 2018): He can deal with what's happening because he's so rational, he's so—what's the word I'm looking for, fuck—competent, he's very *competent* somehow, within all of the madness. "I am known, where I am known, as one cool collected queen, and I am ruffled." All of the hysteria, it feels so brand-new to him, and I think he has to exaggerate it, he has to perform it in certain moments in order to make sense of it and to live with it.

DEBORAH GEIS (co-editor, *Approaching the Millennium*): Camp, campiness, is traditionally a coping mechanism within gay subcultures, a way of showing that something is funny and painful at the same time; so when you get Prior singing fragments from *My Fair Lady*, he's trying to laugh so as not to be devastated.

GARFIELD: For me, growing up, the message I got was "Don't be such a drama queen, don't be so overly sensitive, don't overreact," so I've worked very hard in my life to make sure I am loved by not making big deals out of things. So it's a very liberating, scary place to feel like I'm actually being invited the other way, to be more freely expressive, heightened, over-the-top. It's kind of gorgeous.

SEAN CHAPMAN (Prior in London, 1992): I was playing somebody who had this disease, who was calling out to the only person he could rely on to help him, and this person was slipping through his grasp. I was at sea. I didn't know how to do that without it becoming sentimental. You know, *Oh pity me*. But it's like playing the king in Shakespeare. You don't play being the king, *everyone around you plays that you are king*. So I realized I didn't have to act the illness, everyone around me will act that I have the illness. You let people come into a room where you're on an IV drip and react off of them. In some ways, you actually want to *resist* it, in the way that people resist that when they're ill.

SPINELLA: He never turns his rage into hate. He never gets bitter. He always has things to do that keep him from tumbling over that edge into bitterness, which is what happens when we run out of things to do.

KUSHNER: Stephen and I just have a special kind of understanding. I never really had to tell him anything about how to do it. He just did it.

Prior (Stephen Spinella) in San Francisco, 1991. (*Katy Raddatz/Museum of Performance + Design*)

SPINELLA: The early part of my career was very, very difficult. I weighed, like, 115 pounds! Towards the end of the '80s, before *Angels* started going, I was just doing occasional plays with Tony and beginning to consider whether I should go to law school or something.

McLAUGHLIN: I wrote Stephen a note opening night that said, "Hey, you were already a wonderful guy but Prior has made you a better man. What you have learned from this character has been so significant in your development as a human being. You've let him teach you. You've become a better person by embodying him night after night."

KATHLEEN CHALFANT (Hannah in workshops, San Francisco, Los Angeles, New York, 1990–94): It's not true anymore because Stephen's now a regular-sized person, which is so surprising, but there was a strange dichotomy between Stephen's fierceness and his apparent physical fragility. Which always was kind of a joke, like Stephen was pretending to be the thinnest person there ever was. He's one of the few people I know who doesn't suffer from self-doubt. Which is not to say he didn't think, *I could do this better*, or whatever, but many people in the theater have this radical self-doubt, and Stephen never had that. And it makes you very brave.

F. MURRAY ABRAHAM (Roy in New York replacement cast, 1994): Spinella. That's one of the greatest performances I've ever seen. I would leave my dressing room to watch him in certain scenes. He was astounding. Every night, eight times a week, the same marvelous performance. He used to eat bananas throughout the show backstage to keep his strength up. It was like Superman. Supergayman.

KUSHNER: I mean, nobody could possibly do any better with Prior Walter than Stephen Spinella. It's just not possible. That's just science. But I've seen Justin Kirk and now Andrew take on this part. And Christian Borle and Michael Urie, and every one of them has found something in it that I hadn't seen before.

• • •

CHAPMAN: I remember the scene where Prior shows Louis his lesions. There was a ripple of fear that went out over the audience. Because no one had seen anything like it. Here's this person who looks totally well, he's got this skin disease, what else could it be? And the audience in that time is thinking, *Oh God, I might have this.* And so there was this escalating sense of complicity with the audience, but also their mounting terror on where on earth this was going to go.

MARK BRONNENBERG (Kushner's partner in the mid-1980s): Louis and Prior are together for four and a half years, and that's how long Tony and I were together. I'm assuming that that was something in his head that he took and put in the play.

MARK EMERSON (Prior at Headlong, United Kingdom tour, 2007): I just knew instinctively that Prior's very first scene with Louis was going to be the hardest to do. Because we had a history together at school, I think [director] Daniel Kramer knew that as a person I usually am the nice guy who wants to be well liked in every circumstance. I remember him saying to me one day, "You know, Mark, you *can* be a bitch. You've been a bitch, I've seen it." That was really eye-opening to me. I *do* have that inside of me!

SCOTT PARKINSON (Prior in the Journeymen, Chicago, 1998): On the surface, Louis would certainly not seem to be anyone's idea of a solid, reliable partner, and that to me begs certain questions about who Prior is and what he is drawn to and why.

JAMES McARDLE (Louis in London, 2017, and New York, 2018): It's quite a codependent relationship, and the way we play it, Andrew's almost my mother.

GEORGE C. WOLFE (director in New York, 1993–94): Prior took care of Louis and allowed Louis to live inside of his intellectual and emotional infancy.

KARL MILLER (Prior at Forum Theatre, Silver Spring, MD, 2009): I think Prior loved Louis's gift for analysis and invective and never once imagined those rather sharp tools would be used to gouge out his own heart.

CHAPMAN: The drag scene, the one with Harper, is such a gift.

(Harper appears. Prior is surprised.)

HARPER
Are you . . . Who are you?

PRIOR
Who are you?

HARPER
What are you doing in my hallucination?

PRIOR
I'm not in your hallucination. You're in my dream.

HARPER
You're wearing makeup.

PRIOR
So are you.

HARPER
But you're a man.

PRIOR
(He looks in his mirror, SCREAMS!, mimes slashing his chest with his lipstick and dies, fabulously tragic.)

—Millennium Approaches, Act 1, Scene 7

GEIS: Those moments when Harper and Prior appear together in the threshold of revelation are my favorite moments in the play. It's like these characters have things to say to each other but it's hard to imagine why they would meet up.

CYNTHIA MACE (Harper in Los Angeles, 1992): The great thing about that scene is that they each have a secret. So it takes some gentleness and, on Prior's part, some humor to make someone comfortable enough to talk to you. Harper knows she has to go home and deal with her marriage. Prior knows he has to deal with his illness.

MARCIA GAY HARDEN (Harper in New York, 1993–94): The joy was to have this delightful moment, to then experience the surprise with the audience that Tony had now blended these two moments. The writing would blend, and the audience would gasp at the excitingness of that blending.

KIMBERLY FLYNN (Tony Kushner's friend and dramaturg for *Angels*): When Harper learns from Prior that he is a homosexual, she immediately responds, "In my church, we don't believe in homosexuals." Prior counters "In my church, we don't believe in Mormons." Harper starts "What church . . . ?" but then laughs and declares "I get it!" There is pleasure in the encounter, if not always for the characters, definitely for the audience. There is a sense of excitement and possibility in the new shared space that opens up at the moment when one gets the joke.

MACE: It's also the beginning of where characters you love and believe in start talking about the themes. Prior says, "The limitations of the imagination." Tony is signaling that we will use imagination, but we will get to the heart of things.

I think it's that same scene that talks about how you begin change. They're on the *threshold* of revelation. Things aren't revealed yet. The idea that even America as a country is on the threshold of something, if we just quit lying, is an amazing concept.

SELLA: There's a scene where Prior goes to the doctor and it's indicated that he strips down. It's got a real vulnerability to it, a young man who looks so drawn and is covered in these terrible lesions. I had never done nudity or anything like that before, but it absolutely seemed no question that this was as it was written and as it should be. There were a few moments of "Yikes!" in the theater at Lincoln Center. I remember one older woman turning to her companion and saying, "I thought this was the Juilliard School!"

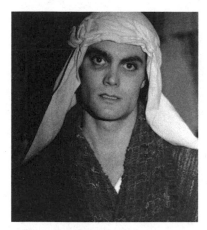

GARRET DILLAHUNT (Prior at American Conservatory Theater, San Francisco, 1994–95): I remember my—I should just say, friends of friends came, and one of them was a professional basketball player in the day, and I remember being really nervous that they were coming—I think he was a Mormon. There's a scene in *Millennium*, the exam scene, and we found a way to put on these really gnarly lesions. I disrobe as the nurse examines me. I just remember peeking out once from backstage and there was such a look of disgust on this guy's face, these people that I had gotten tickets for, and they left at intermission.

And I was talking to Greg Wallace about it, who was my Belize, and I remember feeling so *hurt*. Look, I'm a straight white man. I understand love, I understand shame, I understand guilt and mistakes. But I'm not a gay man, there's a lot I can't imagine. But in that moment, I got a little taste of what many of my friends must have gone through. I remember being so shook by it and so—I don't know what the feelings were, but I identified in a small way. And I remember Greg saying, "Mm-hmm, welcome."

RICHARD FELDMAN (director of Juilliard *Millennium* workshop, 1992): There's that very complicated scene where the two couples are fighting. Prior is in the hospital. Louis and Joe walk out on their spouses simultaneously. Rehearsing those scenes, trying to keep the ball in the air, you have to technically wait while the other scene is playing out.

SPINELLA: I've had people break up with me before and there's a moment when a certain sound comes out of their mouth and you just know. Your peripheral vision disappears and you get tunnel vision and you know your life is gonna change. Tony had written that into the scene. It was a scene I understood very early on, and it never changed throughout the process.

Garret Dillahunt in costume as Prior in ACT's production, 1994. (*Photographer unknown, courtesy of Garret Dillahunt*)

JON MATTHEWS (Louis in Taper Too workshop, 1990): Harper and Joe on one side of the stage, Louis and Prior on the other having their breakup scenes. That's right out of opera.

• • •

AMANDA LAWRENCE (the Angel in London, 2017, and New York, 2018): I come from inside his body, I put a book inside his body, I fuck him. I am his female essence ascendant, I am part of his femaleness.

EELCO SMITS (Prior at Toneelgroep Amsterdam, 2007–15): The Angel is something Prior imagines, because it's inspired by those early days of patients having AIDS medicines and becoming delirious and seeing hallucinations.

KUSHNER: The central tension comes from Prior, and the question of whether this is real or a delusion, AIDS-related dementia, is it some sort of runaway psychological manifestation of something.

GARFIELD: I remember feeling very nervous about the end of *Millennium*, because suddenly he's just alone and onstage in a bed, responding to ghosts, visions, lighting changes, sound changes, sound effects, shaking bed, and it's a big, empty cavernous space at this point. It's the most vulnerable place that Prior has in that first play, and you feel very vulnerable as an actor onstage as well.

SPINELLA: When the magic was great, it was so much easier! He has a total boner, he's completely eroticized, he's humping the sheets. Playing that scene was dealing more with: How nasty can I actually be here in front of all these people?

When the Angel arrives, that's just pretty much: AGOG. When an angel comes into your room, it's very limited, the range of your emotions. It goes from agog to passing out.

The tricky part of that was the line. That he has the wherewithal to use his wit in that moment. That was the thing about Prior. He was so scared all the time, but he had such tenacity. He would be absolutely terrified, this thing coming through his roof, but he would humanize it for himself: "God almighty, *very* Steven Spielberg."

CHAPMAN: "Very Steven Spielberg!" Everyone knows that line now, it's a cliché. But imagine the first audience! Going, *Oh my God, we're going to die of AIDS, oh my God, oh my God oh my God.* Then you say that line and the place would go nuts.

• • •

> HANNAH
> Are you . . . a homosexual?
>
> PRIOR
> Oh, is it *that* obvious? Yes I am. What's it to you?
>
> HANNAH
> Would you say you are a typical . . . homosexual?
>
> PRIOR
> Me? Oh I'm *stereotypical.* What, you mean like am I a hairdresser or . . .
>
> HANNAH
> *Are* you a hairdresser?
>
> PRIOR
> Well it would be *your* lucky day if I was because frankly . . .
>
> *—Perestroika*, Act 4, Scene 6

SPINELLA: Joe Mantello said there were nights where he would clock that laugh.

DAVID CROMER (director and Louis in the Journeymen, 1998): An actor I knew always was critical of the play and said, "*Ugh*, there's a hairdresser joke in the middle of this scene. Why is *that* in there?" But the thing about that joke is that it's immediately followed by Prior realizing he's been mean and crying and being unable to stop.

(Little pause.)

PRIOR
I'm sick. I'm sick. It's expensive.
(He starts to cry.)
Oh shit now I won't be able to stop, now it's started.

—*Perestroika*, Act 4, Scene 6

CROMER: The laugh can't be the *goal*, the line *after* is the goal. So I spent a lot of time trying to get people to deliver the lines not quite as jokingly as people do. Look, it's different if you're Nathan Lane, who is a fucking genius. He could get laughs in *The Crucible*, I bet. But for those of us who aren't Nathan Lane, if you fail at the laugh and you're not playing the moment, it's embarrassing. If you fail at the laugh and you are playing the moment, it doesn't matter because you have the moment.

PARKINSON: While we may have technically missed some of the laughs on the page in our production in favor of a quest for deeper levels of engagement and complexity, there are of course many laughs throughout the two plays that are just so airtight in their writing that I don't think there's any way to deliver them *without* eliciting peals of laughter from an audience.

CROMER: I will say that a scene that is very funny that I *ruined* by overthinking it is the scene where Belize and Prior spy on Joe. "This is an appellate court!" "And I am *appealing* to anyone who will listen!"

K. TODD FREEMAN (Belize in Los Angeles, 1992): We had these big headscarves on, these giant sunglasses.

DILLAHUNT: I had the black robe on and the scarf, Prior's prophet robes, feeling sort of fabulous, and you could swish the scarf around and punctuate the line.

FREEMAN: It was just a classic Lucy-and-Ethel situation.

DILLAHUNT: I think it's in *Perestroika* where Prior and the Angel are wrestling, like Jacob and the angel. She was a gymnastic person, and I was athletic, and she had all these handholds on her rig that I could grab onto. And she would swoop down and we would have these battles way up in the air. We really enjoyed that, the way you do when you're young and immortal.

McLAUGHLIN: When he comes up to heaven and disrupts this chaotic meeting, the thicket of squabbling bureaucracy that the Angels have become, and makes this completely human plea for life, there is this attempt on my part for the first time to understand him. I become curious for the first time. *Why would you want this?* And I have a point: Human life, from our perspective, doesn't make any sense. Why would you *want* to be alive?

JONATHAN BOCK (Louis at Round House/Olney, Bethesda, MD, 2016): Honestly, the Council of Principalities scene was the only part of the entire seven hours where I stood onstage every night and thought, *Come on, Tony, this is a masterpiece and all but couldn't you have just cut this part in half?* I think this part of the play could be fun to perform depending on the director and what he or she chooses to do with it. But in our production, we were given these doofy wings, and it was exceedingly boring to perform.

CAROLYN SWIFT (the Angel in national tour, 1994–95): Michael Mayer had the Council of Principalities scene staged where Robby Sella was way downstage, and the Angel and all the other people dressed as angels were way upstage and we were standing on crates that were hard to get up to and a little scary, and we were in pin spots. We never cracked the scene, we never found the verb. Michael himself would say, in rehearsal, "I don't get this scene, I don't know what to do with it."

MICHAEL MAYER (director of national tour, 1994–95): It was probably too overtly theatricalized, because they couldn't see each other, they couldn't connect. But I was so concerned with establishing what the rules of heaven were in that moment.

SWIFT: Until one night at the Kennedy Center, when I went up on my crate and immediately my pin spot went out. And Robby crossed up, grabbed my hand in the dark, helped me off my crate, and took me into his light. As we were crossing down we had this subterranean conversation where I said, "Don't let go of me, we're gonna arm wrestle through this scene." And we did, and we held on, and I let him win on his last line, "I want more life," and then I let him push me over.

We called Michael Mayer and said, "We finally cracked the scene!"

McLAUGHLIN: Why would anyone want the sheer misery of human life? It goes against all reason. But still, he says, that's all I've got. It's what I want. More life. Which is a deeply moving plea, the most fundamental human desire, something one sees at sickbeds and which all of us had witnessed in Sigrid's last days, that primal desire for more, despite it all, just the raw yearning for that ineffable thing, life itself.

> PRIOR
> But still. Still.
> Bless me anyway.
> I want more life. I can't help myself. I do.
> I've lived through such terrible times, and there are people who live through
> much much worse, but . . . you see them living anyway.
>
> –*Perestroika*, Act 5, Scene 5

GARFIELD: There's an obvious tenderness between Prior and the Angel. She's like a lost child, and I think Prior's heart breaks for her because he can empathize. And even though it's ridiculous what she's asking for, and impossible, there's a part of me that goes: Wouldn't that be wonderful if we could all just stop? If we could all just do that maybe some order could return, if we could all be still for a moment.

McLAUGHLIN: His failure as a prophet is his triumph as a flawed and frail human being who accepts his own imperfect mortal existence, with all its suffering and fleeting beauty.

GARFIELD: That's the great healing at the end of the second play for Prior. That's why I think he feels equipped and allowed to say "I bless you," because he's allowed himself to be blessed. The woundedness that he walks with is as much a part of him as the quote-unquote *fabulousness* that is part of him. It's all one, it's all him.

McLAUGHLIN: I admire so many things about the play, but that moment in the Hall of Principalities is very high on the list.

• • •

PRIOR

It's January 1990. I've been living with AIDS for five years. That's six whole months longer than I lived with Louis.

—*Perestroika*, Epilogue

TONY TACCONE (co-director in Los Angeles, 1992; director at Berkeley Rep, 2018): The audience seeks resolution. The satisfaction that you get from catharsis. Playwrights are always trying to get that balance between reality and artistic truth. Sometimes they're at odds with each other. Tony had the genius to not cut Prior's last speech. Lots of people told him to cut it. It's one of the greatest speeches ever written!

CHRIS GEIDNER (LGBT politics reporter; legal editor, *BuzzFeed*): Different people, I've found over time, dislike aspects of both Harper's and Prior's final speeches. I love them both! I think that they're both so powerful. It's this acknowledgment that—both of those speeches feel as if it's Kushner speaking, not the characters. It's such a Robin Goodfellow sort of moment. You can read it in Tony's voice: This is what we've told you. And this is our story. And this is where it goes from here.

MICHAEL KRASS (costume designer of national tour, 1994–95): Prior needed a coat. They were outside at the fountain, he needed a coat to do the benediction in. I had a brother, who died of AIDS, we think, it was very early on, and I had his coat. So Prior wore his coat for the benediction, for the year of touring. I wore it the other day and thought about it.

SELLA: That moment in the epilogue is one of the most important experiences I ever had. This was a journey, over the course of eight hours, that they've been on with you. And to feel . . . I feel like I could cry about it . . . to feel a room of six hundred, seven hundred, a thousand people, leaning forward and looking up at you, and you knew that some of them had lived it, some of them had lost. It was extremely moving and sometimes I could barely get through it. Because I loved them.

PETER BIRKENHEAD (Louis in national tour, 1994–95): What I remember most of all was the love. The feeling of love for Robby as he spoke those words, for the audience, for my cast-mates, for every man and woman who'd suffered unnecessarily from this plague. For everyone. It was a beautiful experience. Every night.

GARFIELD: It's a privilege to say those words at the end of seven and a half hours. There are some nights I feel like I earn it and some nights I feel like I don't. And that's OK, I think it's inherent in the play, it's inherent in the not-enoughness, it's inherent in that Prior accepts the mystery of just having to show up with whatever he's got and do the best that he possibly can.

DILLAHUNT: I just remember it being very difficult to get through, and looking out there, at that crowd and that city that started the whole thing, when so many of us have lost so many people.

TACCONE: At the same time, it is an optimistic play. It's about people who actually *do* change, and the price is sometimes very high; but the feeling of Harper leaving on that plane, the feeling of Louis and Prior having repaired some form of relationship, of Hannah hanging out with all of them onstage, those are profoundly optimistic events.

McARDLE: It's so important that the chosen characters are Prior, Louis, Belize, Hannah. I love the idea that they've created this family of friends. I was worried, though, at the Bethesda Fountain it would be like . . . *(Sings* Friends *theme song.)*

CROMER: It can't just be a wash of emotions. We're not supposed to sit there with bemused smiles on our faces and let them glisten in the light and show them how moved we are. We're supposed to be arguing about politics on a day in New York. It was decidedly, aggressively unsentimental.

McARDLE: That little last spat between Louis and Belize is so important. It's hopeful and these people have found a way to live together, but that spark is still there.

NATHAN STEWART-JARRETT (Belize in London, 2017, and New York, 2018): I just love the fact that we are all together. Every time I get so emotional, I can't speak.

MONICA PEARL (professor of English and American studies, University of Manchester): I really love it, because it ends with a group of friends arguing. It's a very queer ending. The normal or conventional closure for a story is that it ends with a couple. Normally a heterosexual couple, but we're willing to take a homosexual couple if we're very progressive. A group of friends arguing is a very queer alternative to a normative ending.

People *do* survive. It's seriously underrepresented. You don't want to be pie-in-the-sky about it, but there can be years and years of very productive life. And I thought there was an incredible unwillingness to show that. That it was a widespread form of delectation among those who are not immune-compromised to show over and over again people dying these terrible deaths because it makes you cry. . . . It's terribly important that *Perestroika* ends with an epilogue, five years into the future, and that Prior is still alive.

–Tony Kushner, interviewed by Patrick R. Pacheco in *Body Positive* magazine, September 1993

DALE PECK (literary critic, author of *Martin and John*): You could argue that Prior still being alive at the end of the play a year and a half later, statistically he should be dead by that point. With an opportunistic infection and a diagnosis of AIDS, you generally died within twelve to fourteen months, so to have him alive at the end is an aspirational fantasy.

But this is how fictive narrative works. You create scenarios not because they're the most likely thing that could happen but because they allow readers to work out private psychodramas. We all wanted to believe in 1991 that people were going to live, that being HIV-positive wasn't a death sentence. That play helped create the space for that kind of belief to happen.

EMERSON: We did not do the epilogue in our production. That language in the ending monologue was more fitting to the early '90s, to the height of the AIDS epidemic, and felt a little less resonant in 2007.

McARDLE: I think Prior dies six months after the play ends, but Louis is there with Prior in that last scene.

PRIOR
We won't die secret deaths anymore. The world only spins forward.
We will be citizens. The time has come.
Bye now.

You are fabulous creatures, each and every one.

And I bless you: *More Life*.

The Great Work Begins.

–Perestroika, Epilogue

MADISON MOORE (author of *Fabulous: The Rise of the Beautiful Eccentric*): It's easy to think about *fabulous* as something that is about drag queens or certain kinds of looks. The look is important. The look does political work. But to say "You are all fabulous creatures" is a way of encouraging people to reach their potential, to be there for one another, to create community. That's what fabulousness does. It lifts me up, the person doing it, but it lifts everyone else up as well.

JOE MANTELLO (Louis in Los Angeles and New York, 1992–94): I do believe that. The world only spins forward. I believe that.

PARKINSON: What has resonated with me throughout my life is the final line of the play: "The Great Work Begins." I still think nearly every day in some way about the great work the play asks of us, and what it means for my own life.

JOHN JUDD (Roy in the Journeymen, 1998): Several years after our production I found myself in New York, doing a play Off-Broadway. One day walking through the park I looked up and was standing at the fountain. The beauty and grace of that Emma Stebbins angel, putting her foot down. I sat. I smiled and wept for a long time.

RUSSELL TOVEY (Joe in London, 2017): I have pictures from the last ten years with lovers, friends, my dog, myself, every season, with this angel.

FRANK WOOD (Roy at Signature Theatre, New York, 2010): I will never go to Central Park again without thinking of that play and looking at Bethesda Fountain as a source of solace.

SELLA: It's funny, I've played a lot of parts where I'm the narrator and I talk to the audience. *Side Man, The Glass Menagerie, Cabaret.* It can be hard. You see people yawning or sleeping or sitting with their arms folded. But the end of *Perestroika* was never like that. We're all there with you. We are all exhausted, we're all terrified, we're all elated, we're all delighted, and now what? Good night, and bless you.

Hannah (Kathleen Chalfant), Prior (Stephen Spinella), Belize (K. Todd Freeman), and Louis (Joe Mantello) in the Bethesda Fountain scene, Los Angeles, 1992. (© *Jay Thompson and Craig Schwartz/Center Theatre Group*)

CHAPTER 3

THE WORLD ONLY SPINS FORWARD

THE LEGACY OF *ANGELS*

LARRY KRAMER (writer and activist): What can I say that hasn't been said by many others?

TONY KUSHNER: It's been out in the world now for twenty-five years. There are hundreds of thousands of copies of the play in many languages. I don't know how that feels.

(Pause.)

It feels good. It will be the headline of my obituary: "Author of *Angels in America* is dead."

CAROLYN SWIFT (the Angel in national tour, 1994–95): There are people out there who were suffering alone until they saw *Angels*. I believe *Angels* gave many souls a place to grieve in public and to bury their dead among the living.

FRANK RICH (writer-at-large, *New York*): It's all there. It has everything you want in a play.

GEORGE C. WOLFE (director in New York, 1993–94): Just before we would do a run-through, Ron Leibman would say, "Everything that happens in life happens in this show." And then I'd laugh, and then we'd start.

ZOE KAZAN (Harper at Signature Theatre, New York, 2010): I think it's mimetic. The play does the thing that it prescribes. It requires the same thing from the actors as it does from the characters as it does from the audience.

ADAM DRIVER (Louis at Signature Theatre, New York, 2010): I think it's the greatest play ever written.

CARYL CHURCHILL (world's greatest living playwright): I remember when *Angels in America* was first done in London how happy I was to find this playwright who wrote with politics, imagination, and passion, and on a grand scale.

BEN BRANTLEY (co-chief theater critic, *New York Times*): *Angels* brought theater back into the national conversation, in a way that hasn't happened again until *Hamilton*.

EMILY NUSSBAUM (television critic, *New Yorker*): It reminds me of *Hamilton*, because there was something so startling in seeing the play at this time. It created this set of linked connections that I hadn't thought about.

> *Angels in America* is a second-rate play written by a second-rate playwright who happens to be gay, and because he has written a play about being gay, and about AIDS, no one—and I mean no one—is going to call *Angels in America* the overwrought, coarse, posturing, formulaic mess that it is.
>
> –Lee Siegel, "Angles in America," *New Republic*, December 28, 2003

LEE SIEGEL (cultural critic): I wrote that review in response to the television adaptation of *Angels*. Seeing the play was a very different experience from seeing it on television.

The play left me feeling divided. I was overwhelmed by Kushner's stagecraft. He had created a world of action and ideas—especially ideas—that swept me into it. At the same time, I could feel the action and ideas laboriously rolled into alignment, as if stagehands were moving both around like scenery.

SAM GOLD (director, *A Doll's House Part 2* and *Fun Home*): I saw *Millennium* when I was fifteen. It was the first play I ever saw on Broadway. It was magic, it was poetry, it was enormous.

RICH: All with spectacle, a certain amount of spiritual subtext and meaning, if not classically religious. Also it has great humor and wit. It has the intimate and the grand. It always remains in human scale, even when an angel appears.

CHRISTOPHER SHINN (playwright, *Dying City* and *Against*): Nobody had exposed me to the ideas in that play. For people like me who were young, there was no other mainstream play that had that diversity of inspiration.

KRAMER: It's a very important play and it's wonderful that it's still being performed all over the world. That the two major AIDS plays, *Angels* and my *Normal Heart*, are still being performed so extensively is quite remarkable and a testimony to the power of the theater to deal with gay history.

DAVID FRANCE (director and writer, *How to Survive a Plague*): I remember thinking if I could understand the play, I could understand AIDS. When the movie came out I watched it over and over, trying to see what Tony was telling us about the meaning of AIDS, thinking it was somehow coded in there. I didn't discover it, though, even through the six-year process of writing my book. I don't know how you find meaning in something like that.

JOSEPH HAJ (artistic director, Guthrie Theater, Minneapolis): I can't think of another play in my lifetime that did more to change society's view of an issue than *Angels* did.

OSKAR EUSTIS (artistic director, Public Theater, New York): In that particular mix of high culture and popular culture that is American theater, *Angels* was the tip of the spear. It was the great cultural document that provoked this transition towards full citizenship, as Prior says. One of the very first reviews of *Angels* described Prior as an Everyman, standing in for all of us. When I read that I thought, Oh yes!

Of course there had been other gay protagonists, from *The Normal Heart* and *As Is* to *The Boys in the Band*. But it was the first play where characters who were openly, defiantly, *complicatedly* gay were claiming to speak for all of America. To me, that was the cultural breakthrough, to say that the gay experience is no longer the marginalized experience, it is no longer in an isolated ghetto, but gay people can speak for all Americans.

KARL MILLER (Prior at Forum Theatre, Silver Spring, MD, 2009): Before that, homosexuality was depicted as either some psycho perversion—e.g., *JFK* and *Silence of the Lambs*—or a cheap punch line—e.g., take your pick. Then Kushner comes along and lays down nothing less than a new book of the Bible with five titanic gay leading roles at its center.

DALE PECK (cultural critic): *Angels* asked a question that a lot of gay men, particularly middle-class white gay dudes, asked themselves. OK, for the past couple of decades, we have built a very vibrant subculture that was very much based around being outside the mainstream. This was our little world, and if you could afford to live there, and if you were not suffering, if you were not a woman, a person of color, if you were not trans and dealing with people thinking you didn't actually exist, you could have a really good time there, and have a superior attitude. Ugh, straight people! *So boring.* Mainstream culture! *So limiting.* Here we are, having a fantastic time, not raising children, making a lot of money. It's great!

All that cultural work contributed to the familiarity and the normalizing of homosexuality in America, and the AIDS crisis threw all of that into jeopardy. The gay community responded to that with work that was very politically engaged. By 1991 you had the question: What are we fighting for now? Are we fighting for our own little community on the outside where we get to do our own thing? Or are we fighting to be American just like other Americans?

Angels asked that question at the moment where we actually had to make that choice. We had to ask ourselves what that means. Being outlaws made us interesting. You could use that position to criticize mainstream society, to say what society can't say, but you can't live there forever, particularly once the mainstream starts paying attention to you.

CLEVE JONES (founder, NAMES Project AIDS Memorial Quilt): Those cultural milestones—of which *Angels* is perhaps the most prominent—were important to changing the way we see ourselves in a really powerful way. All this stuff that happened, from the Quilt, to ACT UP, to the Shanti Project and AIDS walkers, coupled with the reality of what we saw in those ICUs, our own living rooms and bedrooms as we emptied bedpans and measured out doses and arranged memorials—out of all of that came a very different attitude. What do you mean this isn't a marriage? Fuck you, this is what a marriage looks like. What do you mean this isn't a community? Fuck you, this is what a community looks like. We want it *all*.

PECK: I feel like gay culture did become a little more boring through that assimilation. I don't know if you've ever had sex in Central Park at night, but it's really fun! Maybe that's the price one pays for full participation in a democracy. I think that was a triumph for the gay community. But it was also, a little bit, a sadness for America. Gay people became more American but America didn't become more gay. That's not *Angels'* fault! This is all of gay culture and gay politics.

SHEILA CALLAGHAN (playwright, *Bed* and *Women Laughing Alone with Salad*): The huge accomplishment of this play was that it became popular. It seems so unlikely that a nontraditional play, epic in nature, discussing sickness and estrangement within a marginalized community, could have such widespread impact. But it did.

WESLEY MORRIS (critic-at-large, *New York Times*): All oppressed peoples want is to be left alone. You want to be included, but also not persecuted due to the attributes that made people want to enslave you, murder you, deny you rights, et cetera. You want to be visible, but you don't want to be conspicuous. But the great thing about this play is that it demanded you be as conspicuous as possible.

BRANTLEY: The phrase that kept coming up with *Hamilton* even before anyone saw it was *game-changer*. That's a very hopeful term, because I'm not sure these things actually change the game.

MICHAEL RIEDEL (theater columnist, *New York Post*): I don't think that this epic play led to more epic dramas. I don't think *Hamilton*'s gonna change theater! God help us if we suffer through ten years of hip-hop musicals. The next thing is gonna be what we don't expect at all.

PETER BIRKENHEAD (Louis in national tour, 1994–95): Within, I don't know, a year of *Angels* opening I feel like I saw maybe half a dozen plays with sprawling, nonlinear, time-traveling structures.

JONATHAN BOCK (Louis at Round House/Olney, Bethesda, MD, 2016): Bad Kushner-esque writing is everywhere and you can immediately feel it. It's that thing when playwrights try to talk politics in a funny and engaging way, with a few long, rambling monologues thrown in. Nobody does it as well, and nobody will ever be as funny.

ELLEN McLAUGHLIN (playwright; the Angel in workshops, San Francisco, Los Angeles, and New York, 1990–94): There were a lot of plays inspired by *Angels* that didn't work, but I'd rather see a big fat mess that attempts something that's out of a playwright's reach than a neat little bundle that stays with me not at all.

EUSTIS: The other thing *Angels* did was help make the claim that theater is something that belongs in the conversation about the great struggles of our time. It's not just for the arts pages. It's grappling with the big issues of who America is and what we would become. So while there's no direct literary lineage, I look at a show like [Lynn Nottage's] *Sweat* and I think its ambition is related. Lin-Manuel would talk about that over the course of working on *Hamilton*.

KIMBERLY FLYNN (Kushner's friend and dramaturg for *Angels*): In *Angels*, Tony stages one debate after another. There is no hesitation on Tony's part to allow his characters to be fully articulate, even philosophical; fully argumentative, even declamatory. The characters speak to each other, but as with Brecht's analogy of the theater as a courtroom, often cited by Tony, they are ultimately always addressing the audience. The audience understands itself as an interlocutor, even an arbiter . . . part of the contestation.

TRIP CULLMAN (director, *Significant Other* and *Lobby Hero*): You can have angels! The bar was set so high in terms of imagination. It's very close to being a kid, playing with your Legos, creating an entire cosmology in your head. That was very influential, thinking that's what I can do as a director: You can make a whole world.

MARK WING-DAVEY (director at American Conservatory Theater, San Francisco, 1994–95): You can write what you want to write, and let other people figure out how to do it.

MONICA PEARL (professor of English and American Studies, University of Manchester): One way to understand what AIDS wrought is to relegate it to a historical moment and to tell stories about it to suggest that it's ended. The other path was one that suggested that AIDS exposed all of the difficulties that were roiling under the surface anyway. Homelessness, drug addiction, oppression against gay people. That's the queer strand. The queer strand has never been able to relegate AIDS into history because none of those problems have gone away.

NICK ORMEROD (designer in London, 1992–93): The great thing about classics is they're about human beings, and the human dilemmas will always be the same, and human beings will always be the same.

TERRY TEACHOUT (theater critic, *Wall Street Journal*): I don't think it's exaggerating to say that *Angels* is a history play. If it continues to live on the stage, then it will undoubtedly be produced in ways that are intended to underline its continuing contemporary relevance. It will be treated with the same flexibility that we treat Shakespeare's history plays. As problematic as I think it is as a work of art, it still works. It really works.

LIN-MANUEL MIRANDA (playwright/performer, *Hamilton* and *In the Heights*): The notion of a country in political, physical, and spiritual crisis is very relatable, very applicable to today. The notion that there are indigenous spirits and they're pissed at us is very relatable. I think the metaphysical stuff couldn't be more relevant. The spiritual crisis that's suffusing the play feels very of the moment.

CYNTHIA MACE (Harper in Los Angeles, 1992): People wanted to see it when we did it because it was long and controversial. Now people want to see it because it's long, and it's magical, and it's *true*. It will never lose its impact because we haven't learned the lessons of it. Our ability to change is still challenged every day.

MARIANNE ELLIOTT (director in London, 2017): It's about people going to the pit of hell and finding a way out. That's an important story for us to hear, that we need to hear again.

SIEGEL: The play could have made itself more relevant by being more angry and less easy to assimilate. There was more to the AIDS crisis than Kushner portrayed, and in many places in this country and in the world, gay survival is not anything that is guaranteed. Great social progress obscures the intense pockets of hatred and resistance that are the backlash to it. The Pulse massacre in Orlando, sadly, is not a revelation. It's a reminder.

KRAMER: I wish that Tony would write more about gay history, but he has a much wider sphere of important interests than I do and we should be grateful for whatever he writes. He is a great writer.

DAVID SAVRAN (distinguished professor, Graduate Center, City University of New York): How do we rediscover it? How do we make it speak to us today? The kinds of utopian hopes that I held twenty-five years ago, that for me were so associated specifically with *Angels in America*, are pretty much dead. Which of course is a good reason to turn back to the play.

KUSHNER: The play doesn't describe a time of great triumph, it describes a time of great terror, beneath the surface of which the seeds of change are beginning to push upwards and through. Apparently, nothing good is happening, but good things *are* happening.

EMILY MANN (artistic director, McCarter Theatre, Princeton, NJ): There are cycles. *Angels* made a huge difference for the theater when it came out. And because it is in the canon now, it will come back as it should when it is needed again.

KUSHNER: It's coming. It's coming to New York. I'm very happy.

> "Angels in America," Tony Kushner's sweeping masterwork,
> will be revived at the Neil Simon Theater next spring, a quarter
> century after its winged title character first hovered over a
> Broadway stage. . . .
>   The revival, directed by Marianne Elliott ("The Curious
> Incident of the Dog in the Night-Time"), was created by the
> National Theater in London, and was staged there earlier this year.
> It is scheduled to begin previews on Broadway Feb. 23 and to
> open March 21; the New York run, produced by Tim Levy of NT
> America and Jordan Roth of Jujamcyn Theaters, is scheduled to
> last 18 weeks.
>
> –Michael Paulson, "'Angels in America' Is Returning to Broadway
> with Nathan Lane," *New York Times*, September 7, 2017

ANDREW GARFIELD (Prior in London, 2017, and New York, 2018): The idea of giving this play in New York, specifically, is deeply humbling, that's for sure. To bring it home to the place of its birth will obviously be a very profound thing.

RUFUS NORRIS (artistic director, Royal National Theatre): It's always a bit dangerous to do. Taking coals to Newcastle, we call it.

KUSHNER: It feels like a kind of a return. I'm very, very happy that American audiences will get to see this production of it because I think it's really wonderful. Not everything is exactly the way I imagined it. And I've seen many other wonderful versions of every scene. But every scene on that stage is rich and alive and you really get the play. You get what *Millennium* does well, and then you get what *Perestroika* does well. You get that they aren't the same play twice.

NORRIS: It will be brilliant to bring it home, not just because of Nathan and Tony, but this is a time in American politics where this play is very important.

DAVID CROMER (director at the Journeymen, Chicago, 1998): I tell ya, I think the play is more terrifying now because it feels like the world is falling apart again.

CALDWELL TIDICUE (Bob the Drag Queen, *RuPaul's Drag Race*; Belize at Berkeley Rep, 2018): During turbulent times, art gets stronger. It's not only Trump. We've got hurricanes. White nationalists marching up and down the street. North Korea. We're feeling desperate, anxious, emotional, and that's where art comes from, you know?

SWIFT: *Angels* reminded us that theater is essentially a political act.

VINSON CUNNINGHAM (culture critic, *New Yorker*): It makes its politics and its stance toward history unavoidable. You can't understand it simply as a lament about AIDS. You have to deal with Cohn.

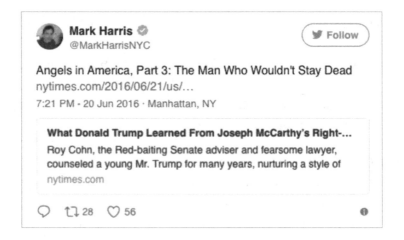

Mark Harris ✔
@MarkHarrisNYC

Follow

Angels in America, Part 3: The Man Who Wouldn't Stay Dead
nytimes.com/2016/06/21/us/...
7:21 PM · 20 Jun 2016 · Manhattan, NY

What Donald Trump Learned From Joseph McCarthy's Right-...
Roy Cohn, the Red-baiting Senate adviser and fearsome lawyer, counseled a young Mr. Trump for many years, nurturing a style of
nytimes.com

💬   ♻ 28   ♡ 56

JENNIFER ENGSTROM (the Angel at Kansas City Repertory Theatre, 2015): I feel like we are in a bizarro Part 3 of *Angels in America*, and the ghost of Roy Cohn is sweetly caressing the nuts of an American president who rides naked on horseback with Vladimir Putin.

EUSTIS: Now, twenty-five years later, it's Tony's vision of the Right that looks so prescient. When Tony wrote Roy Cohn, he was a larger-than-life, demonic figure. Now his pupil is the president of the United States. My God. Talk about the return of the repressed! Here he is, in all his glory. Trump's America is Roy Cohn's America: sharply divided between winners and losers, hatred of the powerless used as a cynical tool to enrich the privileged. Thus proving, as Mark Harris says, that Tony's drag name should be Eera Lee Prescient.

RON LEIBMAN (Roy in Los Angeles and New York, 1992–94): When I read about the Trump-Cohn link I just thought, *Yep! Of course they found each other!*

NATHAN LANE (Roy in London, 2017, and New York, 2018): Tony was rather upset because these articles were starting about Trump and Roy, and he seemed almost insulted on Roy's behalf that these comparisons were being made, because Roy was rather brilliant and this is just a crude version. I was laughing because I said, "I think you're talking more about your character than the real guy."

CHRIS GEIDNER (legal editor, *BuzzFeed*): You see Cohn's influence in Trump's view of the importance of brute force in advancing legal interest. Watch a Trump speech in response to an adverse court ruling: It could be written by Roy Cohn. In a very *Angels* sense, everything remains up in the air, and everything can turn on a dime.

Donald Trump and Roy Cohn, October 18, 1984. (*Bettmann/Contributor via Getty Images*)

TONY TACCONE (director at Berkeley Rep, 2018): There's one factor that's shifted since it was written: the dynamic with AIDS in this country. It's not the same emergency that it was when Tony wrote it. But two other things have actually become more pressing. Climate change. When he was writing about it back then through the voice of Harper, it felt much further down the road in terms of a pressing emergency than right now, when Antarctica is literally melting as we speak. The other issue is Reagan's America. As dangerous and as scary as that was, it really doesn't compare with what's happening with Donald Trump.

NORRIS: I don't want to draw the whole thing to the Trump era, because the play's so much bigger than that. It diminishes the play to talk about it in those terms. The play challenges audiences to be more intelligent.

EUSTIS: *Angels* feels so fresh, twenty-five years after its initial production, because America is still in the life-and-death struggle of figuring out who we are. Will we live in a country that Roy Cohn created, or will we live in the paradise that Belize imagines at Roy's deathbed? Will we choose selfishness and fear and greed, or solidarity and inclusion and love? It is either the end of the world or the beginning.

McLAUGHLIN: What I mostly remember from that time in my life was joy. I felt like we were doing something important with the medium that I had given my life to. That is one of the great privileges, the greatest gift I could have ever been given.

EUSTIS: I think about this play every day, and I have since we started working on it.

STEVEN CULP (Joe at American Conservatory Theater, San Francisco, 1994–95): Great theater—and music, literature, art, film, even acting—works to expand our hearts, minds, and souls. It changes us—slowly, subtly, and incrementally, to be sure, and sometimes that change is difficult to discern. But I believe it's there. Each moment of connecting with something outside of and larger and better than ourselves is a tiny baby step of progress.

MICHAEL MAYER (director of NYU *Perestroika* workshop, 1993, and national tour, 1994–95): If it did nothing else but inspire now two generations of playwrights, then *dayenu*. If it only reminded the American theater that what we do can be important and responsible and responsive to the world that we're in right now, *dayenu*. If all it did was give a community of people who watched their brothers dying year after year after year, if it only gave them a place to come together and feel that in their innermost core, in the very center of their being, that there was no illness—if it gave them an opportunity to imagine a triumph over the disease and the disease of the body politic as well, not just that fucking virus—*dayenu*. I could go on. Just *dayenu* all around.

CULP: As groundbreaking and important as *Angels* was when it opened, its real success, I think, will be incremental, over time. It's part of the great tradition that will continue to nourish and enrich and enlighten us as we stumble forward into what is, hopefully, a better day. "The Great Work Begins." It's always Beginning.

Bethesda Fountain, shot by Tony Kushner in the late 1980s as he was writing *Angels in America*. (*Tony Kushner*)

INTERVIEWER: Think back to yourself, way back in November of 1985, writing the poem based on your dream about Bill and the angel: What would you tell that twenty-nine-year-old guy about the way that the world was going to change?

TONY KUSHNER: What a tough time to ask that question. Well, you know . . . Uh, what would I have wanted him to know, or what would I tell him?

INTERVIEWER: Like, what would you tell him right now?

KUSHNER: *(Long pause.)* I don't think that I would talk to him. I think it's better that we don't know the future. The person that I was at twenty-nine very deeply believed that there would be great progress. I believed back then, with great certainty—I mean I wrote it in the play, "the world only spins forward," "the time has come," et cetera, et cetera.

Sometimes there just are cruel accidents that can cause staggering amounts of damage in the world. Disasters, freaks of nature, and foreign interventions in democratic elections can happen, and we can suffer very severe setbacks. But you have to fight through those.

Working on all this stuff right after Reagan had been reelected, it felt very dark. I'm glad that I didn't know back then that at sixty I'd be looking at some of the same fucking fights that I was looking at at twenty-nine. Nothing, no right, is permanent. These are dark, very dark days. But I believe in the resiliency of our democracy and I think we are going to overcome this motherfucker and all his hateful minions and we'll survive. So, does that answer your question?

June 26, 2017

ACKNOWLEDGMENTS

ISAAC BUTLER (co-author, *The World Only Spins Forward*): When I suggested doing the acknowledgments of the book oral-history style, Dan responded with enthusiasm right away. Dan's been a great collaborator that way.

DAN KOIS (co-author, *The World Only Spins Forward*): I'll be honest, Isaac, I was dubious, but like so many of your cockamamie ideas it ended up working great. Please insert huge parenthetical laughing uproariously here. *(Laughing uproariously.)* Isaac was a fantastic, tireless, gracious partner on the *Slate* cover story about *Angels*, which was published in June 2016. That piece was made possible by a chorus line of people at all levels and in all departments of the online magazine I'm proud to call home: Jeffrey Bloomer, Chelsea Hassler, Aymann Ismail, Andrew Kahn, Lisa Larson-Walker, Greg Lavallee, Evan Mackinder, Natalie Matthews-Ramo, Abby McIntyre, Stephen Metcalf, Catherine Piner, Dana Stevens, David Tran, and Megan Wiegand. John Swansburg edited it with care and good humor. *Slate*'s editor Julia Turner made a magazine where a story like this could be published with love and support, was behind the piece from the first meeting in which I pitched it, and graciously encouraged us to expand it into a book.

BUTLER: When we started working on the *Slate* piece, neither of us knew how much the project would grow, how much of a story there was. It was actually two of our subjects, Ellen McLaughlin and Kathy Chalfant, who first suggested the *Slate* story might just be the beginning. Like so many of our interviewees, Ellen and Kathy gave us way more than we expected. We interviewed, like, two hundred and fifty people for this book. They shared their opinions, their stories, their photos, and their lives with us. Often, they'd help us find the next person to interview or track down some obscure article we'd never heard of that proved to be essential. Some of them played these roles more than a quarter-century ago; some of them would step onstage to play these roles an hour after they finished talking to us. We've both been really overwhelmed by people's generosity around this story and helping us tell it.

KOIS: We've listed everyone we interviewed in the back of the book. If your name is missing, we're sorry! There were a lot of you. We're really proud to share all your stories. Thanks as well to our agents, Alia Hanna Habib and Julie Stevenson; our editor, Ben Hyman; our managing editor, Laura Phillips; and our copy editor, David Chesanow, all of whom have provided wise counsel and careful eyes along the way.

BUTLER: Our research assistant was the incomparable Rae Binstock.

KOIS: Our research assistant Rae has an *Angels* tattoo! That's fucking hard-core.

BUTLER: Additional research was provided by Maddie Gaw and the world's best librarian and younger brother, Lee Butler. Other wise counselors, good friends, and stalwart shoulders include Rob Weinert-Kendt, Jason Zinoman, Helen Shaw, Mark Armstrong, Jason Holtham, Sam Thielman, Jeremy Barnett Reff, Bette Braun, Jonathan Lethem, Kathleen Glasgow, Jason Kaiser, and my writing twin, Sally Franson. This book would never have happened had my parents not brought me to see both parts of *Angels* on Broadway in 1994. For that, and countless other things, I am eternally grateful.

KOIS: This book never would have happened had my mom not sent me more money after I spent my last fifty dollars on tickets to a Sunday night show of *Perestroika* on Broadway only to discover, when I arrived at the theater, that actually my ticket was for a Sunday matinee.

BUTLER: I can't believe you never told me that story until right now. That's . . . ridiculous.

KOIS: Were we ever so young! Emily Breeze was tirelessly helpful in tracking down photos, details, documents, and happy surprises. She was just one of the many assistants whose no-nonsense competence eased our way. Thanks to Erica Daniels, Ray Dooley, Choire Sicha, Paige Williams, and the many other people who gave us interview ideas or helped make connections. Thanks also to the army of publicists and agents who helpfully wrangled clients for this project, especially Emma Hardy at the National who went above and beyond.

(No thanks, obviously, to the publicists and agents who never wrote us back.) Thanks to my work spouses—Allison Benedikt, Laura Bennett, and Forrest Wickman—for their support. And thanks as always to the Virtual Crib.

BUTLER: Anne Love provided much-needed advice, encouragement, support, perspective, and feedback throughout. Our life together is the greatest gift I could ever imagine.

KOIS: Alia Smith is the best. She offered every kind of support from general encouragement to specifically spending a day transcribing a Tony Kushner interview. And speaking of Tony Kushner—

BUTLER: From the start, writing a history of *Angels* as a collage of voices and sources in conversation with each other felt like the only way to tell its story. But that would've been pointless had Tony Kushner not agreed to talk to us. Had he only agreed to talk to us, *dayenu*, but he spoke to us again and again, answering questions that spanned more than four decades of his personal and professional history. Twenty-five years ago, *Angels in America* changed my life. And I know it changed Dan's too.

KOIS: No work of art has moved me, compelled me, baffled me, and taught me the way *Angels* has. It's been a privilege for us to work on this book, and to have Tony's voice be so present in it. His generosity towards us and this project was deeply moving.

All previously published material is noted as such in the text. Some previously unpublished material came from the Robert Altman Collection at the University of Michigan and the National Theatre Archives in London. Interviews were conducted in person, over the phone, over Skype, or over email from April 2016 to October 2017.

CAST OF CHARACTERS

KYLE AARONS: Actor.

OBI ABILI: Belize at Headlong, United Kingdom tour, 2007.

F. MURRAY ABRAHAM: Roy in New York replacement cast, 1994. Oscar-winning actor known for *Amadeus* and *The Grand Budapest Hotel*.

VERONICA ADES: Director of Global Women's Health, NYU Medical School.

JOANNE AKALAITIS: Founder, Mabou Mines; artistic director, Public Theater, New York, 1991–93.

ZAKIYYAH ALEXANDER: Playwright (*10 Things to Do Before I Die*; *Sick?*).

ANNE ALLGOOD: Hannah at Intiman Theatre, Seattle, 2014.

SARAJANE ALVERSON: The Angel at Stray Dog Theatre, St. Louis, 2012.

ANNABEL ARMOUR: Hannah in the Journeymen, Chicago, 1998.

GAIL BEACH: Professor of costume design, Catholic University.

DANIEL BELCHER: Prior in *Angels in America* opera, Théâtre du Châtelet, Paris, 2004.

SCOTT BELFORD: Director of public relations, Charlotte Arts & Science Council, Charlotte, NC, 1995–2000.

CHRISTOPHER BELLIS: Director at Catholic University, 1996.

VIVIENNE BENESCH: Hannah in NYU *Perestroika* workshop, 1993. Now artistic director at PlayMakers Theatre, Chapel Hill, NC.

DEBRA BALLINGER BERNSTEIN: Executive director, Eureka Theatre, San Francisco, 1989–92.

KEV BERRY: Playwright.

PETER BIRKENHEAD: Louis in national tour, 1994–95. Now journalist and author (*Gonville*).

JONATHAN BOCK: Louis at Round House/Olney, Bethesda, MD, 2016.

BEN BRANTLEY: Co–chief theater critic, *New York Times*.

CARY BROKAW: Producer of HBO miniseries, 2003.

MARK BRONNENBERG: Tony Kushner's partner, 1982–86; now a licensed clinical social worker in San Francisco. *Millennium Approaches* is dedicated to him.

SUSAN BROWN: Hannah in London, 2017, and New York, 2018.

FINN CALDWELL: Puppetry designer in London, 2017.

SHEILA CALLAGHAN: Playwright (*Bed*; *Women Laughing Alone with Salad*). Co–executive producer, *Shameless*.

COLIN CALLENDER: President, HBO Films, 1999–2008. Founder, Playground Entertainment.

TIM CARMODY: Journalist.

JACK CARPENTER: Co-lighting designer in San Francisco, 1991.

JIM CAVE: Co-lighting designer in San Francisco, 1991.

KATHLEEN CHALFANT: Hannah in workshops, San Francisco, Los Angeles, and New York (Tony nomination), 1990–94. Also known for her Obie Award–winning roles in *Wit* and *Talking Heads*, and for TV's *The Affair*.

SEAN CHAPMAN: Prior in London, 1992.

JEFF CHRISTIAN: Joe in the Journeymen, Chicago, 1998.

CARYL CHURCHILL: World's greatest living playwright.

SCOTT COHEN: Law student.

KARA LEE CORTHRON: Playwright (*Welcome to Fear City*; *AliceGraceAnon*).

CASEY COWAN: Lighting designer for New Works Festival, 1989, and Taper Too workshop, 1990. Associate lighting designer in Los Angeles, 1992.

NANCY CRANE: The Angel in London, 1992–93.

DAVID CROMER: Director and Louis in the Journeymen, 1998; director at Kansas City Rep, 2015. Obie-winning director of *Our Town* and *The Band's Visit*.

PETER CROOK: Joe at Intiman Theatre, Seattle, 1994–95.

TRIP CULLMAN: Assistant to the director for the HBO miniseries, 2003. Now a stage director (*Significant Other*; *Lobby Hero*).

STEVEN CULP: Joe at American Conservatory Theater, San Francisco, 1994–95. Also known for *Desperate Housewives* and *JAG*.

PADDY CUNNEEN: Composer in London, 1992–93.

VINSON CUNNINGHAM: Culture critic, *New Yorker*.

MARCUS D'AMICO: Louis in London, 1992.

JESSIEE DATINO: Harper at Kansas City Rep, 2015.

ANNE DARRAGH: Harper in San Francisco, 1991.

MASHUQ MUSHTAQ DEEN: Playwright (*Draw the Circle*).

KATHLEEN DENNEHY: Harper at Dallas Theater Center, 1996.

ANNE DENNIS: English professor at Rogers State University, Claremore, OK.

IRA DEUTCHMAN: Co-founder and president of Fine Line Features, 1990–94.

GARRET DILLAHUNT: Prior at American Conservatory Theater, San Francisco, 1994–95. Also known for *Deadwood*, *Justified*, and *The Mindy Project*.

DECLAN DONNELLAN: Director in London, 1992–93.

ADAM DRIVER: Louis at Signature Theatre, New York, 2010. Also known for *Star Wars: The Last Jedi*, *Silence*, and TV's *Girls*.

BOB EGAN: Producing artistic director, Mark Taper Forum, Los Angeles, 1983–2003.

PEGGY EISENHAUER: Associate lighting designer in New York, 1993–94.

MARIANNE ELLIOTT: Director in London, 2017, and New York, 2018.

MARK EMERSON: Prior at Headlong, United Kingdom tour, 2007.

JENNIFER ENGSTROM: The Angel at Kansas City Rep, 2015.

PETER EÖTVÖS: Composer, *Angels in America* opera.

DAVID ESBJORNSON: Director in San Francisco, 1991. Now a Tony-nominated director (*The Ride Down Mt. Morgan*; *The Goat*).

OSKAR EUSTIS: Dramaturg at Eureka Theatre, San Francisco, 1981–88; artistic director, 1988–89. Co-director in Los Angeles, 1992. Now the artistic director of the Public Theater, New York.

RICHARD EYRE: Director, National Theatre, London, 1987–97.

RICHARD FELDMAN: Director of Juilliard *Millennium* workshop, 1992.

JULES FISHER: Lighting designer in New York, 1993–94.

MARY BETH FISHER: The Angel at Court Theatre, Chicago, 2012.

REG FLOWERS: Belize in national tour, 1994–95.

KIMBERLY FLYNN: Close friend of Tony Kushner and dramaturg during the writing of *Angels in America*. *Perestroika* is dedicated to her.

TRAVIS FOSTER: English professor, Villanova University.

DAVID FRANCE: Director and writer, *How to Survive a Plague*.

BARNEY FRANK: Congressman from Massachusetts, 1981–2013.

KEVIN R. FREE: Belize at Charlotte Rep, 1996.

K. TODD FREEMAN: Belize in Los Angeles, 1992.

GRETCHEN KLINEDINST FURST: Harper at Civic Theatre of Allentown, PA, 1997 and 2017.

ANDREW GARFIELD: Prior in London, 2017, and New York, 2018. Oscar- and Tony-nominated actor best known for *The Social Network* and *Hacksaw Ridge*.

EMILY GARSIDE: Scholar of HIV/AIDS-related theater.

KATE GAUDET: Assistant director, University Honors Program, University of New Hampshire.

DEBORAH GEIS: Associate professor of English, DePauw University. Co-editor of *Approaching the Millennium: Essays on Angels in America*.

SAM GOLD: Tony Award–winning director (*Fun Home*).

CHRIS GEIDNER: Legal editor, *BuzzFeed*.

JULIA GIBSON: Harper at American Conservatory Theater, San Francisco, 1994–95; assistant director at Signature Theatre, New York, 2010.

KATE GOEHRING: Harper in national tour, 1994–95.

HENRY GOODMAN: Roy in London, 1992.

DENISE GOUGH: Harper in London, 2017, and New York, 2018.

ENID GRAHAM: Harper in *Millennium Approaches* at Juilliard, 1992.

DAVID MARSHALL GRANT: Joe in New York, 1993–94. Now a television producer (*Brothers & Sisters*, *Code Black*).

JESSE GREEN: Co–chief theater critic, *New York Times*.

JOSEPH HAJ: Louis at Alley Theatre, Houston, 1995. Now artistic director of the Guthrie Theater, Minneapolis.

RACHEL HANKS: Harper at Stray Dog Theatre, St. Louis, 2012.

MARCIA GAY HARDEN: Harper in New York, 1993–94. Oscar-winning actor best known for *Pollock* and *Mystic River*.

MARK HARRIS: Journalist and author of forthcoming biography of Mike Nichols; Tony Kushner's husband.

JORDAN HARRISON: Playwright (*Marjorie Prime*; *Maple and Vine*).

DENNIS HARVEY: Theater critic in San Francisco.

ROBIN HAUETER: Spokesman for ACT UP, 1989–92.

MICHAEL HAYDEN: Roy in *Millennium Approaches* at Juilliard, 1992. Tony-nominated actor (*Judgment at Nuremberg*; *Festen*).

MITCHELL HÉBERT: Roy at Round House/Olney, Bethesda, MD, 2016.

BILL HECK: Joe at Signature Theatre, New York, 2010.

MARIEKE HEEBINK: Hannah at Toneelgroep Amsterdam, 2008–15.

SAM HELFRICH: Director, *Angels in America* opera, City Opera, New York, 2017.

BRIAN HERRERA: Theater professor, Princeton University.

CLARE HOLMAN: Harper in London, 1993.

LORRI HOLT: Company member, Eureka Theatre, San Francisco, 1980–90; Harper in workshops.

ANDY HOLTZ: Business manager, Eureka Theatre, San Francisco, 1987–89.

GITTA HONNEGER: Chair, Catholic University department of drama, 1993–2001.

SAMUEL D. HUNTER: Playwright (*A Bright New Boise*; *The Whale*).

ROBERT HURWITT: Theater critic in San Francisco.

JASON ISAACS: Louis in London, 1993. Known for the *Harry Potter* movies and TV's *Star Trek: Discovery*.

PHILIP EARL JOHNSON: Joe in national tour, 1994–95.

CHERRY JONES: The Angel in New York replacement cast, 1994. Tony Award–winning actor known for *The Heiress* and *Doubt*, as well as her Emmy-winning role on *24*.

CLEVE JONES: Founder, NAMES Project AIDS Memorial Quilt.

JOHN JUDD: Roy in the Journeymen, Chicago, 1998.

TOM KAMM: Set designer in San Francisco, 1991.

STEPHEN KARAM: Tony Award–winning playwright (*The Humans*).

ZOE KAZAN: Harper at Signature Theatre, New York, 2010. Also known for *The Big Sick* and her Emmy-nominated role in *Olive Kitteridge*.

HANS KESTING: Roy at Toneelgroep Amsterdam, 2008–15.

JOYCE KETAY: Tony Kushner's theatrical agent.

HEIDI KETTENRING: Harper at Court Theatre, Chicago, 2012.

JEFF KING: Company member, Eureka Theatre, San Francisco, 1987–90; Joe in Los Angeles, 1992.

JUSTIN KIRK: Prior in the HBO miniseries, 2003. Known for *Other Desert Cities* and TV's *Jack & Jill* and *Weeds*.

MARY KLINGER: Stage manager in Los Angeles and New York, 1992-94.

MIKELL KOBER: Theater producer.

LARRY KRAMER: Playwright (*The Normal Heart*) and activist.

ALICE KRASINSKI: Production manager, Eureka Theatre, San Francisco, 1984–86.

MICHAEL KRASS: Costume designer of national tour, 1994–95.

TONY KUSHNER: Playwright of *Angels in America* (two Tony Awards; Pulitzer Prize). Also known for his Tony-nominated *Caroline, or Change* and his Oscar-nominated screenplays for *Munich* and *Lincoln*.

LAURA KYRO: Hannah at Stray Dog Theatre, St. Louis, 2004 and 2012.

NEIL LaBUTE: Playwright and film director of *Some Girl(s)* and *In the Company of Men*.

ELIZABETH LAIDLAW: The Angel in the Journeymen, Chicago, 1998.

ROCCO LANDESMAN: Producer of New York production as president of Jujamcyn Theaters, 1993–94. Now part-owner and president emeritus of Jujamcyn.

NATHAN LANE: Roy in London, 2017, and New York, 2018. Tony Award–winning actor best known for *Love! Valor! Compassion!* and *The Producers*.

AMANDA LAWRENCE: The Angel in London, 2017, and New York, 2018.

JONATHAN LEE: Production manager at the Mark Taper Forum, 1988–present.

RON LEIBMAN: Roy in Los Angeles and New York, 1992–94 (Tony Award).

JONATHAN LETHEM: Novelist (*Motherless Brooklyn*; *The Fortress of Solitude*).

STEVEN LEVENSON: Playwright (*Dear Evan Hansen*).

MARGO LION: Producer of New York production, 1993–94.

TAYLOR MAC: Playwright (*A 24-Decade History of Popular Music*).

CYNTHIA MACE: Harper in workshops and in Los Angeles, 1989–92.

ANGUS MacLACHLAN: Louis at Charlotte Rep, 1996. Now a screenwriter and director (*Junebug*; *Abundant Acreage Available*).

IAN MacNEIL: Set designer in London, 2017.

IRA MADISON III: Culture writer, *Daily Beast*.

EMILY MANN: Playwright (*Execution of Justice*; *Still Life*); artistic director, McCarter Theatre, Princeton, NJ.

LIZ MANNE: Co-founder and executive vice president, marketing, Fine Line Features, 1990–97.

JOE MANTELLO: Louis in Los Angeles and New York, 1992–94. Now a Tony Award–winning director known for *Assassins*, *Wicked*, and *The Humans*.

KEITH MARTIN: Producing and managing director, Charlotte Rep, 1990–2001.

JON MATTHEWS: Louis in Taper Too *Millennium* workshop, 1990.

MICHAEL MAYER: Director of NYU *Perestroika* workshop, 1993, and national tour, 1994–95. Tony Award–winning director of *Spring Awakening* and *American Idiot*.

JAMES McARDLE: Louis in London, 2017, and New York, 2018.

ELLEN McLAUGHLIN: The Angel in workshops, San Francisco, Los Angeles, and New York, 1990–94. Also a playwright (*A Narrow Bed*).

CRISTINE McMURDO-WALLIS: Hannah at American Conservatory Theater, San Francisco, 1994–95.

DEBRA MESSING: Harper in the NYU workshop of *Perestroika*, 1993. Known for TV's *Will & Grace* and *Smash*.

KARL MILLER: Prior at Forum Theatre, Silver Spring, MD, 2009.

MONICA MILLER: English professor, Middle Georgia State University.

DAVID MILLING: Stage manager in London, 1992–93.

LIN-MANUEL MIRANDA: Tony Award–winning playwright/performer (*Hamilton*; *In the Heights*).

MADISON MOORE: Author of *Fabulous: The Rise of the Beautiful Eccentric*.

WESLEY MORRIS: Critic-at-large, *New York Times*.

ITAMAR MOSES: Playwright (*The Fortress of Solitude*; *The Band's Visit*).

MONICA MURRAY: Drama teacher, Cambridge Rindge and Latin School, Cambridge, MA.

JOSEPH MYDELL: Belize in London, 1992–93 (Olivier award).

ROBYN NEVIN: Hannah at Belvoir St Theatre, Sydney, 2013.

ADAM NEWBORN: Belize at Civic Theatre of Allentown, PA, 2017.

JIM NICOLA: Artistic director, New York Theatre Workshop, 1988–present.

RUFUS NORRIS: Artistic director, National Theatre, London.

EMILY NUSSBAUM: Television critic, *New Yorker*.

HENRY OLSEN: Senior Fellow at the Ethics and Public Policy Center. Author of *The Working Class Republican: Ronald Reagan and the Return of Blue-Collar Conservatism*.

NICK ORMEROD: Set designer in London, 1992–93; Declan Donnellan's partner.

MICHAEL ORNSTEIN: Louis in San Francisco and a Taper workshop, 1991.

R. KURT OSENLUND: Managing editor, *Out* magazine.

MARY-LOUISE PARKER: Harper in the HBO miniseries, 2003 (Emmy award). Known for her Tony Award–winning performance in *Proof* and for the TV series *The West Wing* and *Weeds*.

SCOTT PARKINSON: Prior in the Journeymen, Chicago, 1998.

JEANNE PAULSEN: Hannah at Intiman Theatre, Seattle, 1994–95.

MONICA PEARL: Professor of English and American Studies at the University of Manchester.

DALE PECK: Literary critic; author, *Martin and John*.

DEBORAH PEIFER: Theater critic in San Francisco.

RICK PERLSTEIN: Historian, author of *The Invisible Bridge*.

MICHAEL PETSHAFT: Tony Kushner's assistant, 1991–93. Now a television director.

SANDRA PHILLIPS: Hannah at TAAC, Sacramento, 2010 and 2014.

NICK REDING: Joe in London, 1992.

BEN POWER: Deputy artistic director, National Theatre, London.

GREG REINER: Director, theater and musical theater, National Endowment for the Arts.

FRANK RICH: Chief theater critic for the *New York Times*, 1980–93. Now a columnist at *New York* and a television producer (*Veep*).

MICHAEL RIEDEL: Theater columnist for the *New York Post*.

JOSÉ RIVERA: Playwright (*Marisol*).

BARBARA ROBERTSON: Hannah in national tour, 1994–95.

MAC ROGERS: Playwright (*The Honeycomb Trilogy*; *The Message*).

KIM RUBINSTEIN: Associate director of national tour, 1994–95.

MICHAEL SCOTT RYAN: Joe in San Francisco, 1991.

DAVID SAVRAN: Distinguished professor, City University of New York Graduate Center.

MATTHEW SEIG: Robert Altman's employee; executor, Altman estate.

ROBBY SELLA: Prior in Juilliard *Millennium* workshop, 1992, and in national tour, 1994–95.

RICHARD SEYD: Company member, Eureka Theatre, San Francisco, 1980–88; Sigrid Wurschmidt's husband.

KERRIE SEYMOUR: The Angel at Warehouse Theatre, Greenville, SC, 2013; theater professor, Clemson University.

TINA SHACKLEFORD: Stage manager at Dallas Theater Center, 1996.

BEN SHENKMAN: Roy in NYU *Perestroika* workshop, 1992; Louis at American Conservatory Theater, San Francisco, 1994–95, and on HBO, 2003. Some quotes drawn from a previously unreleased 2010 video interview with the Signature Theatre's David Hatkoff.

CHRISTOPHER SHINN: Playwright (*Dying City*; *Against*).

LEE SIEGEL: Cultural critic.

EELCO SMITS: Prior at Toneelgroep Amsterdam, 2008–15.

STEPHEN SPINELLA: Prior in workshops, San Francisco, Los Angeles, and New York, 1988–94 (two Tony Awards).

BEN STANTON: Lighting designer at Signature Theatre, New York, 2010.

ROBERT STANTON: Actor.

NATHAN STEWART-JARRETT: Belize in London, 2017, and New York, 2018.

PAUL OAKLEY STOVALL: Belize at Kansas City Rep, 2015.

MERYL STREEP: Hannah on HBO, 2003 (Emmy award). Oscar-winning actor known for being Meryl Streep.

CAROLYN SWIFT: The Angel in national tour, 1994–95.

TONY TACCONE: Artistic director, Eureka Theatre, San Francisco, 1980–88. Co-director in Los Angeles, 1992. Now artistic director of Berkeley Rep, and director of *Angels* at Berkeley Rep, 2018.

BRIAN THORSTENSON: Intern, Eureka Theatre, San Francisco, 1990–91.

PERRY TANNENBAUM: Founder and editor, *Creative Loafing Charlotte*.

TERRY TEACHOUT: Theater critic, *Wall Street Journal*.

CALDWELL TIDICUE: Bob the Drag Queen, *RuPaul's Drag Race*; Belize at Berkeley Rep, 2018.

LAWRENCE TOPPMAN: Arts reporter, *Charlotte Observer*, 1980–2017.

RUSSELL TOVEY: Joe in London, 2017. Also known for *The History Boys* and TV's *Looking*.

LOURDES TRAMMELL: Educational consultant.

CATHERINE TRIESCHMANN: Playwright (*How the World Began*; *One House Over*).

JAYCE TROMSNESS: Drama teacher, South Carolina Governor's School for the Arts and Humanities, Greenville.

STEVE UMBERGER: Director at Charlotte Rep, 1996.

KEN URBAN: Playwright.

DAWN URSULA: The Angel at Round House/Olney, Bethesda, MD, 2016.

ABIGAIL VAN ALYN: Member, Eureka Theatre, San Francisco, 1981–91. Hannah in workshops.

IVO VAN HOVE: Director at Toneelgroep Amsterdam, 2008–15.

JAN VERSWEYVELD: Designer at Toneelgroep Amsterdam, 2008–15; Ivo van Hove's partner.

TOM VIERTEL: Producer in New York and of national tour, 1993–95.

KRIS VIRE: Theater editor, *Time Out Chicago*.

MICHELE VOLANSKY: Theater professor, Washington College, Chestertown, MD.

DOUG WAGER: Artistic Director, Arena Stage, Washington, D.C., 1991–98.

ROBIN WAGNER: Set designer in New York, 1993–94.

GREGORY WALLACE: Belize at American Conservatory Theater, San Francisco, 1994–95.

ANNE WASHBURN: Playwright (*Mr. Burns: A Post-Electric Play*; *10 Out of 12*).

HARRY WATERS JR.: Belize in workshops and in San Francisco, 1989–91.

NIKKI WEAVER: Harper at Portland Playhouse, Portland, OR, 2011.

BRUCE WEBER: Reporter, *New York Times*, 1984–2017.

TODD WEEKS: Prior at Alliance Theatre, Atlanta, 1995; in national tour, 1995; at Dallas Theater Center, 1996.

ROBIN WEIGERT: Mormon Mother on HBO, 2003. The Angel at Signature Theatre, New York, 2010.

DAVID WEISSMAN: Director, *We Were Here*.

GARY WILLIAMS: Professor emeritus, Catholic University.

TRACEY SCOTT WILSON: Playwright (*The Good Negro*; *Buzzer*). Co-executive producer, *The Americans*.

MARK WING-DAVEY: Director at American Conservatory Theater, San Francisco, 1994–95.

GEORGE C. WOLFE: Director in New York, 1993–94 (Tony Award). Also known for creating *Bring in da Noise/ Bring in da Funk* and *Shuffle Along*. Artistic director, Public Theater, New York, 1993–2004.

FRANK WOOD: Roy at Signature Theatre, New York, 2010. Also known for his Tony Award–winning role in *Side Man*.

JEFFREY WRIGHT: Belize in New York, 1993–94 (Tony Award), and on HBO, 2003 (Emmy Award). Also known for *Topdog/Underdog*, *A Free Man of Color*, and the *Hunger Games* movies.

TAL YARDEN: Video designer at Toneelgroep Amsterdam, 2008–15.

ELIZABETH ZITRIN: Attorney and board member of the Eureka Theatre, San Francisco, in the early 1990s.

INDEX

Note: Page numbers in *italics* refer to illustrations. Page numbers followed by an *s* refer to sidebars. "London production" refers to the Royal National Theatre productions.

A

Aarons, Kyle, 314*s*
Abili, Obi, 224
Abraham, F. Murray, 39, 114, 119, 213, 215–16, 383
Acker, Amy, 262
ACT UP, 15, 21, 38, *38*, 66–67, 271, 403
Ades, Veronica, 294–95, 365*s*
AIDS
  and activism, 14
  and contemporary students, 279–80*s*
  deaths, 36–39, 66, 96, 173, 396
  early reactions to, 13–18, 37–38
  emergence of (1981), 11–13
  and governmental officials, 13–14, 17–18
  and HBO miniseries, 324
  and HIV testing, 18
  and "immorality" claims, 17–18
  and medical advances, 238, 332
  as metaphor for threats, 362
  and misinformation, 38, 96
  and national tour, 255
  and operatic adaptation of *Angels*, 334
  public awareness of, 13
  and Roy Cohn, 40–41, 115, 119
AIDS Quilt, 15, *41*, 41, 403
Akalaitis, JoAnne, 122, 138–39, 207, 240–41
Albrecht, Chris, 315
Alexander, Zakiyyah, 361*s*, 363*s*, 369*s*
Allgood, Anne, 83
Altman, Robert, 192, 304–6, *305*, 308–12, 316, 323
Alverson, Sarajane, 262–63

Angels in America (Kushner)
  2017 revival of, 407
  Angel character, 259–73, 388
  Belize character, 220–26, 264, 269, 293–303
  Bethesda Fountain scene, 89, 207, *334*, 336, 395, 398
  Central Park scene, 231–32
  coming out scene, 61, 85, 147–48
  concept of, 36
  courthouse steps scene, 149–50
  cultural impact of, 211–12
  decision to divide, 49–50
  Democracy in America scene, 183, 219–26, 321, 358, 366*s*
  Emily character, 271–72
  Emmy Awards, 324
  Epistle scene, 262–66, 269, 335
  Ethel Rosenberg character, 89–91, 118
  first readings of, 127
  Hannah character, 81–91
  Harper character, 144–46, 346–57
  Harper-Joe relationship, 144–46, 351–52
  horror depicted in, 39
  hype and fever surrounding, 177–78
  Joe Pitt character, 112, 142–56
  Kaddish scene, 91, 136, 302–3
  legacy of, 399–411
  Louis-Belize relationship, 219–26, 395
  Louis character, 148–53, 158–60, 195, 219–37
  Louis-Joe relationship, 150–52
  Martin character, 352–54
  and Mormonism, 41–43, 87
  Mormon Mother character, 272
  musical audition for, 45
  and NEA grant, 34–35
  Night Flight scene, 207, 346, *352*, 354–57
  Oldest Living Bolshevik character, 83–84

Prior character, 87–88, 195, 228–29, 380–98
Prior-Harper relationship, 384–86
Prior-Louis relationship, 179, 186, 227, 235–37, 384, 395
protests against, 256, 286–89
Pulitzer Prize, 176*s*, 186–87, 240
Rabbi character, 81–82
reactions to, 59–60
rewrites of, 59, 131, 133–34, 155
rights to, 64–65, 69, 123, 362–63
roles in, 45–47, 56, 82
Roy Cohn character, 40, 89–90, 111–21, 123–24
in schools, 278–83*s*
script delays, 47–48, 200–201
sex scene in Central Park, 59–60, 158–59, 231–32, 321, 403
short scenes in, 104
Sister Ella Chapter character, 86, 271
success of, 213
title of, 33–34, 36, 42
Tony Awards, 126, 140–41, 192
See also Millennium Approaches; Perestroika; specific productions
Arena Stage, 39, 122–23, 278, 281–82
Armour, Annabel, 81, 83–84, 329
As Is (Hoffman), 14, 402

B

Beach, Gail, 276–78, 280–81
Beatty, Warren, 311
Belcher, Daniel, 333–36
Belford, Scott, 286, 289, 291
Bellis, Christopher, 275–78, 280, 282
Benesch, Vivienne, 84, 89–90, *90*, 99*s*, 121, 177–79*s*, 209
Benjamin, Walter, 21, 190
Bennett, Michael, 139–40

A NOTE ON THE AUTHORS

ISAAC BUTLER is a writer and theater director, most recently of *The Trump Card*, a meditation on the peculiar rise of Donald Trump, created and performed by Mike Daisey. He also wrote and directed *Real Enemies*, a collaboration with the composer Darcy James Argue and the video artist Peter Nigrini, which was commissioned by the Brooklyn Academy of Music and named one of the top ten live events of 2015 by the *New York Times*. He holds an MFA in creative nonfiction from the University of Minnesota, and his writing has appeared in the *Guardian*, *Slate*, *American Theatre*, the *Los Angeles Review of Books*, and other publications.

DAN KOIS is an editor and writer for *Slate*'s culture section and a contributing writer for the *New York Times Magazine*. He is the former culture editor at *Slate*, where he launched the *Slate Book Review*. He co-hosted the podcast *Mom and Dad Are Fighting* and is a frequent guest on *Slate's Culture Gabfest*. His previous book was *Facing Future*, about the Hawaiian musician Israel Kamakawiwoʻole, for Bloomsbury's 33⅓ series, and his next book is *How to Be a Family*, a memoir of parenting around the world, for Little, Brown.